Felipe Guaman Poma de Ayala

# THE FIRST NEW CHRONICLE AND GOOD GOVERNMENT

*Abridged*

Part 7 -
Tues., Feb. 12

Felipe Guaman Poma de Ayala

# THE FIRST NEW CHRONICLE AND GOOD GOVERNMENT

*Abridged*

Selected, Translated, and Annotated by
DAVID FRYE

Hackett Publishing Company, Inc.
Indianapolis/Cambridge

11  10  09  08     2  3  4  5  6  7

All images from Felipe Guaman Poma de Ayala's *Nueva corónica y buen gobierno*
(1615) included in this book have been provided courtesy of the Royal Library,
Copenhagen, Denmark.

For further information, please address:
 Hackett Publishing Company, Inc.
 P.O. Box 44937
 Indianapolis, IN 46244-0937


 www.hackettpublishing.com

Cover design by Abigail Coyle
Text design by Carrie Wagner
Composition by Bill Hartman
Printed at Versa Press, Inc.

Library of Congress Cataloging-in-Publication Data

Guaman Poma de Ayala, Felipe, fl. 1613.
     [Primer nueva corónica y buen gobierno. English]
     The first new chronicle and good government, abridged / Felipe
 Guaman Poma de Ayala ; selected, translated, and annotated by David Frye.
          p.   cm.
     Includes index.
     ISBN-13: 978-0-87220-841-4 (pbk)
     ISBN-10: 0-87220-841-9 (pbk)
     ISBN-13: 978-0-87220-842-1 (cloth)
     ISBN-10: 0-87220-842-7 (cloth)
     1. Incas.   2. Indians of South America—Peru—Social life and customs.
 3. Peru—History—Conquest, 1522–1548.   4. Peru—History—To 1820.
 I. Frye, David L.   II. Title.

F3429.G8G82513 2006
985'.02—dc22

# CONTENTS

# INTRODUCTION
## Guaman Poma, an Andean Life

Who was Guaman Poma? An enigma, one is tempted to say. There is little that we know with any certainty about the self-taught artist and writer who styled himself "Don Felipe Guaman Poma de Ayala, Prince and Author." We do not know exactly when or where he was born or died. Doubts were raised during his own lifetime about his status as an indigenous Andean noble; even his name was questioned. But, in contrast to the untold millions of native Peruvians who lived, toiled, and died in anonymity during the Spanish conquest era, Guaman Poma left a trail of documents—above all, his 1,189–page masterwork, the *First New Chronicle and Good Government,* written in Spanish with many passages in Quechua (the "language of the Incas") and completed in 1615–1616.[1] From scattered clues, we can piece together a brief biographical sketch.

Guaman Poma was a native speaker of Quechua, as were both his parents. (His name, too, is Quechua: *waman puma,* Falcon Puma.) His writings and his documented movements support his claim to have been born into an Andean family of the local ruling class in the central Southern Peruvian province of Huamanga. In contrast to fellow Andean-turned-chronicler "El Inca" Garcilaso de la Vega—the mestizo[2] son of a Spanish conqueror and an "Inca princess"—Guaman Poma must have learned to speak, read, and write Spanish late in childhood.

In the *New Chronicle,* Guaman Poma describes himself as being eighty years old, seeming to imply that he was born around the year 1535. It is clear, however, that he considered the number eighty a metaphor for old age, not a figure to be taken literally. From many clues in his book, we can deduce that he was most likely born in 1550 or shortly thereafter, and that he was in his early to mid-sixties when he completed the manuscript. The difference between 1535 and 1550—the transformation of Peru through fifteen chaotic years of upheaval, rebellion, and war among Spanish conquerors and their competing Indian allies—is crucial to understanding Guaman Poma and the world in which he grew up. In 1535, the Spanish conquest of Peru was still in full swing, and strife among the quarrelsome

---

[1] Guaman Poma's full manuscript is available in digitized format (both facsimile and transcribed), along with Guaman Poma's 1615 letter to the king of Spain, the Prado Tello manuscript, and other related documents and studies, on the website of the Royal Library of Denmark, http://www.kb.dk/elib/mss/poma/.

[2] Mestizo: of "mixed" Spanish and Indian descent. The most important Spanish, Quechua, and colonial terms are defined at greater length in the Glossary.

conquerors was beginning. An Andean nobleman born in 1535 would have been raised by parents who knew nothing of Europeans or European ways; as a small boy, he would have witnessed the collapse of his parents' world of comfort and privilege. By the early 1550s, Spanish royal government was established in Lima and order was being imposed on a devastated countryside. Born at that time, Guaman Poma would have been raised by parents with long years of experience with Spanish ways: disillusioned parents who had survived the years of chaos by coming to terms, in one way or another, with the reality of Spanish overlordship.

If Guaman Poma was born in the early 1550s, as I contend, then he came of age together with the maturing of the Spanish colonial system. By 1560, when he would have been a child of five or ten, an archipelago of Spanish settlements stretched from the Pacific coast at Lima to the burgeoning mining city of Potosí in Upper Peru, across a ruralized matrix of Andean pueblos. The old Andean capital of Cusco had become a provincial backwater, filled with memories of past glories. The center of wealth and power had moved to Lima, the newly founded Spanish capital, with its easy access to the sea (and beyond the sea, to the true seat of power in the world that was being built: Europe). The network of Spanish settlements and economic ventures were fueled by a silver mining complex that was established between 1545 (the discovery of the "mountain of silver" at Potosí) and 1563 (the exploitation of mercury deposits at Huancavelica, near Guaman Poma's home territory, which made large-scale refinement of Potosí silver feasible). Spanish cities and Spanish mines alike ran on the forced labor of native Andeans, given too often at the cost of their lives, while a coterie of Spanish potentates reaped fabulous profits. The whole complex was fed and clothed by small farmers and textile producers in the Andean pueblos, as well as by the rich harvests on Spanish-owned estates, which also ran on native labor.

Central Southern Peru in the 1550s and 1560s was a land where Tawantinsuyu, the Inca Empire, was a memory (while Inca culture lived on); where Catholic Christianity permeated indigenous society; where a young and Catholic Guaman Poma could agree with Spanish priests in viewing indigenous Andean religious practices, resurgent among his disillusioned elders in isolated pueblos, as heresy and idolatry. We see a hint of how Guaman Poma's own parents must have dealt with the transition from conquest to established colonial regime in his reference to his mestizo half-brother. He describes this Martín de Ayala (who appears to be some ten to twenty years his senior in the illustrations of the *New Chronicle*) as the son of his mother and a Spanish conqueror. It was Martín, then, not Guaman Poma, who may have been born around 1535, when his mother was perhaps no older than a teenager. At the time of the conquest, indigenous families must have considered the rape of indigenous women and girls by Spanish conquerors a horrific outrage and a deep offense; years later, however, it seems that the children born of this violence had become valuable links with high-ranking Spanish overlords for their indigenous families. For Guaman Poma, a claim to an illegitimate older half-brother was not a topic of shame or outrage, but a family tie linking him with the powerful Ayala name.[3]

Guaman Poma boasts of even more powerful ties on the sides of his Andean father and mother, repeatedly stating that his father's father served as the "second in command" of Tawantinsuyu, the Inca Empire, while his mother was the daughter of the tenth Inca ruler, Topa Inca Yupanqui. Can we give these boasts any credence? We cannot dismiss them out of hand; powerful rulers in the Inca regime had multiple wives and many offspring, and it is at least remotely possible that his parents were born from such liaisons. But again, there is no external evidence for the claims—not surprisingly, given the fragmentary survival of colonial documents and Andean traditions of transmitting history in oral stories, not writing. It is just this fact that makes the *New Chronicle* so precious a document. We should perhaps leave the question of credibility to one side, then, and instead concentrate on Guaman Poma's instrumental use of his alleged family ties in his rhetorical case for having himself appointed as the Spanish king's "second in command" over all of Peru. At our remove, what is important is not the truth or falsity of his claim, but his evident intuition that, if he could not make a claim to high nobility, none of his passionate arguments for reforming the colonial system stood a chance of being heard in patriarchal and hierarchical Spain.

What we do know of Guaman Poma's life on the basis of written sources—the references in his own text and a handful of surviving legal documents—shows that he lived most of his life in or near the central Peruvian district of Huamanga.[4] He spent much of it in the Lucanas province to the

---

[3] Guaman Poma also claims that Martín became an ordained Catholic priest who worked at the hospital (a charitable institution) of the provincial Spanish city of Huamanga, where he taught young Guaman Poma his letters. Whether he actually had such a mestizo half-brother is not recorded elsewhere, but a kinsman of Guaman Poma named Martín de Ayala does appear in a 1595 document (copied in the seventeenth-century Prado Tello manuscript), where he is described as a "*yanacona* [Indian auxiliary] of the hospital of [Huamanga]" (f. 66v). Could this be his actual half-brother? If so, Guaman Poma has doubly inflated Martín's status: by making him a priest, not a mere *yanacona* employee, and by making him the son, albeit unrecognized and illegitimate, of a powerful Spanish conqueror. Could Martín have been born, instead, from his mother's rape by another *yanacona,* an Indian ally of the Spanish during the conquest?

[4] The Spanish city of Huamanga was founded in 1539 by Pizarro's men (or by Guaman Poma's father, if we wish to believe his account on this point) in a populous valley conveniently located between Lima and Cusco. The city was renamed Ayacucho in 1825, but the province is still named Huamanga.

south of the city of Huamanga proper—to be precise, in the twin pueblos of Chipao and Suntunto, where he was probably born, and the nearby pueblo of Apcara, where he says that he and his father before him served as governor. Under Inca rule, the Lucanas valleys were moderately prosperous: well-watered, fertile enough, and well enough connected to the center of the realm at Cusco, 140 miles to the east. A ruling family from Lucanas would likely have kin, friends, and political ties throughout the central Andes. Under the developing Spanish regime, however, Lucanas was becoming an isolated and impoverished rural province, off the highways connecting Lima and Huamanga with Cusco and Potosí. The former ruling elites of Lucanas and similar isolated provinces were being transformed into "Indian *caciques*," the rulers of the lower class, with sharply curtailed privileges and connections. At the same time, the economic forces of the new regime were busily drawing the young, restless, and ambitious out of such back provinces into the commercial opportunities of Spanish cities and estates, if not into the forced labor of the mines.

The first event to take Guaman Poma beyond his hometown appears to have been the *visita* (church inspection tour) of a priest named Cristóbal de Albornoz, who traveled throughout the provinces of Lucanas and Soras in 1568–1570 in an effort to "extirpate idolatries" among the Quechua speakers of the isolated pueblos there. He did this at a time when an Andean religious revival movement known as *Taki Unquy* ("dancing sickness") was advocating a return to the old forms of worship and a rejection of all that was Christian and European. Guaman Poma served as an interpreter on this tour, an experience that deeply marked his understanding of the region and Andean religiosity, and that also stamped him with a fervent Catholic orthodoxy marked by a stubborn nativist bent.

The archives are silent about Guaman Poma's activities for the next decade or so. Then, perhaps in the late 1580s to early 1590s, he served as an assistant to another Spanish cleric: Fray Martín de Murúa, a Mercedarian friar who served as a rural priest in Indian pueblos. Murúa was fascinated with Inca history, and, like a handful of fellow friars, he became a chronicler of that history. Similarities between Murúa's and Guaman Poma's writings—in particular, the parallels between their outlines of Inca history and the uncanny likeness between their illustrations—have led scholars to conclude that Guaman Poma must have collaborated with Murúa, perhaps as an incipient illustrator as well as an informant and translator.[5]

---

[5] Martín de Murúa, *Historia general del Perú*, edited by Manuel Ballesteros (Madrid: Historia 16, 1987) and *Códice Murúa: Historia y genealogía de los reyes incas del Perú del padre mercenario Fray Martín de Murúa* (Madrid: Testimonio Compañía Editorial, 2004). Rolena Adorno and Ivan Boserup, "Guaman Poma and the Manuscripts of Fray Martín de Murúa" (*Fund og Forskning* 44, 2005, pp. 107–258; soon to be posted on the

At some point, however, he had a serious falling out with the friar: in the *New Chronicle,* he uses Murúa as the poster child in his illustrations of the worst abuses meted out by clerics against indigenous Andeans, and even accuses the friar of trying to steal his wife. There is no way to know, at our remove, what actually prompted his break with Murúa. Perhaps it was his resentment and wounded pride at being treated as a mere Indian *lengua* (interpreter), not a nobleman and a chronicler in his own right; perhaps Murúa was truly guilty of the offenses Guaman Poma attributed to him years later; perhaps it was a combination of these factors, or something else entirely. But we suspect that his time with Murúa gave him access to the published accounts of the Spanish conquest and world history that became the models and the foils for the *New Chronicle,* as well as training in the European line drawing styles that he turned to Andean subjects (and wedded with his prose) to such striking effect.

In 1594, Guaman Poma again appears as an interpreter, this time for a different kind of *visitador:* not a church inspector, but the Spanish judge of the city of Huamanga in charge of legitimizing land titles. The language of the document makes it clear that by this time Guaman Poma had moved to Huamanga, some eighty miles north of his home province of Lucanas, and was considered an employee of the judge. Around the same time, he begins to appear as a plaintiff in his own right in a series of lawsuits over title to land and political power. The land in question is in the Chupas valley, on the southern outskirts of Huamanga. Under colonial rule, this region—unlike Lucanas—was swiftly being incorporated into the Spanish-controlled production zone that lined the major inland trade routes of the Andes. Steve Stern comments about the growth of this European enterprise zone: "As usual, those with political power and connections dominated access to the labor, tributes, land rights, and markets needed to realize large profits. . . . Not surprisingly, the landowners who dominated production in this lucrative zone belonged to Huamanga's old elite."[6] It is easy to imagine that, in pre-conquest days, the Guaman family ties to the Chupas valley were just one among many sets of political alliances maintained by a regional ruling clan. Under the new regime, with land almost worthless in Lucanas but soaring in value near Huamanga, the Chupas valley was worth reclaiming. For Guaman Poma and his family, the claims were made too late: newer but already entrenched elites

---

Danish Royal Library website) describe the striking parallels between the two chroniclers and make the case for their collaboration, as does Juan Ossio in the introductory study to *Códice Murúa* and earlier writings.

[6] Steve Stern, *Peru's Indian Peoples and the Challenge of Spanish Conquest: Huamanga to 1640* (Madison, Wis.: University of Wisconsin Press, 1982), 109.

crowded out their claims and ridiculed their pretensions. After several turns in his case (brief losses, briefer wins) between 1594 and 1600, Guaman Poma himself was finally given the humiliating punishment of a public whipping followed by confiscation of all his property and banishment from the vicinity of Huamanga.[7]

This personal disaster occurred late in 1600. Stripped of whatever power, property, and privilege was still left him from his birthright, Guaman Poma took off—in what direction, to what end, we cannot know with certainty, though from the concentration of references in the text to the pueblos south of Huamanga we can guess that he remained in Lucanas and the surrounding provinces. The humiliation of his punishment was so intense that he does no more than whisper hints of these events in his book. However, it was after his banishment from Huamanga that he most likely began the wanderings and questionings that led him to compose his masterwork, which he completed in draft form between 1612 and 1615. It is possible that he spent much time during the same years writing letters—unanswered during his lifetime, and lost to us now—to the king, the viceroy, and other powerful figures. The only one that has been discovered is dated February 14, 1615; writing from the pueblo of Chipao, Guaman Poma informs King Philip (who, he says, will remember his labors "from other earlier letters") that he has completed his chronicle, and asks that the king order the viceroy to have the book shipped to him.[8] He uses the letter to petition the king for a grant, given that "I, my wife and children have suffered much need, poverty, and nakedness because I have neglected my cattle and fields" while writing the book—a plea that implies he was not entirely destitute, but indeed still had a family, cattle, and fields. The fact that he was able to obtain nearly 600 pages of high quality European paper (not a great expense, but not a trivial one either), ink, and a clean, dry area to sit and create the final clean copy of the book over the next year also implies that the poverty of his final years was not

---

[7] See Rolena Adorno, *Guaman Poma: Writing and Resistance in Colonial Peru,* 2d ed. (Austin, Tex.: University of Texas Press, 2000), xxv–xxxvi; Rolena Adorno, "The Genesis of Felipe Guaman Poma de Ayala's *Nueva corónica y buen gobierno,*" *Colonial Latin American Review* 2 (1993): 53–92; the Prado Tello manuscript, transcribed and edited by Elías Prado Tello and Alfredo Prado Prado, *Y no hay remedio* (Lima: CIPA, 1991); and the online facsimile of the Prado Tello manuscript, http://www.kb.dk/elib/mss/poma/docs/tello/index.htm. If there is little reason to believe Guaman Poma's claim of descent from Inca royalty, there is even less reason to believe his opponents' claim that he was just an Indian commoner named Lázaro masquerading as a *curaca* (Andean noble).

[8] The letter is online, in a digital facsimile with Spanish transcription and an English translation, at http://www.kb.dk/elib/mss/poma/docs/carta1615/index.htm.

absolute but relative to the comfort of his youth. In the autobiographical chapter at the book's conclusion (the final addition to the finished manuscript, as Adorno has demonstrated),[9] he described his harrowing journey over snow-covered mountains from Lucanas to Lima and his abandonment along the way by his son and successor. He may have put the final touches on the manuscript in the early days of 1616 in the royal city of Lima. Where he went, and how long he lived, after delivering his book to time and fate is unknown.

## The Andean World in the Time of Guaman Poma

Guaman Poma assumes a fair amount of knowledge about Peru and its history in the *New Chronicle*. It may be useful to summarize some of the major events and figures in that history.

**ANDEAN CIVILIZATION.** The populous civilization of the central Andes had discovered, over the course of thousands of years of history, how to turn the greatest apparent disadvantages of the region—the extreme altitudes, the highly fragmented landscape, the lack of rainfall on the western slopes of the mountain range—into natural resources. Their adaptations and inventions made dense, settled populations possible in the heart of one of the highest mountain chains in the world.

There are several keys to the flowering of Andean civilization. First, Andean farmers domesticated high-altitude plants (potatoes, quinoa, and more) and mountain animals (llama, alpaca, and guinea pig). Second, they invented techniques to exploit the shocking daily temperature swings of the tropical Andes in order to freeze-dry staple foods; freeze-dried potatoes (*ch'uño*), meat (*ch'arki*), and other staples could be stored for years in high-altitude warehouses, giving a huge boost to agricultural societies that would otherwise fall victim to periodic droughts and catastrophic hail storms. Third, Andean societies put their fragmented landscape to clever uses: Andean agriculture became adept at exploiting the microclimates up and down the steep mountain slopes, growing corn at one elevation, potatoes and quinoa at another, and raising llamas and alpacas in the high puna where no crops could grow. The characteristic kin-based Andean communities called *ayllus* preferred to keep fields at a variety of altitudes, in what John Murra called a "vertical archipelago" of settlements, in order to have access to a wide variety of climates and the products that they

---

[9] Rolena Adorno, *A Witness unto Itself: The Integrity of the Autograph Manuscript of Felipe Guaman Poma de Ayala's* El primer nueva corónica y buen gobierno *(1615/1616)* (Copenhagen: Museum Tusculanum Press, 2003; available online at http://www.kb.dk/elib/mss/poma/docs/adorno/2002/index.htm), 76–80.

make possible.[10] Fourth, they developed irrigation techniques and built an extensive infrastructure, including complex canal systems and elaborate terracing, to bring water (and agriculture) from the glacial heights to the arid Pacific slopes of the Peruvian Andes. Scholars have linked the development of large-scale state societies in the central Andes to both the political cooperation needed to make the land productive and the competition generated by the region's highly concentrated ecological resources.[11]

THE INCA EMPIRE. Over the centuries, the Andes went through several cycles of state creation and disintegration. In one of the last rounds of expansion, still within mythic memory during Guaman Poma's lifetime, the city-state of Huari (or Wari), just north of Huamanga, conquered most of western Peru between the years 600 and 1000 to create the "Wari Empire." The Wari state eventually collapsed into many competing kingdoms, each with its own aristocratic ruling-and-warring class, its own peasant agricultural base, its own local pride and sense of identity, and in many cases its own language (or set of languages). By the 1400s, the rulers of one of these warring successor states, the Inca lineage in the city of Cusco, began a new round of aggressive expansion. The exact timing of events is disputed, but most agree that by 1500 the Inca lineage had established a continental empire of unequalled extent in the Americas, and that their armies were continuing to expand—to the north, beyond Quito and into what is now Colombia; to the south, into modern-day Chile and Argentina—for some decades after the Spanish had begun to build an empire of their own in the Caribbean.

The Inca rulers created an empire with four realms, provinces, or sectors (*suyu*): Andesuyu in the north, Condesuyu in the south, Chinchaysuyu in the west, and Collasuyu in the east, all of them adding up to Tawantinsuyu (Four *Suyu* Together), also known as the Inca Empire, with Cusco at its (and the world's) center.[12] Tying the realms together, the Incas expanded the infrastructure built by Wari and other earlier Andean states to create a well-engineered road system spanning tens of thousands of kilometers, lined with

---

[10] John Murra, "The Limits and Limitations of the 'Vertical Archipelago' in the Andes," in *Andean Ecology and Civilization,* eds. Shozo Masuda, Izumi Shimada, and Craig Morris (Tokyo: University of Tokyo Press, 1985), 15–20.

[11] See the review article by Charles Stanish, "The Origin of State Societies in South America," *Annual Review of Anthropology* 30 (2001): 41–64.

[12] These directions are as seen from Cusco, where the Andes range bends from its general north-south direction into an east-west orientation. Following this orientation, Guaman Poma views the "wild" eastern Andes as lying north of the civilized world and the Pacific as located in the south. By coincidence, the Spanish crossed Panama at a point where the isthmus bends east-west, and so they named the Pacific "el Mar del Sur," the Southern Sea, a term that reinforced Guaman Poma's view of world geography.

warehouses and waystations that allowed messengers—and armies—to travel swiftly by foot from one end of the empire to the other. Like all empires, Tawantinsuyu ran on tribute; unlike many, the Inca rulers preferred to collect tribute from their subjects in the form of labor. It was through labor tribute (*mita*) that roads and irrigation systems were built and maintained, staples and luxury goods were produced for the city of Cusco, and warrior armies were raised to continue the expansion of the empire.

The conquered provinces of the expanding empire were governed (as they are in most empires) by the formerly sovereign local rulers, now demoted to regional functionaries. When resentful local rulers rebelled, the Incas did not hesitate to apply other means of control. In some cases, the entire populations of rebel provinces were reduced to the condition of serf-like dependents (*yanakuna,* plural of *yana,* servant or serf) and set to work for the Incas. In other cases, members of an ethnic group that had proved loyal to the Incas were rewarded with land grants and special privileges in an unsettled or rebellious province. In their transplanted settlements, these settlers (*mitmac*) owed their high status, and hence their allegiance, to the ruling Inca, and could be counted on to provide soldiers and officers for the Inca military. According to Guaman Poma, his father's ancestors were *mitmac* settlers from the north-central region of Huánuco.

Tawantinsuyu is regarded by most latter-day observers as a great success. The end of endemic warfare and the general prosperity and insurance against catastrophic famine that the Inca warehouse system made possible may well have seemed a fair trade-off when balanced against the resentments of regional rulers and the hardships of labor tribute imposed on the commoner majority. One aspect of empire was never successfully resolved, however: the problem of succession. The death of a ruling Inca emperor could unleash a wave of bloodletting among his many sons by many wives, with the violence sometimes descending into outright civil war.

This is precisely what happened in Tawantinsuyu around the year 1526 by the European calendar, when the ruling Inca emperor Wayna Capac and a large part of his army succumbed to an epidemic while conquering territories in the far north.[13] (The fact that the first exploratory Spanish incursion into Peru took place at about the same time led to widespread suspicion that Wayna Capac died of an epidemic illness that was unwittingly introduced by the foreigners.) Wayna Capac's son Atawalpa assumed leadership of the army, still headquartered in the north of the empire around Quito. Meanwhile, when news of the emperor's death reached the

---

[13] Wayna Capac's name is spelled Huayna Capac, Guaina Capac, and so forth, in colonial texts; Atawalpa is spelled Atahualpa, Atagualpa, and so on; Wascar is spelled Huascar, Vascar, or Guascar.

imperial capital of Cusco, Atawalpa's half-brother Wascar claimed the throne with the backing of the nobles and warriors who had not followed Wayna Capac and Atawalpa to the north. Wascar's control of the capital city seemed to legitimize his claim in the eyes of many, but Atawalpa launched a war to claim the Inca leadership for himself. This civil war between brothers raged for years and devastated parts of central Peru. Finally, Atawalpa's army captured Cusco and took Wascar captive; the Inca civil war was almost settled. The year was 1532.

**THE CONQUERORS.** Spaniards had been immigrating from Europe to the Americas for four full decades by 1532. Their first stop on the way to creating a Spanish Empire in the New World had been the densely settled Caribbean island of Hispaniola (Santo Domingo), where they established the methods of conquest and settlement (1493–1500) that allowed their late-arriving compatriots to conquer the other American societies with large populations and advanced agriculture in short order: the remaining large Caribbean islands (1508–1512), Panama (1509–1513), Mexico (1519–1524), and finally Peru (beginning in 1532).

One might imagine the Spanish conquerors[14] as soldiers for the Spanish Crown, or perhaps as daring adventurers. Neither image is correct. Spanish expeditions of conquest and settlement in the Americas were generally put together as private ventures by business partners, either in Spain or in a previous settled region of the Americas. The main role played by the Crown was to authorize a venture with the grant of a royal license. Expeditions were staffed by volunteer crews drawn from many walks of life: tailors, shoemakers, notaries, accountants; some may have served in the Spanish army during the Italian wars, but many had not. One thing most had in common was an urban background; only a handful of peasants migrated directly from the fields to the Indies.

The conquest techniques developed on Hispaniola can be summed up briefly. An exploratory expedition would first scout out a new area, looking for the "richest" lands for conquest (that is, the areas with the largest indigenous populations and the most potential booty). Whenever possible, one or more Indians were taken on this first expedition, to serve as sources for information about the land and, crucially, as interpreters. After the target was determined, the enterprise shifted to the conquest itself; the primary goal here was to use a combination of diplomacy (this is where the interpreters came in), surprise, deceit, and overwhelming displays of brute force

---

[14] Or *conquistadores,* as English-speaking historians traditionally write. Keeping the word in Spanish is a distancing technique, a way of implying that the Spanish conquerors were different in kind from their English counterparts. I find little factual support for this view.

to capture the local chief or king and force him to serve the invaders as their puppet ruler. This done, the expedition then shifted to settlement: a Spanish city was founded (on paper, if not always on the ground), a municipal council was elected (legitimizing the enterprise under Spanish legal tradition), and Indian provinces were doled out to the Spanish conquerors as *encomiendas* (sources of tribute and laborers, with the theoretical obligation on the Spanish *encomendero's* part to care for the spiritual needs of his new dependents). The final, inevitable step came when the Spanish Crown sent royal representatives and began the slow process of wresting control of government from the conquerors.

The exploration and conquest of Peru followed this Caribbean model on a grand scale. The venture was financed and led by a pair of well-connected settlers from Panama, Francisco Pizarro (c. 1478–1541) and Diego de Almagro (1475–1538). Pizarro in particular was familiar with Caribbean conquest tactics: born in the hardscrabble western Spanish region of Extremadura, he had moved to Santo Domingo in 1502, served as a leader in the conquest of Panama in 1509, and took part in Balboa's 1513 march across the isthmus to "discover" the "Southern Sea." Pizarro and Almagro's first two expeditions along the South American coast, 1524 and 1526–1528, revealed tantalizing hints of the wealth of the civilization hidden from them in the towering Andes. Pizarro returned to Spain in 1529 to negotiate for a royal license to conquer and govern the land he called Peru; he brought with him a pair of young Indians kidnapped near Tumbes in northern Peru. One of these captives, Felipe, plays a role in Guaman Poma's narrative as Pizarro's interpreter. Pizarro took advantage of his voyage to Spain to recruit a large number of young men from his hometown to serve as "his men" in the conquest. Returning to Panama in late 1530, his title as Governor of Peru in hand (he conveniently neglected to secure any titles for his partner, Almagro), Pizarro launched a third expedition. He then spent nearly two years moving down the coast from modern Ecuador to northern Peru, where he crossed paths with Atawalpa Inca in November of 1532.

On his slow southward march, Pizarro collected information about the war between Wascar and Atawalpa. Learning that Atawalpa was camped nearby, he obtained an embassy with the self-proclaimed emperor. When they met, outside the northern town of Cajamarca, Pizarro dropped the guise of diplomacy. His crew of 168 Spaniards[15] used surprise and steel to

---

[15] One of these Spaniards was a black man born in Extremadura, Spain, presumably a descendant of freed slaves on one or both sides of his family. For a detailed study of Pizarro's men, see James Lockhart, *The Men of Cajamarca: A Social and Biographical Study of the First Conquerors of Peru* (Austin, Tex.: University of Texas Press, 1972). Lockhart's study drives home the point that these "conquerors" were not professional soldiers but a cross-section of urban Spanish society—clerks, merchants, and tradesmen.

decimate the much larger Inca force and capture Atawalpa. Pizarro's men held the Inca emperor hostage at Cajamarca for a fabulous ransom; after the ransom was paid, they divided the treasure among themselves, ignored their pledges, and kept their royal captive. Atawalpa, it was said, feared that the Spanish were plotting to reinstate his brother as emperor, so from his cell he ordered his followers to kill Wascar and to begin planning a counterattack on the Spanish. Such were the charges, true or false, that Pizarro leveled against Atawalpa before having the Inca summarily executed in July of 1533.

Almagro and his men had meanwhile arrived at Cajamarca, where they discovered that they were too late to collect a share of the ransom. Though disappointed and nurturing a grudge against Pizarro's men, they joined together to continue the conquest southward. The rich central Peruvian city of Jauja soon fell, and by November 1533 the Spanish took Cusco with the aid of their growing ranks of Indian allies—their *yanaconas,* as they called them, borrowing the term from the Incas' *yanakuna.* The conquerors anointed Manco Inca, one of Wascar and Atawalpa's many half-brothers, as their new puppet ruler, and then fanned out over the next two or three years to extend the conquest. Some headed north towards Ecuador and Colombia; Almagro went south to attempt the conquest of Chile—a disastrous venture that left his men hungrier than ever for the fortune that had eluded them at Cajamarca. Pizarro, satisfied with what he had already won in Peru, went to the coast to found a new capital city (more to Spanish tastes than mountainous Cusco, and more accessible to Spanish ships) at Lima. All the while, both Pizarro and Almagro distributed conquered Indian communities as *encomiendas* to their followers. After enduring years of hardship, battle, disease, and the risk of death that had robbed them of so many of their compatriots, surviving Spanish conquerors exercised their *encomendero* privileges with a sense of entitlement that led to ruthlessness.

With most of the conquerors gone, the Inca nobles and their loyal followers quietly seethed at the decline of their former imperial capital of Cusco, the disdain of the Spaniards, and the depredations of the *encomenderos.* They erupted into open revolt in April 1536. For the next year, an army of perhaps as many as 200,000 Indians kept Cusco under siege, and for a time they threatened even the new seat of Spanish power at Lima. Ultimately, they did not hold out against the same Spanish advantages that had determined the outcome of the conquest, not even after devising tactics to overcome Spanish steel and horses. Their ranks were thinned by epidemic disease; their troops had to return to their homes and fields for planting and harvests, while the foreign intruders were content to live off the labor of others; and their old enemies, the Andean ethnic lords who had chafed under Inca rule, continued to fight on the Spanish side. Abandoning the siege, many came to terms with the Spanish, but some part of the Inca forces withdrew to the mountain fastness of Vilcabamba under the command of Manco Inca, the former puppet ruler of Cusco, and attempted to build a new Cusco in the forest.

THE ESTABLISHMENT OF COLONIAL PERU. The withdrawal of Inca forces from open battle with the Spanish left the conquerors in full control of the country, except for the inaccessible neo-Inca state of Vilcabamba, a poor imitation of Tawantinsuyu that neither threatened nor much interested them. Ignoring Manco Inca and his successors for the next generation or two,[16] the Spanish turned to a more pressing concern: fighting with each other for a bigger share of the pie. The chronicles of the next decades of Peru's history are a welter of names and dates and a Shakespearean catalogue of pride, treachery, and deaths. Pizarristas against Almagristas; everyone against the representatives of the Spanish Crown. Pizarro's Cusco under siege by Almagro; Almagro executed by Pizarro's brother; Pizarro murdered by Almagro's mestizo son; the first viceroy murdered by another brother, Gonzalo Pizarro; a coup against royal authority and the Crown's efforts to limit the power of the conquerors, led by Gonzalo and supported by the *encomenderos;* the capture and execution of Gonzalo; and a final, lackluster rebellion by dissatisfied *encomenderos* in 1553. The constant turmoil among the Spanish conqueror class between 1537 and 1553 reveals, more than anything, the depth of their conquest of Andean society. The conquerors were free to fight each other over control of the wealth generated by Indian labor precisely because they had nothing to fear from the subdued and subjected Andean Indians.

The chroniclers' entire attention is drawn to the blood and battles of this chaotic time, when both *encomenderos* and Incas could still dream of reestablishing their primacy over Peru.[17] But, behind the battle scenes, the foundations of the colonial state were quietly being laid: Spanish settlements were founded in a continent-spanning network; great silver mines were discovered; royal government and an elaborate legal system, with a special separate track for Indians, were slowly but irresistibly established; a system of Catholic churches, staffed mainly by friars, spread across the indigenous highlands; Quechua, the "language of the Incas," was extended across the Andes by the friars as a lingua franca for Indians,

---

[16] Manco Inca was succeeded as the Inca ruler of Vilcabamba by his sons Sayri Tupac (Sayri Topa), Titu Cusi Yupanqui, and Tupac Amaru (Topa Amaro).

[17] For an entertaining history of the conquest period in Peru, drawn mainly from the accounts of Spanish chroniclers of the era, see John Hemming, *The Conquest of the Incas* (New York: Harcourt Brace Jovanovich, 1970).

replacing perhaps hundreds of former local indigenous languages;[18] and systems for exploiting native labor were regularized. Over the next three decades, and in particular under the active rule of Viceroy Francisco de Toledo (1569–1581), the chaotic social picture of the conquest era gave way to stability, and all the elements of the colonial regime were put in place. To symbolize his establishment of the rule of law in Peru, Toledo kicked off his term of office with a concerted effort to conquer the hold-out neo-Inca kingdom in Vilcabamba. Guaman Poma describes at length the capture and execution of Tupac Amaru, the last ruler of what remained of the Inca Empire, in 1571.

Toledo's ceremonial regicide of the last Inca ruler symbolized the antipathy between the viceroy and native Andean lords. The real source of hostility between them was not this symbolic act, however, but rather Toledo's extension of royal power to the village level. One of his signature efforts was to carry out the *reducción* or resettlement of scattered Andean communities into compact, Spanish-style pueblos, a goal that ran counter to the "vertical archipelago" settlement pattern that Andean societies used to exploit microclimate variations on the mountain slopes. This program was virtually impossible to carry out as intended, but the push to impose *reducciónes* offered provincial authorities endless opportunity for corruption and graft, and caused great hardship to already beleaguered Andean peasants.[19]

The other "Toledan reform" for which the viceroy is most remembered is his imposition of a forced labor draft on Indian communities. The Crown had been pushing to curtail or abolish various forms of Indian forced labor (Indian slavery, *repartimiento, encomienda*) since as early as 1502, but voluntary wage labor proved perennially inadequate to meet the Spanish demand for cheap workers. This was particularly true in the Andes after the discovery of silver at Potosí. Toledo's solution was to adopt the Inca *mita* system of labor tribute, which he justified as a local tradition while reinterpreting it as forced labor. Under the Toledan *mita,* Indian communities located in mining districts were obliged to send a certain number of men to work as miners for months at a time; Spanish agricultural estates could also petition to have *mitayos* (Indians fulfilling their *mita* obligation) work their fields. The mercury mines at Huancavelica took up to 3,000 Indians as its *mitayos* in any given year—one seventh of the Indians from the surrounding region, which by the 1600s was extended as far afield as

---

[18] See Bruce Mannheim, *The Language of the Inka since the European Invasion* (Austin, Tex.: University of Texas Press, 1991), 80–109.

[19] Jeremy Mumford is completing a book that will shed much light on the history of *reducciones* in sixteenth-century Peru.

Guaman Poma's home province of Lucanas, as Indian population declined near the mines.[20]

The colonial regime that came of age under Toledo—a regime that enriched the most unscrupulous of provincial authorities and Spanish intruders while sending so many ordinary Indian workers to their deaths in the mines—is the main object of Guaman Poma's wrath in the *New Chronicle*.

## Reading the First New Chronicle

What, then, is the *First New Chronicle and Good Government?* Physically, it is a heavy, bound manuscript, composed of the 398 fine line drawings that Guaman Poma drew and the nearly 800 pages of text that he painstakingly wrote out by hand.[21] Conceptually, it is a book.[22] Guaman Poma explicitly modeled "this book" or "this chronicle" (as he repeatedly calls it) on the Spanish books that he voraciously read, probably after encountering them in friar Murúa's study. The modeling extends to such details as sequentially paginating his manuscript in the style of printed books, adding running chapter headings in small capitals, printing chapter titles in bold block letters, justifying margins, and repeating the first word of each page at the bottom of the preceding page (a publishing convention for books, not letters, of his time).

Guaman Poma was eclectic in the books that he took as models—particularly from the viewpoint of his Spanish contemporaries, who would have seen histories, chronicles, and official reports as separate genres, each with its own truth value and claim to authority.[23] Perhaps, as a non-Spanish author, Guaman Poma cared little for these distinctions. At any event, his is a book that combines global histories, histories of the Andes, and chronicles of the conquest (compiled or copied from such well-known sources as Zárate and Diego Fernández) with eyewitness accounts (both his own and those of his informants), Catholic moral discourses (some copied directly from devo-

---

[20] Noble David Cook, *Demographic Collapse: Indian Peru, 1520–1620* (Cambridge: Cambridge University Press, 1981), 205–07; Stern, *Peru's Indian Peoples,* 82.

[21] Adorno, *A Witness unto Itself.*

[22] The title and introduction to an earlier abridged English translation of the book—Christopher Dilke, *Letter to a King: A Peruvian Chief's Account of Life Under the Incas and Under Spanish Rule* (New York: E. P. Dutton, 1978)—has led many to misconstrue the manuscript as a lengthy letter to the Spanish king. In fact, Guaman Poma refers to his work throughout as a book (*libro*), never a letter; he divides it into many chapters; he addresses many chapters directly to the king, but he also writes of the king in the third person and explicitly addresses other chapters to different readerships; and he requests more than once to have the manuscript published as a book.

[23] Adorno, *Guaman Poma,* 9.

tional books), satirical interludes, policy recommendations, and personal exhortations directed at the book's readers. From the hypothetical Spanish reader's point of view, the book would have seemed a hopeless mishmash, but read without prejudice it follows a clear, though elaborate, structure.

The book is divided into many chapters, long and short. Better said, the chapters are elastic, constantly expanding and spawning or spinning out into new chapters. Guaman Poma is concerned only with the structural relation among the chapters, ignoring the European convention of dividing books into a linear progression of numbered chapters of roughly equal length. The book opens (again, in imitation of the books of the time) with an introductory series of letters, dedications, and prefaces, which I group under "Introductions." The first major section of the book proper, "The Ages of the World," is a five-part introduction to the theme of the chronicle. The fifth chapter of "The Ages of the World," describing the age that begins with the birth of Jesus (that is, the Christian world in which Guaman Poma himself lives), expands until it becomes a second section in its own right, titled "The Pontiff's Throne." This section concludes with a summary of the Conquest theme, which has not yet been elaborated.

A third major section, "The Ages of the Indians," exactly recapitulates the five-part section on world history. The duplication is so obvious that Guaman Poma must have chosen it for rhetorical effect: through the structure of the book itself, he is arguing that the Indians of the Andes are the equals of the Europeans in world history. Once again, the crowning age, "The Fifth Age of Indians: The Incas," expands into a new section in its own right; indeed, it continues expanding in chapter after chapter (arranged thematically into chapters on the civil hierarchy, on religion, and on government), until it forms the main body of the first third of the book. This section is demarcated by a fifth major section, "The Conquest of This Kingdom," that bridges "The Ages of the World" (which ended with a preview of the Conquest) and "The Ages of the Indians" (which comes to an end—or a transition—with the arrival of the Spanish). The Conquest marks a break in Andean life, but it unites the two strands of the chronicle, world history and Andean history.

The sixth major section, "Good Government," chronicles the viceroys of Peru; their Christian government unites Peruvian with global history. This section expands into a seventh section, in multiple chapters that I group as "Conquest Society in the Andes," which recapitulates the thematic outline of his section on the Incas: the colonial civil hierarchy is presented first, then the Church, and finally a series of critiques of the "good government" of colonial rule. These critiques are followed by a series of chapters on "The Indians," which is both a continuation of the critique of "good government" and a separate, eighth major section in its own right—called here

"Andean Society under Spanish Rule"—that spans the Christian and the Indian sides of the book's structure. The book ends with a series of "Conclusions and Appendices" that mirrors the opening section of introductions and prefaces.

Guaman Poma's interpretations of history and of the Andean world in his own time differ in many ways from the versions offered by Spanish chroniclers and commentators. One difference is based on purely personal or familiar concerns: only Guaman Poma's chronicle mentions the allegedly prominent role of his father, grandfather, and ancestors in the history and government of Peru. Other distinctions are conceptual, based on differences between European and Andean world views; we can see this in Guaman Poma's treatment of time. Like the chapters of his book, time is elastic for Guaman Poma, expanding and contracting according to a structural logic that pays minimal attention to the progression of numbered years (the hallmark of European chronicles). Juan Ossio points out,[24] for example, that Guaman Poma first gives a sum of 6,612 years for all the "Ages of the World" from Creation to the present, and then cites a total of 6,613 years for the "Ages of the Indians." The logic of European chronology insists that the Indian ages, having begun centuries after the Creation, must add up to fewer years than the sum total of world time. But for Guaman Poma, numbers primarily serve a symbolic function. In this case, the numbers *6,612* and *6,613* (that is, the present year in which Guaman Poma wrote each section plus a round 5,000) index the equivalence of the five World ages and the five Indian ages.

A similar distinctiveness in Guaman Poma's approach can be appreciated in his illustrations, the best-known aspect of the book to many students of Latin America. Rolena Adorno has given a thorough analysis of the spatial and structural logic of his drawings and its Andean roots.[25] Without repeating the entire analysis here, one example will give a hint of Adorno's argument. In the illustration titled "God Created the World" Guaman Poma depicts God (recognizable by his long beard, flowing robes, and a triangular halo that represents the Trinity) standing on a landscape marked "World" in the center of the page. Figures marked "Adam" and "Eve" kneel to his right and left. (Adorno emphasizes that in all of Guaman Poma's drawings, right and left are defined from the viewpoint of the people inside the drawing—or from the viewpoint of the drawing itself, as if it were looking out at us—and not from that of the viewer.) God's right hand rests

---

[24] See Juan M. Ossio, *The Idea of History in Felipe Guaman Poma de Ayala,* Ph.D. dissertation, Oxford University, 1970, 200; online at http://www.kb.dk/elib/mss/poma/docs/ossio/1970.

[25] Adorno, *Guaman Poma,* 80–119.

# GOD CREATED THE WORLD.

*He gave it to Adam and Eve.*

on Adam's head, and his left on Eve's. In the sky, the sun appears directly above Adam (to the right of God), the moon appears above Eve (to his left), and the morning star (Venus) is directly above God. The layout of this picture is a virtual diagram of Andean ideas of gender and hierarchy: the female, the left hand, and the moon are associated with each other; the male, the right hand, and the sun are linked. God the Father—the higher, unifying principle—stands both between and above male and female, sun and moon, and is associated with Venus. In Guaman Poma's drawings, the "place of honor" is towards the top right (viewer's left) and the subjected position is towards the bottom left (viewer's right), while balance, synthesis, and justice is found at the center or center top. After establishing this pattern in the sections on world history and the Incas, Guaman Poma can silently critique the colonial regime simply by drawing a corrupt colonial official on the left side of the scene—the position of degradation, visual proof that "the world is upside down."

Other differences between Guaman Poma's approach and those of his Spanish contemporaries are more subtle. Tom Cummins argues that Guaman Poma's goals in depicting Andean life are starkly different from those of the "extirpators of idolatry" for whom he worked earlier in his life, and on whose works he drew in composing his *Nueva corónica*. The friars described Inca religion in order to destroy it; Guaman Poma denounces Indian "idolatry," but in Cummins' view he quietly refrains from describing Andean cultural practices in ways that would give friars such as Murúa greater license to abuse indigenous communities. "Guaman Poma is a Christian, but he is not a cultural iconoclast. . . . The control of knowledge is the exercise of power; the last thing Guaman Poma de Ayala wanted to present to the King of Spain was more power over the Andes, a world that had already been turned upside down." Applying this insight to Guaman Poma's drawings, Cummins concludes that "we see and learn remarkably less at first sight than we think we do about what Guaman Poma knew about the form and operation of objects and images in his Andean culture."[26]

What Guaman Poma does do (and what we presume he wants to do) in his book is to present a persuasive argument for maximum Indian autonomy under royal—but not necessarily colonial—rule. To this end, he insists on a number of points about Andean history that are drawn, in many cases, from Spanish sources, but that in their totality put him at odds with Spanish writers. The Indians, he writes, were evangelized by one of

---

[26] Tom Cummins, "Images on Objects: The Object of Imagery in Colonial Native Peru As Seen through Guaman Poma's *Nueva corónica i buen gobierno*," *Journal of the Steward Anthropological Society* 25 (1997): 263 and 269.

Christ's apostles—a point made by Spanish chroniclers who could not imagine that the apostles could have missed such a large region of the earth. Guaman Poma, however, concludes from this that the Indians were already Christians before the Spanish arrived, that they voluntarily accepted the rulership of the king of Spain, and therefore that there was no need for conquest."[27] Guaman Poma's sophisticated argument on this point, which builds on the work of Bartolomé de las Casas,[28] is aimed not against the king but rather against the conquerors who had become the leading *encomenderos* of the colonial regime. If there was no justification for conquest, then the conquerors' privileges were based on deceit and should be retracted by the Crown.

Readers should note that Guaman Poma does not represent, and indeed would never claim to represent, all Indians. In fact, he would prefer to reject the Spanish-imposed label of "Indian" altogether: he is an "Author and Prince," a *capac apo,* an Andean noble, "*waman,* the king of birds" and "*puma,* the king of beasts," but he is *not* an Indian—a word that, to his ear, means an Indian commoner. He sees Indian commoners, who made up the great majority of Peru's population, as his people: he cries for justice for them, offers them his protection, even speaks of how he lowered himself to walking among them, but he certainly does not see himself as one of them. His attitude throughout is as paternalistic as that of any Spanish friar. Even less does he identify with women, whether commoner or noble; in their case, his paternalism frequently borders on contempt. Going against what most observers see as a longstanding emphasis on gender complementarity in Andean culture, Guaman Poma seems to adopt Spanish concepts of honor and unilateral descent through the male line, and demands that indigenous women be kept safe from the depraved lust of Spanish men, regardless of their own desires.

Finally, the most famous statement in Guaman Poma's writing is one that he repeats throughout the book: *y no hay remedio,* "and there is no remedy." It sounds like a cry of desperation, and in some cases that is just what it is. The reader soon comes to realize, though, that wherever Guaman Poma writes "there is no remedy," he means to imply: "*but yes, there is—there must be a remedy.*" Taken as a whole, the book is not simply a lament for a lost world, but a call to action. Remedies exist, and reforms are possible; Guaman Poma makes substantial and specific policy recommendations, and offers his own service as a kind of reinstated deputy Inca ruler to carry them out.

---

[27] Adorno, *Guaman Poma,* 15.

[28] Ibid. 13–32.

## Notes on the Text and the Translation

Since the discovery of Guaman Poma's manuscript of his book in the Royal Library of Denmark in 1908, it has become more and more available in print: first, with the publication of a photographic facsimile in 1936; then with the first scholarly transcription of the text, by John Murra and Rolena Adorno, with Quechua textual analysis and translations by Jorge Urioste, in 1980; and most recently, with the online publication of the entire text in digital facsimile, together with a searchable version of the Murra-Adorno transcription, in 2001 by the Danish Royal Library.[29] My translation is based primarily on the digital facsimile, though I have had frequent occasion to refer to the Murra-Adorno transcription and notes.[30] The aim of this translation of selected passages from the *New Chronicle* is to make the sweep of Guaman Poma's book and the thinking behind it accessible to a broad English-speaking audience.

"Accessible" is not a word easily associated with this book. The modern reader, accustomed to the standardized spelling and grammar of today's printed books, is confronted in the Guaman Poma manuscript with page after page of run-on sentences with virtually no useful punctuation, words spelled in every conceivable variation, and a lack of concern for leaving spaces between words (rather than in the middle of words, for example). These inconvenient styles hardly reflect limited literacy on Guaman Poma's part. Sparse punctuation and exuberant orthography are the hallmarks of seventeenth-century manuscripts, and in this sense, reading Guaman Poma is mainly a matter of getting used to it. On top of punctuation and spelling, Guaman Poma adds the complication of his idiosyncratic Spanish, which follows a mix of Quechua and Spanish grammatical rules. It is this aspect of his writing, more than his insertion of Quechua phrases (which are often accompanied by Spanish glosses), that has led many readers to throw up their hands in resignation at the perceived "barbarity" of his style. The solution to this problem was pointed out by Bruce Mannheim: although Guaman Poma "followed the conventions for a printed book in assembling his manuscript," Mannheim notes, the text itself (as opposed to its textual layout) is based on *oral* rather than *written* models for Spanish: "His text is written in a Spanish that follows Quechua patterns of rhetorical organization, leaving much of his writing opaque to modern Spanish-speaking readers."[31] Guaman Poma could skillfully imitate, even mock, a

---

[29] The digital project is at http://www.kb.dk/elib/mss/poma/. Readers should note that all 398 illustrations can be viewed online through this site.

[30] The transcription and annotation, *El primer nueva corónica y buen gobierno* (Mexico City: Siglo XXI Editores, 1980; now also available online from the Danish Royal Library), are copyrighted by John V. Murra and Rolena Adorno.

[31] Mannheim, *The Language of the Inka*, 132.

variety of writing styles, but the basic model for his Spanish was the spoken language of the *criollos* of central Southern Peru from his time, deeply informed by Quechua rhetorical patterns. The solution, then, is to treat the text as the transcription of an oral performance. Phrases and passages that seem to make no sense when read by the rules of written language take on new meaning, and often become completely clear, when read aloud.

The lack of punctuation in the text necessarily turns the reader into an interpreter; the oral rhetoric, even more so. In order to read the sentences out loud, a reader must first decide where sentences start and stop, which nouns go with which verbs, where the emphasis falls in each sentence, which sentences are questions or exclamations, and which utterances are quotations or glosses.[32] Once the reader, as an interpreter of the page, has imaginatively transformed Guaman Poma's text into the spoken word, the translator can step in, again in the guise of interpreter, to convey the *meaning* of Guaman Poma's words into another language. In this translation, I have made interpretive decisions based on the flow of the text, the textual hints (such as bold letters and rare punctuation marks) that Guaman Poma proffers, and my own understanding of what it all means. Occasional disagreements with the now-standard Murra-Adorno transcription tell me that such decisions can never be final.[33]

Because this is an abridged translation, a second set of interpretive judgments had to be made: what to leave in, and what to leave out. These decisions were, if anything, even more subjective on the translator's part: my hope was to create an English text that readers would find interesting, and in pursuit of this goal I included the passages that interested me. My own background in Latin American colonial history, not Hispanic literature, Andean studies, or Quechua linguistics, has unquestionably influenced my choices. I see Guaman Poma as a colonial subject, and the aspect of the book that most attracts me is the view it gives us, in our different time and place, of his world and his attempts to make sense of the indignities and deformations suffered by his society under colonial rule. At the same time, I have endeavored to include enough material from each part of the book to suggest its overall structure and the range of details and themes that it covers.

---

[32] An exercise in which readers are in fact greatly aided by Guaman Poma's much-criticized tendency to repeat himself. "Some of Guaman Poma's 'repetition' is in fact parallelism," which derives not from informal verbal communication, but from the formal oral rhetoric of both Quechua and sixteenth-century Spanish (Bruce Mannheim, personal communication, 10 March 2006).

[33] Readers who compare this translation with published transcriptions should be aware that almost all punctuation, sentence breaks, question marks, and paragraph breaks are added by the editors. To envision the book as written, imagine it without punctuation of any kind—or see it in the online facsimile.

**TECHNICAL MATTERS.** Guaman Poma prints his chapter headings and an occasional important line in **bold face**, sometimes in **CAPITALIZED BOLD FACE**. I have tried to replicate this effect in the translation.

Guaman Poma frequently uses the Spanish word *como* ("how") to introduce a new topic, a usage drawn from the titles and chapter headings in Spanish books of his time. This usage translates poorly into English, so I have substituted the mark ◆ for *como* or *de como* at the beginning of many paragraphs.

Throughout the text, I use parentheses ( ) to surround words appearing in Guaman Poma's text that I judge to be parenthetical. In many cases, these are what I interpret as glosses of Quechua terms. I use square brackets [ ] to enclose my own editorial additions. When Guaman Poma writes "nununya y quichimcha – ollin" and I translate this as "*ñuñunya* [the bright red juice of bitter wild cherries] and *quichimcha* (soot)," the bracketed phrase is my explanation of the Quechua term and the parenthetical phrase is Guaman Poma's own Spanish gloss translated into English.

When Guaman Poma inserts single Quechua words and short phrases in the text, I retain (and *italicize*) the Quechua, adding bracketed definitions as necessary. When he has longer passages in Quechua, I sometimes include a transcription of the Quechua with a translation in brackets or a footnote, and sometimes translate only Guaman Poma's own Spanish translation (noting important discrepancies and divergences from his Quechua). In a few instances, I translate his Quechua directly into English and omit the transcription; such passages are marked with footnotes.

Transcriptions of Quechua names, words, and phrases are tricky, given Guaman Poma's inconsistent spelling on the one hand and disagreements among modern Quechua spelling systems on the other. To lend a moderate amount of consistency to the text, I have tried to create a kind of "modernized colonial" Quechua orthography. Southern Peruvian Quechua has only three vowels (*a* as in *father*, *i* as in *bit*, *u* as in *but*), yet Spanish speakers often hear Quechua *i* as *e* and *u* as *o*. Quechua does not have the voiced consonants *b*, *d*, and *g*, yet Spanish speakers often hear them in the sounds *p*, *t*, and *q* or *k*, especially when these follow *n*. Quechua speakers, conversely, cannot tell the difference between the Spanish sounds *u* and *o*, *d* and *t*, and so on; Guaman Poma treats the corresponding Spanish letters as interchangeable. I have made a cautious effort to impose order on the resulting chaos, tending always towards modern Quechua spelling when I make any changes (thus *Suntunto* for *Sondondo*, *Inca* for *Ynga*). On the other hand, Quechua does have a *w* sound, for which Spanish lacks a conventional letter, using instead ad-hoc letters and combinations such as *u, v, gu,* and *hu*. To ease pronunciation for English-speaking readers, I decided to use the very uncolonial letter *w* to transcribe this sound (*Atawalpa,* not *Atahualpa, Atagualpa, Atavalpa,* or *Ataualpa*).[34]

The exceptions to these rules are names and words that passed into common Spanish (or colonial Peruvian Spanish) usage under standardized spellings, which I follow: *Vilcashuaman,* not Guaman Poma's *Bilcas Guaman* or my corrected *Willcas Waman; tambo,* not *tanpu.* Out of respect, I spell Guaman Poma's own name as he always did, not modernizing it to "Waman Puma" (as it is pronounced).

Other conventions: I add tildes (*ñ,* pronounced like *ny* in *canyon*) to Quechua words as appropriate. I inconsistently correct *l* to *ll* (a palatalized *l*) in Quechua words (*willca* not *uilca,* but *Atawalpa* not *Atawallpa*). I use *s* instead of *ç, z,* and *c* (*sapsi,* not *çapci*). In the footnotes, I aim to use modern Quechua spellings (*quipu* in the main text, *kipu* or *khipu* in the notes). I am fully aware that these decisions will repel many and satisfy none. In my defense, I can only point out that the digital facsimile of the full manuscript and the Murra-Adorno transcription are available online.

The page number references to the manuscript refer to the corrected pagination established by Murra and Adorno, which is also used by the online facsimile.

## Acknowledgments

This translation, more than any other I have done, has depended on the work and help of others. First and foremost, my profound thanks to Rolena Adorno, without whom this book would have been literally impossible, for her pioneering work in interpreting Guaman Poma and bringing his words and drawings to the world; to Rolena Adorno, John Murra, and Jorge Urioste for their invaluable transcription of Guaman Poma's manuscript, published in 1980; and to Rolena Adorno (again), Ivan Boserup, Keeper of Rare Books and Manuscripts, and his staff at the Danish Royal Library, for the remarkable labor of creating and publishing the online digital facsimile of the manuscript and the searchable version of the Murra-Adorno transcription. Particular thanks to the Danish Royal Library for their kind permission to reproduce their photographs of Guaman Poma's drawings.

---

[34] I have made no effort to represent Quechua phonemes that have no equivalent in either English or Spanish, notably *q* (pronounced like *k* but at the back of the throat). According to Mannheim, Guaman Poma probably spoke Ayacucho-Chanka Quechua, which does not distinguish the aspirated and glottalized versions of *ch, k, p, q,* and *t* that make life difficult for neophyte speakers of Cusco-Collao Quechua (*The Language of the Inka,* 12–5 and 132).

My thanks as well to the Quechua Program at the University of Michigan. Special thanks go to Bruce Mannheim, who created the program and kept it going through his dedication and force of will, for sharing his deep knowledge of Quechua linguistics and his deep love for the land and people of southern Peru, and for his helpful comments on parts of the translation and an early version of this introduction; to Gina Maldonado and Inés Callalli for teaching me the basics of Quechua grammar; to Margarita Huayhua for tutoring me in the uses of Quechua suffixes; and to Virginia Chávez Mejía for insisting on speaking to me in Quechua, even when it was obvious that I had ceased to follow.

Many thanks to Rick Todhunter of Hackett Publishing for his comments and encouragement; to Sarah Chambers, for her reading of the manuscript of the translation and suggestions for improving it; to Rolena Adorno for her generous comments on this introduction; and to Stella Nair, Maria Gonzalez, Guillermo Salas, Rebecca Scott, and Roland Hamilton for reading parts of the translation and sharing their knowledge with me.

My heartfelt thanks to Ruth Behar, whose request several years ago for a translation of a short selection from Guaman Poma set this project in motion.

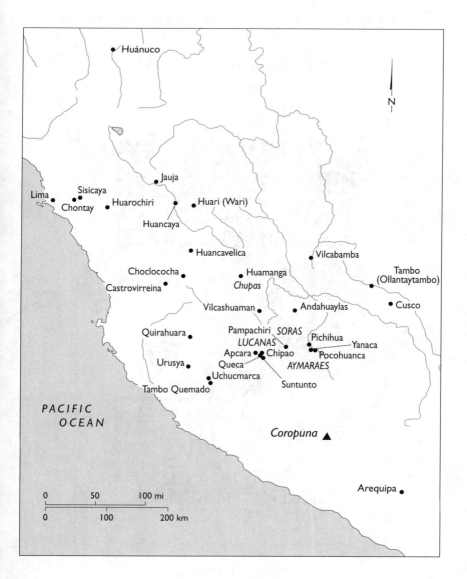

Map of south Peru, the world of Guaman Poma

# THE FIRST NEW CHRONICLE AND GOOD GOVERNMENT

*Composed by*

## Don Felipe Guaman Poma de Ayala

Lord and Noble.

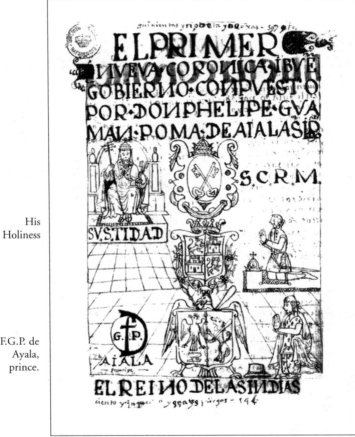

His Holiness

His Royal Catholic Majesty

F.G.P. de Ayala, prince.

1,168 pages.

His Royal Catholic Majesty.

*The kingdom of the Indies*

# CHRONICLE

## FIRST NEW CHRONICLE AND GOOD GOVERNMENT OF THIS KINGDOM

*This book composed and titled by*
Don Felipe Guaman Poma de Ayala

*[Guaman Poma opens his manuscript with a series of introductions that he models on those in the printed Spanish books of his era. The first preface extols the spiritual benefits that readers will derive from his book; next comes an invocation of the Holy Trinity, followed by a plea for the pope's blessing. A letter to the king, purportedly written by Guaman Poma's father, requests to have the book published. A second letter in Guaman Poma's own name imitates the standard sixteenth-century letter of dedication, including such touches as a humble reference to his "crude wit." In this letter, the author briefly outlines his project, his sources, the hardships he has undergone in order to inform the king of the truth, and the contents of the work. The prefaces conclude with a "Prologue to the Reader" (Guaman Poma gives the title "Prologue" to his conclusions).]*

THIS CHRONICLE is very useful and beneficial. Christians and infidels will find it good for amending their lives; Indians, for confessing and for amending their lives, their erroneous ways, and their idolatry; priests, for learning how to take confession from the Indians; and *encomenderos* of Indians, *corregidores,* padres and priests of the *doctrinas* [Indian parishes], mine owners, noble *caciques* and Indian petty authorities, Indian commoners, and other Spaniards and people, for amending themselves.[1] It is good for the audits and general inspection tours of the tributary Indians, and for the general inspection tours of the Holy Mother Church. Christians will find it good for learning new things, and also for restraining their spirits and consciences—as God warns us to do through his divine Scripture and through the voices of the holy prophets. Jeremiah tells us we should repent and change our lives as Christians. The prophet King David tells us the same, in the Psalm *Domine Deus salutis meae* [Psalm 87 (88)], where he paints fearful scenes for us of God's abandonment and of the terrible punishments that he will send us every day. Likewise, the precursor St. John

---

[1] This first sentence contains a catalogue of the social types in Guaman Poma's world (see Glossary for definitions). These types form the subjects of the chapters of the book, and Guaman Poma indicates here his hope that they would also form his readership.

1

the Baptist brings before us the threats, lashings, and punishments of God, so that we might be restrained and amend our ways in this world.

## MOST HOLY TRINITY

**GOD THE FATHER,** God the Son, God the Holy Spirit: one true God, who created and redeemed men and the world; and His Mother, the Virgin St. Mary; and all the saints and angels in heaven: Amen.

Give me your grace to write and record good examples, so that all Christians may select from them, and sow and plant them, that they might yield good fruit and seed in the service of God our Lord, and that sinners might amend their evil ways and restrain their tongues and hearts and spirits and consciences. May the Holy Spirit enlighten all those who read it, and may they counsel each other and learn and understand that there is only one true God, the Most Holy Trinity: in heaven and on earth, one true God.

## MOST HOLY FATHER POPE

**MOST HOLY FATHER, YOUR HIGHNESS,** holder of the keys to heaven and the keys to hell, and of the power of God over all kings and emperors in the world, celestial monarch:

With your key to heaven, open up Glory for us, and lock the gates of hell; send us your holy jubilee and pardon, by Your Holiness's own hand: this great gift we beseech and implore you from this kingdom of Peru in the Indies.[2] We humbly kiss your holy feet and hands, and we bow down before your holy Catholic church, that you might grant us the permission of the holy priestly sacrament, for Your Holiness has already granted us all the other sacraments. We are in the hands of Your Holiness, to serve you in the holy service of God.

And, along with that, I serve you with this small trifle of a book, titled *First Chronicle and Good Government of This Kingdom,*[3] in service to God and to Your Holiness. May you receive it, and I beseech and implore you that you give me your blessing, which is our wish from this kingdom of the Indies of Peru,

Your humble servant,
Don Felipe Ayala,
Author

---

[2] This kingdom of Peru; the Indies: Guaman Poma considers these phrases to be equivalent, and he treats them both as Spanish translations of Tawantinsuyu, the Quechua name for the Inca empire.

[3] Guaman Poma added the words "and Good Government" in the margin after the manuscript was completed. He gives various titles for the book, but they all share the core idea of being a "new chronicle."

Send us, Your Holiness, a letter in your name through your nuncio.[4] We will receive this grant with great relief to our spirit and our health.

## LETTER OF THE AUTHOR'S FATHER TO HIS MAJESTY

A LETTER FROM Don Martín Guaman Mallqui de Ayala, son and grandson of the great lords and kings who ruled of old, and captain general and lord of the kingdom, and *capac apo* (which means prince)[5] and lord of the province of the Lucanas, Andamarcas, Circamarcas, and Soras, and of the city of Huamanga and the jurisdiction of Santa Catalina de Chupas, prince of the Chinchaysuyus, and second-in-command of the Inca of this kingdom of Peru; to His Royal Majesty King Philip II, our lord. It reads as follows:

### YOUR SACRED ROYAL CATHOLIC MAJESTY:

AMONG THE MOST useful things that this great province in these kingdoms has produced, and among the most beneficial to the service of God and of Your Majesty, it has seemed worthy to me to praise the wit, curiosity, and great ability of my legitimate son, Don Felipe Guaman Poma de Ayala, who is the *capac* (which means prince), head governor, and lord of the Indians and other *caciques* and nobles, the administrator of all their common property (*sapsi*), and the general deputy *corregidor* of your province of the Lucanas in the kingdom of Peru.

For the past twenty years or so, he has been writing the histories of our ancestors and grandparents, my forefathers, and the kings from before the Inca and after [ . . . ],[6] based on reports and eyewitness testimony that he has taken from the four sectors of these kingdoms, from very old Indians of 150 years of age—four Indian eyewitnesses from each sector.

His style is simple, serious, substantive, and beneficial to the holy Catholic faith, and the history is very true, as befits the subject and people with which it deals.

---

[4] Nuncio: a church diplomat, the equivalent of an ambassador from the papal court. Ironically, the "Catholic Kings" of Spain refused to allow Vatican nuncios on Spanish territory, for fear that colonial subjects would go over the heads of local Spanish governors and appeal directly to the pope.

[5] At several points, Guaman Poma emends his original wording, "*cacique prencipal*" (the colonial title for an Indian noble) to read "*capac apo (ques prencipe)*." (See Glossary: *caciques, capac apo.*) The Quechua title *qapaq apu* (in modern Quechua spelling), "powerful lord," one of the highest ranks under Inca rule, was untainted by the suggestion of colonial collaboration that marks the word *cacique*. The emended phrase emphasizes Guaman Poma's claim to legitimate Andean noble status.

[6] The sentence continues for half a page, listing the contents of the entire book at length; it is omitted here, because Guaman Poma's own letter in the following section repeats it nearly verbatim.

Beyond the service to Your Majesty that will result from publishing this history, it will be the first to celebrate and immortalize the memory and name of the former great lords who were our ancestors as their great deeds deserve.

In the hope that all of this may be achieved, I humbly beseech Your Majesty be pleased to grant your favor to my son, Don Felipe de Ayala, and so help all my grandchildren by allowing his plans to move forward: this is what I hope to see. May Your Majesty, our lord, live and prosper for many happy years, and may you add many more kingdoms and dominions, as your most humble vassal desires.

From Concepción de Huayllapampa and Apcara,[7] in the province of the Lucanas and Soras, jurisdiction of the city of Huamanga, on the 15th of May, 1587.

YOUR SACRED ROYAL CATHOLIC MAJESTY,
I kiss your royal feet and hands,
Your humble vassal,
Don Martín de Ayala

## LETTER FROM THE AUTHOR

A LETTER FROM Don Felipe Guaman Poma de Ayala to His Majesty King Philip:

Many times I have doubted, Your Sacred Royal Catholic Majesty, whether to accept this enterprise, and many more times after taking it up I have wished to go back, judging my intentions to be reckless and finding my capacities insufficient to the task of finishing it, in accordance with its reliance on histories written in no script whatsoever, but solely on *quipus*[8] and on the reports and accounts of the oldest Indian men and women elders and eyewitnesses, that they may swear to it, and that any sentence that may be passed be thereby valid.

And thus I spent countless days and years amidst discourses that go back to the beginning of this kingdom, until, overcome by my advanced years, I accomplished this age-old desire, which was always to investigate, despite the crudeness of my wit, my blind eyes, little sight, little learning, and my lack of a graduate degree, a doctorate, a master's, or even Latin. Yet, as the

---

[7] Apcara (Aucara) is about three miles from Guaman Poma's home town of Chipao, also in the province of Lucanas (Ayacucho).

[8] *Quipus* (*khipu* in the Cusco-Collao Quechua of the Incas; *kipu* in Guaman Poma's Ayacucho Quechua) are the knotted cords used as recording devices in pre-conquest Andean society. See Jeffrey Quilter and Gary Urton, eds., *Narrative Threads: Accounting and Recounting in Andean Khipu* (Austin, Tex.: University of Texas Press, 2002); Gary Urton, *Signs of the Inka Khipu: Binary Coding in the Andean Knotted-String Records* (Austin, Tex.: University of Texas Press, 2003); and Frank Salomon, *The Cord Keepers: Khipus and Cultural Life in a Peruvian Village* (Durham, N.C.: Duke University Press, 2004).

first in this kingdom with the occasion and the ability to serve Your Majesty, I resolved to write about the history, descendents, and famous deeds of the first kings, lords, and captains, our grandfathers; and about the nobles and the lives of the Indians, their generations, and their descent from the first Indians—the *Wari Wiracocha Runa* and *Wari Runa* (the descendents of Noah of the Flood), the *Purun Runa,* and the *Auca Runa.*[9]

I would also write about the twelve Incas, their idolatries and errors; about their wives, the queens (*Coyas*); about the princesses (*ñustas*), noblewomen (*pallas*), wives of nobles (*curaca warmi*), and captains general (*sinchecunas*); and about the dukes, counts, marquises (*capac apocunas*), and other Indian petty authorities. And about the contest between the legitimate Inca, Topa Cusiwalpa Wascar Inca, and his bastard brother Atawalpa Inca;[10] and about his captains general and majors, Chalco Chima Inca, Awa Panti Inca, Quisquis Inca, Quiso Yupanqui Inca, and Manco Inca, who defended himself from the damage inflicted by the Spaniards in the days of the Emperor.

---

[9] These four *runa,* "people," were the inhabitants of the first four "worlds" or eras of human life in the Andes according to Guaman Poma's chronology: (1) *Wari Wiracocha:* Guaman Poma identifies these as descendents of Noah after the flood; (2) *Wari:* descendents of the primordial *Wari Wiracocha;* (3) *Purun* means "fallow land, meadow land, untilled land"; metaphorically, it connotes "ancestral"; (4) *Auca* (*awqa*) means "enemy, rival, adversary"; these were the people of the era of war preceding the Inca conquest.

[10] The people named here and in the next paragraph are well-known figures from the conquest era and will be introduced later in the book. The word "bastard" applied to Atawalpa and others is not necessarily an insult. Spanish law recognized three levels of legitimacy: *hijo legítimo,* the "legitimate child" of a couple married by Church law; *hijo natural,* the "natural child" of a couple unmarried at the time of birth, but who could get married by Church law and thereby legitimate the child; and *hijo bastardo,* the "bastard child" of a couple who cannot marry by church law without a dispensation, either because they are too closely related (siblings, first cousins) or because one partner is married to another person. In contrast with English law, which stripped all illegitimate children of inheritance rights, Spanish law let all children be recognized, though on a sliding scale. There is some evidence that Andean kinship rules specified three degrees of descent for nobility and royalty (depending on the status of the mother), in which case Guaman Poma may have used the Spanish terms to refer to the Andean concepts, perhaps unaware that the Spanish and Quechua concepts were not equivalent. The internal evidence of Guaman Poma's manuscript suggests that he used "natural child" and "bastard" to refer to offspring of secondary wives of high-ranking men. For the theory of three ranks of descent in Andean nobility, see R. T. Zuidema, *The Ceque System of Cuzco: The Social Organization of the Capital of the Inca* (Leiden: Brill, 1964), p. 80, and note 4 to ms. p. 183 of John Murra and Rolena Adorno, eds., *El primer nueva corónica y buen gobierno* (Mexico City: Siglo XXI Editores, 1980). Hereafter, this transcription of the Guaman Poma manuscript will be referred to as Murra and Adorno; to ease consultation with various editions of the work, page number references are to the corrected pagination of the manuscript.

And then about the conquest of this your Kingdom of the Indies of Peru; about the uprisings against your Royal Crown by Don Francisco Pizarro, Don Diego de Almagro, Gonzalo Pizarro, Carvajal, Francisco Hernández Girón, and the other captains and soldiers; and about your first Viceroy, Vasco Núñez de Vela; and about Viceroy Don Antonio de Mendoza of the Order of Santiago,[11] Viceroy Don Martín Enríquez, Viceroy Don Luis de Velasco of the Order of Santiago, Viceroy Don Gaspar Zúñiga y Acevedo, Count of Monterrey, and Viceroy Marquis Don Juan de Mendoza y Luna.

And about the lives of your *corregidores,* notaries, deputies, *encomenderos,* and parish priests; about the mine owners, the Spanish travelers who stay in the royal *tambos,*[12] and the roads, rivers, boundaries, and the whole Kingdom of Peru of the Indies; about the inspectors and judges; and about the noble *caciques,* the poor common Indians, and other matters.

To this end, I have toiled to obtain the most truthful accounts I could, taking the essence from all the people who were brought to me; even though they came from many different places, I finally reduced all their accounts to the most common opinion. I selected the language and the wording, whether in Castilian, Aymara, Colla, Puquina Conde, Yunca, Quechua, Inca, Wanca, Chinchaysuyu, Yauyo, Andesuyu, Condesuyu, Collasuyu, Cañari, Cayanpi, or Quito.[13] I have labored hard to complete this book, with the hope of presenting it to you. It is entitled *First New Chronicle of the Indies of Peru, Profitable to Faithful Christians,* written and illustrated by my hand and wit in such a way that the variety and inventiveness of the pictures and illustrations, to which Your Majesty is inclined, may lighten the weight and trouble of a script that is lacking in invention and in the ornamentation and polished style found among the great talents. As an example and for the conservation of the Holy Catholic Faith and correcting errors and profit for the infidels through the salvation of their souls, as an example and corrective for the Christians, whether they be priests or *corregidores, encomenderos,* mine owners, or Spanish travelers, noble *caciques* or common Indians, may Your Majesty benignly receive this

---

[11] Order of Santiago (St. James the Great): membership in this military-religious order was restricted to the upper elite of Spanish and Spanish colonial society and was considered the highest order the crown could bestow on a person, short of a grant of high nobility.

[12] *Tambos* (*tampu*): The Spanish retained the way stations (*tampu*) that the Inca rulers had established along their extensive highway system, particularly between Lima and Cusco, transforming them into inns known in Andean Spanish as *tambos.* Guaman Poma saw these *tambos* as dens of immorality.

[13] These are names of diverse Andean languages and regions.

humble small service, together with my great hope; for me, this will be a blessed and restful reward for my toil.

In the province of Lucanos, on the first of January of 1613,
Your humble subject,
Don Felipe de Ayala,
Author

## PROLOGUE TO THE READER[14]

TO THE CHRISTIAN who happens to read this book, having occasion to find this writing in your hand:

Making a clean copy of these histories cost me much hard work, for they were not written in any kind of letters, but rather solely on *quipus* and in reports in many languages, together with Castilian—Quechua, Inca, Aymara, Puquina Colla, Canche, Cana, Charca, Chinchaysuyu, Andesuyu, Collasuyu, Condesuyu, all the speech of Indians. I undertook this hard labor in the service of God our Lord and of His Sacred Catholic Majesty, King Don Philip III.

I spent much time and many years reminding myself that this book should be useful to faithful Christians, for amending their sins, bad living, and erroneous ways. Indians will learn to make confession, and priests will learn how to confess the Indians and find salvation for their souls, through the printing and enjoyment of this book, *First New Chronicle and Right Living of Christians,* one of the first titles to be skillfully chronicled and printed by one of the Indian princes[15] and lords of the kingdom of the Indies.

This is the favor that is begged and entreated of
HIS MAJESTY:
the printing of this book, composed by the author,
Don Felipe Guaman Poma de Ayala, lord and *capac apo* (which means prince),
for no less than this is merited by his skill
AND HARD WORK.

---

[14] Throughout the manuscript, Guaman Poma marks his concluding texts for each part, section, and chapter with the title "Prologue." Most of these prologues are exhortations directed at a specific audience; here, the intended audience is the king of Spain himself.

[15] Indian princes (*indios prencipes*): a late emendation; the text originally read *indios prencipales,* "Indian nobles."

# GENERATION[16]

*[The introductions to the manuscript conclude with brief chapters on the origin of the book and its basis in the Christian religiosity of Guaman Poma's family. The emphasis on the faith and nobility of his family are key points in his bid for the attention of the ruler of Spain, whose official title was "the Catholic King."]*

*[The illustration of God, Adam, and Eve on ms. p. 12 is described and reprinted in the Introduction on p. xxiv.]*

SO THAT YOU MIGHT SEE, Christian reader, the marvels and mercies that God performed for the good of men:

♦ God created the world in six days, and to redeem the world and the men in it, he worked for thirty-three years and died and lost his life. Knowing which were the best times and years, he created our father Adam and our mother Eve, heaven and earth, water and wind, fish and animals—all for men; and heaven, to fill it with us, with men. For men's sake, our Lord Jesus Christ died, and he sent the Holy Spirit so that we would be enlightened with his grace. It is posited and written that 2,000,612 years must have passed since the world was founded.[17] This is what has been written of the ages, months, and years, according to the planets and their courses, by the poets and learned philosophers Aristotle, Pompeii, Julius Caesar, Marcus Flavius, and Claudius, and by the holy apostles and the doctors of the holy church.

## HOW GOD ORDERED THE FIRST BEGINNING OF THIS CHRONICLE

*[An illustration on ms. p. 14, shows "Don Martín Ayala, Most Excellent Lord, Prince," sitting on a low throne in the center. He holds a rosary and gestures to his right, towards a young boy dressed in European children's clothing, "Martín de Ayala, Hermit,"[18] who kneels and bows to the elder Don Martín. "Doña*

---

[16] *Generación:* Guaman Poma uses this word in two related senses: genesis (the process of coming into being) and lineage (the descendents of a founding father). Here, it refers to both the biblical story of Genesis and the genesis of this book, which Guaman Poma relates to his own "generation" (descent) from his father.

[17] 2,000,612 years: Guaman Poma uses "millón" to translate *hunu*, the largest number in the Quechua number system, though elsewhere (see ms. p. 456) he specifies that it refers to 100,000. In many contexts, *hunu* refers to an abstract large quantity ("myriad"), not a specific number. The final digits of this number, 612, suggest that the passage was originally penned in 1612.

[18] There is no biographical evidence about the younger Martín de Ayala apart from the evidence of this manuscript. "Hermit" (*hermitaño*): a man who voluntarily withdraws from the secular world for a life of contemplation, either on his own or as a member of

*Juana Curi Oclla Coya"* sits cross-legged on a carpet behind the father figure, and a dove (sign of the Holy Spirit) descends from a window towards the boy. The caption reads, "In the city of Cusco."]

**THE HISTORY OF HOW** this book, the *First Chronicle and Good Living of Christians,* first came to be written.

This is the history of the Christianity of Don Martín de Ayala, second-in-command of Topa Inca Yupanqui, and his wife, Doña Juana Curi Oclla Coya, daughter[19] of Topa Inca Yupanqui, and of the lives that they spent in God's service. It is the history, too, of Don Martín de Ayala's children, to whom he gave his example, punishments, and doctrine. One of these was his stepson, the saintly mestizo Martín de Ayala, whom he encouraged to enter into the service of God, who received the hermit's habit at the age of twelve, and whom he bid study doctrine. He punished this stepson with his own hands.

Through his teaching, that saintly man was able grow up and teach his brothers, including the author of this book. This was how this *First Chronicle* came to be written: it was because of that splendid mestizo's virtues and because of the prayers that he said.

The noble *cacique* Don Martín de Ayala and his lady, although they were Indians, served God for thirty years, serving the poor in the hospital of the city of Cusco and that of the city of Huamanga. In this way, the saintly, noble *cacique* gave himself over to the service of God and left the world to raise his stepson and his children and to punish them; he gave up his mestizo stepson, Martín de Ayala, entrusting him to God.

For Don Martín Guaman Mallqui de Ayala was one of the greatest Indian nobles, a lord and gentleman of this kingdom, a great servant of His Majesty, and the second-in-command of the Inca himself throughout this kingdom. As a lord, he went to the port of Tumbes, in the city of Cajamarca, to receive the emperor Don Carlos's ambassadors, Don Francisco Pizarro and Don Diego Almagro; there, he kissed their hands and offered his peace and friendship to His Majesty. Don Martín de Ayala, second-in-command, went there as the deputy viceroy of this kingdom, on behalf of Wascar Inca, the legitimate king, and appeared before the Christians.

---

an Augustinian order. Of the Catholic religious orders in colonial Peru, Guaman Poma consistently singles out hermits, Franciscan friars, and Jesuits as the most ethical and charitable.

[19] Doña Juana Curi Oclla Coya, daughter: this is emended from the original, "Doña Juana Aua, granddaughter." Likewise, in the illustration on ms. p. 14, Guaman Poma added the phrase "Most Excellent Lord, Prince" after his father's name. Both emendations serve to bolster his claims of high status.

Afterwards, Don Martín de Ayala returned to his province, where, as a powerful man,[20] he served in all of His Majesty's wars and battles, combating uprisings against the royal crown. At that time, he began to serve a gentleman named Captain Luis de Ávalos de Ayala, who was a captain general and great servant of His Majesty. (This captain was the father of the aforementioned saintly hermit, Martín de Ayala, mestizo.) During a battle in Huarina Pampa, Collao, while they were waging combat in His Majesty's service, Luis de Ávalos de Ayala (the father of this saintly man) was knocked down from his horse by a lance blow, in an encounter with the traitor Gonzalo Pizarro. Don Martín de Ayala saved him from death and killed the enemy traitor Martín de Olmos; he unnerved him and killed him, and in this way he saved Luis de Ávalos de Ayala, who stood up and shouted out loud: "O lord of this kingdom, Don Martín de Ayala, servant of God and of our lofty emperor Don Carlos of glorious memory! Though you are an Indian, His Majesty will be sure to give you your *encomienda*." Thus, through this service, Don Martín, the second-in-command of the emperor in this kingdom, gained honor and merit as a lord and gentleman of the kingdom, and he took the name Ayala: Don Martín Ayala.[21]

## PADRE MARTÍN DE AYALA AND HIS NOBLE STEPFATHER DON MARTÍN

### THE EXAMPLE OF THE PADRE AND OF CAYCEDO IN THE SERVICE OF GOD

*[An illustration, ms. p. 17, shows a very young Guaman Poma, labeled "Don Felipe Ayala, author, prince," kneeling with a rosary in his hand and a hat indicating native Andean lordship on his head. Behind him kneel his father, "Don Martín Ayala, father of the author, most excellent lord," and his mother, "Doña Juana Coya," who enters the picture from stage left. Standing in front of the three, "Padre Martín de Ayala, mestizo hermit and priest who performed*

---

[20] Powerful man: this is a direct translation into Spanish of *capac* (*qapaq*), the Incaic term for a high lord. The implication is that Don Martín did not merely fight himself but rather commanded an army of followers. All indications are that Guaman Poma invented his father's titles and his participation in these events.

[21] Guaman Poma expresses here the deep sentiment among Andean nobles that they were at least as deserving of receiving royal grants and *encomiendas* as were their Spanish allies. Students of colonialism will not be surprised to learn that Andean nobles were rarely if ever successful in their attempts to press for such grants, however. Murra and Adorno note (ms. p. 16, n. 2) that this story conflicts with historical evidence suggesting that events could not have happened in the order, times, and places described here.

*Mass," preaches from an open book. The headline reads, "Saintly, beloved of God," and the caption reads, "In the city of Huamanga."]*

AFTER BEING ORDAINED as a priest to say Mass, Padre Martín de Ayala, mestizo, was a great, saintly man. He never wanted to have an Indian parish, but rather remained, his whole life, with the poor people in the hospital of the city of Huamanga, where he was their chaplain. He performed much penitence: he slept little; he had only a woven straw mat for a blanket and mattress; he kept a rooster by the head of his bed as a clock, so that he would wake up at the Angelus and visit the poor sick people; he prayed the Angelus at matins, nones, and vespers.[22] He often scourged his flesh: he wore a hair shirt his whole life, and he never wore a plain shirt against his body. He never laughed in his life. He never gazed at women with his eyes; he lowered his eyes and his face towards the ground whenever a woman spoke to him. He gave great alms and charity, showing his fear of God and his love for his fellow men. He never said a bad word to men or women, nor to any creature. He never allowed an animal to be killed; he did not want people to kill so much as a louse. He greatly rejoiced when the poor married, and he gave them dowries so that they could marry well and serve God. Every morning, many birds would come to sing to him and receive his blessing, and the mice would be humble and cease their scurrying while he was at the Angelus. The angels of the Lord revealed themselves nightly to this saintly man.

*[An illustration, ms. p. 19, comes in the middle of the next paragraph. It shows "Padre Ayala" kneeling in the center before an altar with a crucifix; he is scourging his shirtless body with a triple lash, and a small angel hovers above him, holding a halo over his head. Behind him kneels "Diego Beltrán de Caycedo, hospital administrator, companion of Padre Ayala," whose clothes indicate that he is a Spanish noble. The heading reads, "Penitence," and the caption reads, "In the city of Huamanga."]*

Afterwards, he would teach his stepfather Don Martín de Ayala (the Inca's second-in-command) and his mother and siblings about the holy commandments, the holy gospel of God, and the good works of mercy.[23] Through his teaching, his stepfather Don Martín de Ayala and his mother

---

[22] These are the traditional services held in cloisters and monasteries before dawn, at midday, and at twilight.

[23] Good works of mercy (*buenas obras de misericordia*): a key concept for Guaman Poma, this phrase appears forty-five times in the manuscript. He distinguishes between *misericordia* (mercy or loving kindness) and *caridad* (charity); both are good and pious qualities, but the latter is only made necessary by the existence of poverty, which he contends was not a problem before the coming of the Spanish colonial regime.

Doña Juana came to grow [in their faith], and, together with all his siblings, they served God and had much expertise and faith in God.

During this time, there was much contention among the Indians of the pueblo of Gran Canario, which belonged to the *encomienda* of a most Christian man named Jerónimo de Oré, a citizen of the city of Huamanga.[24] The Indians asked His Lordship Don Fray Gregorio de Montalvo, bishop of the city of Cusco,[25] to appoint Padre Martín de Ayala as their interim parish priest. Padre Martín did not want to leave his poor people in the hospital, but His Lordship threatened him with excommunication, so he went weeping to that *doctrina*.[26] He stayed there for several months with little relish, for it seemed to him that there he was doing more to earn money than to win souls. He fled the world, even though that most Christian man, Jerónimo de Oré, and his brothers and all the Indian men and women were very happy with him as their padre. The poor, the sick, the old, and the orphans were the happiest of all. Still, he returned to his poor people in the hospital and chaplaincy. When the Indians in that pueblo saw him leave, they all shouted and wept out loud. All the poor people trailed after him, and they returned home filled with sorrow and grief.

A few months after he returned to the city of Huamanga, this saintly man Ayala died in the hospital and was buried very honorably in the church of San Francisco, in the side chapel of Our Lady of the Immaculate Conception. He left the little he owned to the hospital, as his heir. All the poor people of the city wept when he died, and all the noblemen, citizens, and ladies were sorrowful. The Indians, and his companion Diego Beltrán de Caycedo, a most Christian man who was the hospital administrator, grieved the most. Ayala was then buried there, as has been mentioned.

In the same way, the life of his stepfather Don Martín Ayala, prince,[27] came to an end, after thirty years of serving the poor; the life of his

---

[24] Pueblo, city, citizen (*vecino*): In colonial Peru, the word *pueblo* (which in Spain simply means "town") was used exclusively for Indian towns; *ciudad* and *villa* were used for cities and towns founded by and for Spaniards. Only members of the very highest levels of conquest society were given the title of *vecino*, "citizen of a Spanish city." Most inhabitants of colonial cities (even among the Spaniards) were considered mere "residents." The Indians of the pueblos, who formed the vast majority of the colonial population, had even lower status. Murra and Adorno (ms. p. 20, n. 1) and others note that the *encomendero* Guaman Poma has in mind was actually named Antonio de Oré. The well-known author Jerónimo de Oré was one of Antonio's four sons, all of whom became Franciscan friars.

[25] Bishop of Cusco, 1590–1592.

[26] *Doctrina:* a colonial Indian parish. Just as colonial vocabulary distinguished between Spanish towns (*villas*) and Indian towns (pueblos), it also distinguished between Spanish parishes (*parroquias*) and Indian parishes (*doctrinas*).

[27] Prince (*prencipe*): originally, the text read *prencipal* (noble).

mother Doña Juana Coya also ended. They were buried in San Francisco. Blessed be the Holy Trinity and His mother, the virgin St. Mary, and all the saints and angels, Amen. The portrait of Padre Martín de Ayala and Diego Beltrán de Caycedo [still] hangs in the hospital of the city of Huamanga.

## THE DEVOTIONAL MASSES OF PADRE AYALA

### THE ORDER AND SAINTLINESS THAT PADRE MARTÍN DE AYALA KEPT IN SAYING MASS EACH DAY OF THE WEEK THROUGHOUT THE YEAR

IT SEEMS THAT the other Christian priests should keep this same order and saintliness in saying Mass; all the parish priests of all the *doctrinas* should follow this order. The most illustrious-in-Christ bishops and prelates should decree that this order be kept, imposing serious penalties and excommunication [on those who fail to do so]. The general inspectors of the Holy Mother Church should keep the order of this padre in mind.

It went as follows:

On Sundays, he would say Mass for the Christian kings and princes and for the people.

On feast days, he would say the same Mass.

On Mondays, he would say Mass for the conversion of the infidels who persecute the Holy Mother Church of our Christianity; and he would perform the marriage ceremony for all those who asked.

On Tuesdays, he would say Mass for all those who gave him alms, and for those who gave offerings for the prayer for the dead.

On Wednesdays, he would say Mass for his father, mother, brothers, sisters, and close kin, and for those who do good, and for evildoers, for whom we should pray to God, because that is right and proper.

On Thursdays, he would say Mass for the dead, for the souls in Purgatory— High Mass for those who left alms, or Low Mass for those who did not.

On Fridays, he would say Mass for all the souls in Purgatory, the poor saintly souls who suffer there. We should pray to God without requiring alms from those in need, as an act of mercy, because God is so merciful that he left his apostles and saintly priests in this world; thus, those priests of God should be merciful.

On Saturdays, the Mass should be said for the ever-virgin Mother of God, St. Mary, Our Advocate, that she might pray to her precious son, our Lord Jesus Christ, and for the Most Holy Trinity, one true God, without need for alms.

Adam

Eve

*In the world.*

# PART 1.
## THE AGES OF THE WORLD

*[Guaman Poma begins his chronicle with a summary of what he calls five successive "worlds," or alternately, the five "ages of the world" or "generations of the world." The equivalence of these terms reflects the Quechua word* pacha, *meaning both "world" and "time" or "era." In this opening history, Guaman Poma presents brief histories of five "worlds" or eras derived from Christian biblical history. The "first world" of Adam and Eve is translated here.]*

## THE FIRST GENERATION OF THE WORLD

ADAM AND his wife Eve were created by God, body and soul.

Adam begot Seth; Seth begot Enos; Enos begot Cainan.[28]

Cain killed Abel; from him came the stock of blacks, because of envy, he built the first city and named it Enoch after a son of his.[29]

Cainan begot Mahalalel; Mahalalel begot Jared; Jared begot Enoch, who is in paradise. His father, Lamech, was of the lineage of Cain. He had three sons and a daughter: Jabal invented the tent; another son, Jubal, invented the organ and guitar and playing the organ. Tubalcain invented the art of forging iron; the daughter, Naamah, invented spinning.

Enoch begot Methuselah. Methuselah lived longer in the world than anyone else—1,040 years and more—but even so, Adam and Eve lived longer.

Methuselah begot Lamech; Lamech begot Noah.

These men, each one of them and their offspring, lived for a very many years. Only Adam and Eve lived 2,000 or 3,000 years. They must have given birth by pairs, as was necessary in order to fill the world with people.[30]

All this is written with the consideration that it is impossible to know what happened so long ago, for the world is old, and only God in his secrets knows what was and what will be. It cannot be known, but only

---

[28] Here Guaman Poma presents a summary of Genesis 1–5. King James Version spellings are used in this translation for biblical names.

[29] Guaman Poma repeats the racist European interpretation of Cain as the ancestor of the "stock" (*casta*) of blacks. Elsewhere, he writes sensitively about the harsh lives of enslaved black men and women. The phrase "because of envy" is ambiguous (hence the ambiguous punctuation in this translation): it may refer either to the origins of the "race of blacks" or to the founding of the first city.

[30] The birth of twins was a significant event in the Andean world: twins of identical sex were an ill omen, while twins of opposite sex augured fertility and increase. On the life spans mentioned here, compare Genesis 5:5: Methuselah lived 969 years; Adam lived 930 years; Eve's life span is not mentioned, nor indeed is that of any woman.

imagined, what God determined in the millions of years from the founding of the world until God's punishment. The world was so filled with men that they no longer fit, and they no longer knew the Creator and Maker of men. So God ordered that the world be punished; everything created within it, for their sins, was punished by the waters of the flood. It was determined by God that Noah and his children would be saved in the ark of God.

*[The brief histories of the next three "worlds"—Noah and the Flood; Abraham and the binding of Isaac; King David—are omitted here. Guaman Poma elaborates the longer history of the fifth world, the Christian age that began with the birth of Jesus and still continues today, into a separate section.]*

# PART 2.
## THE PONTIFF'S THRONE

*[Our present "fifth world" is marked by the universal rule of the pope. This chapter begins with a dry listing of the first two hundred–odd popes from Peter to Urban VI, pausing only to note that the reign of the earliest popes in Rome coincided with that of the first Incas "in this kingdom." During the era (tiempo) of the next set of popes, from Boniface IX to Innocent VIII (1389–1492), as Guaman Poma tells us in the selection below, the "pontifical world" was expanded by the discovery of the Indies, leading to the conquest of Peru. In this chapter he introduces an idiosyncratic etymology of "the Indies" (Las Indias, the usual Spanish term for the Americas). This land, he argues, is called Indias because it is higher than Spain, and thus "in the day" (en día)—that is, closer to the daylight sun. He briefly presents his view of the conquest history of Peru, which he will elaborate later in the book.]*

IN THIS ERA the Indies of Peru were discovered, and the news ran through- 42–7 out Castile and Rome that there was a Land-In-Day, *India,* at a higher level than all of Castile and Rome and Turkey: therefore it was called the Land in Day, "India," a land of gold and silver riches.

IN THIS ERA the popes were: Pope Boniface IX from Naples, Pope Inno- cence VII, Pope Gregory XII, Pope Alexander V, Pope John XXII, Pope Martin V, Pope Eugene IV, Pope Nicholas V, Pope Callistus III, Pope Pius II, Pope Paul II, Pope Sixtus IV, and Pope Innocent VIII.[31]

Philosophers, astrologers, and poets who know the land, the altitude, and the riches of the world, know that there is no other land in the world that God has created that holds so many riches, because it lies in the highest level of the sun. This means, according to astrology, that it should be called the child of the sun, and should call the sun its father. Thus the king can rightly claim with pride that he is very powerful and [. . .].[32]

---

[31] These were the popes from 1389 to 1492; Alexander V of Avignon and John XXII (or XXIII) of Pisa are now considered antipopes.

[32] Guaman Poma added this paragraph after the manuscript was finished, writing it over a flourish (*rúbrica*) that signaled the importance of this page. The line added at the very bottom of the page has been lost. The final paragraphs of the next two text pages are also late additions by the author. In the final surviving words, Guaman Poma uses *rico,* "rich," a literal translation of Quechua *qapaq,* which in this context (and others that fol- low) is better translated as "powerful." The "king" mentioned is the Inca ruler, who claimed the sun as his father, and also the king of Spain, who in Guaman Poma's inter- pretation inherited the Inca's throne.

The Indies
of Peru,
above Spain

Cusco

Below the
Indies

Castile

IN THIS ERA an embassy from the glorious emperor Don Carlos, king of Castile, was enlisted and armed to embark for the Indies, and Don Diego de Almagro and Don Francisco Pizarro were chosen as captains. The greed for the gold and silver of the Indies caused tumult throughout Castile; 172 soldiers joined up, with Hernando de Luque as first mate and Felipe (a *Huancavilca* Indian)[33] as general interpreter. His Holiness the Pope sent his ambassador, the reverend padre Fray Vicente of the order of St. Francis.[34]

This was the era of Pope Alexander [VI], the Spaniard, Pope Pius III, Pope Julius II, Pope Leo X, Pope Adrian VI, Pope Clement VII, Pope Paul III, and Pope Julius III.[35]

During this era, Don Carlos had good fortune. As a holy man of God, he was aided by the Holy Trinity, the Virgin Mary, and all His saints and angels—most of all, the glorious St. Bartholomew, who was the first of all to win [the Indies], and who set up the Holy Cross in Carabuco; and St. James of Galicia won it for the emperor Don Carlos, that holy man.[36]

IN THIS ERA the Spanish Christians embarked and landed in the Indies at the port of Tumbes: 172 soldiers, and captains Don Diego de Almagro and Don Francisco Pizarro, and Fray Vicente of the order of St. Francis, ambassadors of the glorious Don Carlos and of the most holy father, the pope of Rome; the pope being Marcellus II.[37]

They disembarked in the port of Tumbes. They were first received by the ambassador of Wascar, the legitimate Inca; this was the second-in-command

---

[33] Felipe was one of several coastal Indians who were kidnapped as boys and sent to Castile to learn Spanish so that they could serve as interpreters during the planned conquest of Peru. Guaman Poma follows Garcilaso in calling Felipe a *Huancavilca* (*Wanka Willka*) Indian from near Guayaquil, Ecuador. As Murra and Adorno point out (ms. p. 85, n. 1), the *Huancavilca* ethnic group is not to be confused with the high Andean mining town of Huancavelica, located 150 miles inland from Lima, though Guaman Poma uses the same transcription for both names.

[34] Vicente Valverde, who later became the first bishop of Cusco (that is to say, of Peru), was a Dominican friar, not a Franciscan. For more information on Fray Vicente, Felipe, and the conquerors present with Pizarro at Cajamarca, see James Lockhart, *The Men of Cajamarca: A Social and Biographical Study of the First Conquerors of Peru* (Austin, Tex.: University of Texas Press, 1972).

[35] These were the popes from 1492 to 1555.

[36] St. Bartholomew and St. James the Great were two of the twelve apostles or disciples of Jesus. An old tradition held that Bartholomew went to India to preach the gospel, leading some chroniclers (including Guaman Poma) to conclude that he must have also preached to the "Indians" of the Americas. The story of the Cross of Carabuco is told below. St. James the Great (Santiago de Galicia) similarly set out to evangelize Spain, according to tradition, and became the country's patron saint. See footnote 162.

[37] Guaman Poma's timing is off here: Pizarro landed (without Almagro) at Tumbes, the starting point of the conquest of Peru, in 1532; Marcellus II reigned as pope in 1555.

## The Columbus Fleet
## Over Seas, to the Indies of Peru.

Juan Diaz de Solis, Pilot

Columbus

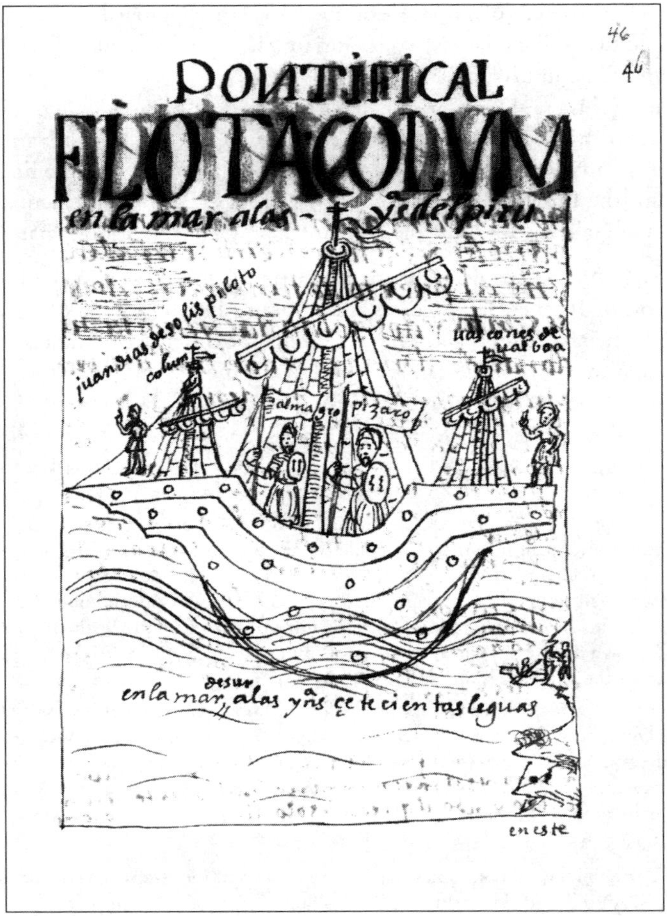

Vasco de Balboa

Almagro

Pizarro

*Over the Southern Sea to the Indies, 700 leagues.*

of the Inca, the viceroy (*capac apo*), Don Martín de Ayala. He kissed the emperor's hands, and they exchanged the sign of peace. Later, [Wascar] sent his brother Atawalpa, the bastard Inca.

First they won Panama, Nombre de Dios, and Santo Domingo; then they went further on and entered this kingdom of the Indies in the era of Pope Martin II, Pope Paul IV, Pope Pius IV, Pope Pius V, and Pope Gregory XIII.[38]

Thus this New World was discovered. When they landed in the port of Tumbes, Pizarro knew in his heart that he was sent as an ambassador merely to kiss the hands of the king (*Inca*); but as soon as he saw the gold and silver riches, his greed drove him to kill the Inca Atawalpa.

---

[38] These were the popes from 1555 to 1585. Murra and Adorno suggest (ms. p. 47, n. 2) that Guaman Poma probably used a source such as Gonzalo de Illescas, *Historia pontifical y cathólica* (Barcelona, 1589), which ends with the reign of Gregory XIII.

# PART 3.
## THE AGES OF THE INDIANS

*[Guaman Poma now returns to the beginning to retell the history of the Andean world, which he structures as a precise mirror of his biblical history of the world. His first four "worlds" (Adam, Noah, Abraham, and David) are paralleled by the first four "generations of Indians" (Wari Wiracocha, Wari, Purun, and Auca Pacha peoples). He has two apparent aims in describing these four "generations of Indians." First, in keeping with Andean notions of kinship and legitimate rule, he emphasizes the unbroken line of legitimate, first-born male heirs from Adam and Noah to the "first Indians" and thence to the royal families of the four sectors of the Inca empire—including, not incidentally, his own family. His point is that the indigenous rulers of Peru had a legitimate right to their rulership over their kingdoms, which they ultimately inherited from God's grant of the earth to Adam. Second, he argues that each generation of Indians continued to worship God, despite their faults and their distance from the revealed word of Scripture, in a more direct and honest way than most Christians do; his point here is that the indigenous rulers never gave up their legitimate ownership of Peru through apostasy.]*

## CHAPTER OF THE FIRST GENERATION OF INDIANS

48–52

*[The first of the four sections is presented here in its entirety. In it, Guaman Poma presents (or perhaps invents) an early history for native Andeans that reconciles two meanings for the term* Wiracocha: *the name of a major Andean deity,* Wiracocha *also served as the colonial Quechua term for the Spanish.[39] To reconcile the two usages, Guaman Poma attaches the name of the god to that of an early Andean civilization, the* Wari,[40] *to create the* Wari Wiracocha Runa, *a people who, he argues, descended from the biblical Noah and were sent by God to Peru. Their descent from a "Spanish" (that is, non-Indian) lineage made them* wiracocha; *this foreign origin is evident in the illustration on the*

---

[39] *Wiracocha* (*wira qucha*) literally means "Lake of Fat"; metaphorically, "Place of Power." *Wira*, fat or grease, is a sign of vital power in the Andes. See Glossary.

[40] Wari (or Huari) was an empire centered in Guaman Poma's homeland near Ayacucho. It expanded between A.D. 500 and 800 to cover much of central Peru, and collapsed suddenly around A.D. 1000. For a similar argument, see Jean-Philippe Husson, "La idea de nación en la crónica de Felipe Guaman Poma de Ayala: Sugerencias para una interpretación global de *El primer nueva corónica y buen gobierno*," *Revista Histórica* 25, no. 2 (2001): 99–134.

# THE FIRST GENERATION OF INDIANS,
## *WARI WIRACOCHA RUNA.*

The first
Indian of
this kingdom

*Wari
Wiracocha
Warmi*
[woman]

*In this kingdom of the Indies.*

*opposite page, which depicts the man as bearded (like all the other "Spaniards," and unlike the other "Indians" in the text). But these people, he says, also worship God under the name* wiracocha. *In Guaman Poma's cosmology, the* Wari Wiracocha *can be seen as culture heroes and divine messengers who gave birth to an Indian world. His arguments for the legitimacy of Indian possession of the land and rulership in the Andes rests on this history.]*

### WARI WIRACOCHA RUNA, THE FIRST GENERATION OF INDIANS, FROM THE MULTIPLYING OFFSPRING OF THE SPANIARDS[41]

BROUGHT BY GOD to this kingdom of the Indies, these were the ones who left Noah's ark following the flood, and who multiplied, by God's command, and filled the world.

This first generation lasted and multiplied for only a few years, eight hundred years,[42] in this new world called the Indies, where God sent these Indians called the *Wari Wiracocha Runa*. They were descended from those Spaniards; that is why they were given the name *wiracocha*.

The people of this generation began to multiply, and their descendents multiplied; later, these people were called gods and were held as such.

Counting the 6,613 years mentioned earlier,[43] and taking away the 800 years just mentioned, they lasted and multiplied very quickly, being the first generation of Indians. They did not die, and they did not kill. People say that they gave birth in pairs, boy and girl. From these there multiplied all the generations of Indians that were known as *Pacarimoc Runa* [founding people]. Those people did not know how to do anything, not even how to make clothes; they wore tree leaves and straw mats. Nor did they know how to make houses; they lived in caves and under cliffs. Their only work was to worship God, like the prophet Habakkuk, and thus they shouted: "Oh Lord, how long shall I cry and you will not hear, shout and you will not respond?" (*Capac*, Lord, *haycacamam caparisac, mana oyariwanquicho? Cayariptipas, mana hayñiwanquicho?*)[44] With these words they worshipped

---

[41] Spaniards (*españoles*): Guaman Poma uses this as a generic word for non-Indians. Here he means the not-yet-Indian descendants of Adam and Eve. See Glossary: *Spaniard, Wiracocha*.

[42] The original has "eight hundred and thirty," but the words "and thirty" are crossed out both here and below.

[43] In an earlier chapter, Guaman Poma dated Noah's Ark and the Flood at 6,612 years before the present; perhaps he was estimating the date of the Flood by adding a round 5,000 years to the present date at the time of writing each chapter.

[44] Compare Habakkuk 1:2, "How long, O Lord, shall I cry, and thou wilt not hear? Shall I cry out to thee suffering violence, and thou wilt not save?"

the Creator, with the shadowy understanding that they had of Him,[45] and they did not worship the demonic idols, the *wacas*. They began to work, to plow like their father Adam, and they went about as if lost—wild, in a land that had never been known before, a lost people.

**FOR IN THIS LAND, THERE FIRST LIVED** snakes (*amaro*), savages (*sacha runa, uchuc ullcu*), tigers (*otoronco*), imps (*hapi ñuño*), lions (*puma*), foxes (*atoc*), bears (*ucumari*), and deer (*lluycho*). These first Indians, the *Wari Wiracocha*, killed them, conquered the land, and ruled over them. They entered this kingdom of the Indies by the will of God.

**THESE PEOPLE, THE** *Wari Wiracocha Runa,* completely lost their faith and their hope in God and in his scripture and commandments; they lost it all, and so they themselves were lost, even though they kept a shadowy knowledge of the Creator of men and of the world and of heaven. Thus, they worshipped God, calling him *Runa Camac Wiracocha* [*Wiracocha,* Creator of People].

**THESE PEOPLE NEVER KNEW** where they had come from, nor how, nor in what way, and so they did not idolize the *wacas,* nor the sun, the moon, or the stars, nor the demons. They did not remember that they were descended from Noah of the Flood. They were, however, aware of the Flood, because they called it the *uno yaco pachacuti*[46] [water world-reversal]: it was a punishment from God.

◆ **THESE PEOPLE WERE EACH** married to their own wives, and lived without bickering or quarrels. Nor did they live bad lives; rather, all was worshiping and adoring God, together with their wives, like the prophet Isaiah, who in the psalm prayed to God for the world and the sinners, or like the prophet Solomon, who said that we should pray for the conversion of our fellows in the world. That was how these people taught each other, among themselves; that was the way these Indians spent their lives in this kingdom.

---

[45] Shadowy understanding: this is an interpretation of Guaman Poma's recurrent phrase, *poca sombra,* literally "little shadow."

[46] *Pachacuti* is an important Quechua concept. The word *pacha* can be translated as both "world" and "age, era"; *kuti* means "turn," both in the sense of "taking turns" and of "turning over." A *pachakuti,* then, is a time when one world age is overturned or gives way to the turn of the next world age. In this passage, the biblical Flood is assimilated to this Andean notion of world-reversal. As Guaman Poma notes (ms. p. 94), rulers who had achieved a transformation of the settled order sometimes took the name Pachacuti—notably, the ninth Inca ruler, Pachacuti Inca Yupanqui, who led the expansion of Tawantinsuyu north into Ecuador and south into Chile. The Spanish phrase *mundo al revés,* "the world turned upside-down," that runs throughout the second half of this book draws on the concept of *pachacuti* and the belief that the disorder of the conquest era presages an imminent new era of harmony.

◆ **THEY HAD SPECIAL PLACES** for calling God (*Runa Camac*), even though they were a lost people; and those places they kept clean.

◆ **THOSE FIRST INDIANS,** the *Wari Wiracocha Runa,* wore the same clothes and dress, and plowed in the same way as Adam and Eve: the custom of plowing the earth comes from the first people.

**THESE FIRST INDIANS, CALLED** *Wari Wiracocha Runa,* worshipped *Ticse Wiracocha, Caylla Wiracocha, Pacha Camac, Runa Rurac* [Foundational Wiracocha, Nearby Wiracocha, Creator of the World, Maker of People]. Kneeling down, holding their arms and faces up towards heaven, they would beg for health and grace, and would cry out loudly, saying, "*Maypim canqui, maypim canqui, yaya?* [Where are you, where are you, Father?]"

**FROM THESE INDIANS, THE** *Wari Wiracocha*—the legitimate and older ones, known as the *pacarimoc capac apo* [founding powerful lords]—came the great lords; and from their bastards and younger ones came the common people.[47] They multiplied, and [their offspring] were known as the *Wari Runa* and the *Purun Runa;* many people came from them.

**THE BURIALS OF THESE INDIANS, THE** *Wari Wiracocha Runa,* were simple; they did not do anything. In the time of the *Wari Wiracocha* people, the *Wari* people, the *Purun* people, and the *Auca* people, they simply had burials, without any idolatries or ceremonies whatsoever.[48]

## PROLOGUE TO "THE FIRST INDIANS, THE PEOPLE CALLED *WARI WIRACOCHA RUNA*"

**OH, WHAT GOOD PEOPLE,** though they were barbarians and infidels, because they had some shadowy knowledge, some spark of understanding of the Creator and Maker of heaven and earth and all it contains! They would say "*Runa Camac, Pacha Rurac* [creator of people, maker of the world]." That alone showed faith, and was one of the most serious things—even if they did not know the rest of the laws and commandments and God's gospel—because that point contains everything. See this, oh Christian readers, about these new people! Learn from them how to show true faith and service for God, the Most Holy Trinity.

End of the history of the first Indians, the *Wari Wiracocha Runa.*

---

[47] On "bastard" as a translation of an Andean descent category, see footnote 10.

[48] Guaman Poma stresses the simplicity of early Andean burials so that he can make the case that the Inca customs of mummifying the dead and of worshipping mummified ancestors were later aberrations.

## 56 PROLOGUE TO THE READERS OF *WARI RUNA,* THE SECOND PEOPLE, WHO RECEIVED FROM THEIR FATHERS THE LAW OF RECOGNIZING THE CREATOR (*TICSE* AND *CAYLLA WIRACOCHA,* AND *RUNA CAMAC*)

THEY WENT SO FAR AS TO SAY, "*Allpamanta Rurac*" [maker out of clay], saying and shouting it out loud. They never used to say anything else, nor did they worship idols and *wacas*. But it seems that doing this was enough for them to keep all the laws and commandments and the good works of mercy of God, even though they were barbarians and knew nothing other than to build the first of those stone huts (*pucullo*) that remain standing to this day. Look, Christian reader, at these barbarous people! You do not keep [God's law] as they did, and so you will be lost. Learn from them and serve God our Lord, who created us.

End of the history of the second people, the *Wari Runa*.

## 62 PROLOGUE TO THE READERS OF "THE INDIANS OF *PURUN RUNA*"

LOOK, CHRISTIAN READER; look at these people, the third men, who went so far with the ancient laws and commandments of God the Creator, even though they were not taught. They kept the Ten Commandments and the good works of pity, alms, and charity among themselves.

They also gave rise to many more peoples than there had been. Beginning with fights over firewood and the hay that they harvested, and over their lands, fields, tilled plots, meadows, and corrals, and over who had the right to take more water, and their coveting of the riches of this people or the other people, they started wars and looted clothes and dress, gold and silver. And in the midst of the plunder, they danced and sang with drums and fifes.

In spite of all this, they never abandoned the law, and never stopped praying to the God of heaven (*Pacha Camac*). Each people had their own king. These *Purun Runa* Indians were never involved with matters of idolatry and lies, nor was there any of that in this era; rather, everyone was simple and well-behaved.

Look, Christian reader, and learn from these barbarous people that the shadowy understanding they had of the Creator was no small thing. And so, be sure to involve yourselves with the law of God, in his holy service.

End of the third age of Indians, the *Purun Runa*.

## PROLOGUE TO THE READERS OF "THE INDIANS CALLED *AUCA PACHA RUNA* [WARTIME PEOPLE], THE FOURTH AGE"

**ALTHOUGH THEY KEPT** the law of their ancestors, calling and recognizing God from the heights and the mountains, these people abandoned their pueblos and went to settle in the heights of the mountains and crags, where they built fortresses because of the great wars they had, which is why they were called *auca runa* [Enemy People or War People]. They killed and finished each other off, took each others' wives and children, and captured each other, because of the many battles between one king and another; but, despite all this, they never ceased to worship the God of heaven, and they kept the commandments they had and the good works of mercy. Before going into battle, they first would pray, all of them asking out loud for victory, proclaiming like the prophets: "How long, Lord, shall I cry and you will not hear, shout and you will not reply? If you, Lord, are blind, you will not see me. Help me, Lord, Father. [. . .]"[49] The whole kingdom worshipped God with their hearts and words, even if they were rich people with gold, silver, cattle, and clothes. Even so, they worshipped God and held fiestas.

End of the *Auca Runa,* and the Incas begin to enter, bit by bit.

---

[49] Guaman Poma gives the Quechua equivalent for this prayer, as above.

*Inti Raymi* [Festival of the Sun]

*Coya Raymi* [Festival of the Queen]

*Choqui illa willca* (sacred lightning, or gold-flashing deity; refers to Venus, the morning star)]

[Idol of Wanacauri]

Pacaritambo Tambotoco

Idols of the Incas and coat of arms of Cusco .

**Royal arms of the kingdom of the Indies of the Inca Kings.**

# PART 4.
# THE FIFTH AGE OF INDIANS: THE INCAS

*[As he did with the "fifth world," Guaman Poma elaborates his history of the "fifth generation of Indians" into a section that stands on its own. This 290-page part, one of the longest in the book, contains a wealth of details about the social institutions of the Andes under Inca rule; underpinning it all is Guaman Poma's profoundly ambivalent attitude towards the Inca rulers. On the one hand, he subtly refers to the anti-Inca traditions that were current (we infer) among the regional nobles who had been sidelined by imperial rule. For example, he highlights the Incas' "idolatry" and "sorcery," as well as the ritual incest practiced by the royal family. On the other hand, he constantly highlights the orderliness and charity of Incaic society, which he compares unfavorably with the chaos, greed, and violence of Spanish colonial rule. In an effort at reconciling this ambivalence, Guaman Poma notes that the best practices of the Incas were the ones they inherited from their predecessors. This section is represented here by a few short excerpts.]*

## CHAPTER ONE OF THE HISTORY OF THE INCAS

79–95

*[In this opening chapter, Guaman Poma outlines the histories of the twelve rulers in the Inca dynasty. He begins by elaborating on an alternate tradition about the foundation of the Inca dynasty, which states that there was a "first Inca," Tocay Capac–Pinau Capac (it is unclear whether this was one person or two dual rulers), whose kingship was usurped by Manco Capac, the traditional founder of the Inca line. The ruling Inca were therefore descended from a usurper, whose illegitimacy as a ruler was compounded by a scandalous genealogy. It is easy to see how this scurrilous portrait of the Incas might have appealed to regional rulers itching to regain personal control over their lost kingdoms.]*

### TOCAY CAPAC, THE FIRST INCA

**HERE BEGINS THE HISTORY** of the first Inca kings, who were legitimate descendents of Adam and Eve, and offspring of Noah and of the first people, the *Wari Wiracocha Runa*, the *Wari Runa*, the *Purun Runa*, and the *Auca Runa*.

Their descendent was the Capac Inca, Tocay Capac–Pinau Capac, the first Inca. This generation and lineage then came to an end, and with

31

them, the personal coat of arms that his lineage painted and considered to be truest.

◆ The first chroniclers declared that the Inca was the "son of the sun" (*intip churin*). They claimed that, from the beginning, he had said that his father was the sun, his mother was the moon, his sister was the morning star, his idol was Wanacauri, and the place from which the Incas had emerged was Tambotoco (also known as Pacaritambo);[50] the Incas worshipped and made sacrifices to all these things, it was said. But the very first Inca, Tocay Capac, had no idol and no ceremonies; the Incas were free of such things until the reign of the mother and wife of Manco Capac Inca, followed by his lineage, who were descended from *amaros* (serpents). Everything else that is said and painted about these Incas is simply laughable.

**These first Incas came to an end,** and Manco Inca began his reign. Back in the time of the *Wari Wiracocha Runa,* the *Wari Runa,* the *Purun Runa,* and the *Auca Runa,* this Manco Inca had no people, no land, no fields, no fortress, no lineage, and no ancient kin (*pacarimoc*). Because he had no way to prove that he was a son of the first Indians (the *Wari Wiracocha Runa* who descended from Adam and Noah in the time of the Flood), and that he therefore belonged to the *capac apo's* lineage, he claimed instead that he was the son of the sun.

**This first Inca, Manco Capac,** had no known father; that is why he was called a "son of the sun" (*intip churin, quillap wawan* [the sun's son, the moon's child]).

But actually, his mother was Mama Waco. This woman was, they say, a great deceiver, idolater, and sorceress, who spoke with the demons of hell and who performed ceremonies and sorcery. She could make stones and cliffs and sticks and hills talk, because the demons replied to her. Thus, this woman was the first inventor of *wacas* (idols), sorceries, and enchantments, and she used them to fool the Indians. First she deceived the Indians of Cusco, and she kept them deceived and submissive, because the Indians saw it as a miraculous thing for a woman to be able to talk with stones and cliffs and mountains. Thus this woman, Mama Waco, was obeyed, and so they called her *Coya* (queen) of Cusco. They say that she slept with every man she wanted to in the whole pueblo, and she kept this fraud going for many years, according to the stories told by very old Indians.

**They say that at first this Mama was** called Mama; when she became a lady, she was called Mama Waco; after she married her son and became

---

[50] Tambotoco (*tampu t'uqu,* "Cave Inn") and Pacaritambo (*paqariq tampu,* "Dawning Inn" or "Origin Inn") were the legendary places of origin of the Incas. See Gary Urton, *The History of a Myth: Pacariqtambo and the Origin of the Incas* (Austin, Tex.: University of Texas Press, 1990).

lady and queen, she was called Mama Waco Coya. She discovered that she
was pregnant with a son by casting the demon's lots, and they say that the
demon taught her that she should give birth to this boy and not let the
people see him, and that she should give him to a nurse named Pillco Sisa.
[The demons] told her to take [the boy] to the cave called Tambotoco and
bring him back when he was two years old. She was to give him nourish-
ment, and she was to announce that a *Capac Apo Inca* (king) named Manco
Capac Inca would emerge from Pacaritambo—the son of the sun and his
wife the moon, and the brother of the morning star. [The demons said]
that his god would be Wanacauri, that he was to rule the earth as king, and
that he was to be *Capac Apo Inca* like them. This is what was declared and
ordered by the *waca willcas,* which are the demons of Cusco.

**They say that this Inca had no land** or pueblo that he could call his
own; nor did any father or lineage claim him. They say that his mother was
a worldly woman and an enchantress, the first woman who began serving
and dealing with the demons. How could the sun and the moon make a
child from thirteen degrees up in the sky, which is the highest point of the
sky? That is a lie, <and kingship and having the kingdom did not come to
him by God-given right nor by justice>.[51] They say that he is *amaro,* <a serpent and demon; he does not have the right to be lord and king> as has
been written. First, because he had no land nor ancient house <to make
him king>. Second, because he was a son of the <demon, the enemy of
God and men, the evil> serpent (*amaro*). Third, because it is a lie to say
that he is a son of the sun and the moon. And fourth, because he was born
fatherless and his mother was a worldly woman, the first sorceress, the
greatest master servant of the <demons. He had no lineage or honor, nor
can any man in all the generations of the> world <depict any for him. No
other father can be found for him, not even a wild animal, other than the
demon—that is, the *amaro* (serpent).>

*[An illustration, ms. p. 83, depicts the "second coat of arms of the Incas," which
depicts a golden hummingbird at top left, a jaguar behind a palm tree at top
right, a "royal tassel" at bottom left, and two* amaros *(serpents) with tassels in
their mouths at bottom right. The story of Manco Capac continues.]*

---

[51] The words enclosed by <brackets> in this paragraph were crossed out by Guaman
Poma, but left clearly legible. Murra and Adorno (ms. p. 82, n. 1) suggest that this "self-
censorship" was Guaman Poma's way of agreeing with an anti–Manco Inca tradition
while at the same time distancing himself from it. It might also be noted that the words
he crossed out are those that draw on Catholic associations between serpents and the
devil to malign Manco Inca; the Andean serpent (*amaru*) is not an image of evil, but
rather an ambiguous or amoral image of power.

**They say that the Incas came from** Lake Titicaca and from Tiahuanaco, and that they entered into Tambotoco, from which eight Inca brothers and sisters emerged: four brothers (the first, Wanacauri Inca; the second, Cusco Wanca Inca; the third, Manco Capac Inca; the fourth, Topa Ayar Cachi Inca) and four sisters (the first, Topa Waco Ñusta; the second, Mama Cora Ñusta; the third, Curi Ocllo Ñusta; the fourth, Ipa Waco Ñusta).[52] These eight siblings emerged from Pacaritambo and went to their *waca* (idol) Wanacauri; they moved from Collao to the city of Cusco (which at first was called Acamama and later called Cusco). Thus the Inca ordered that they worship and make sacrifices to their *pacaricos* [places of origin] and *wacas*—the hills, caves, and crags.

*[Guaman Poma explains that, contrary to Spanish understandings, "Inca" is the "general term" for the lineage, not the specific word for "king"; and not all who wear large earplugs (*orejones, *in Spanish) are Incas. He gives several examples of non-Incas who wore earplugs, as well as "imperfect" Incas who did not wear them.]*

**They say that the Anca Wallo Chanca**—fifty thousand million Indians, not counting women, old men, or children—emerged from lake Choclococha. Their king, Anca Wallo, wanted to be Inca in the time of Manco Capac, the first Inca. So Manco Capac Inca presented his sister Tupa Waco to him, and this *warmi auca* [enemy woman] deceived and killed the lord, king, and captain Anca Wallco. After the captain general had been killed, all his people went up into the mountain range and into the land beyond the mountains—a cold, harsh land—where they live to this day. They are infidel Indians, and they are governed by their king and Inca lord. They say that there are many Indians there, with a great many clothing styles and lineages, and that they make war among themselves, just as the *Chuncho* and *Ande* Indians do. They say that there is a lot of gold and silver there, and much land and many cattle. The land is fertile and the Indians hostile, as I have said, for these Indians are up towards the Northern Sea.[53]

## MANCO CAPAC, INCA

FROM THE FIRST INCA, Manco Capac Inca, who ruled for 160 years at the beginning, through the last legitimate Inca, Topa Cusiwalpa Wascar, and his bastard brother Atawalpa Inca—from when these Incas began to

---

[52] Ñusta (*ñusta*): princess, daughter of the Inca lineage.
[53] Towards the Northern Sea (the Caribbean): that is, on the other side of the Andes, a region that Guaman Poma only knew through its mythical reputation as a wild land of indomitable peoples.

parasol

*This Inca ruled over only Cusco (Acamama).*

rule, until their reign ended and was finished—the legitimate, rightfully ruling Incas and kings were sovereign over this land for 1,515 years. They were the first to worship idols (*wacas*) and demons. But they and their *wacas* and demons have come to an end. These Incas conquered half of Peru, and the other half is yet to be conquered, up around the mountains.[54] So, from the *Wari Wiracocha Runa,* the *Wari Runa,* the *Purun Runa,* and the *Auca Runa,* through these people of the *Inca pacha* [Inca Age], to the end of the Incas, there were 6,015 years. The reign of the Incas themselves lasted no more than 1,515 years: from the time of the Inca Cinche Roca Inca until today; from the birth of our Lord and savior Jesus Christ to the year 1613.

Manco Capac Inca, the first father of the Incas, wore his green *llauto* [headdress] with its feather visor, and his pure gold ear[plug]; his *mascapaycha* [royal tassel] and *wayoc tica* [ornamental flower]; in his right hand, his *conca cuchuna* [ceremonial ax], and a parasol in his left; his scarlet mantle; his blouse: red on top, three *tocapo* [embroidered] stripes in the middle, and light blue on the bottom; and two leg bands on his legs. This Inca built Curi Cancha, the temple of the sun; he began to worship the sun and said that it was his father. He brought all of Cusco (not including the surrounding area) under his control, and he did it without war or battle; rather, he won it through deceit and idolatrous enchantments, casting the devil's lots—he was the first to worship *wacas* (idols).[55] After giving his dowry to the sun and the moon, he got married to his wife, who was his mother, the lady Mama Waco Coya, by order of the *wacas* and demons. He died at the age of 160 in Cusco. He was a very fine gentleman,[56] he knew many tricks and ways to divine by lots, and he was extremely poor.[57] He had legitimate royal children—Cinche Roca Inca, Chinbo Urma Coya, Inca Yupanqui, and Pachacuti Inca—and also many bastard sons and daughters (*auquicunas* and *ñustacunas* [princes and princesses]) in Cusco.

---

[54] The Spanish is unclear here. Reinterpreting this statement by taking "these Incas" to be the object rather than the subject of "conquered," it would mean that the Spaniards had conquered the Incas in half of Peru, leaving only the last Inca redoubt in the mountains around Vilcabamba.

[55] Worship: here Guaman Poma uses the word *mochar,* a verb in Spanish form taken from Quechua *muchay,* "to kiss; to worship." The word had evidently been adopted into the local colloquial Spanish of the time.

[56] "A very fine gentleman" (*muy gentil hombre*): considering Guaman Poma's implicit criticism of Manco Capac's idolatry, this may be intended as a pun. *Gentil* in Spanish means both "gentleman," a noble status in Guaman Poma's day, and "gentile, pagan."

[57] Poverty, voluntarily embraced by the powerful (as by friars and monks), is a sign of morality and goodness in Guaman Poma's view of the world.

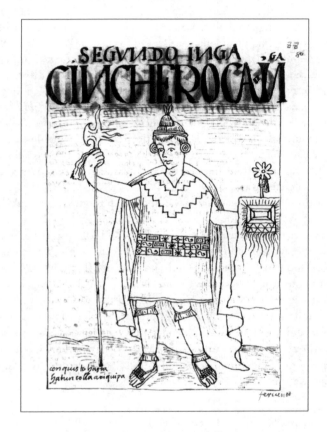

*He conquered up to Hatun Colla, Arequipa.*

## CINCHE ROCA, INCA

A FERVENT AND GENTLE MAN, he wore his red *llauto,* his feather visor, his blouse, which was rose-colored, with its *awaqui* [woven section] and three stripes of *tocapo* [embroidery] in the middle, and red at the bottom, and his light scarlet mantle; in his right hand, his *conca cuchuna* [ax], and his shield and *champi* [scepter] in his left, and four leg bands on his legs. He was a very fine gentleman, and his face was fierce and darkish. He governed Cusco and conquered all the big-eared people; he won all of Collasuyu, Hatun Colla, Puquina Colla, Pacaxi, Quispi Llacta, Poma Cancha, Hatun Conde, and Cullahua Conde.[58] This Inca killed the first, legitimate Inca, the descendent of Adam and Eve and of Wari Wiracocha Runa, the first king Tocay Capac–Pinau Capac, who was the Inca from Jaquijaguana to Quiquijana.[59] He had not yet subjugated or conquered the *Chilque* and *Aco* Indians. The first to be conquered, with few people, were the *Colla* Indians, on account of their being lazy, fainthearted, and worthless people; he decreed and made it a law and a commandment that they worship the *waca* (idols) and make sacrifices to them, and so the first province that the demons entered was Collao.

This Inca was a great man of war and began to grow powerful.[60] He was married to Chinbo Urma Coya.

This Inca died in Cusco at the age of 155, and left great riches to the temple of the sun and to his *wacas.* He had royal children—Mama Cora Ocllo Coya, Lloqui Yupanqui Inca, Wari Tito Inca, and Topa Amaro Inca—and a great number of bastard sons (*auquicuna*) and daughters (*ñustacunas*).

As it has been said, when Cinche Roca Inca was eighty years old, our Lord and savior Jesus Christ was born, and in his life he ascended into heaven and the Holy Spirit descended upon the apostles. The apostles then spread out across the world; the apostle St. Bartholomew was given the Indies of this kingdom of Peru, and so this apostle came to this kingdom.

The two Incas ruled for 315 years.

---

[58] "The big-eared people" (*los orejones*) were those who, like the Inca lineage of Cusco, wore earplugs that distended their earlobes. Collasuyu was the southeastern quarter of Tawantinsuyu, the Inca empire; the other places and peoples listed, to the degree that they can be identified, are in southern and central Peru. Collao, mentioned below, is the area around Puno and Lake Titicaca in southern Peru.

[59] Jaquijaguana and Quiquijana (in Guaman Poma's spelling, Xacxauana and Quiquixana): pueblos within fifty miles of Cusco.

[60] Began to grow powerful: *comenso a rrequezer* (*comenzó a enriquecer*), literally "began to enrich." This is based on a translation of the Quechua term *capac (qapaq),* "powerful; rich," and refers to the fact that the Inca was becoming a powerful lord who could command many men in war.

*[Illustration, ms. p. 90: a Nativity scene of the infant Jesus in Bethlehem with Joseph and Mary.]*

## THE BIRTH OF JESUS CHRIST IN BETHLEHEM

### ON THE BIRTH OF OUR LORD AND THE SAVIOR OF THE WORLD JESUS CHRIST

HE WAS BORN during the time and the reign of Cinche Roca Inca, when the Inca was eighty years old. It was in the time of Cinche Roca Inca that He suffered martyrdom and was crucified, died, and was buried, and He was resurrected, ascended into heaven, and was seated on the right hand of God the Father. He sent the Holy Spirit to give his grace to the holy apostles, so that they would go throughout the world preaching his gospel. Thus it was that the holy apostle St. Bartholomew got the fortunate task, departed for Collao, and through his holy miracles left the Holy Cross ✠ of Carabuco.[61]

From the time of Manco Capac Inca to the end of the Incas, with the deaths of Wascar the legitimate Inca and of his brother Atawalpa the bastard Inca—from beginning to end—the Incas reigned for 1,548 years, not counting the 80 years from the birth of the Inca Cinche Roca [to the birth of Jesus] and the 160 years of Manco Capac Inca, for these two Incas reigned 240 years. Since the birth of Jesus Christ, there have been 1,613 years; that was during the reign of Cinche Roca Inca. After Cinche Roca Inca's death, he was succeeded by his legitimate son, Lloqui Yupanqui Inca, in his kingdom.

As it has been said, it was in the time of Cinche Roca Inca that the baby Jesus was born in Bethlehem. The ever-virgin St. Mary gave birth, and [Jesus] was adored there by the kings of the three nations that God put in this world: the three wise kings, Melchior the Indian, Balthasar the Spaniard, and Gaspar the black; for he was adored by the three kings of the world. As Scripture and experience demonstrate, the birth of the Creator of the world was adored in this way.[62]

---

[61] Carabuco is a small town on the Bolivian shore of Lake Titicaca. According to legend, a regional culture hero named Tunupa carried a large wooden cross over the Andes and set it up in Carabuco in the age before the Incas. After the conquest, several writers identified Tunupa as St. Bartholomew, St. Thomas, or Christ himself. A relic of the cross is said to be kept in the church of Carabuco; the cathedral of Chuquisaca (Sucre), Bolivia is said to have the entire cross mounted on its dome.

[62] This paragraph was added after the manuscript was completed. Melchior, Balthasar, and Gaspar are the names given by medieval legend to the wise men of Matthew 2:1–12. The identification of the three with different continents (usually Africa, Asia, and Europe) was a recent innovation in Guaman Poma's time.

## MIRACLE OF GOD

*[Illustration, ms. p. 92: St. Bartholomew places the Holy Cross of Carabuco in the province of Collao and baptizes the Colla Indian, Anti Wiracocha. An addendum notes that the miracle occurred 1,570 years ago.]*

THE FIRST MIRACLE PERFORMED BY GOD in this kingdom, through his apostle St. Bartholomew, was as follows:

- The pueblo of Cacha would burn with fire from heaven.
- The saint would be attacked with slings and stones, to kill him, to chase him out of the pueblo.
- The saint would bring a miracle from God to that province.
- Through a **singular miraculous deed** of the Holy Cross ✠, an Indian, a native of Carabuco named Anti, would be converted and later baptized with the name Anti Wiracocha.

St. Bartholomew was traveling in the province known as Collao. He entered a cave, for it was the cold time of year. An Indian sorcerer named Anti kept his idol in the same cave, where he spoke to it. But now he got no reply from the devil, for it left the cave as soon as Lord St. Bartholomew entered; it no longer responded to his questions.

When the cliff of sacrifices fell silent, Anti took fright and left. The demon later appeared to Anti in his dreams and told him that by no means, and in no way, should he reenter that cave. Anti ran in anger after the blessed St. Bartholomew; when he caught up with him, he told him everything that had happened. St. Bartholomew ordered him to return and speak again to the idol that he kept in that cave.

Anti did return and spoke to it; the demon replied, telling him that the poor man he had run after was more powerful than the demon himself, with all he knew.

On hearing this reply, the Indian sorcerer Anti returned to the apostle St. Bartholomew and began to follow him wholeheartedly. He caught up with the saint, embraced him, kissed his hands and holy feet, and begged him for mercy and restitution, because the poor man and his God were more powerful [than the idol].

As a sign of the holy miracle and baptism, St. Bartholomew left the Holy ✠ Cross of Carabuco, which stands to this day as witness to this holy miracle and to the arrival of the blessed apostle of Jesus Christ, St. Bartholomew. The feast day of the apostle saint and of the Holy ✠ should be annual holidays, for God wished to decree these two holy miracles in the kingdom.

**Many other miracles** that occurred among the Indians of this kingdom were never recorded in the old times. They say that God sent poor hermits and poor Franciscan friars among the Incas, to tempt them and find out if they were charitable towards their neighbors. No one left a record of this, because there was no one who could write it down; but they say that God sent them in the form of poor friars who, they say, would beg for alms in the name of God, asking to be given food and drink. When these poor people came, the Incas would put on great festivities (*taquíes*). If the Incas gave no alms to the poor, they say that God would punish them. On hearing their prayers, he would burn them with fire from heaven, and in some places he covered the hills, turned their pueblos into lakes, and made the earth swallow them: such were the great punishments and miracles of God in the world, from the beginning.

One great judgment was the fall of that angel with his followers: so high-ranked, so handsome.[63] [Another judgment was] the fall of all humankind through the fault of one. [A third judgment was] the punishment of the entire world with the waters of the Flood. Other great judgments were: the election of Jacob; the rebuke of Esau; the dismay of Judas Iscariot; the calling of St. Paul; the rebuke of the Jewish people; the election of the gentiles; and likewise, other miracles and punishments that happen among the sons of men in the world. Likewise, there were many other miracles and punishments in the time of the Inca. These punishments were not recorded in writing, yet the fallen hills and tumbled crags bear witness to them, and so the final account is written: that is why God's punishment is called the *pachacuti pachaticra;*[64] for this reason, some kings were named Pachacuti.

In this life, we have seen volcanoes erupt and rain hellfire and sand, laying waste to a city and its region. It could be called nothing other than a miracle when an earthquake killed many people, along with a friar—a Dominican prior. More than a league of the mountain range along the coastline was laid waste and turned into just another league of seawater. Nothing like this has ever happened again, not since the time that God ordered this to happen.[65]

This also can only be called a miracle: the plagues that God still sends—measles, pox, croup, and mumps; from these, a great many people have died.

This, too, could only be called a miracle: the great snowfall and hailstorm that fell from heaven and covered all the hills. The snow fell two

---

[63] Referring to the fall of Lucifer. This and the following series of "judgments" are drawn from standard Catholic interpretations of biblical history. Guaman Poma equates these biblical events and legends with Andean legends of supernatural punishment.

[64] *Pachacuti pachaticra:* "end of the world, great destruction, pestilence, ruin," according to González Holguín (1586); literally, "world reversal, world upside-down." See footnote 46.

[65] The volcano of Huaynaputina erupted in a massive explosion in February 1600, covering a vast area in ash and destroying the ancient city of Arequipa, fifty miles to its west. This was the only significant volcanic eruption in the central Andes in historical times.

yards deep upon the earth, and in some places four yards, killing many people and cattle.

This, too, can only be called a miracle from God: the punishment and plague of mice upon the plains, and the great damage done by birds in the planted fields throughout the mountain range of the Northern Sea; for many people have died of hunger and plagues of mosquitoes, flies, lice, and fleas (*piqui niwa*). It is also a plague and punishment from God when the corn and potatoes freeze and hail falls on the food crops.

Another plague, sent by God to bad Christians, is when poor men are robbed of their possessions and their wives and daughters are taken and forced to be servants.

This is also called a miracle and a plague from God: when the Indians abandon their pueblos in this kingdom and leave to wander.

It is also a punishment from God when many Indians die in the quicksilver and silver mines, and when others die of quicksilver poisoning[66]—they fall very ill, suffering terrible labors for five or six years, until they die, leaving their wives and children orphan-poor after their deaths.[67]

With all these things, God is telling us to remember and call out to Him. God sends his punishments to each man and each house in the world, so that we might call out to him and thank him, and so that he might bring us to his Glory, where the Most Holy Trinity resides.

*[Following this interlude, Guaman Poma returns to the history of the Inca kings. The brief histories of kings three through eleven are omitted here. In his chronicle of the final legitimate Inca king, Wascar Inca dies and leaves the trappings of his office to the king of Spain, thus legitimating Spanish imperial rule in the Andes.]*

115–119                        **THE TWELFTH INCA**

WASCAR INCA TOPA CUSIWALPA was the name of this Inca. He was chosen and named by his father the sun, and was the legitimate and eldest heir of this entire kingdom of Peru, the *Capac Apo Inca*. This Inca wore his helmet (*uma chuco*), *añaspacra* [helmet fringe], and *mascapaycha*

---

[66] Quicksilver (*azogue*) or mercury, a highly toxic mineral, was a crucial ingredient in the most productive silver refining process of the time. Thousands of tons of mercury were spilled in the silver mining regions of the Andes, while the mercury miners themselves generally contracted debilitating mercury poisoning within months and died after only a few years of hard labor. Large deposits of mercury were discovered in the south-central Peruvian region of Huancavelica in 1559, revolutionizing the silver mining industry in Peru. On mercury poisoning, see Kendall Brown, "Workers' Health and Colonial Mercury Mining at Huancavelica, Peru," *The Americas* 57, no. 4 (April 2001): 467–96.

[67] Orphan-poor (*guerfanos y pobres*): the Quechua word *wakcha* means both "orphan" and "poor," two concepts that are frequently entwined in Guaman Poma's writing.

Quisquis Inca
Andamarca

[On Wascar's tunic:] His rule ended; he died in Andamarca.

Challcochima Inca

He died.

*He began to rule and he died..*

[royal tassel], and his *champi* [scepter] and *wallcanca* [shield]. He wore his light blue mantle, and his blouse was iridescent blue, with three *tocapos* in the middle and green at the bottom; and he wore four leg bands on his legs. His face was darkish and long, and he was long-limbed, ugly, and evil-hearted.

This Inca governed and ruled from the Jauja valley of the *Wanca* Indians.[68] He was very fierce and miserly, and he had no children at all, neither legitimate nor bastard, male nor female. He was married to Chuquillanto Coya and died at the age of twenty-five in the settlement of Andamarca, in the hands of his enemy.

The captains Challco Chima Inca and Quisquis Inca, acting on the orders of his bastard brother Atawalpa Inca, executed justice upon Wascar Inca.[69] When they held him prisoner, they mocked him: they gave him the filth of people and dogs to eat; for *chicha* [corn beer], they gave him llama and human piss to drink; for coca, they offered him packets of *chillca* leaves [a bitter plant]; and for *llipta* [ash, chewed together with coca leaves], they gave him powdered human filth. They mocked him crudely. Then, after Wascar Inca had died, they went to the city of Cusco and killed everyone in his lineage—all the Inca *auquicunas* [princes] and *ñustas* [princesses], even the pregnant women. Those who escaped and hid remained the bastard *auquicunas* and *ñustas* of Hanan Cusco and Lurin Cusco. He died at the age of twenty-five.

As has been said, the line of the kings—of the legitimate *Capac Apo Incas,* by the law of Peru—came to an end in this kingdom with the death of Wascar Inca. He left his royal tassel (the *mascapaycha*) and his crown to His Sacred Catholic Majesty, our lord and king, who rules the entire world.

This Wascar Inca was bad-hearted and bad-tempered, and therefore he came to a very bad end. When his bastard brother Atawalpa tried to honor Wascar by sending him presents and riches with his ambassador and by showing him respect, he in turn sent his brother Atawalpa women's clothing, pots, gold *chamillcos* [cooking pots] and pitchers, and *acxo, lliclla, wincha, topo, pines, lirpo, naccha, chumpis,* and *oxotas* [skirts, shawls, ribbons, shawl pins, jewels, mirrors, combs, sashes, and sandals], all for women. Thus, through his pride, Wascar gained trouble, strife, and death. His pride caused the deaths of many noble lords, captains, and poor Indians,

---

[68] Jauja: in central Peru, 150 miles east of Lima and 230 miles northwest of Cusco. This was one of the richest and most densely populated valleys in Peru, and briefly served as Peru's first Spanish capital due to an alliance between Pizarro and the *Wancas* (or *Huancas*) against their common enemy, the Incas.

[69] According to other chronicles, the capture and assassination of Wascar occurred in late 1532, while Atawalpa himself was being held for ransom by Pizarro's men.

and the destruction of all the wealth of this kingdom. To this day, the poor Indians are lost and have been sold.

In the middle of this furor, the Spaniards came from Castile to this kingdom, but the Indians did not defend themselves as the Indians of Chile have done.[70] Instead, the Indian lords of this country put themselves in the service of the royal crown of His Majesty.

**The law of the Incas lay down the rules** for being king (*Capac Apo Inca*). For "Inca" does not mean king; rather, there are low-class people who are Inca, such as the *Chilqui* Inca (who are potters); the *Acos* Inca (who are frauds); the *Waroc* Inca, otherwise known as the *llulla* [lying] *Waroc* (who are liars); the *Mayu* Inca (who are false witnesses); and the *Quilliscachi* and *Equeco* Inca (who are gossips and liars).[71] All of these are Incas, so "Inca" does not mean "lord," "king," "duke," "count," "marquis," or "gentleman," for there are commoner and low-class Incas.

*Capac Apo Inca* means "absolute king." "Gentlemen" are *auquicunas,* and "ladies" are *ñustacunas.* The name *wiracocha* is applied to all Castilian foreigners alike, whether they are Jews, Moors, Turks, English, or French, for they all are Spaniards (*wiracochas*).[72] It is just the same for Incas. To be "king" (*Capac Apo Inca*), one had to be the legitimate son of his own wife, the "queen" (*Capac Apo Coya*)—he had to be married to his sister or his mother. He also had to be chosen by his father the sun in the temple and named to be the king. They paid no attention to whether he was old or young, only to who was chosen by the sun to be legitimate. The bastard *auquicunas* were called *mestizos.*[73]

---

[70] The *Araucans* of Chile fiercely resisted the Spanish invaders, holding off the conquest of the southern half of the country from 1533 until 1886, centuries after Guaman Poma wrote these line. His argument here, and through much of the book, is that the Andeans voluntarily joined forces with the Spanish and therefore were not conquered. The rule of the king of Spain was thus legitimate, but the rule of the Spanish conquerors was not.

[71] Guaman Poma elsewhere identifies these Inca *ayllus* (semi-localized lineages), which were centered in pueblos near Cusco, as the *allicaccuna,* people who had been promoted by the ruling Incas in honor of their service as soldiers in the Incaic conquests. In his section on the "ordinances of the Inca," (pp. 57–68) Guaman Poma associates several of these *ayllus* with specific government functionaries under Incan rule. His comments here point to resentment among non-Inca nobles over the way that these "low-class Incas" had been "raised up" (*allicac*).

[72] Again, in an inversion of the European habit of calling all the peoples of the Americas "Indians," Guaman Poma calls all the peoples of Europe, Africa, and Asia "Spaniards" or "Castilians." He seems to assume that this was the normal usage in Spain as well.

[73] *Mestizo* or "mixed" usually refers to people of mixed Spanish and Indian ancestry, but here it refers to those of mixed royal and non-royal Inca lineages. "Bastard" here seems to refer to the children of male rulers by secondary wives (see footnote 10).

All of this has been declared for the sake of good justice and so that it may be known how the kings (*Capac Apo Incacunas*) came to an end with Topa Cusiwalpa Wascar Inca. Then the *wiracocha* king Don Philip III Inca succeeded, may God save him, amen.

The twelve Incas finished their reign in the year 1522. At that time, Don Francisco Pizarro and Don Diego de Almagro, ambassadors of the king Emperor Charles, landed in this kingdom, before the death of these two kings: Wascar Inca and Atawalpa Inca.

♦ **These Incas and other lords** and nobles and common Indians, these people of old, kept and lengthened their health and their lives.

♦ They lived to be 200 or 150 years old; their lives were long because they followed an order and a rule for living and raising their children. When they were young, they were not allowed to eat anything with grease, nor anything with honey, hot pepper, salt, or vinegar. Nor were they allowed to drink *chicha;* nor did they sleep with women until they were fifty years old; nor were they given bleedings. They purged themselves every month with three pairs of *willca tauri* [a purgative] and a sizeable portion of *maca* [a medicinal root]; they took half of it by mouth, and half was given to them as medicine. This increased their health and their lives. Until the age of thirty they did not have wives or husbands or obligations, and so they had a great deal of strength.

## To the Reader of "the Incas"

**SEE HERE!** From your beginnings, with Manco Capac Inca, until the end of the legitimate Wascar Inca (oh, wayward Inca!), this is what I have wanted to ask you: Why, from the moment you entered, were you idolaters, enemies of God? Why haven't you followed the ancient law of knowing the Lord and Creator, God, maker of men and of the world? What was it that the Indians of old called out? "*Pacha Camac* (God), *Runa Rurac*" [Creator of the earth, maker of men]. That was how they knew him; that was what they declared him to be; that was what the first *Capac Apo Incas* of old called God.

What was it that entered into your hearts, and into the hearts of your grandmother Mama Waco Coya and Manco Capac Inca? It was the demon, the evil serpent. That is what made you masterful and heretical idolaters (*waca mucha*); that is what imposed and impressed the law of idolatry and ceremonies upon you. At least you were never induced to abandon the Ten Commandments and the good works of mercy! If only you were to abandon idolatry and take up the way of God, what would become of you? You would become the greatest saints in the world! From now on, serve God and the Virgin Mary and His Saints.

## THE FIRST COYA

*[A chapter on the twelve Coyas, female rulers of the dynasty, parallels the chapter on the twelve male Inca rulers. The pages on the first and twelfth Coyas are presented here.]*

HERE BEGINS THE HISTORY of the queens (*Coyas*), the wives of the Inca kings, the first of whom was named Mama Waco. She was very beautiful, and her whole body was dark and fine of figure. They say she was a great sorceress; according to the tales told of her life and history, she spoke with the demons. They say this lady made the rocks, crags, and idols (*wacas*) talk.

It was from this lady that the first Inca kings descended. They say that neither her father nor the father of her son, Manco Capac Inca, was known; rather, she claimed to be the daughter of the sun and the moon, and she married her first son, Manco Capac Inca. To get married, they say that she asked her father the sun for her dowry; he gave the dowry, and mother and son were married.

This Mama Waco Coya wore her rose-colored dress, and she had her large, silver *topos* [pins for holding her shawl]. She died in Cusco at the age of two hundred, in the time of her son, Cinche Roca Inca. She had royal sons, Inca Yupanqui, Pachacuti Inca, and Chinbo Urma; her husband had other bastard *auquicunas* and *ñustacunas* [princes and princesses].

Although this lady left the demon's law well-established for all her sons and grandsons and descendents, she was a good friend of gentlemen and other people. She governed more than her husband Manco Capac Inca did. The whole city of Cusco obeyed and respected her throughout her life, because she performed demons' miracles unlike any that men had ever seen. She spoke with the crags and stones as if they were people.

This concludes the life of this lady (*Coya*), Mama Waco. She was a most beautiful woman, greatly learned, and did much good for the poor in the city of Cusco and throughout her kingdom. The realm of this lady's husband grew mainly because she ruled in Cusco and its territory.[74]

*[The brief histories of the next ten Coyas are omitted here.]*

## THE TWELFTH COYA

CHUQUI LLANTO COYA, they say, was exceedingly beautiful and fair. She had no blemish on her body or face and was very cheerful, full of song, and fond of raising little birds. She owned no possessions of her own, even though her husband was avaricious. Out of sheer greed, he would eat in the

---

[74] The final lines of this sentence, beginning with "in the city of Cusco," were added after the manuscript was completed.

## THE FIRST HISTORY OF THE QUEENS
### MAMA WACO COYA.

*She ruled in Cusco.*

*She began to rule and she died.*

middle of the night, and he could be seen in the morning with his mouth stuffed with coca.

She wore her light blue *liclla* [shawl], dark green in the middle, and her green *acxo* [skirt], with *tocapo* [embroidery] at the bottom.

She was so good and cheerful that she pleased her husband, even though he was stubborn and thus did not live many years. Her husband, Wascar Inca, died first; she wore mourning clothes and died in Yucay, in the time of the Christians' conquest. Nothing is written about her sons or daughters, whether she had legitimate or bastard children. Thus, with this king and queen (*Inca* and *Coya*), the kings (*Capac Apo Incas*) came to an end. She died at the age of fifty-nine; the sad life of this lady came to an end.[75]

## PROLOGUE

To the Readers of "Women (Coya, capac warmi, curaca warmi, allicac warmi, waccha warmi)"

**DO NOT BE SHOCKED, WOMEN!** Woman committed the first sin: Eve sinned with the apple, breaking God's commandment. Thus you began the first idolatry, woman, and you served the demons. All of that is a matter of mockery and lies. Leave it all behind, and devote yourself to the Most Holy Trinity—God the Father, God the Son, God the Holy Spirit, the one and only God—and to the Mother of God, St. Mary, ever Virgin. May she favor you and pray for you in heaven, that we may delight and join together in heaven and in this world, and that Satan might not tempt us. Arm yourself with the cross and pray the Our Father and the Hail Mary, and recall the passion of our Lord Jesus Christ.

Let us say the Credo so that we may be with the Most Holy Trinity, with Jesus Christ, with his mother St. Mary, and with his saints and angels in the court of heaven. To this end, let us arm ourselves with the sign of the Holy ✠ Cross. From our enemies deliver us, Lord: from all the evil of the world, from the flesh, and from the demon.

*[Two chapters give brief descriptions of deeper layers of authority under Inca rule. The chapter on the fifteen "captains" who led the Inca conquest of the Andes is omitted here. In the chapter on the "ladies" of the four suyus (provinces or sectors) of the Inca empire, Guaman Poma shows his preference for his ancestral homeland, Chinchaysuyu, by presenting a personal account of the "great lady" of that region. In fact, he claims that the great lady was his own grandmother. The "ladies" of the other three sectors of Tawantinsuyu are represented by titles, not the names of individuals.]*

---

[75] A final paragraph, omitted here, lists the titles of noble women in Cusco and the other provinces of Tawantinsuyu.

# CHAPTER ON THE LADIES OF THE FOUR SUYUS

## THE FIRST LADY

### *CAPAC WARMI* [POWERFUL WOMAN] POMA WALLCA OF CHINCHAYSUYU

SHE WAS A LADY AND A QUEEN, both before there was an Inca and afterwards. She was a very splendid and beautiful woman, who was so good that she governed the whole kingdom. She was the wife and lady of *capac apo* Waman Chawa, second-in-command of the Inca; she was of the Yaro Willca–Allauca Wanaco lineage and was the author's grandmother.[76] This lady was the greatest in all the kingdom.

After this lady came other noble ladies, named Chuqui Timta, Asto Carwa, Carwa Quillpa, Waman Chisque, Wamancha Poma, Churay Pariama, Waman Chunbe, Lauca Chuque, Maywa Poma, Churay Maclla, Paria Wanay, Suyuma Awama, Collque Timta, Carwa Churay, Citcama Chunbi, Cuti Quisllama, and Misa Warmi.[77] Besides these ladies, there have been other noblewomen to whom Your Majesty should bestow grants[78] in this kingdom.

## THE SECOND LADY

### CAPAC MALLQUIMA OF ANDESUYU[79]

ALTHOUGH THESE LADIES are fine of figure, very beautiful, and whiter than Spanish women, even so, they go around dressed only in loincloths. Some lineages go completely stark naked—both men and women—for they are of the lineage of nature, and they eat human flesh. But all of them

---

[76] There is also some self-promotion here. Elsewhere, Guaman Poma describes his ancestor Waman Chawa as "the most excellent viceroy" of Tawantinsuyu, "like the most excellent Duke of Alva in Castile" (ms. p. 343), and emphasizes that he also belonged to the noble Yaro Willca–Allauca Wanaco *allyu*.

[77] These appear to be titles for noble women in several Andean languages and social hierarchies, not the names of individual women. The same is true of the lists of "other noble ladies" at the end of each of the following three sections.

[78] Bestow grants (*hacer merced*): during the colonial years, royal *mercedes* (grants) usually came in the form of land grants, sometimes of large expanses of territory that had been emptied by the wars of conquest and subsequent epidemics. Guaman Poma's arguments throughout the manuscript are framed to support the case that the native lords of the Andes were more deserving of land grants and *encomiendas* than the Spanish conquerors. Legal appeals making the same argument in colonial courts were almost uniformly rejected.

[79] *Capac mallquima* combines the terms *qapaq* (powerful, rich, noble, royal), *mallqui* (noble, lord), and *-ma* (woman), which occur in several Andean languages. Andesuyu was, from Guaman Poma's perspective, a wild northern province that stretched from the Andes (to which it gave its name) into the Amazonian jungle.

# THE FIRST QUEEN AND LADY
## CAPAC ♦ POMA WALLCA.

*Chinchaysuyu.*

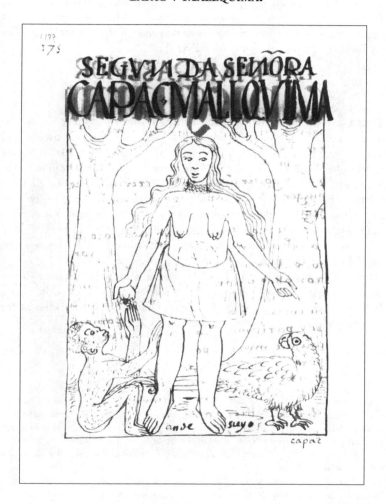

*Andesuyu.*

paint and daub their whole bodies with *mantor* [a red dye] and stay in the mountains. They are as yet unconquered Indians and, with so many mountains surrounding them, they cannot be conquered.

Other ladies are named Awa Mana, Cucar Mana, Cuca Mallquima Tazama, Awama, Loroma Supama, Tirania Awa Paria, and Pillco Challwa Mapiscoma. There are many other ladies in each village in the mountains. There are many people on the other side of the mountains, and a land of riches where there are infidel Indians named *Anca Wallo, Warmi Auca.* They say there is a great deal of gold and silver there.

## THE THIRD LADY

### CAPACOMI TALLAMA[80] OF COLLASUYU

THIS LADY WAS very splendid and beautiful, but from sheer fatness she became ugly, for all those of her lineage are extremely fat, lazy, useless, and fainthearted but rich people. Those people are called Colla Capac. They are rich in silver from Potosí and gold from Carabaya, the purest gold in all the kingdom; they are rich in cattle—*wacay* and alpacas—and cattle from Castile—sheep, cows, pigs; and they are rich in potatoes, *chuño, moraya,* and quinoa, but poor in corn, wheat, and wine. The saying is: *Capac colla, mapa colla, poquis colla* [rich/powerful Colla, dirty Colla, stupid Colla]. They are tremendous brutes, all the men and women alike: they are great, fat, flabby, lazy beasts, good only for sleeping and eating.[81]

There have been other ladies: Talla Warmi, Cayuma, Wizama, Chunbima, Cucama, Anama, Chuqui Timta, Timtayaca, Tallatimta, Pacllama, Pulloma, Zurima. Apart from these, there have been other ladies in the province of the Collas, Canas, Canches, and Charcas.

---

[80] *Capacomi tallama:* an Aymara title, the equivalent of Quechua *Coya,* rendered in Bertonio's 1612 vocabulary as *ttalla ccapkhomi,* "Queen; Wife of the chief lord of the pueblo; and the close female relatives of the *mallcos* [nobles]." (Ludovico Bertonio, *Vocabulario de la lengua aymara,* facsimile of the 1612 edition [Cochabamba, Peru: Ediciones CERES, 1984], 347, my trans.)

[81] As a partisan of his ancestral region, Chinchaysuyu, Guaman Poma makes several invidious comparisons with the rival region of Collasuyu, for example: "The Inca . . . found the most strength in the Indians of Chinchaysuyu; though small in stature, they are spirited Indians, because they live on corn and drink corn *chicha,* which gives strength; while the Indians of Collasuyu have little strength or spirit, and they have great, fat, flabby bodies, and are of little use, because they only eat *chuño* and drink *chicha* made from *chuño*" (ms. p. 338).

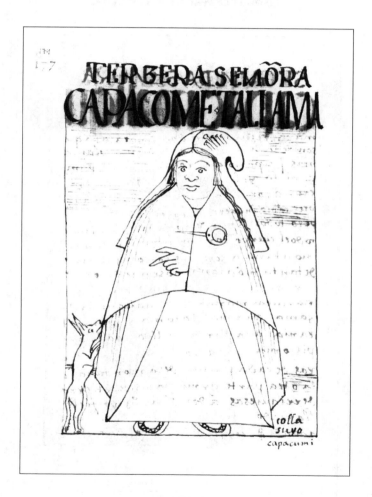

*Collasuyu.*

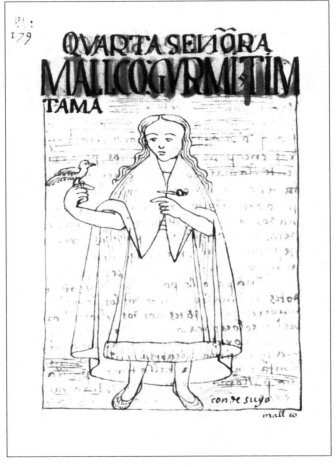

*Condesuyu.*

## THE FOURTH LADY

### MALLCO WARMI TIMTAMA OF CONDESUYU

THIS LADY WAS very beautiful and brave, because she was of the good sort. Her land, however, is very poor. The district of Arequipa has no gold, silver, or cattle; only the district of Coropuna Conde has cattle. The other districts live from the peppers and cotton that they bring from the *yungas* [tropical lowlands] and plains. These districts are Palta Conde, Hatun Conde, Callawa Conde, Cusco Conde, Alcatoro, Waynacota, and Pomatambo.

These districts belong to the Condes, and they have other ladies, who are called Timta Carwa, Timta Churay, Churama Auzama, Cusima Illama, Ayayama, Anyama, Chuquipana, Panallo Sequema, Pusimapana, Timta Carwama, and Mulloma Culima. There have been other ladies, wives of the noblemen of Condesuyu, whose names have not been written. Grants should be bestowed upon all of them, for they descend from the great nobles of this kingdom.

*[The chapter on "The Ladies" concludes with a page that lists some eight descendents of the Incas who were assigned salaries or* encomiendas *by the Spanish. In this page (omitted here), Guaman Poma again argues that the right to rule Peru had properly passed to the Spanish crown after the death of the last Inca king, and he ties this argument to an implicit argument that the king of Spain should resume Incaic governing policies and restore the wealth of regional nobles.]*

*[The long and pictureless chapter that follows, presented here in its entirety, claims to be a codification of Inca law enacted by the tenth Inca, Topa Inca Yupanqui. It can serve as a synopsis of much of the material presented in the remaining chapters on the Inca world.]*

## THE ORDINANCES OF THE INCA    *184–195*

### THE GREAT GOVERNMENT OF THE INCAS OF THIS KINGDOM, AND OF THE OTHER LORDS AND GREAT NOBLES OF THIS KINGDOM, WHO EXISTED AT THAT TIME AND WHO GOVERNED THE LAND IN THIS KINGDOM

#### *THE LAWS AND ORDINANCES OF THESE KINGDOMS OF PERU*

THE FIRST LAWS were as follows. The Incas later added their idolatries, feast days, holy days, and fasts, to be kept each month and each year (*warachicos, rotochicos, pacaricos,* and *wacachicos*); as well as the sacrifices, the selection of virgins, the storehouses, and other matters of the demons' ceremonies that the Incas kept. The first laws, however, ran as follows:

**TOPA INCA YUPANQUI,** the other *auquicunas,* and the great lords (*capac apocunas, curacacunas,* and *allicac camachicoccunas*) who form the *tawantinsuyu camachiconchic* [our authorities of Tawantinsuyu] declare:

We ordain and decree in these kingdoms and domains that these laws be kept and carried out, under penalty of death. Those who do not keep them shall be punished, killed, and condemned to death, along with their children and descendents. All their offspring shall be destroyed; their villages shall be consumed and sown with salt, and animals will live there—*lluycho, puma, atoc, usco, condor,* and *waman* [deer, pumas, foxes, wildcats, condors, and hawks].

(These penalties were imposed, decreed, and executed for all time throughout this kingdom, and thus there were never any quarrels: this sentence established law and justice in this kingdom.)[82]

**I ORDAIN AND DECREE** that in this great city, the capital of these kingdoms, there be a pontiff, a high sorcerer (called *walla wisa, conde wisa*), and that there be others in Chinchaysuyu, Andesuyu, Collasuyu, and Condesuyu.

(These sorcerers were called *wisa layca camascacuna;* they were kept in the temple of the sun, and there were many more in the other temples and *wacas* of this kingdom, such as Pariacaca, Carhuancho Huallullo, Sahuasiray, Pitosiray, Coropuna, Suriurco, and Titicaca.[83] In other temples they had priests, as well as bishops, canons, and sextons, who performed services, confessed, and did burials; these were the *laycacunas, wisacunas,* and *camascacunas.* They served the temples and gods throughout the kingdom, and this law of idolatry and ceremonies for the demons was well established in this kingdom.)

Item: I ordain and decree that in this city there be a royal council, with two Incas—one each from Hanan Cusco and Lurin Cusco [Upper and Lower Cusco]—four great lords from Chinchaysuyu, two from Andesuyu, four from Collasuyu, and two from Condesuyu.

*(These were called the* tawantinsuyu camachiconchic.*)*

---

[82] The statements in round parenthesis, here and following several of the other laws, are Guaman Poma's own comments on the Incas' practices.

[83] These are imposing features of the natural landscape: tall mountains and the largest inland lake in South America, all of which were pilgrimage sites and identified with (or as) deities. Pariacaca and Carhuancho Huallullo are in Chinchaysuyu, near Jauja; Sahuasiray and Pitosiray are north of Cusco, in Andesuyu; Coropuna (the third highest mountain in Peru) is in Condesuyu, northwest of Arequipa; Suriurco and Lake Titicaca are in Collasuyu, about 100 and 200 miles southeast of Cusco. Together, these sites enclose an area nearly the size of Spain, which formed Guaman Poma's area of personal geographic knowledge.

**Item:** I decree that there be an *asesor*[84] (*incap rantin rimaric capac apo* [great lord who speaks in the Inca's place]).

*(This* asesor *was a nobleman.)*

**Item:** I decree that there be a viceroy who shall act as my second-in-command.

*(He did not allow his viceroy to be a commoner; rather, his viceroy was* capac apo *Waman Chawa. This lord was carried in a litter,* chicche ranpa; *he was carried like the Inca when he went to the provinces, and he was called* incap rantin, *the Inca's lieutenant.)*

**Item:** We decree that in each province there be, for good justice, a district magistrate.[85]

*(This official was called the* tocricoc; *he was chosen from among the Incas with torn earlobes of Hanan Cusco and Lurin Cusco.)*

**Item:** We decree that there be justices of the royal court,[86] who shall be from the Anta Inca, to arrest nobles, captains, great lords, and gentlemen in this kingdom.

*(These officials carried, as a token of justice, a tall staff with the Inca's* mascapaycha *[royal tassel]. They were called* incap camachinan wataycamayoc *[jailers at the Inca's command].)*

**Item:** We decree that there be justices of the peace[87] in each settlement.

*(These were called* incap simin oyaric *[those who hear the Inca's word]; [they were chosen from the* ayllu *of] Quilliscachi.)*[88]

**Item:** We decree that there be local magistrates.[89]

*(These were called* surcococ; *[they were chosen from the] Equeco Inca.)*

---

[84] *Asesor:* in the Spanish state of the time, this was a chief legal advisor to the governor, viceroy, or king, who exercised judicial as well as executive authority. The *asesor* would, in effect, stand in for the chief executive at trials and hearings, and would draw up sentences and legal findings, which in most cases the executive would authorize with a signature. The closest equivalent in the U.S. legal system is the Attorney General.

[85] *Corregidor,* the title of colonial Spanish provincial governors.

[86] *Alcaldes de corte.*

[87] *Alcaldes ordinarios.*

[88] Quilliscachi was an Inca *ayllu* centered in a pueblo near Cusco. Guaman Poma associates a particular *ayllu* with many of the government functionaries he lists (see footnote 71 for his opinion of these *allicac,* "people raised by the Inca").

[89] *Regidores,* the title of colonial Spanish town council members.

**Item:** We decree that there be a chief constable and minor constables.[90]

*(These were called* watacamayoc *[jailers]; [they were chosen from the] Lulla Waroc.)*

**Item:** We decree that there be a secretary[91] to the Inca.

*(This man was called* incap quipucamayocnin *[overseer of the Inca's kipu]; [he was chosen from the] Chillque Inca.)*

**Item:** We declare that there be secretaries to the royal council.

*(These were called* tawantinsuyu quipoc *[kipu-keepers of Tawantinsuyu]; [they were chosen from the] Quewar Inca.)*

**Item:** We decree that there be a public scribe in each pueblo.

*(These were called* llactapi quipococ camachicoccuna *[kipu-keeping authorities of the pueblos], that is, petty authorities.)*

**Item:** We decree that royal scribes shall be appointed.

*(These were called* caroman cachasca quipococ *[kipu-keepers sent afar]; [they were chosen from the] Pabri Inca.)*

**Item:** We decree that there be chief accountants.

*(These were called* tawantinsuyu hucho, tasa, ima hayca wata quillatawan quipococ yupacoc *[counters and kipu-keepers of the amounts of fines, taxes, and so on in Tawantinsuyu]; [they were chosen from the]* curaca churicuna *[sons of* kurakas, *nobles].)*

All these things I ordain and decree for the government, good justice, and well-being of Peru in this kingdom.

**Item:** We decree that in this our kingdom, no person should blaspheme my father the sun, my mother the moon, the stars, the morning star *(chasca cuyllor, waca willcacunas)* nor the gods *(wacas).* Likewise, no one should blaspheme myself, the Inca, nor the *Coya.*

*(This item went as follows:* Ama ñacaconquicho intiman, quillaman, choqui illa waca willcacunaman, noca incayquitapas, Coyatawanpas. Wañuchiquimanmi, tucuchiquimanmi. *[Do not curse the sun, the moon, the gold-flashing* waqa willkas, *nor me your Inca, nor the* Coya. *I would surely have you killed; I would surely have you finished off.])*

---

[90] *Alguaciles mayores y menores.*

[91] *Escribano.*

**Item:** We decree that you shall blaspheme no person, neither the council, the nobles, nor the poor Indians. (*Ama ñacaconquicho pitapas.* [Do not curse anyone.])

**Item:** We decree that there be another Cusco in Quito, another one in Tumi, another in Huánuco, another in Hatun Colla, and another in Charcas; and that the capital be in Cusco, and that provincial councils should meet in these capitals; this should be law.[92]

**Item:** We decree that no woman shall be allowed to be a witness, because woman is a dissembler, a liar, and fainthearted (*pisi sonco*).

**Item:** We decree that no one who is poor should be a witness, for a poor man might be bribed (*pagar-asca runa, llullamanta rimac runa* [a paid man, a man who speaks in lies]).

**Item:** We decree that in this kingdom, no fruit tree, lumber tree, or hay be burned or cut without permission, under penalty of death and punishments.

**Item:** We decree that these animals not be hunted: *lluycho, taruco, wanaco, wicuña, <wachawa>,*[93] nor should they be killed, so that they might increase. Only the mountain lion and the fox should be killed, because of the damage they cause.

**Item:** We decree that a widow should not uncover her face or leave her house for six months. She should wear mourning for one year, and should not know any man for the rest of her life. She should be chaste and secluded, and should raise her children in her estate, her house, her *chacras* [fields], and her *lucri* [family or *ayllu* cornfields], and she should weep there as a widow and a poor woman.

**Item:** We decree that all people should bury their dead in their own vaults (*pucullos*), and that they not bury them in their houses. They should bury their dead according to their natural customs, with their utensils, food, drink, and clothing.

**Item:** We decree that children and youth shall be very obedient to their fathers and mothers, and to the other adults, elderly people, great lords, and firstborn heirs throughout this kingdom. A child

---

[92] Murra and Adorno note (ms. p. 187, n. 2) that, with the anachronistic exception of Quito, the cities mentioned were major Incaic cities: Tumipampa in Ecuador, Huánuco Pampa in central Peru, Hatun Colla in southern Peru, and Paria in Charcas, Bolivia.

[93] These are two species of deer, two camelids (guanaco and vicuña), and the Andean duck; the last of these is crossed out in the manuscript.

should be whipped the first time he disobeys, and banished to the silver or gold mines for a second offense.

**Item:** We decree that no thieves (*suwa*) shall be allowed in this kingdom, nor shall any highwaymen (*puma ranra*).[94] The former shall be punished with five hundred lashes, and the latter shall be stoned to death and their bodies left unburied, to be eaten by foxes and condors.

**Item:** We decree that those who find anything should return what they find, and the find should be repaid.[95] By following this law, the finders shall not be punished as the thieves they might otherwise appear to be.

**Item:** We decree that no one who has died should be asked to repay a debt, nor should the wife or husband of the deceased be forced to pay it, nor a father for his son, nor a son for his father. Rather, debts should be called in while the person is alive, for to do otherwise is suspicious and deceitful. If the deceased includes the debt in his will, it should be paid from his estate; if the deceased is poor, [the debt] should be forgiven.[96]

**Item:** We decree that Indian men and women who have been banished or imprisoned shall be made to work hard, so that they might receive chastisement and punishment, serve as examples, and make amends for their faults.

**Item:** We decree that in this kingdom, no one shall possess any poison, venom, or sorcery of any kind that can be used to kill another person, nor should anyone kill another. We shall condemn any killer to death by hurling him from a cliff to be broken to pieces. If the crime is against the Inca or the great lords, the rebels and traitors shall have their skins made into human drums,[97] their bones made

---

[94] *Puma ranra:* literally, "rocky wasteland mountain lions," a metaphoric term for the hazards of travel.

[95] It is unclear whether this means that the person who lost the object should pay a reward to the finder, or simply that the finder should "repay" the find by returning the lost item to its true owner.

[96] These ambiguous sentences could alternatively be interpreted as: "It is suspicious and deceitful to mention a debt in a will, forcing it to be paid by the estate of the deceased. If the deceased is poor, [the estate] might then perish."

[97] Guaman Poma writes that the Inca kept several of these *runa tinya* ("people drums"), which were made from the skins of rebellious nobles. "These were drums made from the entire body, and dressed in their own [ethnic] clothing style. . . . They looked alive, and [the Inca ruler] would beat the drum, which was made from the stomach, with his own hand" (ms. p. 336).

into flutes, their teeth and molars made into necklace beads, and their skulls into *mate* [drinking gourds] for drinking *chicha*.

*(This is the penalty for the traitor who rises in public revolt; he is called* iscay sonco auca *[two-hearted enemy]).*

**Item:** We decree that any killer should die in the same way that he killed, whether by stoning or by beating. May he bear the punishment, and may the sentence be carried out.

**Item:** We decree that a woman who is in her period should not enter the temple nor the sacrifice of the gods (*waca willca*). If she enters, she shall be punished.

**Item:** We decree that the woman who aborts her son should die. If the aborted child is a daughter, the woman should be punished with two hundred lashes and be banished.

**Item:** We decree that the woman who is corrupted, or who has consented to being corrupted, or who is a whore, should be hung alive by her hair or by her hands from the crag called Anta Caca[98] and be left there to die. The man who deflowered her shall be given five hundred lashes and shall endure the torment of *hiwaya,*[99] which shall be dropped from the height of one yard onto the man's back. (This punishment kills some men, while others remain alive.) A rapist of a woman shall be sentenced to death. If both [the man and the woman] consented [to the sexual act], both shall die by being hanged: equal punishments.

**Item:** We decree that the woman who is widowed should not remarry nor should she cohabit with a man after her husband has died. If she has a son, he shall be the heir of her entire estate, houses, and *chacras* [fields]; if she has a daughter, she shall be the heir of half the estate, and the other half shall be inherited by her father, mother, or brothers.

**Item:** We decree that the man who has one son shall be honored (*yupaychasca*). The man with two sons shall be given grants.[100] The man with three sons shall be given fields, pasture, and lands. Those

---

[98] Anta Caca (*anta qaqa*), "Copper Rock." This place, depicted in the graphic illustration of this punishment on ms. p. 310, has not been identified.

[99] *Hiwaya:* Guaman Poma describes this as a "stone about half the size of an adobe," adding that those who survived the ordeal were crippled for life (ms. p. 315).

[100] Grants (*merced*): such as the land grants made by the colonial administration in the name of the king.

with four sons shall be exempt [from labor tribute obligations]. Those with five sons shall be made lesser authorities over their sons (*pichica camachicoc*).[101] Those with ten sons shall be lords of grant.[102] And those with thirty, forty, or fifty sons shall settle in the place of their choosing, whether a pueblo or vacant land, and shall be the lord therein.

**Item:** We decree that lazy, dirty pigs[103] shall be punished with the filth from their *chacra* [fields], their houses, or the plates they eat on, or from their heads, hands, or feet. They shall be washed and shall be forced to drink their own filth from a *mate* [drinking gourd], as chastisement and punishment.

*(This punishment was carried out throughout the kingdom.)*

**Item:** We declare that all those who bury their dead inside the houses where they live shall be banished.

**Item:** We declare that the noble lords shall have 50 women to serve them and increase the number of people in the kingdom. A *hunu curaca* [great lord over myriads] shall have 30 women. A *wamanin apo* [district lord, or captain], 20 women. An *waranca curaca* [great lord over 1,000] shall have 15 women. A *pisca pachaca* [man of 500] should have 12 women. A *pachaca camachicoc* [authority over 100] should have 8 women. A *pisca chunca camachicoc* [authority over 50] should have 7 women. A *chunca camachicoc* [authority over 10] should have 5 women. A *pisca camachicoc* [authority over 5] should have 3 women. And a poor Indian should have 2 women.

*(The others who were placed as* mitmacs *[settlers]*[104] *had two women. Soldiers at war were given more or fewer women depending on their victories, so that they might multiply.)*

---

[101] *Pisca camachicoc (pichqa kamachikuq)* "five-authority," was the lowest rank in the Incaic hierarchy, which is spelled out in detail below. The person who held this office ruled, in theory, over five households.

[102] Señor *de merced:* either a lord over a land grant, or someone who has the power to make grants himself.

[103] Pigs (*puercos*): given that pigs were European animals, the fact that this common Spanish insult had entered Guaman Poma's vocabulary is perhaps a sign that it was often on the lips of Spaniards in Peru.

[104] *Mitmaq:* "colonizer, settler," a person sent by the Inca regime from an allied province to colonize land granted to them in a distant province as a means of controlling potentially rebellious subjects.

**Item:** We declare that no man shall marry his sister, his mother, or his first cousin, nor his aunt, niece, relative, or *comadre*,[105] under penalty of being punished by having his eyes gouged out, being quartered, and having his body placed on the mountains as a reminder and as punishment. For by law, only the Inca shall marry his full sister.

**Item:** We declare that captains shall be of good blood, pure, and loyal, and that soldiers shall be loyal not treacherous, and shall be thirty to forty or fifty years of age. They shall also be Indians, tough, strong, powerful, and fit for war and battle.

**Item:** We declare that no person should spill corn, other foods, or potatoes, nor should they peel them; for if they understood, they would weep when they are peeled.[106] Therefore, they shall not peel them, under penalty of being punished.

**Item:** We declare that in times of plague, sacrifice, storms, famine, thirst, the death of the Inca or of some great lord (*capac apo*), or uprisings, the people should not have festivities and should not dance, sing, play drums or flute, nor should men touch women. Nor, in times of fasting and penitence, should they eat salt, peppers, meat, or fruit, nor should they drink *chicha*, nor eat any food other than simple, raw white corn during their penitence.

**Item:** We declare that in times of frost or hail, or in times when the corn dries up for lack of rain from the sky, everyone together should beg God (*runa camac*) for water: they should all dress in mourning and paint their faces black with *ñuñunya* [the bright red juice of bitter wild cherries] and *quichimcha* (soot). All the adult Indians, together with the women and older children, are to walk in procession through the mountains, weeping and begging God (*Pacha Camac*) for water, shouting out this hymn:[107]

| | |
|---|---|
| *Ayawya, wacaylli.* | [Ay! oh! hearken to our tears! |
| *Ayawya, puypuylli.* | Ay! oh! hearken to our weeping! |

[105] *Comadre:* a Spanish term for the godmother of one's child, or conversely the mother of one's godchild. The Catholic category of godparents (for baptized children) had an Andean counterpart in the sponsors for the ritual of the first haircut (*rutuchikuy*).

[106] This ambiguous phrase could mean either that the foods themselves would cry in pain if they were conscious, or that the people doing the spilling and peeling would weep over their own wastefulness if they only understood the consequences of their acts.

[107] Guaman Poma includes four versions of this chant in the book, each of them cited in Quechua without Spanish translation; compare the version on p. 93.

| | |
|---|---|
| *Lluto puchac wamrayqui,* | We, your tender, suffering young children, |
| *lluto puchac wacchayqui* | we, your tender, suffering poor, |
| *wacallamusumquim.* | weep only for you. |
| *Unuc sayquita* | Please send us |
| *yacuc sayquita,* | your water, |
| *cachallamuway,* | your rain, |
| *wacchayqui, runayqui,* | for us, your poor, your people, |
| *llacta runa camascayquiman.* | your townspeople whom you created.] |

They are to obey this rule in this kingdom.

**Item:** We ordain and decree that all skilled workers not be idle nor lazy. This includes both those in charge of salaried offices (governors, pontiffs, priests, and the great lords who rule over the land) and those who live from their crafts, such as wall painters (*cuscoc*) and painters of *quiro* [wooden cups] and *mate* [drinking gourds], who are called *llinpec; amautacuna* (artisans); *llacllac* and *quiro camayoc* (woodworkers); *rumita chichoc* (stoneworkers); *manca llutac* (potters); *tacac* (silversmiths); *cumpi camayoc* (embroiderers and silk workers); *pachaca* (plowmen); herders (*michic*); *awa camayoc* (weavers); *sirac* (tailors, but not including seamstresses); bakers (*sara tanta rurac* [makers of corn bread]); cooks (*micuy rurac*); *suyuyoc* (overseers); *collca camayoc* [granary masters] and *sapsi camayoc* (administrators of the commons); *quillca camayoc* (scribes of the *quipu,* knotted cord); singers and musicians (*taquic* and *cochochic*); *pincollo camayoc* (flutists); and *auca camayoc* (warriors). These skilled workers shall not go absent in this kingdom, for if they do, they will be punished as lazy and thieving.

**Item:** We decree that throughout the kingdom there shall be an abundance of food. Much corn, potatoes, and *ocas* shall be planted. People shall make *cawi, caya, chuño, tamos,* and *chochoca.*[108] All types of food—quinoa, *ulluco, maswa,*[109] even leafy greens (*yuyos*)—shall be dried so that people may have food to eat all year round. The common lands (*sapsi*) should be planted with corn, potatoes, peppers, *macno,* and cotton. People shall pick *pawau quewencha* flowers and other leaves to make dyes for *cumpi* [fine weaving] and *awasca* [coarse weaving]. They shall burn *marco* and quinoa to make *llipta* [ash for chewing with coca]. Let the district magistrates (*tocricoc*) give accounts each year; those who fail to do so shall be cruelly punished in this kingdom.

---

[108] Preserved foods made by drying potatoes, other root crops, and corn.

[109] Quinoa is a grain; *ullucos, maswas,* and *ocas* are root crops similar to potatoes.

**Item:** We decree that all houses, garments, pots, guinea pig pens, and *chacras* [fields] shall be inspected twice a year. Those who fail to do so shall be punished with one hundred lashes for each omission.[110] The inspector shall also demand an accounting of the manure from the fields (*chacras*). The people shall keep in their houses an abundance of firewood, hay, and [. . .].[111] They shall keep barrels (*cullonas*), [. . .], and [. . .] of potatoes for themselves, to serve the Inca, the *capac apocunas*, and the captains, and to supply to the *tambos* [inns] and *chasquis* [couriers] on the royal highways. They shall clean [the *tambos*], maintain the bridges, and [keep supplies] for festivities. We set down and decree this law and ordinance in these kingdoms.

**Item:** We decree that the barbers and surgeons (*hampi camayoc, sircac,* and *quichicawan*) shall heal with herbs.

*(These men were called* hampi camayoc *[herb masters], and the devout women midwives were called* wawa wachachic *[birthers of babies] and* wicsa allichac hampi camayoc *[stomach-healer herb masters].)*

**Item:** We decree that the wet nurses of orphans (*waccha rurocha ñuñuchic*) be exempt from everything, and that they be given an older girl to help them raise the orphans.

*(These women were called* mamacuna.*)*

**Item:** We declare that no Indian in this kingdom shall change his attire and clothing from that of his particular band (*ayllu*), under penalty of one hundred lashes.

**Item:** We decree that in this kingdom, in every pueblo, all shall eat in the public square—noble lords, Indians great and small—so that all the poor and orphaned, the widows, the sick, the old, the blind and lame, the pilgrims and the travelers might join them. All may eat, for this is charity, and it has been the tradition and custom since the first people. This is the law and good works and mercy of God in this kingdom.

**Item:** We decree that, in this kingdom, there be temple virgins (*wayrur aclla, chaupi aclla,* and *pampa aclla*).

*(These nuns died with their virginity inviolate.)*

---

[110] Presumably it was the *tuqrikuq* (district magistrate) who was to be punished for failing to make the required inspection. This law contains an implicit criticism of the lack of accountability and the unconcern for people's welfare demonstrated by the Spanish magistrates (*corregidores*) who replaced the Incaic *tuqrikuq*.

[111] Much of this sentence is illegible.

These general ordinances of this kingdom were set forth by Topa Inca Yupanqui and by his royal council in this kingdom. After Don Francisco de Toledo, the viceroy of these kingdoms, reviewed them, he spread the word of these ancient laws and ordinances, selecting the best of them. Our Catholic lord and king Don Philip II then ordained and confirmed them, and for that reason he decreed that all should dine in the public square and celebrate a feast there.

From all of this: I believe in the One God of the Most Holy Trinity, God the Father, God the Son, and God the Holy Spirit, and in his blessed mother, St. Mary, and in all the saints and holy angels of heaven and of all that I believe and that the Holy Mother Church of Rome holds. With true faith, I hold and believe that I have written of everything. May God be served by what is good in it, may Christians correct what is bad, and may the Christians who read these ancient ordinances of the Indians be moved to repent of their sins.

*[The next chapter presents descriptions of the "streets" or "paths" (*calles, *Guaman Poma's curious Spanish term for age-ranked groups of people) in the Inca's world. Sketches of ten male age groups are followed by ten parallel female age groups. The descriptions come in the guise of an inspection tour carried out by the Inca's royal council, as if each age group actually lived on a separate street. Inspection tours (*visitas*) were a prominent tool of colonial statecraft, and one that Guaman Poma frequently advocates, as it was one of the few checks on the often arbitrary exercise of power by local governors and priests. In this chapter, he projects the Spanish* visita *model onto a presumable pre-conquest method of ascertaining who was obligated to give labor tribute to the Inca. He suggests that the Spanish crown would be well-served to reinstate the orderly and traditional age-group system of categorizing people.]*

*195–236*    # THE GENERAL INSPECTION TOUR

## OF THE INDIANS OF THIS KINGDOM BY THE INCAS AND OTHER NOBLE LORDS WHO MAKE UP HIS ROYAL COUNCIL IS AS FOLLOWS:

TEN PATHS FOR Indians to apply themselves in work, so that they may not be idle and lazy in this kingdom, for otherwise they would not be able to support themselves, nor would the other nobles and lords, nor His Majesty the Inca and his government.

*[The first illustration, ms. p. 196, shows a young warrior, labeled "Auca camayoc" (master of war), holding his ax and shield in his left hand and the head of an enemy in his right. The caption reads: "From the age of thirty-three. Brave young Indian tributary."]*

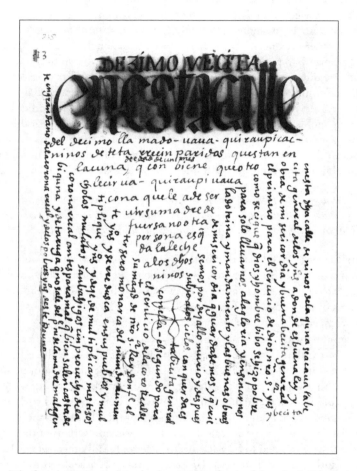

[The first short paragraph in the descriptions of each of these "paths" formed the entire original text. Guaman Poma wrote this first paragraph in the form of a descending triangle. He later came back and added the subsequent paragraphs in each description at a perpendicular to the main text. As several commentators have noted, the added lines hang down the page like the cords on a quipu, the knotted writing device of the Incas. ]

**THE FIRST PATH** was that of the brave men, the soldiers of war (*auca camayoc*). They were thirty-three years of age (they entered this path as young as twenty-five, and left it at fifty). These brave men were held very much set apart and distinguished in every manner possible.

The Inca selected some of these Indians to serve in his battles and wars. He selected some from among these brave Indians to settle as *mitmacs* (foreigners) in other provinces, giving them more than enough land, both pasture and cropland, to multiply, and giving each of them a woman from the same land. He did this to keep his kingdom secure; they served as overseers. He selected some of these brave Indians to serve as plowmen and as skilled workers in every task that was necessary for the Inca and the other lords, princes, noblemen, and ladies of this kingdom; those selected in this way were called *mitmac* (foreigners). Others of these brave men were selected to work in the mines and for other labor, toil, and obligations. Thus, in the general inspection, this first path was titled *auca camayoc* (able men of war).

*[The illustration of the "second path," ms. p. 198, shows an old man walking with a load of firewood on his back and a dog at his feet. The caption reads: "From the age of sixty. Past paying tribute, one who serves the nobles."]*

**THE SECOND PATH** was that of the *puric macho* [old walkers]—old men, advanced in age, from sixty to seventy or eighty years old. They served in the *chacras* [fields], in carrying firewood and hay, and in cleaning the houses of the Inca or of some lord and noble. They also served as valets, stewards, gatekeepers, and *quipucamayoc* [*kipu* masters].

Beginning with the year in which they reached the age of fifty years from their birth (that is, the year they turned fifty-one), these Indians became exempt from going to war or to battle, or from doing any kind of personal service that involved leaving their houses and lands and going with the *auca camayoc* (brave man) Indians. But they were obligated to serve in every kind of errand, not only in the houses of their lords but also in their croplands. These men were called *pachaca* (plowmen). Others of these aged Indians were selected to be valets (called *apocuna*); still others were selected to be authorities and stewards (*surcocuc*); others were selected to be footmen for the noble lords (called *curaca catic*); and others were selected to be squires for the ladies (*curaca warmita pusac*). In this way, these Indians did every kind of service they were commanded to do in their pueblos, whether it was for the noble chief, his children, or his women, in this kingdom.

*[The illustration of the "third path," ms. p. 200, shows an old man hobbling with a cane. The caption reads: "From the age of eighty. Deaf old man, exempt from everything, sleepy."]*

THE THIRD PATH was that of the so-called *rocto macho* (deaf old men), who ranged from 80 up to 100 or 150 years of age. These *rocto machos* are old men who live only to eat and sleep. Those who could do so would make *wasca* (rope) and blankets (*apa*); they would also guard the houses of the poor and raise guinea pigs[112] and ducks.

These old men were widely feared, honored, and obeyed. Their tasks included whipping the boys and girls and giving good advice and doctrine. Even with the shadowy understanding that they had of God, they were able to shed much light and clarity on the service of God, and they would preach good examples. [That is why there is a saying,] *alli cunacoc alli yachachic macho yaya,* which means, "good example-giver, good teacher, old man." Those who could would work as gatekeepers for the maidens, the virgins, and the noble ladies. All the rich men would give these men alms and make their clothes. Their whole band would cultivate their croplands, and the whole pueblo would serve them. Their *compadres* (*wayno*) and their *compadres'* spouses (*socna*) would give generous gifts.[113] Thus there was no reason to keep hospitals,[114] for their croplands were cultivated and their llamas were watched over, and so there was no need to have hospitals for the poor, the old, the lame, the blind, or the crippled, in the . . .[115]

*[The illustration of the "fourth path," ms. p. 202, shows a one-legged man walking with a walking stick. The caption reads: "These sick people have no specific age for being grouped here. Those who can serve are to serve the nobles."]*

THE FOURTH PATH was that of the sick and wounded, the lame, the handless, and the crippled: *upa* (the deaf), *ñausa* (the blind), *uncoc* (the sick), *wiñay uncoc* (the crippled), *maquin paquisca* (the armless or handless), and *hanca* (the lame). [Some of] these men served as entertainers with their talk and jests, such as the dwarfs (*tinre wayaca*), *cumu* (the hunchbacked), and *chicta sinca* [the cleft-nosed]. All those who could do so would work and help. Those who had eyes served as watchmen; those who had feet, walked;

---

[112] Guinea pigs were domesticated in the Andes as sources of meat. Guaman Poma uses the Spanish word *conejo* (rabbit), which was how the Spanish identified them.

[113] In Latin American Catholicism, *compadres* and *comadres* are spiritual kin; when a couple's child is baptized, for example, the child's parent and godparents become each others' *compadres* and *comadres*. Murra and Adorno note (ms. p. 201, n. 1) that there is no independent evidence that such a relationship existed in the Quechua-speaking world before colonization and Christianization.

[114] Colonial hospitals were shelters more than medical centers, run by charity for the destitute and the dying.

[115] The end of the line is cut off.

those who had hands, wove and served as servants and *quipucamayoc* (overseers). Each of these was married to his equal so that they could multiply and serve in every way they could.

The rule that [the Inca] kept for these Indian men and women was very good for the service of God and the multiplication of people, so that the land might be filled with people, towards the greatness, increase, and service of His Majesty the Inca and the princes, dukes, counts, and marquises of this kingdom. He married the blind man to a woman who was also blind, the lame man to a woman who was also lame, the mute man to a woman who was also mute, the dwarf to a dwarf, the hunchback to a hunchback, the cleft-nosed man with a woman who was also cleft-nosed, for the multiplication of the world. These people had their croplands, houses, estates, and the help of their service. Because of this saintly rule and orderliness, there was no need for hospitals or for begging in this kingdom, for no other kingdom in Christianity nor among the infidels has ever been nor could be so [orderly], no matter how Christian . . .[116]

*[The illustration of the "fifth path," ms. p. 204, shows a young man running with a* kipu *(knotted recording device) in his hand, which is labeled "letter." The caption reads: "From the age of eighteen. Indian who pays half tribute; young men."]*

**THE FIFTH PATH** was that of the *sayapayac* [those who stand upright]. These were the Indians of the watch, aged from eighteen to twenty years. They served as messenger boys (*cachacuna wayna*) between one pueblo and another, and to other nearby places in the valleys. They also herded flocks and accompanied the Indians of war and the great lords and captains. They also carried food and served the nobles and petty authorities of their pueblos.

Good manners and good breeding; studying to know poverty, lack, and obedience, so as to be submissive to the service of God: such were the customs in the time of the Incas and before, by the ancient law that came from the first people (from *Wari Wiracocha Runa, Wari Runa, Purun Runa,* and *Auca Runa,* up to the time of the Incas). But between the time of Chalco Chima Inca, Wascar Inca, and Atawalpa Inca and the present, this good law has been lost—this way of bringing up children and youths with these exemplars, the *sayapayac macta.* These skillful young men, these squires, were ordered to eat raw corn. They would not taste salt, pepper, honey, or vinegar, nor would they eat sweets, meat, nor any fattening food, nor would they drink *chicha.* For a special present they would be given a bit of *mote* (cooked corn), a blouse, and a thick poncho; that was all they needed.

---

[116] The end of the line is cut off.

If one of them was the son of a noble, he would be punished even more strictly. These young men never slowed down, until the age of thirty, nor did they know woman, throughout the kingdom.

[*The illustration of the "sixth path," ms. p. 206, shows a boy with a two-handled net in his right hand and three small birds in his left; a herd of llamas stand behind him. The caption reads: "From the age of twelve. He serves the community* (sapa).*"*]

**THE SIXTH PATH** was that of the boys aged twelve to eighteen years, who are called *mactacuna*. These boys were sent out to watch over the herds. While out there, they would use ropes and snares to catch the birds called *wachiwa, yuto, quiwyu, tacami, awas,* and *recrec* [Andean goose, partridge, small tinamou, flightless black duck, parrot, bird that sings "rec-rec"], and they would make jerky from the meat and save the feathers for the Incas (the *capac apocuna*) and the captains; this was their task.

They did all these chores out of love for the republic and to increase the greatness of the Inca's majesty. Before there was an Inca, each pueblo had its own Inca (king and lord) to assist. The older boys (*macta*) would take part in helping their commons (*sapsi*) and the estates of the Inca, of the lady (Coya), and of other great lords in their kingdom, as well as those of the sun, the moon, the stars, and the idols (*wacas*). They would help keep watch over the herds and the crops, and their service to the great *caciques* in this kingdom taught these young men humility, obedience, and that they should serve throughout the kingdom and be very obedient in their kingdom. If this law were to be followed now, God and His Majesty would be well served, and the commons (*sapsi*) would grow in this kingdom. All this is hindered by the *doctrina* priests, the *corregidores*, and the *encomenderos*, under the pretext of getting their own personal service throughout the kingdom . . .[117]

[*The illustration of the "seventh path," ms. p. 208, shows a boy with a small* bola *(a stick with two foot-long strings, weighted with small balls or stones attached at the end) in his right hand and a dead bird in his left, chasing a flock of ground birds. The caption reads: "From the age of nine. He serves his father and the* cacique.*"*]

**THE SEVENTH PATH** was that of the so-called *tocllacoc wamracuna* [hunter boys], aged from nine to twelve years. They were said to be hunters of small birds, which they would catch with ropes and snares and other methods—

---

[117] The end of the line is cut off.

the birds called *pulidos, quinte, waychau, chayna, urpay* [unidentified bird, hummingbird, blackbird, goldfinch, dove], and other sorts of birds. They would make the meat into *charqui* (jerky)[118] and save the feathers for making *cumpi* ([fine weavings] of feathers), and for *wallcanca, chasca chuqui, uru cawa* [decorated shields and lances], and other elegancies for the Inca, the nobles, the captains, and the *auca camayoccuna*.

So that they would get instruction and be taught to work and to take up an occupation and learn virtue, these boys were told to be hunters. That is why they were called *tocllacoc wamra* (hunter boys) throughout the kingdom; for, over here, boys were never sent to school to learn an occupation at these ages, but rather when they were young men of twenty or thirty years, so that they could learn well without playing. These boys spent their time catching birds with ropes, snares, or stones in the countryside. This was their usual occupation; otherwise, they would watch the herds, carry firewood and hay, twist and spin yarn, assist in other errands for the nobles, and meet the just demands of their fathers, mothers, and older brothers. They were well acquainted with the lash, and there was much cleanliness in this kingdom.

*[The illustration of the "eighth path," ms. p. 210, shows a small boy playing with a sling and stone, and wearing what appears to be a headdress decorated with a bat skin. The caption reads: "From the age of five. A catechism boy."]*[119]

**THE EIGHTH PATH** was that of boys aged from five to nine years. These were the "boys who play" (*pucllacoc wamracuna*). They served their mothers and fathers in whatever ways they could, and bore many whippings and thumpings; they also served by playing with the toddlers and by rocking and watching over the babies in cradles.

Today we would call them "catechism boys," for they are the proper age for going to school and being instructed in the catechism. They were set aside by the general inspection for helping out in their houses and raising their younger siblings (children in cradles and toddlers) by playing with them, for helping to raise orphans, and for doing other household chores, such as watching the house. Such were the tasks of these boys, who were

---

[118] *Charqui (charki;* in Cusco Quechua, *ch'arki*): the English word "jerky" is derived from this Quechua word for dried, smoked meat.

[119] Catechism boy: *niño de doctrina*, a boy sent to learn the Catholic catechism before his first communion. In other contexts, *doctrina* refers to the parishes and churches established in Indian pueblos under the colonial regime; this is because Indians of all ages were viewed as needing to learn the catechism, even decades after their ancestors had been incorporated into Catholic life. As Guaman Poma goes on to explain, "catechism boy" is an anachronism in a discussion of Incaic times, but one that he finds appropriate.

called *pucllacoc wamra* (boys who play)—catechism boys, schoolboys. It is right for these boys to be punished and instructed throughout the kingdom for the order of the kingdom; this is a good law. Let the *fiscales* of the pueblos[120] gather together those of this age, that they may be of help to the tribute-paying community, in service of God and of His Majesty in this kingdom.

*[The illustration of the "ninth path," ms. p. 212, shows a baby or toddler crawling on the ground. The caption reads: "From the age of one. Unproductive."]*

THE NINTH PATH was that of those called *llullo llocac wamracuna* (babies at the breast who are beginning to crawl), aged from one, two, or three years up to the age of five. They do nothing; instead, others serve them, allow them to play with other boys, and look after them so that they do not fall down or get burned. They are well watched.

In this general inspection of the Indians called *llocac wamra* (crawling children), it is very proper for their mothers to be exempted for raising them; if they are fatherless, even more so. If two are born from a single womb, their father and mother should both be exempted for two years, by the law of God and their position: this was a very ancient law of this kingdom, just as it is a law of Christianity due to the fact that it was brought by God our Lord Jesus Christ and his mother our Lady of the Rosary. In spite of being barbarians and pagans, the Inca lords decreed that people should obey this law of the ancient Indians they called the *Pacarimoc Runa* (which means "the first men who emerged"). They did keep it, so there was less need for charity [than there is now], because of these decrees and these works of mercy in the world, in this kingdom.

*[The illustration of the "tenth path," ms. p. 214, shows a small baby strapped inside a wicker cradle. The caption reads: "From the age of one month. Others serve him."]*

THE TENTH PATH was that of those called *wawa quirawpi cac* (newborn babies at the breast, in cradles), from the age of one month. It is right for others to serve the *quirawpi wawacuna;* their mothers must necessarily serve them, for no other person can give milk to these children.

With this, the path of babies in cradles, the general inspections of the Indians comes to an end. It is a good law, a work of mercy, and a good general inspection tour. In the first place, it serves God as follows: God as a living man made himself poor, solely to bring us to Glory and teach us

---

[120] *Fiscales* were Indian officials who ran the lay religious hierarchy in Indian pueblos.

the catechism, the commandments, and the good works of mercy, that we might keep them and believe; he died in order to leave them here, and then he rose into heaven. This general inspection tour was therefore in line with [God's teachings]. In the second place, it serves the royal crown of His Majesty our lord and king Don Philip III, the monarch of the world, that the number of Indians should increase, that they should congregate into their pueblos,[121] that the Indians should multiply, and that the mestizos, *cholos*, mulattos, and *zambaigos* should cease multiplying, for they are of no benefit to the royal crown. The [mestizos] turn out worse rather than better, like offspring of *wicuña* and *taruca* [wild camelids and deer], for they take after neither their fathers nor their mothers: bad people, and very damaging to the royal crown and to the poor Indians of this kingdom.[122]

*[The ten "paths" of men are followed by ten parallel "paths" of women.]*

## FIRST INSPECTION OF WOMEN

THREE DAYS AFTER inspecting these ten paths, [the inspector] would leave and then would enter [the paths of] the women. After completing all his inspections, he would return every six months to inspect them, move from path to path, in accordance with the age of each person. This was the task of each district magistrate (*tocricoc, michoc inca*). He would perform it twice each year, every six months; he never forgot this general inspection, composed by His Majesty the Inca and his council (*capac apo, apocuna, coracuna, camachicoc*). "*Camachinchic Tawantinsuyu runanchicta—Chinchaysuyu, Andesuyu, Collasuyu, Condesuyu—cay camachicoyninchicta wacaychanca. Sapa ayllunpi uchuc churinpi quipunca runa quiputa.* [We decree to our people of Tawantinsuyu—Chinchaysuyu, Andesuyu, Collasuyu, Condesuyu—who shall keep these, our ordinances. People shall keep records on *kipus* of each *ayllu*, of their smallest children.]"

---

[121] Congregate into their pueblos (*se reduzca[n] en sus pueblos*): Guaman Poma refers here to the colonial policy of *reducciones,* by which the crown attempted to force Indians who lived in houses dispersed across the countryside to move to consolidated, Spanish-style towns. See footnote 207.

[122] Mestizos (children of Spanish and Indian descent), *cholos* (Indians living in Spanish settlements), mulattos (of Spanish and African descent), and *zambaigos* (of Indian and African descent): Guaman Poma consistently argues that these mixed populations are damaging to the interests of the Indians. Here, as Murra and Adorno note (ms. p. 215, n. 1), he compares them to unproductive vicuñas (wild camelids) and *taruka* (wild deer), in implicit contrast with domesticated alpacas, which produce wool and meat, much as settled Indians produce tribute.

*[The illustration of the "first path," ms. p. 217, shows a woman kneeling to weave fine cloth on a backstrap loom. The caption reads: "From the age of thirty-three. Tributary woman."]*

THE FIRST PATH was that of the married women and widows called *auca camayocpa warmin* [the warriors' women], whose occupation is weaving fine cloth (*cumpi awasca*) for the Inca, the other lords (*capac apocuna*), the captains, and the soldiers. They were thirty-three years of age when they married; up until then, they remained virgins and maidens. These women, like men of the same age, got married; up until then they were called girls (*wamra tasqui, purun warmi*).

According to the general inspection of the first path of women, these so-called *auca camayocpa warmi* ("wives of the brave men," or as we might say today, "like the wives of taxpaying commoners[123] and soldiers in Castile") were not free [from tribute obligations]. These women had the occupation of weaving fine *awasca* cloth and spinning yarn for *cumpis;* they assisted the commons in their pueblos and provinces; and they assisted with everything their titled noble lords decreed—until their husbands were beyond tributary age, for then the women passed beyond tributary status as well. That was why no noblewoman was allowed to marry a tributary commoner. If she did, she became as much a commoner as he was, throughout the kingdom, and was lowered from being a "Doña." When women were called *mama,* that was an honor [equivalent to the Spanish title *Doña*] throughout the kingdom.

*[The illustration of the "second path," ms. p. 219, shows an old woman kneeling in the same pose as the previous illustration, weaving coarse cloth on a backstrap loom. The caption reads: "From the age of fifty. Woman who serves the nobles."]*

THE SECOND PATH was that of those called *payacuna* (old women), fifty years of age. These were old women whose occupation was weaving coarse cloth for the community. These Indian women went in to serve the noble women as doorkeepers, stewards, chambermaids, cooks, and head maids; they also served the virgins (*acllacunas*), and did everything mandated in their occupations and offices. They were called *mama,* and they were required to keep *quipus* (accounts) of all these things.

These women of the second path were called *paya,* which means "old woman," by which one should understand "somewhat old woman, or

---

[123] Taxpaying commoners (*pecheros*): Spaniards liable for paying a tributary tax to their king or provincial lord. See Glossary: taxpayers.

widow." All widows and deflowered women were called *paya iquima wacllisca* (which means "old woman, widow, fallen woman"), even if they were girls. No attention was paid to such women: they went onto the rolls of the widows. But no fallen woman was ever found to have married after having fallen, nor was any woman ever an adulterer. Any young man and young maiden who broke [the sexual prohibitions] were killed by being hanged alive from a crag—the man and the woman alike—when caught in adultery. This was serious justice. Everything having to do with this sin was brought here by the Spanish.

These women served by weaving sackcloth and other things for the nobles, and they assisted the commons and other obligations of their pueblos, which they never left. They were respected as honorable old women, and they had the maidens in their charge, and they assisted in other *mitas* (obligations)—whatever was demanded of them as tributary women in this kingdom.

*[The illustration of the "third path," ms. p. 221, shows a very old woman resting on her knees. She holds a walking stick in her left hand, and her right hand rests on her temples. The caption reads: "From the age of eighty. Sleepy old woman, past all [obligations]."]*

**THE THIRD PATH** was that of those called *puñoc paya* (old women who only know how to sleep and eat), eighty years of age. Those who could, served as doorkeepers and companions, and some who were able to do so wove sackcloth, spun thick yarn, and did whatever else they could, such as watching guinea pigs, raising ducks and dogs, looking after houses, and helping to raise children.

Each great lady had two or three of these old women (who were called *puñoc paya*). The greatest ladies had ten or twenty old women to keep their houses in order and watch over the maidens. The best of these old women were employed as stewards, chambermaids, doorkeepers, and for punishing the girls of the house. All this aside, these and other women had their croplands, for which they made *minca* so that others would help cultivate them.[124] Thus old women and orphans who were unable [to work the land] had no need of begging for alms; rather, these old women would feed and raise the orphaned children.

[Today,] under the Christians' law, no one does this much to help boys and girls. Old women who are still capable of working don't even bother to

---

[124] *Minka* is work done for another person with an expectation of reciprocity. In this case, an old woman would perform some kind of labor for another family, such as weaving or guarding animals, and in return would expect the others to reciprocate by cultivating her fields.

walk downhill, and so they become poor. When they are poor, they fanta-size that they are nobles; taxpaying commoner women make themselves into ladies and Doñas, which they are not. In this way, the world is turned upside down. So it was that there was great charity for these old, sick women in these kingdoms.

*[The illustration of the "fourth path," ms. p. 223, shows a hunchbacked woman spinning yarn while walking. The caption reads: "These sick women were gathered from all ages, so no age is given. They serve the noble caciques."]*

THE FOURTH PATH was that of the women called *ñausacuna* (blind women), *hanca* (lame women), *opa* (deaf women), *wiñay concoc* (cripples), *tinre wayaca* (dwarfs, like hunchbacks), and *chicta sinca, cacya* (cleft noses). The Inca would marry these women to others like themselves. All those who were able to work, he would set to spinning and weaving—these Indian women knew a thousand handicrafts, such as weaving *chumpi* and *wincha* [sashes and ribbons]. The Inca would distribute the rest as concu-bines, so that they would give birth, multiply, and increase their population so the land would not be left empty and alone. They used to be great weav-ers of cloth, cooks, *chicheras* [makers of corn beer], and jesters for the enter-tainment of the Inca and the great lords.

On this path, the women inspected were the sick: lame and blind, wid-ows, hunchbacks, and dwarfs. All of them had fields, croplands, houses, and pastures, from which they made a living and were able to eat, so that they did not need to beg for alms. Those who could, worked; and those who could, married and gave birth and multiplied. These sick women were well loved and highly respected, and the best of them worked, so they had no need for alms. Spanish women who have strength become poor because they do not work, and they must beg for alms when they are blind or aged, eighty years old, and orphan-poor: such women ought to be given alms and charity for the sake of God in this world.

*[The illustration of the "fifth path," ms. p. 225, shows a young, long-haired woman standing upright and spinning yarn. The caption reads: "Aged thirty-three. Maiden, as yet unmarried; they assist the commons (sapsi)."]*

THE FIFTH PATH was that of the young women of marriageable age, called *allin sumac sipascuna* [good, beautiful young women]. These were virgin maidens (*purum tasqui*) and were thirty-three years of age. Some from among them were chosen to be the perpetual virgins for the sun and the temples of the moon and the morning star. [Others were chosen] for the Inca, the gods (*waca willcacunas*), the *capac apocunas* and *curacacunas* (princes), the *allicaccunas* [those raised in rank by the Inca], and the *camachicunas* [petty authorities]. [Others were chosen] for the brave Indians *(auca camayoccuna)* and for the *pircac, lucric,* and *chicoc* [builders, stone masons, and plowmen]. They were distributed without wronging anyone. No one, not even the Inca himself, ever took a woman without her consent, because the penalties and laws in place at that time prescribed a fixed sentence of death.

What greatness there was in this New World of the Indies, to have women who were maidens at the age of thirty-three! Some women remained virgins and maidens until they died: such women could stay in their houses or wander through the countryside without being touched by so much as a fly. Oh, what a lovely law, not only of this world but also of God! If only the Christians' law would allow young women to go out into the street and remain virgins! No emperor or king in the world has had such a lovely law. These women served in every way they were ordered by the Inca and by justice. All the bad things—adultery and other mortal sins—were brought in by those Christians, who, under the cover of teaching catechism, deflowered all the maidens; because of this, many mestizos are born in this kingdom.

*[The illustration of the "sixth path," ms. p. 227, shows a short-haired girl spinning yarn, carrying a load of firewood, and herding llamas. The caption reads: "From the age of twelve. They serve their parents and the community."]*

THE SIXTH PATH was that of those called *coro tasquicunas, rotusca tasqui,* which means "young girls with short-cropped hair." They were from twelve to eighteen years of age and served their fathers, mothers, and grandmothers. They also began to serve the great ladies so that they could learn to spin yarn and weave delicate materials. They served as animal herders and workers in the fields *(chacras),* and in making *chicha* [corn beer] for their fathers and mothers, and they assisted in other occupations insofar as they could, helping out. They were sent out for firewood and hay, served their parents as cooks, and cleaned the house.

These *coro tasqui* (girls with cropped hair) went about unkempt, barefoot, and in short dresses. They greatly helped their fathers and mothers, the noble women, and the community. They were filled with obedience and respect, and were taught to cook, spin, and weave. Their hair was kept cropped until they reached the age of thirty, when they were married and given the dowry of their destitution and poverty. This was true for both men and women: until the Inca or his viceroy gave the command, they never knew woman or man, under penalty of death, by the laws and ordinances of these kingdoms and the upbringing of sons and daughters, in the way they were punished and instructed. So should it still be in the world, in this kingdom.

*[The illustration of the "seventh path," ms. p. 229, shows a young, short-haired girl picking flowers. The caption reads: "From the age of nine. For the community, and they serve the noble ladies."]*

THE SEVENTH PATH on the inspection tour was that of the girls called *pawau pallac* (flower pickers). They picked *tire, quewencha, onquena, llachoc, paconca, pinau, siclla, llullucha, morcoto,* and *escana* [various flowers]; they were *chullcota pallac* [iris pickers]. These girls picked flowers to dye wool for *cumpis,* cloth, and other things, and they picked the edible herbs mentioned above, which they dried out and stored in the warehouse (*cullca*) to be eaten the following year. These girls were from nine to twelve years of age. With these herbs, they served the sun and the *capa cocha;*[125] the Inca, the great lords, and the captains; the ladies (*Coyas* and *ñustas*); and the noblewomen, who used the herbs for dying the *cumpi, awasca, compana, llauto, ojotas, wicha, chumpi,* and *chupa curo* [fine and coarse cloth, weavings, headdresses, sandals, ribbons, sashes, and flounces]. Apart from this, they helped their fathers and mothers in everything they were ordered to do, and they were very obedient young maidens; they were punished.

These young girls, as the daughters of taxpaying commoners, were given this job and occupation so that they would learn, in this kingdom. These girls were *pawau pallac,* which means "girls who pick flowers." This was so that they would not be idle (unlike [Spanish] ladies, who are accustomed to luxury from a very young age and learn the sin of fornicating).

*[The illustration of the "eighth path," ms. p. 231, shows a very young girl carrying a water jug on her back. The caption reads: "From the age of five. She serves her mother."]*

THE EIGHTH PATH was that of the girls from five to nine years of age, called *pucllacoc warmi wamra* ("girls who go around playing"). These young maidens served as handmaids to the Coya, the *ñustas,* the great ladies, the virgins, or the *mamacunas,* and they served their mothers and fathers by carrying firewood and hay. These girls would begin to work, spinning delicate silk, and doing whatever they could, such as collecting *yuyos* [herbs] to eat from the plowed fields, helping to make *chicha,* serving to raise the younger children, and carrying the babies.

Girls of this age should be taught cleanliness, and they should learn from a young age how to spin, carry water, wash, and cook. Such are the occupations

---

[125] Guaman Poma indicates that *capa cocha* (*qapa qucha*) was the name of a sacrifice to the sun mandated by the Inca, and suggests that it involved burying "innocent children" (ms. p. 249) and dressing the *waqas* in fine clothing (ms. p. 267). The flowers would have been used as dyes for the *waqas'* clothes.

of women and maidens, so it is useful for their fathers and mothers to instruct them in how to do them. They were inspected in the general inspection tour, and were exempted [from the labor tribute] so that they could help their mothers raise their siblings in every way they could. [But today,] using these young girls as a pretext, the *doctrina* priests, *corregidores,* and *encomenderos* gather all the maidens and deflower them. The Spaniards enjoy themselves, and thus the numbers of mestizos multiply—even though the ordinances of good government and the Holy Council[126] never decreed that girls or maidens should be gathered together to be deflowered under the pretext of teaching them the catechism; instead, [only] boys of five [should go to catechism], and they should leave at the age of six in this kingdom.

*[The illustration of the "ninth path," ms. p. 233, shows a crawling baby who wears a tasseled head covering; a sleeping dog lies behind her. The caption reads: "From the age of one. Unproductive."]*

THE NINTH PATH was that of the girls aged one and two, who were called *llucac warmi wawa* ("young girls who crawl"). They do nothing; instead, others serve them. Better said, they ought to be served by their mothers, who should be exempt [from tribute] because of the work of raising their children. Their mothers have to walk around carrying them, and never let go of their hands.

These girls were exempt, and others were to serve them. This is only just, as everyone knows, even if the girls are daughters of commoners. If a girl is the daughter of a gentleman, she should be served even more, as is her due by the law of God in this world: she is a child of God. If she is an orphan, she deserves even more. Thus these girls (*llucac wamra,* which means "girls who crawl") were exempt from the moment they emerged from their mothers' wombs. They were issued fields and croplands, which were cultivated by their bands and by all their *compadres* and *comadres* (*wayno, socna*); everybody supported them and looked after them, whether or not they had fathers and mothers. The great mercy that existed in this kingdom was never seen in all Castile, nor could they have so much, being such scoundrel people; for, if one [of them] is a commoner, he wants to become a lord; if he is of a poor lineage, he wants to make himself king, though he does not deserve it by right, by lineage, by blood, nor by courtliness towards these poor people, as can be seen in this general inspection tour of this kingdom.

[126] Holy Council: the Third Council of Lima (1582–1583), at which Spanish church leaders from across the colonized Andes met to discuss the process of evangelizing native Andeans and implementing the reforms of the Council of Trent, and as a result published the first catechisms in Quechua and other indigenous languages.

*[The illustration of the "tenth path," ms. p. 235, shows a small baby strapped inside a wicker cradle. The caption reads: "From the age of one month. Others serve her."]*

**THE TENTH PATH** was that of the young girls in cradles, called *llullo wawa warmi, quirapi cac wawacuna*—newborn girls from one month to two, three, four, or five months. They give no help; instead, their mothers serve them, and they are helped by their little sisters, their grandmothers, their aunts, or by some close kin of these girls.

As is known, these girls were registered as commoners on this general inspection tour of the Indian women of this kingdom. They required that others serve them, and so their mothers were exempt; if there were two girls from one womb, both their fathers and mothers were exempt, throughout this kingdom. If a girl were the child of a noble, much more so; and if she were an orphan, even better. These laws and ordinances were kept in place because of His Majesty the Capac Inca. This general inspection should be made known; the inspection was done for the service of God, the royal crown of the Inca, and the welfare of the natives of this kingdom. Peace to all.

**END OF THE GENERAL INSPECTION** composed of Topa Inca Yupanqui, his royal council, and the *capac apo* Waman Chawa.

*[Over the next 130 pages of the manuscript, Guaman Poma describes the customs and institutions of the Andean world under Inca rule. These pages can be divided into several chapters:*

1. *"The Months of the Year": a monthly description, January through December, of the rituals and agricultural tasks that took place throughout the year (ms. pp. 237–62).*

2. *"The Idols (Wacas)": a description of the gods and "idols" of the Incas, Chinchaysuyus, Andesuyus, Collasuyus, and Condesuyus (ms. pp. 263–75).*

3. *A set of short chapters on religious practices and practitioners: "The Common Sorcerers; the Great Sorcerers of the Past; Sorcerers of Dreams; Superstitions and Omens; Processions, Fasts, and Penitence" (ms. pp. 276–88, translated on pp. 84–95).*

4. *Burial practices of the Incas, Chinchaysuyus, Andesuyus, Collasuyus, and Condesuyus (ms. pp. 289–99).*

5. *"The Nuns (Acllacunas)" (ms. pp. 300–2).*

6. *"The Inca's Justice": prison, jail, stoning of adulterers, torture and killing for rape and fornication, and death for poisoners (ms. pp. 303–16).*

7.  *"Festivities": songs, music, and festivities of the Incas,* Chinchay-suyus, Andesuyus, Collasuyus, *and* Condesuyus *(ms. pp. 317–29).*

8.  *The Inca's royal palaces, royal litters, warehouses, and service tribute (ms. pp. 330–41).*

9.  *The Inca government: descriptions of various offices and officers, such as "Viceroy," provincial administrator, postal service, and governors of bridges and roads (ms. pp. 342–69.)]*

*[The set of chapters on religious practitioners is included here as an example of Guaman Poma's writing in this section. Guaman Poma, it is thought, developed his knowledge about these "sorcerers" (hechiceros) and his negative attitudes toward them while he served as an interpreter for the Church inspector Cristóbal de Albornoz, during the latter's campaign for the "extirpation of idolatries" in the Andes (1568–1570).*[127] *Guaman Poma's condemnation of coca chewing is striking, given the important place of that mild narcotic in later Andean culture, and perhaps indicates that members of the Andean nobility, with which Guaman Poma identified, considered coca chewing an uncouth habit of Indian commoners. The number of untranslated Quechua phrases in this presentation of Andean "superstitions" is noteworthy, and reflects Guaman Poma's stated purpose (in his introduction to the book) of helping Indian commoners to "amend their erroneous ways."*

*276–288*  **CHAPTER OF THE COMMON SORCERERS**

THE COMMON SORCERERS who used to be in this kingdom—and they still exist—are as follows. First: very evil sorcerers who administer venoms and poisons in order to kill; they are called sorcerers (*hampicoc*). They use these [poisons] to kill. Some die quickly, others slowly—they dry out for a year, become thin as sticks, and then they die. At first, only the Inca had this poison and no one else; he ordered any Indians who had it killed. They were killed by stoning, together with all their offspring, until none were left alive but the babes at the breast.

◆ **The Indian sorcerers made** *tinquichi*—uniting a man and a woman so that they would fall in love and the man would waste away. They say that they would burn fat mixed with filth in a new pot (called *ari manco*) over a hot fire. Afterwards, they say, the sorcerer would call the demon, and the sorcerer would do this by the arts and deeds of the demon.

◆ **They break up marriages** and make married and unmarried men fall out of love, in the same way as described above. These sorcerers speak with the demons from hell and approve of them.

---

[127] On Albornoz and Guaman Poma, see footnote 257.

◆ **They place curses on various people** by performing ceremonies. They say that they blow on corn meal mixed with ashes and the hairs of the person upon whom they wish evil. To this end, they say that they endeavor to steal a few of their hairs so that they can burn it and blow [on the ashes].

◆ **To save themselves from the hands** of justice, the thieves, killers, or sorcerers blow on their adversaries by using the same corn meal, which they call *wayrap saran* [corn of the wind], mixed with the [ground] bones of dead men. They blow on this mixture, and they say that with it they are blowing on the judges and on their adversaries.

◆ **It is a custom of the Indians** that, when they have been robbed, or when someone has stolen a handful of corn cobs or potatoes from their *chacras*, they take the leaves, tie them to sticks from the trees, and place them—uttering curses—along the highways or paths where people will have to pass, so that they can see who the culprit is. They place a curse on them, to shame them. This was an ancient custom.[. . . .]

**Other sorceries that are still practiced today:** they take a toad, they remove the venom from a snake, and with it they say that the toad speaks and sends poison to men. Others, speaking with the demons, take a toad and sew its mouth and eyes shut with thorns; they bind the toad's hands and feet, and they bury it in a hole under the seat of their enemy or the person to whom they wish ill, so that he will wither and die. The toad does not die there; it simply withers. To this end, they raise toads and snakes, and they feed them and serve them. This is what one Indian did: Don Diego Suyca from the pueblo of Santiago de Chipao. His own sister was a sorceress; when Martín de Mendoza was the *corregidor,* he burned their snakes in Hatun Lucana and banished these Indians to Huancavelica.[128]

**Other sorcerers take a piece of yarn** that has been spun in a left-handed direction from white and black [wool], and they place it on the roads. They stretch it out and place it, like a leash for the demons, along the path that their enemies will take so that the yarn will cripple them with the sorcery they have placed on it, created through their enchantments, so that whoever breaks the yarn will fall into the danger of illness and will wither and die. That is why they watch carefully to see when an enemy will pass by; the sorcerer lies in wait for that moment.

**Other sorcerers take ears of corn** that they call *cuti sara* ["twisted corn," an ear of corn with individual grains covered with husk-like leaves] mixed with fat, hair, and thorns—they manage to steal the hair from their enemy,

---

[128] Santiago de Chipao was Guaman Poma's hometown. He has more to say about his experiences with Diego Suyca at the end of the book. Huancavelica was the site of the largest mercury mines in Spanish America.

or they pay another person to take it from the enemy himself. They bury all this in their enemy's *chacra,* or in his house, or under the place where he sits, performing a thousand ceremonies so that he will die and suffer troubles and poverty along with all his household and family. This was punished by the *corregidor* Martín de Mendoza.[. . . .]

**Other sorcerers are the *wacanqui*** *camayocs* [masters of *waqanki*]. About these *wacanquis* [amulets], some say that they are the Andean birds known as *tunqui* [Andean cock-of-the-rock]. Others say that they are thorns; others says that they are water; others say that they are stones; others say that they are the leaves of trees. Others say that they are dyes, *ichima* [annatto, a bright red dye]; these kinds of *wacanquis* are worn by haughty Indian women, the *chinaconas* (serving girls) of the Spaniards, who are whores, tavern girls, and *tambo* girls. They say that some Spanish women also wear them to trick men out of their estates. These *wacanqui*-wielding women make men kill themselves by spending all they own on them until they are poor.

**Other sorcerers say, when they enter** the caves to sleep and to worship the caves, "*Machay mama, ama micuwanquicho, allilla puñochiway*" ([Mother] cave, do not eat me; let me sleep well and keep me tonight). After saying this, they feed it masticated corn or coca leaves, which they spread over the cave. Even today the Indians do this.

**Other sorcerer-priests declare,** when two children are born from a single womb, or when a child is born with a cleft nose (*waca sinca*), or when a child is born feet-first—a *yayuma, wisama,* or *awalla*—that he is a son of Santiago, a son of *illapa* [lightning] and of *curi* [gold]. During that time, they avoid visitors, they fast from eating salt and other foods, and men do not sleep with women. Likewise, they fast from eating salt, when a man or woman dies, and they do the other things mentioned: that night they take ashes and spread them on their house doors, and they stay up all night, sitting vigil and drinking and getting drunk and making *pacarico.* For five days they do all this over again, and they all dance and eat raw meat and drink raw blood. They do these things even today, as I have witnessed with my own eyes, and they say "*Camiwanchicmi ricuwanchic*" [They will reproach us if they catch us]. That is why the people who do these things do not wish me well.

## THE PONTIFFS (*WALLA WISA, CONDE WISA*)

*[An illustration on ms. p. 279 shows "the former great sorcerer" talking with a devil, drawn in the European style, that is perched on a boiling cauldron. A woman, to the sorcerer's right, stokes the fire.]*

THE SORCERER PONTIFFS (*laycacunas, umucunas, wisacunas, camascacunas*) whom the Inca kept, and who were worshipped and respected: they say that these sorcerers took a new pot (called an *ari manca*) that has been fired without any decorations, and they took human fat mixed with corn meal (*sanco*), feathers, coca leaves, silver, gold, and all sorts of food, and they say that they put it all in the pot and burned it over a high fire, and through this the sorcerer spoke, because the demons spoke from the interior of the pot. The pontiffs would ask about matching men with women, or about killing any person by giving him poison to eat; and they would learn about what was going to happen and come to pass—things about which [the demons] know. Because every sorcerer, whether man or woman, knows and speaks first with the demons of hell to learn what is happening around the world. May God save the Christians and keep them in His hands! Jesus and Mary, be with me, amen. This is being written here in order to punish and inquire after these things among the idolaters against our Holy Catholic faith.

These pontiffs appointed by the Incas performed ceremonies with llamas and guinea pigs and with human flesh that was given to them by the Incas. They took fat and blood, and with those things they blew on the idols (*wacas*) and made their *wacas* and demons speak, these pontiffs (*walla, conde wisa,* and *laycacunas*).

Other sorcerers take the fat from llamas and from snakes and from pumas and from other animals, and [mix it with] corn and blood and *chicha* [corn beer] and coca leaves, and they burn it and make the demons talk through the fire. They ask questions, and [the demons] reply and tell them what will come to pass and what is happening; through them, they find out. Everyone who chews coca is a sorcerer who speaks with the demons; whether they are drunk or not, those who chew coca go mad. God save us! For this reason, the sacrament must not be given to those who chew coca.

During the time of the Incas, imps and evil spirits wandered among the Indians. Thus, the ghosts of the *Chinchaysuyus* and *Andesuyus* were in Anllay Pampa, and those of the *Collasuyus* and *Condesuyus* in Caray Sinca and in the Puquinas; because they used to say that those places were where all the spirits of the dead wandered, suffering from hunger and thirst and heat and cold and fire.

## ILLNESS-SUCKING SORCERERS

OTHER SORCERERS speak with the demons and claim to suck out the illnesses from people's bodies, claiming to suck out silver, pebbles, twigs, worms, toads, straw, or corn from the bodies of men and women.[129] These men are false sorcerers: they fool the Indians and the demon, with the sole aim of tricking them out of their estates and teaching the Indians to be idolaters. These sorcerers claim that there are such illnesses as *taqui oncoy, chirapa oncoy, pucyo oncoy, pacha macasca, capac oncoy, waca macasca, pucyop tapyascan, sara papa acoya urmachiscan oncoycuna:*[130] all these are idolatrous sorceries of the Inca, who taught them to the sorcerers.

**Other sorcerers sleep, and while** half asleep they talk with the demons, who tell them everything there is and everything that is happening and all they desire and demand to know. These are the dream sorcerers, and at dawn they make sacrifices and worship the demons. They are subtle and secretive sorcerers, and in this way they fool the people.

**Pontiffs, like cardinals and bishops,** were appointed by the Incas to the major *wacas,* except for the *waca* (idol) of the Inca, as has been mentioned. For Pacha Camac, Aysa Willca, Lati, Sullco, Pariacaca, Muchuca Willca, Watacocha, Paucaray, and other major *wacas* they kept these lesser pontiffs at great salaries, the seconds-in-command to the main pontiffs of the sun and of Wanacauri (*walla wisa, conde wisa*).

**The sorcerers who were like canons** served major *wacas* such as Sawasiray, Pitusiray, Ausancata, Coropuna, Suriwillca, and Quichicalla—all the volcanoes in this kingdom. These sorcerers served for salaries paid by the Incas.

**The sorcerers who were like priests** served in the *wamaníes* [provinces], at the *apachitas* [sacred piles of stone], and the common *wacas* (idols, gods), of which there were many in the kingdom. They served as confessor-priests. They tricked men, telling them that the *wacas* ate and drank and talked, when they did not. Thus, all across the kingdom people kept *wacas* (idols), and those who did not keep them were immediately ordered to be killed.

I know about all that I have written on the pontiffs because I used to serve Cristóbal de Albornoz, the inspector general of the Holy Catholic Church, who burned all the *wacas* (idols) and sorceries in the kingdom. He was a Christian judge.

---

[129] This is a common technique used by healers and shamans around the world. See Claude Levi-Strauss's life history of a man who set out to debunk this "trick" and ended up understanding its power: "The Sorcerer and His Magic," *Structural Anthropology* (New York: Basic Books, 1963), 167–85.

[130] These are: dancing sickness (see footnote 257 on the *Taki Unquy* movement of the 1560s), rainbow sickness, spring water sickness, being beaten by the earth, major sickness, being beaten by a *waqa,* being cursed by spring water, and sicknesses caused by dropping corn or potatoes.

*Llulla Layca, Umu* [Lying *layqas* and *umus*]

Dream
sorcerer

Fire
sorcerer

Illness-
sucking
sorcerer

*False Sorcerers.*

## SUPERSTITIONS ◆ OMENS

*[The illustration on ms. p. 283 shows a man in priestly Inca garments surrounded by animals of ill omen, saying, "Go away! I am going to die!"]*

THERE ARE SUPERSTITIOUS PEOPLE who believe in the omens that the Indians used to have in the time of the Incas, and which they still have—such things as *atitapya, tapyawanmi, acoyraqui, tiyoraqui* [bad omen, I have been cursed, calamity, misfortune]:

- When snakes cross their paths or appear in their houses.
- The songs of horned owls, pygmy owls, and bats calling out to them—*"Tuco, chusic, pacpac, pecpe, chicollom cayaycuwan* [The horned owl, the barn owl, the pygmy owl, the nightingale, the screech owl has called to me]."
- *"Taparanco yaycuwan* [A *taparanku* moth has entered into me]."
- *"Uro nina ayacta aysaycuwan* [The fire wasp has brought me a corpse]."[131]
- *"Ichapas maycan wañusun, atocmi supayta aysan warmitam ichapas carita* [Which of us might die? The fox is dragging a *supay* (spirit or demon)—perhaps a woman, perhaps a man]."

When they hear foxes or some other animals barking, the Indians who believe in omens say that the heads of the living are rising up and wandering about, or else the arms or legs or guts of men or women. They used to say that those Indians would die if they did not leave the land of their wives or husbands—or, in the case of children, the land of their mothers and fathers; otherwise, they would die by drowning in a river, or falling off a cliff, or burning up in a fire, or else they would have to hang themselves by their own hands, as the *Changas* still do when they hang themselves after becoming very drunk, and are carried off by Satan and all his demons to his house, which is hell.

**They have another ill omen and superstition** (*atitapya, acoyraqui*). When a horned owl, a bat, a moth, or a snake enters their house, or when mushrooms spring up, or there are many fleas inside the house, they say *"Carcowanchicmi, wañusunmi, tucusunmi* [We are being expelled; we will die, we will perish]." They say that they are all going to die, and that is why [the animals] entered their house. Believing this superstition, they consume and eat up everything they own, and every day they go about drunk, without bearing in mind God or the Virgin Mary and his saints.

---

[131] The illustration of this omen (ms. p. 283) shows a wasp carrying a dead insect; the superstitious Inca is saying, "A *nina nina* is bringing me an insect: my wife is dying."

**Superstitious people!** The Indians—from the time of the Inca and from this time alike—believe in dreams. When they dream of an *uru nina* [fire wasp], they say they are going to fall ill. When they dream of an *ande chicollo*, a *waychau*, or a *chiwaco* [three kinds of birds], they say they are going to fight. When they dream of an *acoyraqui* [calamity], *mayuta chacata chimpani* [approaching a river or a bridge], or *inti quilla wañun* [an eclipse of the sun or moon], they say that their father or their mother is going to die.

When they dream: "*Quiroymi llocsin* [My tooth is falling out]," then their father or their brother is going to die. "*Llamata ñacani* [I am butchering a llama]," the same. When a woman dreams, "*Rutuscam cani* [My hair is being cut]," then she is going to be widowed. "*Moscospa yana pachawan pampascam cani, callampatam riconi, sapallotam paquini moscuypi* [While dreaming, I am being buried in black clothes, I see a mushroom, I break a gourd in my dream]." They believe the superstitions about these dreams— that they, or their fathers, mothers, or brothers are going to die or, if they live, that they will have to leave their land.

They had another set of superstitions. They would say, ". . . If I see someone with my right eye, I will cry about whomever I see. If I twist my foot while someone is approaching, I will leave. If my good ear is burning, perhaps a good person will talk to me. If my left ear is burning, perhaps someone will tell me bad news. If my back quivers, I will be beaten."[132] These are superstitions and omens that the Indians still keep today, and in which they believe.

**The curses they hurled** at each other: to begin with, they would say,

| | |
|---|---|
| *Supay apasunqui:* | [The *supay* (spirit, devil) shall carry you off, |
| *maypi ismoc:* | in the place of rottenness, |
| *tantay warina puric:* | beggar, wandering mountain deer, |
| *mana pacuspa causac:* | living unable to graze, |
| *ayamanpas chunca mita cutic:* | becoming ten times over a corpse, |
| *runa-camacniquip micuscan:* | devoured by your Creator, |
| *intip llacsascan:* | debilitated by the sun, |
| *pachap millpuscan:* | swallowed up by the earth. |
| *amatac cay watawanpas causanquicho:* | Nor shall you live out this year: |
| *hinantiqui colloc:* | your kind shall be extinguished, |
| *mana pacuspa causac maypi ismoc:* | living without fodder in the place of rottenness, |
| *wachapucuspa wañoc, mana surcayoc, wachoc, suwa:* | stillborn, fainthearted, adulterer, thief, |
| *misti wasa pacusca:* | mestizo's backside, grazed like grass, |

---

[132] These sayings are translated directly from the Quechua; Guaman Poma does not provide Spanish translations. Part of the first line is missing in the manuscript.

| | |
|---|---|
| *misti watanaypi yumasca:* | engendered on the mestizo whipping post, |
| *misti palla pacusca:* | mestizo lady, grazed like grass, |
| *isullaya:* | bastard, |
| *upsa pacusca.* | cattle, grazed like grass.][133] |

All of these curses were hurled back then, and they are still hurled now in these times, with little fear of God Our Lord and Creator.

**About the omen they look for every year** when they pick corn, potatoes, or *ocas* [a root crop] and find two ears of corn born together, or two potatoes together, or much larger than normal: they say that this is a very bad sign, that they are all going to die and perish. For this reason, so that they might not die, they decree that everyone dance all night long, making *pacarico.* They stay up all night without closing their eyes, singing, "*Arawayu, arawayu, arawayu.*" For an entire day, they sing and drink until they are drunk, and chew a lot of coca and eat raw meat without salt; this is what they call "making *pacarico.*"

They do the same custom, staying up all night singing and drinking, for the health of someone who is ill.

They do the same thing when they ward off pestilence: they make *pacarico.*

They do the same when they make *warachicos* and *rotochicos* [rituals celebrating, respectively, a boy's coming of age at puberty, and a child's first haircut at the age of about three years]. All alike are idolatrous ceremonies, customs of the Inca, the *ñawpa pacha* [ancient times] of the Indians *waca muchas* [who worshipped *wacas*], yet they still keep these customs in these times, something deserving of punishment.

All that is said here about the sorcerers I saw when the inspector of the Holy Church Cristóbal de Albornoz punished a great many Indians. He was a Christian judge: he punished the padres along with everyone else.

## PROCESSIONS, FASTS, AND PENANCES OF THE INCA

*[An illustration, ms. p. 286, shows a procession of many Inca nobles draped with mourning cloth, barefoot, carrying spears with small banners, and all weeping profusely.]*

THE PROCESSIONS that the Incas performed—and the fasts—and the penances for the sacrifices: for one month, they ate no cooked food and tasted no salt. They ate uncooked white corn together with the green herbs that they call *siclla.* They would eat this twice a day, for breakfast and supper, and they would not laugh or sleep with women, and they were always sad,

---

[133] This curse is in Quechua, without Spanish translation.

without conversation, their eyes downcast, and all the men and women in the kingdom were covered in mourning cloth. This penance was enforced with stiff penalties imposed by the law of the Incas.

**The procession to expel illnesses** and plagues: they would use slings to throw fireballs, armed as if they were fighting a battle. In this way they expelled [the plagues] from the cities, towns, and pueblos throughout the kingdom, by order of the Inca.

**The procession for storms: they would walk,** all dressed in mourning, with small flags flying from their *chunta* [palm wood] spears, crying and howling so loud that the hills and mountains echoed their cries.

**The procession for hail, frost,** and lightning: they expelled these with weapons, drums, flutes, trumpets, and bells, while shouting, "*Astaya, suwa runa, wacchachac! Cuncayqui cuchuscayqui. Ama ricuscayquichu!* [Begone, thief, impoverisher! I will cut your throat. May I never see you again!]"

**Their fasts and penances, practicing Lent** in the month of penance, January (*Camay Quilla* [the month of rest]): they would do this penance with their faces daubed with black; all the men and women would color themselves with *ñuñunya* [wild cherry] and *quichimcha* [soot] all over.

Weeping, covered with mourning cloth, howling, screaming, and shouting, they would cry out, "*Quilla Mama* [Mother Moon]," in the month of October:[134]

| | |
|---|---|
| *Uma raymi quilla,* | [Month of the main festival, |
| *quilla Coya mama,* | Mother *Coya* month: |
| *yacuc sallayqui,* | your rainwater lovers, |
| *unuc sallayqui,* | your lakewater lovers, |
| *ayawya wacaylli,* | ay! oh! hearken to our tears! |
| *ayawya puypuylli.* | Ay! oh! hearken to our weeping! |
| *Llutu puchac wamrayqui* | We, your tender, suffering young children |
| *micuymanta* | are weeping, |
| *yacumanta* | are weeping, |
| *wacallasunquim,* | for food, |
| *wacallasunquim.* | for rainwater. |
| *Pacha Camac Yaya,* | Creator of the earth, Father, |
| *may pachapim canqui.* | in which world are you? |
| *Hanac pachapichu.* | In the upper world? |
| *Cay pachapichu.* | In this world? |
| *Caylla pachapichu.* | In the nearby world? |
| *Yacullayquita cacharimuway* | Send just a little of your rainwater |
| *wacchayquiman,* | for us, your poor, |
| *runayquiman.* | for us, your people.] |

---

[134] *Quilla* (*killa*) means both "moon" and "month." The following chant is in Quechua without Spanish translation; compare the version on p. 65–66.

And so the young men have continued until today the law and custom of begging God for water and of dyeing their bodies and daubing their faces. This is an ancient custom of the idolaters, and therefore Francisco de Toledo decreed in his ordinances that those who daub their faces should be punished with fifty lashes. There has been no remedy for this, because the alcaldes are to blame for it.

◆ **The sun and the *wacas* (idols) had Indians** who were exempt from tribute, called *yanayacu,*[135] and they had *wayrur aclla,* the nuns of their gods. These women [. . .][136] all their lives. The never spoke with men. They had pastures, called *intip muyan wayrur aclla* [the select women's orchards of the sun]. They had cattle and herders and croplands. All their guanacos and vicuñas were called *intip llaman* [the llamas of the sun]. Among fowl, they had the *wachiwa* [Andean geese], which in those days were set aside as the property of the idol gods of this kingdom.

**The plagues that God sent in the time of the Incas**—and in these times as well, God sends his plagues:[137]

- In the time of the Incas, fire rained down and devastated the pueblo of Cacha de Collao, and sand rained down when the Putina volcano erupted and devastated the city of Arequipa and its entire district and province.
- The terrible plague of measles and smallpox: In the time of Wayna Capac Inca, a large number of people died, and they say that the Inca had hidden himself inside a stone cave out of fear of the plague and of death, and that he died in there.
- Earthquakes, and many people dying from them.
- In the time of the Inca, not raining for ten years during the reign of Pachacuti Inca, like the seven years of famine in Egypt; and at that time, they say that stones cracked open.
- When crops freeze.
- When hail falls on the crops.
- The plague of worms that destroy crops in the fields.
- Inside the houses, woodworms.
- The plague of mice that destroy everything from the mountains to the plains.
- And the plague of birds—of partridges, parrots, parakeets, and *chi-willos*—and of deer, skunks, and foxes:

---

[135] *Yanayacu:* the original form of *yana* (servant); this Quechua term entered colonial Spanish in the plural form (treated in Spanish as singular), *yanacona.*

[136] The page is partially torn here.

[137] Guaman Poma lists ten "plagues," no doubt recalling the ten biblical plagues of Exodus.

All these plagues came in the time of the Inca, and in these days God continues to punish.

**The old men and women from the past say, moreover,** that God used to test the Indians in every pueblo, and that he used to come in the form of a poor hermit who begged by God for clothing and food and drink. These beggars, they say, came especially to the pueblos where they were celebrating fiestas in the public squares, and, if no one gave them alms, they would return. It was for this reason, they say, that so many great ills and punishments were sent by God (*Pacha Camac Ticse Caylla Wiracocha*) that those miserly pueblos were swallowed by the earth, or else covered over by the mountains or turned into lakes in the foothills of Pariacaca or Isua de Apcara, like the pueblo of Cacha. This is why the Indians of this kingdom so love the hermits and Franciscan friars.

◆ **The Incas imposed steep penalties** and ordained that it be established that their whole kingdom should have *wacas* (idols). Out of fear, people made certain to keep idols that they created out of stone or wood. Those who were unable to do this created theirs out of clay, at least. They made sacrifices to them, and gave them names, and held fiestas for them. In this way, the demons entered among them, through the ceremonies that the Inca ordained in this kingdom.

*[The section on the Inca world ends with a description of the "royal council of Tawantinsuyu," followed by Guaman Poma's statement on how he gathered information about the Incas from the different regions of the empire and corroborated oral reports with data from* kipu *(records made with knotted cords), and finally his general concluding "prologue" to this part.]*

## THE ROYAL COUNCIL OF THIS KINGDOM     *368–369*

*[The illustration on p. 97 shows the Inca ruler (the* Capac Inca*) dressed in full regalia, in the center, surrounded by a large crowd of Andean nobles. The Chinchaysuyu lord (recognizable by his headdress) stands immediately to the Inca's right, with the Andesuyu lord behind him and to his right. The Collasuyu lords stand to the Inca's left, with the Condesuyu lord behind them and to their left. At the far left and the far right, framing the ensemble, stand two lesser Inca lords, presumably representing Hanan and Lurin (Upper and Lower) Cusco.]*[138]

---

[138] This illustration is analyzed by Rolena Adorno, who contrasts its "orderly portrayal" of Tawantinsuyu with the distressed image of the kingdom two pages later, in which the lords of the four quarters stand in the wrong places (Adorno 2d ed. *Guaman Poma: Writing and Resistance in Colonial Peru,* [Austin: University of Texas Press, 2000], 116). In the latter, Guaman Poma portrays himself in the Inca's mediating central position, attempting to knit together the fabric of society by asking questions of the elders.

## ♦ CAPAC INCA TAWANTINSUYU CAMACHICOC APOCUNA.

[The *Capac Inca,* authorities, and lords of Tawantinsuyu.]

*The royal council of this kingdom.*

THE ROYAL COUNCIL of this kingdom resided in the great city, capital, and court of Cusco, in the center of the entire kingdom, which stretches from Chile, Tucumán, and Paraguay to Nuevo Reino [Bogotá], Panama, and Santo Domingo. All of these places go under the name of Tawantinsuyu: Chinchaysuyu, Andesuyu, Collasuyu, and Condesuyu. It is also divided, through Cusco, into two parts: Hanan Cusco (Chinchaysuyu) and Lurin Cusco (Collasuyu).

These noble lords, viceroys, and princes (*capac apo, apo curaca, allicac*) and other gentlemen lived and resided in the great city of Cusco. They formed the royal councils (*tawantinsuyu camachicoc, capac apocuna*) for good government, for punishing bad people justly, and for showing mercy to the good. Two Incas, the noblest Incas of Hanan Cusco, governed it, together with two other Incas from Lurin Cusco, four great lords from the region of Chinchaysuyu and two lords of Andesuyu, and four lords of Collasuyu and two lords of Condesuyu.

These were the lords of the royal council of this kingdom. When one of them left, his place would go to one of his sons or brothers. As has been said, no poor man, no man who did not descend from a noble lineage, was ever chosen [to serve on the council], not even if he were talented and well off, if he was not rich.[139] This was because His Highness, His Royalty, and His Majesty could not communicate with the sons of poor taxpaying commoners, lest the lords become commoners and the majesty of the Inca be disdained. No poor Indian man or woman ever spoke to the Inca. Instead, he kept an interpreter and an *asesor* [chief legal advisor] to hear their [pleas for] justice; but he would greatly favor the poor, the orphan, and the widow.

## THE AUTHOR QUESTIONS: TELL THE AUTHOR

THE AUTHOR QUESTIONS: "Tell the author and show him the *quipus*. Tell him about the Incas, the Chinchaysuyus, the Andesuyus, the Collasuyus, and the Condesuyus; give your reports on these things to the author, Don Felipe Guaman Poma de Ayala, administrator-protector and deputy *corregidor* of the province of Los Lucanas, lord and prince of this kingdom. Tell him everything, beginning with the first Indian whom God brought to this kingdom from the offspring of Adam and Eve. Tell him about Noah of the Flood; about the first Indian, called Wari Wiracocha; and about *Wari Runa, Purun Runa, Auca Runa,* and *Inca Pacha Runa*."

The author was given an account of everything so that he could write it and set it down in this book, and so that good public order could move forward.

---

[139] Rich: this translates the Quechua term *capac* (*qapaq*), "rich, powerful, noble."

# THE AUTHOR QUESTIONS
## MA WILLAWAY ♦ ACHAMITAMA.

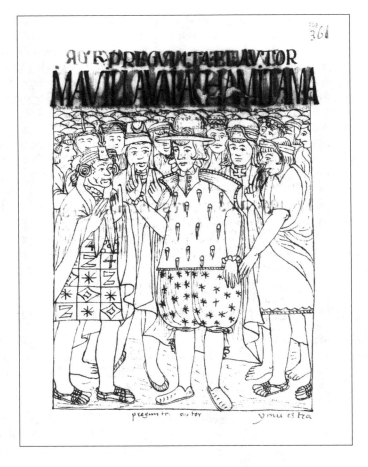

["So, tell me." (in Quechua) ♦ "Tell me." (in Aymara)]

*The author asks.*

He learned all the rest by walking around and serving Their Excellencies the viceroys, and the Reverend-in-Christ bishops, and the general inspectors. He went on, writing it all down and learning it with understanding and with the skill and grace that God gave him, in order to serve God and His Majesty.

## PROLOGUE TO THE SPANISH CHRISTIAN READERS

HERE YOU SEE, Christian, all the law, good and bad. Now, Christian reader, divide it in two parts: set the bad aside that it may be punished, and use the good to serve God and His Majesty.

Christian reader, here you see the whole Christian law. I have found no Indians who are greedy for gold nor silver, nor have I found any who owe a hundred pesos, nor liars, nor gamblers, nor sluggards, nor whores, nor buggers, nor any who steal from one another. But you have all these ills among yourselves: you are disobedient to your fathers, mothers, prelates, and king; and when you blaspheme God, you blaspheme him wholeheartedly. You have all these ills, and you teach them to the poor Indians.

You claim—when you skin[140] each another, and much more so when you do it to the poor Indians—you claim that you will repay what you have taken, but I do not see you repaying it, neither in life nor in death.

It seems to me, Christian, that you are all condemning yourselves to hell.

His Majesty is so great a saint that, when his prelates and viceroys come over here to take care of the poor natives, throughout the long sea crossing they think only of the poor Indians' best interests. But then as soon as they step ashore, all of them—even the prelates—turn against the poor Indians of Jesus Christ.

Do not be shocked, Christian reader, by the idolatry and error of the old pagan Indians who strayed from the true path. Just as the Spaniards also had their idols—as the reverend padre Fray Luis de Granada has written, a pagan Spaniard had a silver idol, which he had forged with his own hands, and another Spaniard stole it, whereupon he went weeping in search of his idol, weeping more for the idol than for the silver[141]—so the Indians, being barbarians and gentiles, wept for their idols when they were smashed in the time of the conquest.

But you have your own idols—your treasuries and your silver—all over the world.

---

[140] *Desollar,* to skin, to flay; used by Guaman Poma in the sense of "cheat, plunder, rob blind."

[141] Murra and Adorno (ms. p. 369, n. 1), trace this anecdote to Fray Luis de Granada, *Memorial de la vida cristiana* (1566; trans., *A Memorial of a Christian Life* [London, 1688], 66]), which cites an incident from Judges 18: 18–24 involving the Israelite tribe of Dan. Again, for Guaman Poma, all non-Indians are "Spaniards."

*"Cay curitacho micunqui?"* ["Is this gold what you eat?"]

"This gold is what we eat."

*In Cusco.*

Castile is the new Jerusalem?

# PART 5

# THE CONQUEST OF THIS KINGDOM

*[Guaman Poma's history of the conquest marks the point where the two roots of his chronicle—world or biblical history and Andean history—join together. In this part, he plays off the Spanish chronicles to present his own moral view of what happened when Pizarro, Almagro, and their men invaded Tawantin-suyu. (See the Introduction, for a brief summary of conquest history.) In contrast to the Spanish chroniclers, Guaman Poma places less emphasis on the internal politics of the Spanish factions during the civil wars that violently divided the conquerors between 1537 and 1553, and he pays almost no attention to the details of military history. Skipping easily over long years of the military action that absorbed Spanish memoirists, he focuses instead on a few events that place the emphasis on Andean roles in the conquest. (He dwells on the tragedy of Atawalpa, and also on the alleged exploits of his own grandfather during this period.) His lesser aim is to claim a higher position for himself in early colonial society; his higher aims are to demonstrate the rebellious and uncharitable character of the Spanish conquerors, and to illustrate his contention that Peru was already Christianized before the Spaniards' arrival, that the Incas willingly submitted to the Spanish king, and that therefore the encomenderos could not truly claim the rights of conquest. The logical legal consequence of this argument, if admitted, would be that Spanish royal rule in Peru was legitimate, but the status and the authority of the Spanish conquerors and their descendents—the ones who actually ruled and exploited Peru on a daily basis—were illegitimate.]*

## THE CONQUEST OF THIS KINGDOM

### THE CONQUEST THAT WAS MADE OF THIS KINGDOM; ITS DISCOVERY; AND THE FIRST SPANIARD FROM CASTILE, FROM JERUSALEM [142]

**THIS KINGDOM WAS DISCOVERED** by the apostle of Jesus Christ, the lord St. Bartholomew, who went out to this land and returned during the time when the Inca Cinche Roca ruled only Cusco and part of Collao.

[142] Once more, Guaman Poma uses "Spaniard" and "Castile" as generic terms for non-Indians and the world outside of the Americas, much as Europeans of his time used "Indian" and "the Indies" to refer to all the peoples and places of the Americas. There were many theories that the Americas had been evangelized by one or another of the apostles, with St. Bartholomew and St. Thomas being the most frequent suspects.

101

Later, in the era when Boniface IX, the Neapolitan pontiff, was pope, the route of the sea was discovered. This happened in the year 1493, when the pope was the Spaniard Alexander VI,[143] the Emperor of Rome was Maximilian, and the Queen of Spain was Doña Juana. The route to the Southern Sea[144] became known—700 leagues to Paraguay and to the Indies. The news spread throughout Castile and Rome that the *New World* had been found, for that was what the men of Castile called it. This land was in the highest altitude; thus they called it "the Indies," which means "the land in the day." That is why they gave it the name "Land In Day" (*In Dies*), not because the natives were called Indians: they got "Indians" from "Indies."[145] This same land is higher than all Castile and the other lands of the world. The first term for it was "New World." That is its title and true name, and its people are called "Natives." Therefore, only the greenhorns[146] call them Indians. Even now they call them so, and they err. All Spaniards in general are called Spaniards (*wiracocha*), and so they call each other *wiracocha*. The same is true of "Indians." But each band[147] has its own name: Castile, Rome.

◆ **Two Men Discovered It:** the companion of Columbus,[148] and Candia.[149]

---

[143] Boniface IX (1389–1404) was pope at the beginning of the century in which the sea route to the Americas was discovered; Alexander VI (1492–1503) was pope at the time of the discovery.

[144] Southern Sea (Mar del Sur) was the Spanish term for the Pacific. Balboa famously "discovered" the overland route from the Caribbean to the Pacific in 1513 in Panama, where a twist of geography puts the Caribbean in the north and the Pacific in the south. The term makes sense to Guaman Poma, who writes from a part of Peru where a similar geographical twist puts the Pacific on the southern rather than western shore. From his perspective, the Caribbean is therefore "the Northern Sea," and in his mental map of the region he locates it directly across the Andes, which he sees as a northern mountain range.

[145] This inventive etymology seems to be Guaman Poma's own. Columbus in fact insisted that he had discovered a route to India (by which he meant Asia) and had not found a "new world."

[146] Greenhorns: *chapetones*, a label used in South American Spanish for newcomers from Europe who are inexpert in the ways of the new country.

[147] Band (*parcialidad*): Guaman Poma uses this word to translate the Quechua concept *ayllu*. In his terms, Castile was the general name for the world outside of the Andes, and Rome was an *ayllu* of Castile.

[148] Gonzalo Fernández de Oviedo, the first chronicler of the Indies (*Historia general y natural de las Indias*, 1535), invented the story that America had been accidentally discovered by a Spanish or Portuguese sailor who revealed his secret to Columbus on his deathbed, in order to explain why such a capable navigator as Columbus would persist in trying to reach Asia when educated persons of the time knew that Asia lay too far west of Europe to be safely reached by sea. The anecdote was repeated as fact by later chroniclers. (D. A. Brading, *The First America* [Cambridge: Cambridge University Press, 1991], 12.)

[149] Pedro de Candia, a Greek artilleryman and one of the thirteen companions of

The companion of Columbus died and left his papers to his companion, to this same Columbus. And Candia reported in Castile that they had gone ashore in Santa.

There he had spoken by signs. A report had been sent to Wayna Capac Inca in Cusco, saying that the first men had gone ashore, that they wore very long beards, and that they were shrouded, like corpses; Wayna Capac then had them carry him on a *wando* [litter] by *chasqui* [messenger], so that the Inca greenhorn and the Spanish greenhorn could meet.[150] They spoke by signs; Wayna Capac asked the Spaniard what was it that he ate. He replied in the language of the Spaniards and by signs, pointing at things, that he ate gold and silver. And so [the Inca] gave him a lot of gold dust, silver, and gold utensils; with all this, [the Inca] ordered him to turn back, escorted by the *chasqui*, to the port of Santa.

When Candia arrived [at the port], he was told that his companion had died, so he left for Spain with his gold and silver and riches.

◆ **CANDIA ARRIVED** with the riches in Spain, with all he had brought, and proclaimed the news of the land and its riches. He said that the people there wore clothes and shoes all of gold and silver, that the ground they walked was made of gold and silver, and that they wore gold and silver on their heads and hands. He was speaking of the clothing they wear to dance the *taquies* (dances), which the Indians dance with clothes of silver and gold (*cullqui curi cusma, cacro, chipana, canipo, culqui wayta, topos*). And he said that there were small camels, speaking of the local sheep [llamas and alpacas].

At this news, this greed, this announcement of gold and silver, people began to come. These people kidnapped a *Huancavilca* Indian, who was later named Felipe, and they brought him along as an interpreter to the conquest of this kingdom.[151] The captains and the soldiers were very happy to arrive. They had no gold; they yearned to arrive for their greed of gold and silver.

*[The illustration on ms. p. 373 shows "Don Diego Almagro," stage right, and "Don Francisco Pizarro" with two unnamed Spaniards, stage left. All four wear full armor, and one carries the flag of Castile. The caption reads, "in Castile."]*

---

Pizarro during his second expedition to northern Peru in 1526–1528, later took part in the 1532 capture of Atawalpa and was rewarded an *encomienda*, only to be killed fighting for Almagro in 1542. By focusing on Candia as the "discoverer" of Peru and hinting that he had landed long before 1526, perhaps Guaman Poma was trying to take away some of the glory of discovery that accrued to Pizarro.

[150] Inca emperor Wayna Capac undoubtedly received reports of the strangers' landing in 1524, but he certainly did not travel to the coast to meet them himself.

[151] On Felipe, see footnote 33.

DON FRANCISCO PIZARRO and Don Diego de Almagro, the two captains general, and the rest gathered together 350 soldiers. Throughout Castile there were great tumults. It was like a dream, both day and night; everyone said, "The Indies! The Indies! Gold, silver! Gold, silver from Peru!" Even musicians sang the ballad, "Indies! Gold, silver!" And these soldiers gathered with the message from our Catholic lord the king of Spain and from His Holiness the Pope.

**In the year 1512,** the seventh year of Pope Julian II in his pontificate, the seventeenth of Emperor Maximilian II in his empire, the fifth of Queen Doña Juana of Spain in her reign:[152] Vasco Núñez de Balboa received news of the Southern Sea. With this report, the tumults grew in the land, so that, if the Queen had let them come, it seems to me that all Castile would have come for this rich new source of coveted gold and silver. Everyone was saying that the people here went around dressed all in gold and silver, that all the ground they walked on was solid gold and silver, and that they piled up gold and silver like rocks. The yearning for gold and silver endures to this day. The Spaniards still kill each other and skin the poor Indians over gold and silver, and in some parts of this kingdom the pueblos of the poor Indians have been depopulated because of gold and silver.

**In the year 1513,** the seventh year of Pope Julian II in his pontificate, the seventeenth of Emperor Maximilian II in his empire, the fifth of Queen Doña Juana of Spain in her reign: the pilot Juan Díaz de Solís, citizen of the town of Lebrija, discovered the River Plate—a route of 700 leagues to Paraguay and the great river was discovered.[153] The captains began to prepare their voyages and their ships' stores. They brought large quantities of food and arms—for food, nothing but biscuits, bacon, and dried beef; and they made sure to bring other gifts and white clothing, but of poor make. All they wanted to bring was arms and guns, with their greed for "Gold and silver! Gold and silver of the Indies! To the Indies, to Peru!"

*[The illustration on ms. p. 375 is a copy of the allegorical ship on ms. p. 46, with the addition of one more figure at the stern, "Martín Fernandez Enciso," and a new headline, "They embarked for the Indies."]*

---

[152] Guaman Poma is off by two years; the seventh year of Pope Julian II (and so on) was 1510. (The Holy Roman Emperor, too, was Maximilian I, not II). He repeats the tag line of rulers, unchanged, for the next two years. His larger point is correct, though: Balboa got word of the Pacific in 1512, though he did not lead his expedition to "discover" it until 1513.

[153] Solís led the expedition to South America in 1515 and named the River Plate ("River of Silver"), where he was killed shortly afterward, in 1516.

THE SOUTHERN SEA to the River Plate, 700 leagues to the city of Paraguay. But first, the Northern Sea, the route to the Indies, was discovered by the companion of Columbus. He died then and left his papers to Columbus. Santo Domingo was won, and then Panama; from there, they went ashore in the Indies, in the Kingdom of Peru, during the time and reign of Wayna Capac Inca. That was when it was discovered; it was conquered in the time when Topa Cusiwalpa Wascar Inca reigned, when he had a disagreement with his bastard brother Atawalpa Inca.

Thus, Don Francisco Pizarro, Don Diego de Almagro, his brother Gonzalo Pizarro, the factor Illán,[154] Martín Fernández Enciso, Columbus, the pilot Juan Diaz de Solís, and Vasco Núñez de Balboa heard the news of the sea.

In the year 1514, the seventh year of the pontificate of Pope Julius II, the seventeenth of Emperor Maximilian II in his empire, the fifth of the Queen of Spain Doña Juana in her reign: Don Francisco Pizarro, Don Diego de Almagro, Fray Vicente of the Order of St. Francis, and Felipe, the *Huancavilca* Indian interpreter, joined with Martín Fernández Enciso. Together with 350 soldiers, they embarked for the kingdom of the Indies of Peru, and they did not wish to rest a single day in any port. Every day, they did nothing but think of "Gold, silver, and the riches of the Indies of Peru!" They were like desperate men, foolish, crazy, out of their minds with their greed for gold and silver. At times they could not eat for thinking about gold and silver. At times they had great feasts, for it seemed they had all the gold and silver within their grasp. They were like a house cat: when he has the mouse in his claws, then he rejoices; if not, he constantly sets up ambushes, and he labors, and all his care and thought is set on this goal until he catches it. He never stops, and always returns to his one goal. That was what the first men were like: they did not fear death, with their self-interest in gold and silver. Worse still are the men of this life today—the Spanish *corregidores*, priests, and *encomenderos:* with their greed for gold and silver, they are going to hell.

In the year 1525, the third year of the pontificate of Pope Clement VII, the seventh of Emperor Don Carlos V in his empire and the fifth in his reign:[155] Don Francisco Pizarro and Don Diego de Almagro (the two captains general

---

[154] Illán: Guaman Poma spells this name "Gelin." The royal factor in Peru (that is, the personal representative of the king's commercial interests in the conquest enterprise) was Illán Suárez de Carvajal, an alderman of Lima and a prominent partner of Hernando Pizarro. His death at the hands of the first viceroy of Peru in 1544 inflamed a civil war among the conquerors.

[155] The grandson of Ferdinand and Isabela inherited the Spanish crown in 1516 (as Charles I) and the Holy Roman Empire in 1519 (as Carlos V, his preferred title). Guaman Poma calculates the years of his reign inconsistently.

## THE FIRST AMBASSADOR FROM WASCAR INCA TO THE
## AMBASSADOR FROM THE EMPEROR.

The Most Excellent Lord Don Martín Guaman Mallqui de Ayala, viceroy and second-in-command of the Inca in this kingdom.

Don Francisco Pizarro

Don Diego de Almagro

*The sign of peace was exchanged between the king-emperor of Castile and the legitimate king of the land of this kingdom of Peru, Wascar Inca; in his place went his second-in-command and viceroy, Ayala.*

in the discovery of this kingdom of Peru) and shipmaster Hernando de Luque went ashore in this land.

Soon they began quarreling over the discovery of this New World of the Indies of this kingdom, and with their greed for "Gold and silver!" it seems that they already had "I'll kill you or you'll kill me" in their hearts. They began their backbiting, and all the soldiers were frightened.

**In the year 1526,** the fifth year of the pontificate of Pope Clement VII, the ninth of Emperor Don Carlos V in his empire and the tenth in his reign: there were great festivities in Spain and throughout Castile and Rome for the birth of Don Philip, the second of this name.

**In the year 1532,** the tenth year of the pontificate of Pope Clement VII, the fourteenth of Emperor Don Carlos V in his empire and the fifteenth in his reign: Don Francisco Pizarro and Don Diego de Almagro received the first ambassador, whom the legitimate king *(Capac Apo Inca)* Tupa Cusi-walpa Wascar Inca, king and lord of this kingdom, sent to give passage in the port of Tumbes to the ambassador of the king of Castile. The Inca sent his second-in-command, the viceroy of this kingdom, *capac apo* (Most Excellent Lord) Don Martín Guaman Mallqui de Ayala: he was the ambassador from the great city of Cusco, the capital of this kingdom.

The Spaniards, Don Francisco Pizarro and Don Diego Almagro, and Don Martín de Ayala knelt, embraced, and exchanged the sign of peace and friendship with the emperor. They honored him, he ate at their table, and they spoke and conversed. He gave presents to the Christians, and they likewise gave [presents] to Don Martín de Ayala, who was the first ambassador from Atawalpa Inca in the port of Tumbes, where they first came ashore.[156]

---

*[The illustration on ms. p. 379 shows the Inca sitting, eyes closed, in the center of his royal litter, with the Coya seated behind and a priestly figure in front. We know that the Inca is dead because of the headline, "The Late Wayna Capac Inca–Illapa [lightning]." The litter (labeled, "they carry him to bury him in Cusco") is carried on the shoulders of four men. The caption reads, "They bring the deceased from Quito to bury him in the royal mausoleum in Cusco."]*

**THE LATE WAYNA** Capac Inca was carried to the city of Cusco, the capital of this kingdom, to be buried. They brought him there from the province of Quito.

---

[156] "First ambassador from Atawalpa Inca": this may be a slip on Guaman Poma's part. He usually identifies his father, Don Martín Waman Mallqui de Ayala, as the ambassador of Wascar, Atawalpa's brother and rival. (In any event, Guaman Poma apparently invented the entire episode.) The phrases "in the port of Tumbes" and "in the port of Tumbes, where they first came ashore" are late additions to the manuscript.

At that time there were ongoing skirmishes between the two Incas, the legitimate Wascar Inca and the bastard Atawalpa Inca, who fought from Quito. There was contention among their captains, and the kingdom was divided in two: the part from Jauja to Quito and Nuevo Reino [Bogotá] went to Atawalpa, and from Jauja to Chile was Wascar's. There were great confrontations between them, and battles and deaths among the captains and Indians of this kingdom.

It was then that the body of Wayna Capac Inca was carried to the great city of Cusco. They gave the Inca Wayna Capac the name "Illapa" [lightning]. The Indians of Quito thought the Inca was traveling alive, so they did not revolt, nor was there any tumult in the kingdom on the death of the Inca; they were carrying him embalmed to his royal mausoleum. It was only when they reached Jauja that they discovered he was dead, as it happened. A great wailing and weeping then went up in the city of Cusco over the death of Wayna Capac Inca. A prophecy, which the demons had revealed to the Inca from the time of his Inca ancestors, was then made public: some men called *wiracocha* would soon step forth.

As it was said, so it occurred: the *wiracocha* (Christian) men emerged at that time, during the disturbance in this kingdom. God was served, and the Virgin Mary was venerated, and all the saints and angels were called to go to the conquest during the tremendous disturbance between Wascar and Atawalpa, the two Incas.

[*The illustration on ms. p. 381 shows two young women in the center, kneeling before "Don Francisco Pizarro" and "Don Diego de Almagro," both in armor. "Captain Rumiñawi," an important military leader under Atawalpa, kneels behind the women, pointing at them. The headline gives the dialogue between Pizarro and Rumiñawi: "These maidens were sent to me by Atawalpa." "Caymi, apo (Here they are, lord)." The caption reads, "Maidens, presented to the Christians."*]

**THE SECOND AMBASSADOR** was the one sent by Atawalpa Inca, the bastard brother of Wascar Inca: his captain general, named Rumiñawi, whom he sent to the port of Tumbes to meet the ambassadors of the emperor, Don Francisco Pizarro and Don Diego de Almagro. They had very polite and ceremonious exchanges. Rumiñawi had been sent to request that the Christians return to their lands, and he told them that he would give them a great deal of gold and silver so that they would return. They did not take advantage of [the offer], however, replying instead that they wanted to see and kiss the hands of the king (*Inca*), after which they would return. They said that they were there as the ambassadors of their emperor-king, and so they marched onward.

◆ **Atawalpa Inca ordered** that *mitayos*[157] be given to Don Francisco Pizarro, Don Diego de Almagro, and the factor Illán. They gave *camaricos* (presents) and women to [the Spaniards] and also to their horses. This was because they said the horses were people, since they ate corn. Horses were unknown, and no one alive had ever seen them before, and therefore it was ordered that they be given provisions.

**In the year 1533,** the eleventh year of the pontificate of Pope Clement VII, the fifteenth of Emperor Don Carlos V in his empire and the sixteenth in his reign: Don Francisco Pizarro and Don Diego de Almagro marched on the city of Cajamarca against Atawalpa Inca, with 160 soldiers against 100,000 Indians. Hernando de Soto, Sebastián de Benalcázar, Hernando Pizarro, 20 [other] horsemen,[158] and Felipe—the *Huancavilca* Indian interpreter whom they brought along for the conquest—entered Cajamarca. But the Inca Atawalpa was not in the city; he was at the baths.[159] It was from those baths that Atawalpa sent his ambassador, the captain Rumiñawi, to the city, where he told them that the Spanish Christians should return to their land. Don Francisco Pizarro and Don Diego de Almagro replied that they did not accede to the request for them to return.

◆ **The Spaniards reached** the city of Cajamarca, but with the Inca Atawalpa absent, they did not lodge there. Rather, they set up their tents outside the city, arraying themselves like spirited warriors, to attack him. In those days, they did not wear [ruffled] collars; instead, they wore collars like those of priests. They all wore red caps, tight breeches, quilted doublets with long sleeves, and short capes with long sleeves, similar to Biscay cloaks. *[conflict w/ Incas]*

◆ **Atawalpa Inca was informed,** as were the noble lords, captains, and the other Indians, about the lives of the Spaniards. What they heard frightened them: *[myths about the Spaniards]*

The Spaniards never slept—they were told this because the Spaniards set watches. They ate silver and gold, both the Spaniards and their horses. They wore silver *ojotas* [sandals]—they said this because of the horseshoes and bridles, and because of their steel weapons and red caps. Each of them talked with his papers (*quilca*), night and day. They all wore funeral

---

[157] *Mitayos* (*mitayu*): tributary Indians who can be called upon to perform a specified labor task. Under colonial rule, the Andean system of labor tribute devolved into one of virtual slave labor, in which Indian *mitayos* were forced to work for long periods of deadly labor in the silver and mercury mines, while the Spanish completely ignored their duty to reciprocate the *mitayos'* offerings.

[158] In this context, *caballero* means both "gentlemen" (the usual translation) and the more literal "horsemen" (or even "knight"). Men with horses were the aristocrats among the Spanish invaders; when the spoils of war were divided, horsemen commanded a double share.

[159] The hot springs are located about 3.5 miles southwest of the town of Cajamarca.

*[handwritten annotations in margins: "gave women to Spaniards, executed women who laughed" at top; "Spaniards refused to turn back" at left; "scared" in middle]*

shrouds. Their whole faces were covered in wool, and only their eyes could be seen. They wore some kind of red pots (*ari manca*) on their heads, with *suri wayta* [feathered decorations]. They had very long pricks, which they wore dangling behind them—they said this because of their swords. They were dressed all in pure silver. And, finally, they had no senior lord, because they all seemed like brothers in their clothes, speech, conversation, eating, and dressing, and they all had the same face; but it seemed to [the Indians] that they had one old gentleman with a dark face and white teeth and eyes, and that only this man spoke a lot to all of the others.

Hearing this news, the Inca was frightened, and he said, "What news is this you're bringing me? A bad message!" So they were frightened by this unheard-of news. Atawalpa Inca therefore ordered that the Spaniards and their horses be given the services of women. The women laughed about the pricks of the Christians, because of their swords, so Atawalpa Inca ordered the execution of the Indian women who laughed. Once more, he gave them new Indian women and services. All along, he insisted that the Spaniards should turn back and leave. But there was no remedy:[160] the Christians insisted on meeting His Majesty the Inca.

## HERNANDO PIZARRO AND SEBASTIÁN DE BENALCÁZAR[161]

♦ **ATAWALPA INCA WAS IN THE BATHS.** These two gentlemen went there, mounted on two furious horses. The horses were harnessed, armored, and decked out with many bells and plumes, and the gentlemen were armed and finely dressed. They spurred their horses until they were galloping so furiously that they seemed to be dissolving, and they were enveloped in a loud jangling of bells. They say that this scene frightened the Inca and the Indians who were at the baths of Cajamarca. As he was witnessing a sight that had never been seen before, Atawalpa Inca fell down to the ground in fright from high in his litter.

The Spaniards were galloping towards him; all his people were shocked and frightened. Each one took flight on seeing how those huge animals galloped, and how they were ridden by men whose likes had never before been seen. Everyone went about in bewilderment.

---

[160] *No hubo remedio*, "there was no remedy": this is one of Guaman Poma's most characteristic phrases, repeated in various forms some ninety times throughout the text, sometimes meaning "there has been no reform," and other times, "there was no way out." Despite the seeming pessimism of the phrase, the point of his book is precisely to seek a "way out" and to "reform" the ills of conquest society and the colonial regime.

[161] Hernando Pizarro (1502–1578) was one of two younger brothers of Francisco Pizarro who played prominent roles in the conquest. Sebastián de Benalcázar (1480–1551) participated in the rapacious conquest of Nicaragua (1525) before joining the Peru expedition. He later led the conquest of Quito (1533) and parts of modern Colombia.

*At the baths of Cajamarca.*

Sebastián de
Benalcázar

Hernando
Pizarro

Then the Spaniards galloped back, and were happier as they galloped, saying, "By Holy Mary, a good sign! By Lord Santiago,[162] a good sign!"

Thus, they had a good sign for beginning the battle and for making war against Atawalpa Inca. Don Francisco Pizarro reached his brother and told the gentlemen, "Hurrah, my brothers! I've got the Indians convinced and frightened. God willing, we'll begin the battle, because they're all frightened. They've left their king sitting on the ground, and each of them has fled. A good sign! A good sign!"

## DON FRANCISCO PIZARRO, DON DIEGO DE ALMAGRO, AND FRAY VICENTE OF THE FRANCISCAN ORDER

◆ **THE INCA ATAWALPA** went from the baths to the city and court of Cajamarca. Having arrived, His Majesty was surrounded by his captains and many more people—twice one hundred thousand Indians—in the city of Cajamarca. In the public plaza, in the middle of it, on his throne and stepped seat (called *usno*), sat the Inca Atawalpa.

Don Francisco Pizarro and Don Diego de Almagro then began telling him (through the interpreter Felipe, the *Huancavilca* Indian) that they were the messengers and ambassadors of a great lord. They said that he should be their friend, and that this was the only reason they had come.

He replied very politely to what Don Francisco Pizarro had said, through the words of the interpreter, Felipe the Indian. The Inca replied with majesty; he said he believed it was true that, having come from so distant a land as messengers, theirs must be a great lord. But, he said, he did not have to make friendship; for he, too, was a great lord in his kingdom.

On hearing this reply, Fray Vicente made his own point, carrying a cross ✠ in his right hand and a breviary in his left. He told Atawalpa Inca that he, too, was an ambassador and a messenger from another lord—a very great lord: he was, he said, a friend of God. He said that [Atawalpa] should be his friend; he should adore the ✠ cross, believe in the Gospel of God, and worship no objects, for everything else was a matter of mockery.

The Inca Atawalpa replied, saying that he had no need to worship anyone but the Sun, who never dies. Nor do his *wacas* (gods) die; they were also in

---

[162] El Señor Santiago: that is, St. James the Great; his Spanish and English names are used interchangeably in this translation. The tomb of St. James (who died in Palestine in the year C.E. 42) was miraculously discovered in Galicia, northwestern Spain, in the ninth century, during the wars between resurgent Christian kingdoms and the Muslim rulers of most of the peninsula. According to legend, St. James would appear in battle against the "Moors" when his name was invoked by Christian fighters; as a result, "Santiago!" became the Spanish battle cry, and was often shouted in battles during the Spanish conquests in the Americas. More than one Spanish conqueror alleged that Santiago appeared in those battles, fighting against the Indians.

# ATAWALPA INCA, NOW IN THE CITY OF CAJAMARCA, ON HIS THRONE.

386

Almagro
Pizarro

Felipe,
Indian
Interpreter

Fray Vicente

*Usno* (throne of the Inca)

**City of Cajamarca: Atawalpa Inca is seated on his throne.**

his law, which he did keep. The Inca asked Fray Vicente who it was who had told him otherwise.

Fray Vicente replied that the Gospel, the book, had told him so.

Atawalpa said, "Give me the book, so that it will tell me." And so Fray Vicente gave it to him; Atawalpa took the book in his hands and began to look through its pages. Then the Inca said, "Well, why doesn't it tell me? The book doesn't even talk to me!" Speaking with great majesty, seated in his throne, the Inca Atawalpa threw the book down from his hands.

◆ **Fray Vicente shouted and said:** "Here, gentlemen! After these heathen Indians—they are against our faith!"

Don Francisco Pizarro and Don Diego de Almagro, for their part, shouted and said: "Come, horsemen! Against these infidels, who are against our Christianity! For our Emperor and King, let us have at them!"

Then the horsemen began to fire their harquebuses and to give skirmish, and the soldiers began to kill Indians like ants. With the fright of the harquebuses, the noise of the horse bells, and the sight of the arms and of men who had never before been seen, and with the plaza of Cajamarca being so full of Indians, the walls of the enclosure of the plaza of Cajamarca came falling down. The Indians were killed, between being squeezed, being stepped on, and being trampled by the horses. Many people died, so many Indians they could not be counted. On the Spanish side, five people died—of their own will, for no Indian dared [attack them], astonished as they were by the fright. They say that the five dead Spaniards were found among the dead Indians. They must have been knocked senseless, like the Indians; they must have been trampled by the horsemen.

So it was that Don Francisco Pizarro and Don Diego de Almagro took the Inca Atawalpa prisoner. They carried him from his throne without wounding him, and he was imprisoned, put in the custody of Spaniards under Don Francisco Pizarro. He was left sad, disconsolate, dispossessed of his majesty, sitting on the ground, his throne and kingdom gone.

◆ **There was a struggle in** this kingdom between brothers—the legitimate king (*capac apo*) Wascar Inca, and his brother, prince (*auqui*) Atawalpa Inca—after the death of their father Wayna Capac Inca; this struggle and war lasted thirty-six years.[163]

Since childhood, Wascar had been very haughty, miserly, and badly inclined. He would order his captains killed at the drop of a hat, and so they fled from him. Afterwards, he never wished to show favor to any captain or soldier. Here you can see how a kingdom can be lost through pride.

---

[163] The war between Wascar and Atawalpa lasted less than five years. Murra and Adorno comment: "One of many curious errors in Guaman Poma" (ms. pp. 388, n. 1, and 114, n. 1).

Whosoever is king or captain, if he be haughty and avaricious, he will lose his kingdom and his life, as Wascar Inca did.

It so pleased God that, at just that time, the king-emperor should send his ambassadors and messengers, the captains Don Francisco Pizarro and Don Diego de Almagro, [to Peru]. A battle was fought between the legitimate [Inca], on behalf of Cusco, and the bastard, on behalf of Quito. Many captains and soldiers died in that battle, and a great deal of the treasure of the Incas and of the temples was lost; it remains hidden to this day, throughout this kingdom. And so [Peru] was conquered, and was not defended.

◆ **THEY DETAINED** Atawalpa Inca. While he was being held prisoner, Don Francisco Pizarro, Don Diego de Almagro, and all the other soldiers and Spaniards stole all his treasure from him. They also took all the wealth from the Temple of the Sun (Curi Cancha) and from Wanacauri—so many millions in gold and silver, it couldn't all be counted, for the walls, the ceiling, the floor, and the windows of Curi Cancha alone were all lined with gold. They say that the person who entered that place, with its rays of gold, looked like a corpse in the midst of the golden color. [They also stole from] all the Inca Atawalpa's captains, and all the noble lords of this kingdom. They stole [the Inca's] golden and silver litter, the beams of which weighed more than 20,000 marks of pure gold and 20,000 marks of pure silver. [Altogether, they took] 1,326,000 escudos of purest gold.[164]

They likewise took away his services, going so far as to take away his legitimate wife (*Coya*). On seeing such mistreatment, harm, and robbery, the Inca felt great grief and sorrow in his heart; he wept, and would not eat. He saw his lady (*Coya*) weep, and he wept with her. For his sake, there were great laments in the city; the Indians sang this song:

| | |
|---|---|
| *Aray arawi, aray arawi!* | [*Aray arawi, aray arawi!* |
| *Sapra aucachu, Coya,* | Could this wicked enemy, Coya, |
| *atiwanchic, llasawanchic?* | be what defeats us, what afflicts us? |
| *Ma Coya, suclla wañusun.* | Well, Coya, we will die only once. |
| *Amatac acoyraqui cacachunchu.* | May the ill omen not be set in stone. |
| *Parasinam, wequi payllamanta urman,* | Like rain, tears fall of their own accord. |
| *Cam, Coya, hinataccha.* | You, Coya, will do the same.] |

---

[164] Guaman Poma is not exaggerating in this instance. According to other accounts, the Inca's ransom at Cajamarca amounted to nearly 20,000 marks of 22-karat gold and 40,000 silver marks. (One mark weighs 8 ounces; a gold mark made 50 gold pesos). When the treasure was divided among Pizarro's men, the average footman got 548 ounces of gold and 1,117 of silver. Pizarro also claimed as his own the Inca's golden seat, which contained 180 pounds of 15-karat gold. For a detailed analysis of the booty, the division, and each of the men involved, see Lockhart, *The Men of Cajamarca*.

# ATAWALPA INCA WAS IMPRISONED.

Guard

*Atawalpa Inca, imprisoned in the city of Cajamarca..*

Atawalpa Inca asked Don Francisco Pizarro to read him a document. He said he did not know how to read, and he told a soldier to read it, which he did. Atawalpa said . . .[bottom line in manuscript is cut off.]

◆ **While imprisoned, Atawalpa Inca** conversed with Don Francisco Pizarro, Don Diego de Almagro, and the other Spaniards. He played the chess game that they call *taptana* with them. He was a very peaceful prince, and so he made himself agreeable with the Christians; he gave them his treasure, and did not know how else to make them happy and indulge them.

*[handwritten: native people deserted Atawalpa]*

◆ **While Atawalpa Inca** was imprisoned, all his vassals, Indians, and captains, and the great lords of his kingdom deserted him and did not serve him.

◆ **Atawalpa Inca endeavored** to ransom his life and all his captains. He gave Don Francisco Pizarro, Don Diego de Almagro, and all the soldiers a great deal of gold. For Don Francisco Pizarro pointed out a house with his own sword and measured half way up its wall; it was eight yards long by four yards wide. It was filled with gold, and Don Francisco Pizarro, Don Diego de Almagro, and all the other Spaniards took it all. They divided up the treasure and sent it all to the emperor, to Spain, and to each of their kinsmen, relatives, and friends.

*[handwritten: Atawalpa gave Spaniards treasures]*

◆ **The Inca Atawalpa,** while imprisoned, sent his ambassadors and captains—the captains-major Challco Chima and Quisquis Incas, and other captains—to make war and battle on his legitimate brother Wascar Inca. In this way, Atawalpa defeated Wascar Inca and bodily captured him. Then he abused Wascar, giving him rotten corn and *chuño.* For coca, he gave him *chillca* leaves; for *llipta,* he gave him powdered human filth and llama dung; for *chicha,* llama piss; for bedding, a mat; and for a woman, a long stone dressed as a woman. In the place called Andamarca, the *Cañaris* and *Chachapoyas* killed Wascar, while they sang, "*Poluya poluya, uwiya, uwiya.*" They also killed all his *auquicunas* and *ñustas* [princes and princesses], opening the wombs of the Indian women who were pregnant. They did all this in order to consume Wascar Inca and finish off him and all his generation, so that there would be no legitimate Inca king. The Christians had demanded to see the legitimate Inca king, so Atawalpa ordered him killed.

*[handwritten: bro feud]*

*[handwritten: yikes]*

◆ **In the time** of this quarrel between the two brothers Wascar Inca and Atawalpa Inca, when new men (the Spaniards) appeared, unlike any who had ever been seen before, so much treasure was lost: the treasure of the sun, of the moon, of the stars, of the gods (*waca willcas*), of the Temple of Curi Cancha, of the Inca, of the virgins (*acllas*), of the high priests, of the great lords and the captains general, and of the common Indians. So many momentous things were [lost] throughout the kingdom, it is impossible to count so high.

◆ **The Indians felt** abandoned by their gods (*wacas*), by their kings, and by their great lords and captains during this time of the conquest. Nor did they have the God of the Christians, nor the king of Spain; nor did they have justice.

*[handwritten margin notes: "Attacking + robbing Spaniards", "Pizarro ordered that Atawalpa be decapitated", "Killed natives", "more treasure"]*

They therefore went in for stealing and robbing the Spaniards. Challco Chima, Quisquis, Awa Panti, Rumiñawi, and many other captains, and all the *Cañari, Chachapoya,* and *Wanca* Indians went about attacking and robbing, for they were abandoned and had turned into *yanaconas.*[165] That was how the *yanaconas* began acting as scoundrels and thieves. As a result, there was a very great deal of hunger and tumult, many people died, and there was commotion through the kingdom: "Give me gold, hand over that gold."

◆ **SENTENCE** was passed by Don Francisco Pizarro: they were to behead Atawalpa Inca. Don Diego de Almagro and the others did not wish to sign this sentence, because Atawalpa had given them all his wealth in gold and silver, but Pizarro sentenced him. Everyone said that he should send him off to the emperor as a prisoner, so that, over there, [the emperor] might restore all the wealth of this kingdom.

**Atawalpa Inca was** to be decapitated. He was sentenced and ordered beheaded by Don Francisco Pizarro. The Indian interpreter, Felipe, a *Huancavilca* native, notified him of the sentence. This interpreter gave bad information to Don Francisco Pizarro and to the others, who were unhappy with the sentence. He did not let them know that Atawalpa Inca pleaded for justice and mercy, for he loved the *Coya,* his legitimate wife. This was the reason why they killed and beheaded Atawalpa Inca. He died a martyr; his life came to a most Christian end, in the city of Cajamarca.

◆ **On the orders** of Don Francisco Pizarro, Don Diego de Almagro, and their generals, two Spaniards were sent to bodily capture the captains Chalco Chima and Quisquis. They captured Chalco Chima and executed justice on him in Jauja; they hanged him from a pair of poles, and Chalco Chima died. The rest of the captains fled: Quisquis, Quiso Yupanqui, Rumiñawi, Awa Panti, Wanca Auqui, and Colla Tupa.

◆ **All the wealth** that they had hidden was discovered: gold, silver, jewels, and precious stones. They sent it all to the emperor and Catholic king of Spain; Don Francisco Pizarro, Don Diego de Almagro, and the other soldiers sent him all the wealth that belonged to the *wacas* and the sun—as much as they could get their hands on. Each of them also sent [some of the treasure] to their own houses—to their wives, children, and relatives, in this kingdom and in Castile.

Out of greed, many priests and Spaniards and ladies and merchants embarked for Peru. Everywhere one heard "Peru!" and more "Peru!," "Indies!" and more "Indies!," "Gold and silver! Gold, silver!" in this kingdom.

---

[165] *Yanacona:* an Indian commoner who became a personal servant in a Spanish household and was thereby removed from his Indian community and from tribute responsibilities. See Glossary.

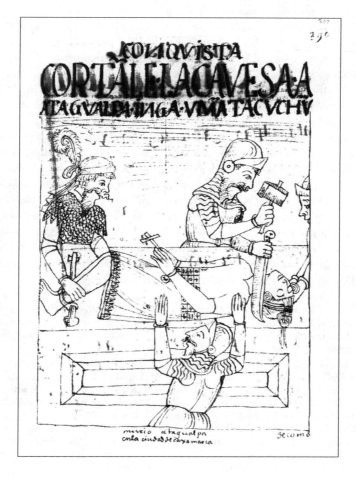

*Atawalpa died in the city of Cajamarca.*

◆ **Because of this** wealth, the emperor sent governors and magistrates, presidents and bishops, priests and friars, Spaniards and ladies. Everywhere people were saying, "Peru!" and more "Peru!" There was a tremendous increase in numbers, from the [original] 160 Spaniards and one Congo black.[166] Spaniards, merchants, barterers, petty hawkers, and dark-skinned people came. Mestizos—the children of priests—now multiply much more than Indians. "Gold and silver in Peru!"

Here you see how an emperor came to ruin through pride; how a gentleman could sentence his king. And if he had not been killed, all the wealth would have belonged to the emperor, and all the mines would have been discovered.[167]

CAPTAIN LUIS DE Ávalos de Ayala, Don Pedro Luján, Rodrigo Niño, Gómez Arias, and the other captains and soldiers who were in the troop and service began the battle.[168]

Being a valiant captain, Luis de Ávalos de Ayala charged in against captain Quiso Yupanqui Inca, the [grand]son of Topa Yupanqui and the author's uncle, who came with a dozen captains and a thousand Indians.[169]

For his own part, Quiso Yupanqui leapt into battle, for he ran swiftly as a deer and was so light on his feet that he could pass right under the horses. While fighting, he jumped over a water canal at Lati in the city of Lima and fell; just then he was speared and killed by captain Luis de Ávalos de Ayala. This captain was the father of the author's brother, Padre Martín de Ayala, an ordained priest who died in the hospital of the city of Huamanga, where his portrait still hangs, as has been mentioned.

---

[166] One of Pizarro's men at Cajamarca was a black town crier from Seville. He was a free man (not, as Guaman Poma assumes, a "Congo black," that is, an enslaved African), and was treated as a Spaniard in the division of Atawalpa's ransom. See Lockhart, *Men of Cajamarca*, 380–84.

[167] Emperor: Guaman Poma usually reserves the word *emperador* to refer to Carlos V in his dual role as Holy Roman Emperor and king of Spain. Taken in this sense, the argument here is that if the king (Atawalpa) had not been killed, he would have pledged loyalty directly to the emperor (Carlos V), and then the gold that was lost and stolen by the quarrelsome Spanish conquerors would have gone directly to the latter, saving him from financial ruin. Guaman Poma is deliberately ambiguous in this passage, however. By not naming the emperor, he leaves open the interpretation that the Inca himself could have reclaimed the title of emperor in Peru. In the same way, he is ambiguous about the "pride" that caused the ruin: was it Atawalpa's, or Pizarro's?

[168] Guaman Poma's narrative jumps from the events at Cajamarca (1532–1533) to an imagined account of the 1536 siege of Lima. Murra and Adorno note (ms. pp. 394 and 395) that the historical Ávalos de Ayala arrived in Peru in 1548, and Gómez Arias in 1547, more than a decade after the siege.

[169] In his description of the Incas (ms. p. 114), Guaman Poma identifies Quiso Yupanqui's parents as Wayna Capac and a sister of Guaman Poma's grandfather Waman Chawa.

# CAPTAIN LUIS DE ÁVALOS DE AYALA KILLED THE CAPTAIN QUISO YUPANQUI INCA.

Quiso Yupanqui died when he slipped by the canal; his life came to an end, and the other captains fled, each in his own direction, to their pueblos; they did not want to wait.

It was after this battle that people began to settle [in that place]. The first name it had was Lima. Today it is called Los Reyes de Lima, because it was in the month of the wise kings, Balthasar, Melchior, and Gaspar, that this city was won, and thus it was ordained by God that it should be the city of His Majesty the king and of his viceroy and royal council in this kingdom, and its main capital.[170]

It was there that the Inca was conquered, for he had not defended himself in any city. This was a miracle from God and from the three holy wise kings. Therefore, today this city is Seville,[171] a royal court like that of Castile or any court in the world, for God has taken possession of it. Its patron is St. James the Greater,[172] and the patron of this kingdom is St. James the Greater, Apostle of Jesus Christ.

◆ **THE SPANIARDS** spread all across the land in this kingdom, two by two or more. Each Spaniard went about turning people into *yanaconas* (Indians)[173] and seeking out his own fortune. They each sought for income, doing great harm and much damage to the Indians along the way—demanding gold and silver from them, taking away their clothes and food. The Indians were frightened to see new people, unlike any who had ever been seen before. Therefore, they hid and fled from the Christians, throughout the kingdom.

◆ **The first conquerors** wore different clothes [in those days], for fear of the cold: red doublets and caps, tight breeches, short collars like a cleric's, and they wore long sleeves, undershirts, and short capes. Likewise the women, like the Indian men in the old days, wore long blouses and short

---

[170] Guaman Poma has changed the order of events, placing the 1536 battle over Lima before its foundation in 1535. The Spanish moved the colonial capital of Peru from the mountain city of Cusco (nearly one month's journey from the coast) in order to improve communications with Spain. Francisco Pizarro selected the Lima plain, near one of the best natural harbors in Peru, as its site, and he supposedly laid the cornerstone for its cathedral on January 6, 1535, the feast day of the Three Kings. Colonial Spaniards knew the city as *la ciudad de Los Reyes,* the City of the Kings. Lima came under siege by resurgent Inca forces one year later.

[171] Seville: the largest city in Spain at the time. Spain did not establish its capital at Madrid until 1561.

[172] See footnote 162. By claiming Santiago, patron saint of Spain, as the patron of Peru as well, Guaman Poma is arguing for the equality of the two kingdoms.

[173] *Yanaconas:* see Glossary. The Spanish settlers took people out of their communities, turning them into their personal servants and treating them as generic "Indians," not as members of their own distinct ethnic groups.

CONQVISTA
PRIMER AVITO DE'S
PAÑA·QTRAJOENLACONQVISTA

*el uso antigo*          *como*

*The old style.*

mantles. Then they went around consuming and laying waste to the land more than ever, in this kingdom.

◆ **The first conquerors** were greenhorns; the Indians were the same. Neither understood the other. A Spaniard would demand "*agua* [water]," and an Indian would bring wool.[174] A Spaniard would shout, "*Anda, puto!* [Move it, bugger!]," and the Indians would bring copper and gourds, because *anda* means "copper" and *puto* means "gourds."

But some Indians would become *ladinos* [bilingual]; such *yanaconas* would say, "Sheep *chinc*-ing, *pacat, tuta* searching, *mana tarinchos, wiracocha*."[175] Like the mestizos of Cusco, Jaquijaguana, and Cochacalla,[176] they would say, "Ah, señor, corn is *parway*ing [ripening], chicken is roasting, we eating everything, my mother go up, me now looking to shoe the mule." Both sides thus had great difficulties—the Indians and the Christians alike.

In the province of the Collas, when they said, "*Anda, puto*," the Indians would say, "*Putu sapi hiley haccha puto sapi hila*."[177]

◆ **After they had** conquered and stolen, the Spaniards began taking the women and maidens and deflowering them by force. If they resisted, they killed them like dogs and punished them, without fear of God nor of justice; nor was there any justice.

◆ **The first Spaniards** conquered the land with just two words that they had learned. They would say, "*Ama mancha, noca Inca*" ("No be afraid, I'm the Inca").[178] They would shout this at the Indians, who would flee from them in terror. They did not conquer with arms, nor did they spill any blood or labor hard.

The *Cañaris, Chachapoyas,* and *yanaconas* only joined up with the Spaniards so that they could rob and steal alongside them; they did not join up to serve His Majesty.

They say that one Spaniard, with his greed for gold and silver, ordered [his *yanaconas*] to carry him in a litter, and to put earplugs and the Inca's garb on him. He would enter each pueblo asking for gold and silver. When the Indians saw a bearded Inca, they would be frightened and would rush to flee—especially the women—throughout this kingdom.

---

[174] Wool: because Quechua *awa* (woven cloth) sounds like Spanish *agua*.

[175] The sentence mixes Quechua and Spanish; roughly: "The lost sheep is hiding; in the afternoon they searched for it but did not find it, sir."

[176] The mestizos of these highland towns were known for their Quechua-inflected Spanish.

[177] A difficult phrase, presumably in an Aymaran language.

[178] Like the Spanish of the *yanaconas,* the Spaniards' Quechua is grammatically incorrect; more correct would be *ama manchakuychu,* "do not be afraid."

*[handwritten margin note: burned a chief alive]*

**DON FRANCISCO,** Don Diego de Almagro, and the other Christians ordered them to wall up the most excellent lord (*Capac Apo*) Waman Chawa, the second-in-command of the Inca, who was alive and very old, along with the other great lords. They walled him in, demanding gold and silver. In their self-interest and greed for gold and silver, those conquerors set fire to the house and burned him up. His life came to an end.

In the same way, with various tortures they killed the Incas, all the great lords, the captains general, and the nobles of every province in this kingdom, demanding gold and silver from them. They would imprison them and punish them quite cruelly, holding them with chains of iron, with twisted cow leather, and even with cows' yokes. They say that they used cow harnesses and restraints made from cow leather to imprison the Indians of this kingdom. Many noble lords, out of fear of being tortured, therefore said that they were poor Indians so that they would not be tortured and go through such suffering, in this kingdom.

◆ **In the time** of the Incas there were highwaymen (called *puma ranra*); their captain was called *chuqui aquilla inca*. These runaway Indians, these so-called *puma ranra,* would hide out in the deep gorges, rocky places, crags, and ravines, and they would rob people on the royal highways. In the times of the conquest, these highwaymen, the so-called *puma ranra,* became *yanaconas* for the Spaniards. Then they carried out even more assaults and robberies on the poor Indians; afterwards, they would live in the cities, where they registered as *yanaconas* during the general inspection tours. Now they are *yanaconas* in Quito, Huánuco, Lima, Huamanga, Cusco, Arequipa, Potosí, and Chuquisaca; in all the cities, they are tributary Indians and pay taxes to the king in this kingdom.

**MANCO INCA** rebelled when he was king (*Inca*), because that was what his captains and the council of this kingdom demanded: Quisquis Inca, Awapati Amaro, Wanca Auqui Illatopa, Collatopa Curiñawi Yuto Inca, and Yucra Wallpa (these captains were Incas from Hanan Cusco and Lurin Cusco); Calla Aymara Chuquillanqui, Supawamani, Chuwiwaman Chanbi Mallco, Apo Mallco Castillapari, Apo Mollo Condorchawa, and Cullic Chawa Cusichaqui Wayanay.[179] *[handwritten margin note: rebelled b/c of death of then chief]* The councilors rebelled because of the death of *capac apo* Waman Chawa, the second-in-command of the Inca, a very old lord of the kingdom who was burned and killed by Don Francisco Pizarro, Don Diego de Almagro, and the other Spaniards. They rebelled against the Spaniards because of

---

[179] Manco Inca, a younger half-brother of Atawalpa and Wascar, was set up by the Spanish to be the new puppet ruler of the Inca Empire under indirect Spanish rule, but continued insults, imprisonments, and provocations by Spanish *encomenderos* who dreamed of Atawalpa's treasure, led him to revolt in April, 1536.

## DON FRANCISCO PIZARRO BURNS *CAPAC APO* WAMAN CHAWA IN A HOUSE, DEMANDING GOLD.

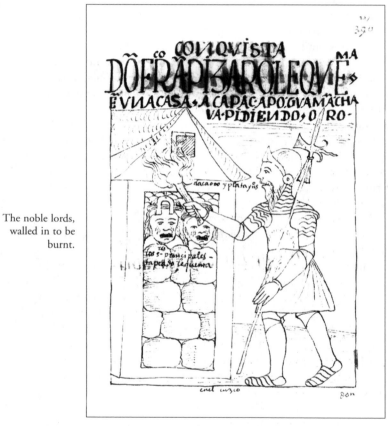

"Give me gold and silver, Indians!"

The noble lords, walled in to be burnt.

*In Cusco.*

Throne and seat of the Inca, called *usno.*

**In Cusco.**

their ill treatment and mockery, for they told crude jokes about the Inca and the other lords of this kingdom. The Spaniards, with their bad opinions and little fear of God or justice, would take the Indians' wives and maiden daughters in plain view. The Indians suffered many other offenses at the Spaniards' hands as well.

Therefore, the Indians defended themselves. So many Indians laid siege to the Spaniards that they were beyond counting; there must have been a hundred thousand million Indians, who came from all over this kingdom.[180] When they had all gathered together, the Christian soldiers begged for mercy, kneeling and calling out, with tears and cries, to God, the Virgin Mary, and all the saints. They cried out loud, "Lord Santiago, save me! Santiago! St. Mary, save me! St. Mary! Help us, God!" That was what the horsemen shouted in the skirmish: they would cry, "Santiago!" The foot soldiers in their midst would kneel and cry, "St. Mary!" with their hands clasped in prayer.

**MANCO INCA SET FIRE TO** the house of the Inca, called *Cuyus Manco,* which the Christians had set aside as a temple of God, and where they had placed the holy cross ✠ on the roof and on an altar. First, the Indians set fire to the Christians' houses, burning them down while the Christians were besieged. They set fire to all the housing, even the storehouse and palace of the Inca, the *Cuyas Manco,* which today is the main church of the city of Cusco. People say that, when they were setting fire to this house, the fire would fly up, and the house would absolutely refuse to burn. It frightened them to see how the fire refused to come near the holy ✠. They say that this was a miracle from God our Lord. It was a sign from God that, at that time, the Holy Church was already established in the kingdom.

**THEN, AT THAT TIME,** God performed another miracle. It happened while all the Christians were besieged in the plaza of Cusco. They were praying, kneeling, shouting, and crying out to God, the Virgin Mary, and all his saints and angels: "Help me, Virgin Mary, Mother of God!" He then performed another great miracle, a miraculous apparition of the Mother of God in this kingdom. She was seen by the Indians of this kingdom with their own eyes; they have testified and sworn to it, for at the time there was no other [Spanish] lady anywhere in the kingdom, nor had anyone ever seen or known one. Rather, the first lady that they came to know was the Virgin Mary.

---

[180] Most chroniclers of the siege of Cusco (1536–1537) and the country-wide rebellion estimate Inca forces at between 100,000 and 200,000 (John Hemming, *The Conquest of the Incas* [New York: Harcourt Brace Jovanovich, 1970], 190). There were fewer than 200 Spaniards in Cusco at the time (Lockhart, *Men of Cajamarca,* 15).

With the Holy Cross ✠ God performed a miracle, and it did not burn.

*In Cusco.*

## SANTA MARÍA DE PEÑA DE FRANCIA[181]

A VERY BEAUTIFUL WOMAN, dressed all in a very white gown, whiter than snow, and with a radiant face, more radiant than the sun: at the sight of her, the Indians were frightened. They say she threw dirt in the infidel Indians' eyes. For God performed a miracle, and so did his blessed mother, to show mercy to the Christian Spaniards. Better said, the mother of God wished rather to show mercy to the Indians so that they would become Christian, and to save the Indians' souls by pleading with her precious Son and with the Most Holy Trinity—God the Father, God the Son, and God the Holy Spirit, one God.

Therefore, it is very just that all the universal world should adore and honor the Virgin Santa María de Peña de Francia. This is especially true of the Indians and Spaniards of this kingdom, because of the great mercy she showed in that time of need, and for the miracles of the mother of God, Our Lady of Peña de Francia and of Copacabana in this kingdom.

## ST. JAMES THE GREATER OF GALICIA, THE APOSTLE OF JESUS CHRIST

IN THAT HOUR, when the Christians were under siege, God performed another great miracle in the city of Cusco. People say that they saw the saint with their own eyes—that Lord Santiago descended with a great clap of thunder, falling like a bolt of lightning onto the Inca's fortress, Sacsawaman (that is the Inca's *pucara,* above San Cristóbal). When St. James fell to earth, the Indians were frightened and said that *illapa* (a bolt of thunder and lightning, *caccha!*) had fallen in the Christians' favor.[182]

In that way, St. James descended to defend the Christians.

They say he came mounted on a white horse. They say his horse was wearing a plume (*suri*) and many bells on its harness, and the saint was well-armed, bearing his shield, his banner, his red mantle, and his naked sword; and they say he brought great destruction and death upon many Indians, and undid the Indians' siege of the Christians, which Manco Inca had ordered.

[181] Guaman Poma writes elsewhere (ms. pp. 933, 946–47) about his devotion to this fifteenth-century Spanish image of St. Mary. Santa María de Peña de Francia was apparently the patron saint of his birth pueblo, Suntunto, and was also venerated in an early-seventeenth-century image at the major Andean pilgrimage site of Copacabana. It is perhaps significant that her name incorporates the Spanish word *peña,* crag, the same term that Guaman Poma uses to describe the sites of native Andean worship.

[182] Meteor fragments are generally identified with bolts of lightning, which in turn are seen as manifestations of Illapa, the lightning deity, or of Santiago, his Catholic counterpart.

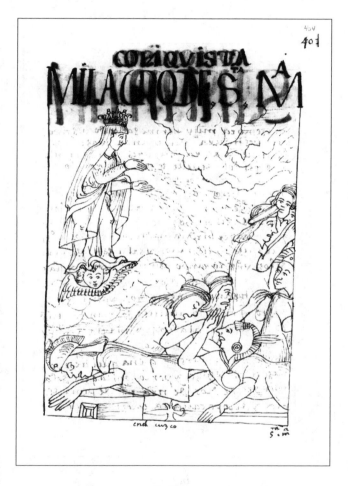

*In Cusco.*

# MIRACLE OF ST. JAMES THE GREATER, APOSTLE OF JESUS CHRIST.

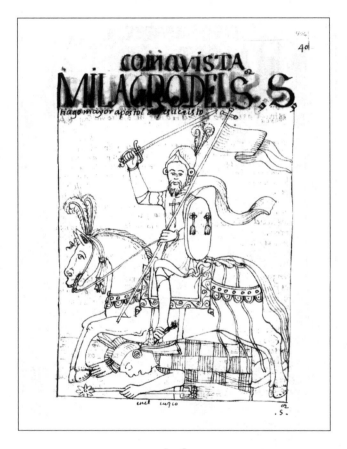

*In Cusco.*

And they say the saint made so much noise that the Indians were frightened. Manco Inca and the other captains and Indians fled the noise, heading for the pueblo of Tambo with his captains and all the other Indians who could flee.

Ever since, the Indians have called the thunder "Santiago," because the saint descended to earth like a lightning bolt (*illapa*). They call it "Santiago" because that is what the Christians were shouting out—they were crying, "Santiago!" The infidel Indians heard their cries, and they saw the saint descend to earth like a lightning bolt. Thus, the Indians are eye-witnesses to Lord Santiago, and the feast day of St. James should be kept in this kingdom as a holiday because of the miracle won by God and Lord Santiago.

### ◆ MANCO INCA WAS ROUTED BY THE CHRISTIANS' LORD SANTIAGO

◆ **MANCO INCA WAS FRIGHTENED,** and he fled with his captains, bringing many Indians to the pueblo of Tambo.[183] There he built many houses and halls, and commanded [the Indians to cultivate] many *chacras*, and ordered them to create a portrait of himself, Manco Inca, with his coat of arms, on a very tall crag, so that there would be a memorial [to him].

But he could not stay in that pueblo of Tambo. He withdrew from there deeper into the mountains of Vilcabamba[184] with his other captains. He brought Indians and his wife, the *Coya;* and he left his kingdom and crown, his *mascapaycha* and *champi* [royal tassel and scepter], to the emperor and king, our lord Don Carlos of glorious memory, who is now in heaven, and to his son Don Philip II, who is now in heaven, and to his son Philip III, our king.

**Captain Quisquis rose up** once more, after Manco Inca, on behalf of the Inca Paullo Topa, a bastard son of Wayna Capac Inca, and defended him against the Spaniards. Although [Paullo Topa] later began to serve and help [the Spanish], he never was wholehearted about it, and there was constant suspicion about him until his death. Paullo Topa Inca died a very Christian death in the city of Cusco, leaving his son, Don Melchor Carlos.[185]

---

[183] Ollantaytambo, a pueblo about thirty miles northwest of Cusco.

[184] Vilcabamba (Willka Pampa), a mountain fastness sixty miles west of Ollantaytambo, became the site of the last Inca redoubt until its conquest in 1572.

[185] Paullo Topa was yet another half-brother of Atawalpa, Wascar, and Manco. He joined forces with Almagro, took part in the attempted conquest of Chile, was rewarded with an *encomienda* south of Cusco, and became the Spanish colonial government's puppet Inca in Cusco after Manco's rebellion. He married a Spanish woman. His son, Don Melchor Carlos, spent the later years of his life in the court of Philip III of Spain. According to Guaman Poma (ms. p. 948), he was banished from Peru on trumped-up charges.

**The captain mentioned,** Quisquis, always pursued the Christians, both because of his sins and because he never made peace with the Christians. So his own captains—the Indians that he had on his own side—killed him. He died in Cusco and left his position to other captains in this kingdom.

♦ **Manco Inca moved** further into the mountains of Vilcabamba, because he did not feel safe in the pueblo of Tambo. He went with several captains—Curi Paucar, Mana Cutana, Atoc, and Rumi Sonco—and he brought along Indians from various lineages. He moved further inland until he reached a large river, where they built a bridge of plaited ropes and crossed over to the other side, reaching the valley named Vilcabamba. They settled there, building a city, a second Cusco. They built a temple there— its own Curi Cancha. But the city was poorly armed and had very few people. There were Indians of several lineages (*ayllus*) in the city of Vilcabamba and in its *chacras* (planted fields) and pastures. Manco Inca was reduced to poverty in Vilcabamba.

♦ **By Manco Inca's orders,** his captains robbed the Spaniards, as well as the Christian Indians who were on the king's side, along the highway at Apurimac. When they passed by on the royal highway from Cusco to Lima with their mule trains and merchandise, Manco Inca's captains would kill them and take their treasure, clothes, and everything they carried. They would also rob and capture the Christian Indians. They kept this up for many years—robbing the highway from the pueblo of Vilcabamba, where Manco Inca lived with his wife and children.

♦ **A mestizo, named** Diego Méndez, used to enter the city of Vilcabamba with his tricks and lies. This mestizo would let the Inca, Manco Inca, know when the king's mule train, or the mule train of some rich Spaniard, was going to pass, so that Manco Inca could rob them on the royal highway. That way, they were constantly robbing and causing great harm to the Christians along that highway. Then, one day when Manco Inca and the mestizo Diego Méndez were both very drunk, they began to play games of daring. The mestizo killed him; he stabbed Manco Inca and left him dead.[186] Then the captains killed the mestizo, leaving the Inca Sayri Topa as heir [to the throne], and Cusi Warcaya as Coya. Sayri Topa died in Cusco, leaving behind Topa Amaro Inca.

---

[186] In 1545.

## DAMIÁN DE LA BANDERA, GENERAL INSPECTOR OF THE INDIANS OF THIS KINGDOM

### THE FIRST GENERAL INSPECTION TOUR ORDERED BY THE EMPEROR AND KING OF SPAIN, DON CARLOS[187]

◆ THE LAND WAS DESTROYED, and both Christians and Indians wandered about lost, after the confrontation between the two brothers (the legitimate Wascar Inca and his bastard brother Atawalpa Inca), followed by the conquest (when people unlike any ever before seen came here), the destruction it caused, and the deaths of the king (*Inca*), of lords who were as great as the Duke of Alva (the counts, marquises, gentlemen, and lords of this land), and of Indians and nobles (*curacas*).

◆ The land was lost. Low Indians and petty authorities made themselves into *caciques,* when that was not what they were. They were enrolled in the inspection as such. Tributary Indians (*mitayos*) made themselves out to be noble *caciques,* and they styled themselves "Don" and their wives "Doña," because the land was lost.

The world was lost as well: the same things occurred among the Spaniards. Greengrocers, peddlers, tailors, shoemakers, pastry cooks, and bakers were calling themselves "Don" and "Doña."[188] Jews and Moors now use the title of "Don": the world is upside down. The judges do nothing to remedy this, because they have been paid off.

◆ Priests and padres call themselves doctors, licentiates, bachelors, and masters,[189] even though they have earned no titles, have no rights, and know no letters. Some people make crude jokes, mocking them with the name *licensiasnos* ["licentiate asses"]. That is to say: the world is upsidedown. Justice, however, ought to deal justly and issue punishments.

**Don Francisco Pizarro, pursuing** his own interests in the conquest, in governing this kingdom and in gold and silver riches, revolted and killed

---

[187] Bandera inspected (*visitó*) the province of Huamanga and the valley of Yucay, near Cusco, in 1557–1558. Rolena Adorno notes that this *visita* is the earliest post-conquest event mentioned in the manuscript, and suggests that it is a memory from Guaman Poma's youth (*Guaman Poma and His Illustrated Chronicle from Colonial Peru: From a Century of Scholarship to a New Era of Reading* [Copenhagen: Museum Tusculanum Press, 2001], 32).

[188] Guaman Poma paints an accurate portrait of the Spanish conquerors: the majority were neither professional soldiers nor nobles, but petty merchants and artisans from the small cities of Castile. The honorific Spanish titles *don* and *doña* were once reserved for recognized members of the nobility, but became more widespread in the Americas as conquerors and their families claimed privileges based on their roles in the conquest.

[189] These were college and university degrees, roughly equivalent to Ph.D., B.A., high school, and M.A., respectively.

"This one is a nobleman's son."

*"Caymi, siño, sapra inca. Nocap waway, capac apop churinmi."*

["This one, señor, is the Sapra Inca. He is my own child, and the son of a powerful lord."]

***General Inspection Tour.***

Don Diego de Almagro the elder. Don Francisco Pizarro then rose up as governor of this kingdom. Don Diego de Almagro the younger, mestizo, then killed Don Francisco Pizarro and rose up as governor of the land.[190]

**Don Francisco Pizarro was killed** by his own interests in the conquest, in governing this kingdom, and in gold and silver riches. Don Diego de Almagro the younger came and killed him, and then rose up as governor of this kingdom. Don Francisco Pizarro died, and Don Diego de Almagro the younger, mestizo, was killed by Don Gonzalo Pizarro, who rose up as governor of the land.

Gonzalo Pizarro and the other conquerors and magistrates killed Don Diego de Almagro the younger. Gonzalo Pizarro then rose up and killed the viceroy, Blasco Núñez, in Quito. Gonzalo Pizarro then rose up as king and governor of the land, loudly proclaiming from his house that he was rebelling against the royal crown.

He was then conquered and killed by the president and magistrates of the Audiencia [the high court of colonial Peru] and by the captains, archbishops, bishops, and prelates sent by the emperor.

After that, Francisco Hernández Girón revolted against the royal crown. He was undone by the lords of this kingdom. The first battle against him was led by Don Martín Guaman Mallqui de Ayala, the Inca's second-in-command and a most excellent lord of this kingdom; and by Apo Wasco, a noble of the province of Andahuaylas, Chanca, in Huancacocha, close by Ora Yaoma. After that battle, [Hernández Girón] was captured by Apo Alanya Chuquillanqui of the *Wanca* Indians. He then met justice in Lima.

Still later, Carreño and the people in Quito tried rising up; they met justice in Cusco.

*[The paragraphs above provide a brief outline of the histories of ambition, conflict, revenge, and murder that marked the Spanish civil wars in Peru (1537–1553). The following twenty pages of the book (omitted here) elaborate on these stories. We return to the text with the account of the final battle against Girón, in which Guaman Poma turns away from his source material[191] in order to expand upon his own father's purported role in establishing order in the kingdom. The story of Girón's rebellion and capture closes the chapter on the conquest, which Guaman Poma ends with a reflection on the mysteries of time.]*

---

[190] This paragraph represents the story as Guaman Poma originally wrote it. He later heavily emended these lines to produce a second version, which overlays the first; that version is presented in the following paragraph.

[191] Guaman Poma gathered most of his information on the Spanish civil wars in Peru from Agustín de Zárate's 1555 chronicle, *Historia del descubrimiento y conquista del Perú* (*The Discoverie and Conquest of the Provinces of Peru,* London, 1581), according to Murra and Adorno (ms. pp. 415–30).

*434–437* **DON MARTÍN GUAMAN MALLQUI DE AYALA, *CAPAC APO*,**
SECOND-IN-COMMAND OF THE INCA, AND HIS VICEROY
IN THESE KINGDOMS, THE MOST EXCELLENT LORD
DUKE OF THIS KINGDOM; AND DON LEÓN APO WASCO OF
HANAN CHANCA; AND DON JUAN WAMAN WACHACA
OF LURIN CHANCA, FROM THE PUEBLO AND
PROVINCE OF ANDAHUAYLAS

THESE NOBLE LORDS personally waged battle in His Majesty's service
against the traitor Francisco Hernández Girón. On their side, there were
100 Indian soldiers; on Francisco Hernández's, there were 400 soldiers:
300 Spaniards and 100 *yanaconas,* mestizos, and mulattos. They closed battle near Huatacocha, Urayauma, and Huancacocha, in the heights of Hua-
chahuapite. Among the traitors, 200 soldiers died, and the rest ran off,
each fleeing in a different direction. Francisco Hernández himself fled
without his weapons, very poor, with six captains and no other people. He
traveled along the royal highway of the Inca, going to Quilcata, Ura
Pampa, Yawar Pampa, Caracha, Choclococha, and Astaputi before reaching Huancavelica. From there, he went on to Vilcabamba, and from there
to Los Chongos, where he was captured, utterly destitute, naked, and
unarmed.[192]

The hoof prints and bones of the horses can still be seen today, as testimony to the battle that the nobles gave in His Majesty's service. But
[Hernández Girón] ran away, saying that he was going to kill those nobles
and their Indians, that he was going to sow salt in their pueblos, and that
deer, foxes, and lions would live there as their memorial. He claimed there
had been no war and no battle, but rather that he had fought against the
emperor-king over the Indians and their tribute.

In that way, he fled from Huatacocha and got to Jauja without any gunpowder or shot, and thus the *Wanca* Indians caught him, like a woman.

APO ALANYA Chuquillanqui of Hanan Wanca and Apo Waccra Paucar of
Lurin Wanca, the Cusichac of Jauja,[193] captured Francisco Hernández
Girón and his six captains, whom they discovered very poor, unarmed,
bereft of gunpowder and shot. [Hernández Girón] was sitting in the hut

---

[192] Most of the places mentioned in this paragraph are just east of Lima, in the region
stretching 150 miles from Junín (the area where the battles take place) to Huancavelica.

[193] The *Wancas* of the Jauja valley in central Peru were the first important allies of Pizarro
in the conquest of Peru. Their leader in 1532 was Don Francisco *Cusichac* (John Murra,
"Litigation over the Rights of 'Natural Lords' in Early Colonial Courts in the Andes," in
Elizabeth Hill Boone and Tom Cummins, eds., *Native Traditions in the Postconquest
World* [Washington: Dunbarton Oaks, 1998], 55). I am assuming here that *Cusichac*
was the *Wanca* equivalent of *Inca,* referring to a ruler or ruling lineage.

## THE BATTLE FOUGHT.

434

The battle fought in the service of His Majesty by the Most Excellent Lord
*(capac apo)* Don Martín de Ayala, Father of the Author, as leader of the
Chinchaysuyu, and by Apo Wasco and Apo Waman Wachaca, as leaders of
Hanan and Lurin Chanca, at the head of one hundred soldiers. Francisco
Hernández and his three hundred soldiers were defeated and fled.

Waman Wacha

Apo Wasco

*Capac apo*
Don Martín
Guaman
Mallqui de
Ayala

Francisco
Hernández
Girón

*In Huatococha.*

# APO ALANYA CHUQUILLANQUI.

Apo Alanya Chuquillanqui of Hanan Wanca and Waccra Waman of Lurin Wanca, the *Cusichac* of Jauja, captured Francisco Hernández with his six soldier-captains, whom they found unarmed and very poor.

Girón

Waccra Waman

Alanya

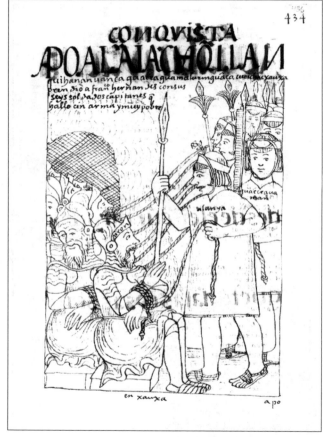

*In Jauja.*

(*chuclla*) of a *llama michi* [llama herder] when they caught him. Like a woman, he gave himself up to the *Wanca* Indians of the Jauja valley. From there, they took him to Lima (the city of Los Reyes). After they arrived, Francisco Hernández was sentenced to be beheaded and the others to being hanged and quartered. Justice was done to them, and their heads were exhibited along with those of all the other traitors who were executed with them. In this way, the rebellion against the royal crown came to an end.

**From the confrontation** between the two brothers Wascar and Atawalpa in the year 1532, to the conquest of this kingdom, followed by all the uprisings against the royal crown—by the traitors Don Francisco Pizarro, Don Diego Almagro (the elder and the younger alike), Gonzalo Pizarro, Carvajal, Francisco Hernández Girón, and the others who rose up with them, conquering and battling against each other—and up to the point when good justice was established, there were a total of twenty-four years of restlessness, pestilence, uproar, and attempts by poor men to turn themselves into lords. God did not will it so. One hundred and fifty years have passed since the discovery; 112 more years have passed since the conquest, counting up to the year of our Lord 1613.

**For all things belong** to God and to our lord the king, may God save him. God alone knows the times and the years, although astrology speaks of them. The astrologers wrote of them; the apostles of Jesus Christ wrote of them; so did the apostle and prime doctor Deudorito, a very ancient doctor and bishop of the Church.[194] So did other wise men, who were enlightened by the grace of the Holy Spirit, in order that God might reveal to us the secrets that He created in heaven, on earth, and in hell: the secrets of heaven, that we might fill it; the secrets of the earth, that we might praise Him and give him thanks for them; and the secrets of hell, that the wicked might be punished, and that we might fear being punished in the bad world that God created.

---

[194] Murra and Adorno suggest (ms. p. 437, n. 2) that "Deudorito" refers to the fifth-century Greek historian Theodoretus of Cyrrhus, whose church history was printed in Spanish translation in the 1500s.

# THE BEGINNINGS OF GOOD GOVERNMENT AND JUSTICE.

Don Antonio de Mendoza,[195] of the order of Santiago, Gentleman, the second viceroy of this kingdom.

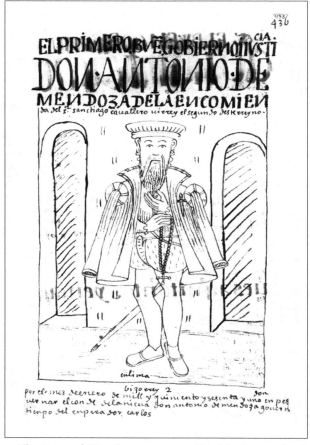

The Count of Nieva began to govern [Peru] in the month of January, 1561.[196]

Don Antonio de Mendoza governed [Peru] during the reign of emperor Carlos V.

### In Lima.

---

[195] Antonio de Mendoza was the second viceroy of Peru (1551–1552). The first viceroy, Blas Núñez Vela, was deposed by an uprising of Spanish *encomenderos* soon after his arrival at Lima in 1544 and was killed in battle against the de facto ruler of Peru, Gonzalo Pizarro, in 1546.

[196] Guaman Poma added this marginal note to correct his omission of the fourth viceroy, the Count of Nieva (1561–1564), in his history of the viceroys.

# PART 6.

## GOOD GOVERNMENT

*[Guaman Poma's chronicle of the conquest continues into the post-conquest period with a sequential description of the Spanish viceroys and the major events under their rule. Structurally, this section parallels his chronology of the twelve Incas, which he similarly used as a transition between his description of a time of war (the world of the* Auca Runa*) and his detailed description of the Incan world. His focus on what he calls "good government"—government that enforces justice and maintains a separation between the Spanish and Andean worlds—makes this a transitional section between his history of the violent era of the conquest and his prolonged social analysis of Peru's "Christian era" in the second half of the book.*

*In keeping with Guaman Poma's hierarchical view of society, "Good Government" focuses on the top echelon of post-conquest Spanish society: the viceroy, who served as the Spanish king's personal representative in the distant "kingdom of Peru." The viceroys come across as representatives of good government—with the notable exception of Don Francisco de Toledo (1570–1581), widely recognized as the architect of the government and social order of colonial Peru. By criticizing Toledo and praising the viceroys who came before and after, Guaman Poma accomplishes his rhetorical goal of condemning the entire Spanish order as contrary to the very Christian principles that the Spanish themselves claimed to follow. The keystone event in this section is the capture and execution under Toledo of the last Inca emperor, Topa Amaro, an event that Guaman Poma depicts as regicide, the betrayal of a Christian king by a low-born Spanish interloper.]*

## GOOD GOVERNMENT *438–463*

**DON ANTONIO** de Mendoza, a knight of the order of Santiago and the second viceroy of this kingdom, was sixty years of age, very Christian, a friend of the poor, and a servant of God and of His Majesty.

Though an old man, he had no fear of death or the troubles that might befall him. As for dealing with the conquerors who were in revolt, he brought that same spirit of serving God and the holy Catholic faith to establishing God's law and His Majesty's law in the land. If that did not please the conquerors, his intention was to punish the bad ones, but to do it quietly, one at a time, and thus to take away their appetite. I believe he could have accomplished this goal; I even think he might have been able to establish expeditiously all the laws of Castile here, including the mining taxes, excise taxes, and commoner taxes owed to His Majesty.[197]

Even though he lived to serve for only a short time, he established the law that Blasco Núñez Vela, the first viceroy, had brought here. He died a most Christian death in the city of Los Reyes de Lima. He performed good works and a great deal of charity, and he died serving His Majesty as a gentleman and a Christian.

**See here, you** poor, foolish, and incompetent Spaniards, who are as proud as Lucifer: Luzbel became Lucifer, the great devil.[198] You are the same as he. I am shocked to see how you yearn to hang yourselves, to behead yourselves with your own hands, to draw and quarter yourselves, to hang yourselves like Judas and hurl yourselves into hell. You yearn to be more than what God decreed you should be. If you are not kings, why do you yearn to be kings? If you are not princes, dukes, counts, marquises, or gentlemen, why do you yearn to be such? If you are taxpaying commoners—shoemakers, tailors, Jews, or Moors—then do not rise up and disturb the land; rather, pay what you owe. Did you own slaves in Castile? Did you have Indians? Then eat by your own labor and by the sweat of your brow, as God has commanded, and you shall be free: give thanks for this to God and to His Majesty.

*[An illustration, ms. p. 440, shows the third viceroy standing with an open book in his left hand and a rosary in his right, in his palace in Lima.]*

**DON ANDRÉS,** Marquis of Cañete, lord of the town of Argete, the third viceroy of this kingdom, was a most Christian man who governed peacefully.[199] Being such a Christian man, he did no harm to anyone, offending

---

[197] Mining taxes (*quintos*): a tax of one fifth of the precious metals extracted from the earth in the king's domains. Excise taxes (*alcabalas*): a tax on the total value of goods sold in each jurisdiction. Commoner taxes (*pechos*): annual tribute paid in Spain by Spanish commoners (*pecheros*) and distinct from the tribute (*tributo*) charged to Indians in the conquered territories. One of Guaman Poma's major complaints is that Spanish commoners were not forced to pay tribute in the Americas.

[198] Luzbel is an old Castilian variant of the name Lucifer—in Christian legend, an angel of light who rebelled against God and became the leader of the fallen angels. Guaman Poma uses "Luzbel" to signify Lucifer's name before the fall. It is perhaps significant that Luzbel/Lucifer is often identified with the morning star (Venus), a major Andean deity.

[199] Andrés Hurtado de Mendoza, second Marquis of Cañete, was viceroy from 1556 to 1560 and died in Lima the following year, either heartbroken at being removed from his post or poisoned by his enemies. His period in office is often remembered for the discovery of the mercury mines of Huancavelica in 1559, but Guaman Poma focuses on his negotiations and relations with Sayri Topa (Sayri Tupac), leader of the neo-Incan state of Vilcabamba from 1545 to 1561, during the last three years of Sayri Topa's life.

neither the conquerors nor the Incas, the great lords, or the nobles of this kingdom. He favored the Indians and defended them from the Spaniards. He helped the soldiers,[200] and gave what he had to the poor, being such a charitable person.

He ordered that bridges of stone and mortar be built in the city of Lima, in Jauja, in Ango Yaco, and in Amancay. All of these were masonry bridges. [He also ordered] other bridges made of plaited ropes. He ordered that all the roads be kept clean and that the churches be ornamented. He was peaceful and never arrogant towards great or small in this kingdom. He well knew the land and all that it contained.

◆ **Sayri Topa Inca,** the legitimate son of Manco Inca, left the mountains of Vilcabamba when he learned that the Marquis of Cañete was a most Christian friend of the lords and gentlemen of this kingdom. He left the mountains with his people, his *Chuncho* and *Andesuyu*[201] Indian captains, solely to meet the marquis, the viceroy. He did not even pass through the city of Cusco; he went straight from Vilcabamba to the city of Lima, leaving his son Topa Amaro Inca to take his place in the city of Vilcabamba.[202] All along his way, he was served and honored as the king and lord of this land. Then, at last, he arrived.

**Sayri Topa Inca** was received very well by the marquis, by the nobles, and by all the people in the city of Los Reyes de Lima, and there was a great feast for his reception. The marquis went out on horseback, together with the other nobles, to meet him on the road, and there were many fireworks and other amusements, and the Inca entered the city on his litter as the lord and king of all Peru. He was received by the whole Audiencia and court, and was very honored. He embraced the marquis, and the other nobles and gentlemen kissed his hand in accordance with ancient custom. From there, he went to the houses of the town council to rest.

◆ **Sayri Topa Inca** and the Marquis of Cañete each sat on his own seat, and they began to converse, speaking through interpreters, and the Inca king was very eloquent and discerning. The Inca and the marquis found great enjoyment and festivity in these talks; they loved each other very

---

[200] That is, the common Spanish soldiers who received no privileges or tribute after the conquest. As viceroy, the marquis established a standing militia (*guardia contínua*) in Lima in 1557.

[201] These are not the names of specific ethnic groups. *Chuncho (Chunchu)* is a generic Quechua term for "savage," and *Andesuyu (Antisuyu)* refers to the mountainous region north of Cusco, the homeland of people who were feared, respected, and despised for their "barbarity" by the peoples of central and southern Peru.

[202] Sayri Topa left Vilcabamba in November, 1557, and arrived in Lima in January, 1558. Topa Amaro (Tupac Amaru) was his brother, not his son; both were sons of Manco Inca.

# DON ANDRÉS, MARQUIS, VICEROY, AND SAYRI TOPA INCA, KING OF PERU

He received him and honored him and spoke with him; both the marquis and Sayri Topa were seated.

*In Los Reyes de Lima.*

much and spoke often. Likewise with the other noble conquerors, who rejoiced. The most illustrious-in-Christ bishops, prelates, and priests, for their part, went to see him and to speak with him. Likewise, the noble Indian lords of this kingdom went to see him and serve him from all over this kingdom.

*[An illustration, ms. p. 444, shows Archbishop Don Juan Solano blessing the marriage between "Don Cristóbal Sayri Topa Inca and his sister Doña Beatriz Coya" in the city of Cusco. The Inca and Coya are each dressed in the traditional clothing that denotes their rank.]*

### THE MARRIAGE OF DON CRISTÓBAL SAYRI TOPA INCA AND DOÑA BEATRIZ COYA IN THE CITY OF CUSCO

◆ **[Sayri Topa] bid farewell** to the marquis and left the city of Lima. The marquis and the [Spanish] noblemen and conquerors of the city accompanied him on his journey to his own city, the capital of this kingdom, Cusco. On his entrance into the city of Cusco he was solemnly received by the [Spanish] noblemen and conquerors, by the Inca lords of Hanan Cusco and Lurin Cusco, and by all the great noble lords of the kingdom. The Inca was highly esteemed.[203]

He was baptized and married, and there was a great celebration. Now, Sayri Topa Inca and Doña Beatriz were brother and sister, both of them children of Manco Inca and his mother Cusi Warcaya Coya. Therefore, they were married with a dispensation from Archbishop Don Juan Solano,[204] by the public authority and commission of Pope Julius III.

Don Carlos Inca, Don Alonso Atauchi, and the other *auquicunas* (princes), together with the *Cañari* captain Chillchi, then killed Sayri Topa Inca. They poisoned him because they were vexed to see the Inca, Sayri Topa, leave the mountains; it grieved them even more to see how he was honored and respected throughout the kingdom. In their vexation, they gave him a potion from which he died a most Christian death in Cusco.

---

[203] Other chroniclers depict Sayri Topa's negotiations with the viceroy as a capitulation under military pressure (see Hemming, *Conquest of the Incas,* 291–96). Sayri Topa, they write, renounced his right to the Inca throne, and in exchange was given a large *encomienda* near Cusco. Guaman Poma, in contrast, depicts this scene as a virtual Spanish recognition of the legitimacy of continued Inca rule. He pictures Sayri Topa and Beatriz being married in traditional Inca royal clothing, not Spanish dress; he states that both Spanish and Andean nobility proclaimed his entry to Cusco; and he pointedly refers to Cusco as "his [the Inca's] own city" and as "the capital of this kingdom"—a title usurped by the Spanish colonial capital of Lima.

[204] A Dominican friar, Juan Solana was the second bishop (not archbishop) of Cusco, 1544–1561.

He had no son to be his heir, only a legitimate daughter, Doña Beatriz, who married Martín García de Loyola.[205] Topa Amaro Inca remained, however, in the city of Vilcabamba, as legitimate as Sayri Topa.

And thus, his life ended.

*[An illustration, ms. p. 446, depicts the fourth viceroy, Don Francisco de Toledo, who "ruled from the year 1570 to July of 1581, in the time of King Philip II."]*

## DON FRANCISCO DE TOLEDO, STEWARD TO HIS MAJESTY, THE FOURTH VICEROY OF THIS KINGDOM[206]

HE BROUGHT HIS titles with him, as His Majesty's steward and tax officer, and as the general inspector in charge of congregating and settling[207] these kingdoms of Peru, and as such he entered the city of Los Reyes de Lima, where he was very well received.

From Lima, he went out to the cities of Huamanga and Cusco, where he made the Indians congregate into new settlements, some in good places and others in bad, depending on how their luck fell out. Because of this, the Indians were torn from their desire to maintain very distant croplands, as Indians do.[208]

---

[205] Martín García Óñez de Loyola (a nephew of St. Ignatius Loyola, founder of the Jesuit order) participated in the capture of Topa Amaro, as Guaman Poma depicts on p. 153, and was rewarded with the governorship of Chile and marriage to Doña Beatriz Clara Coya. A commemorative seventeenth-century painting of their wedding hangs in the Jesuit church of Cusco.

[206] "Steward to His Majesty" was a title of honor, but Guaman Poma uses it to good rhetorical effect to portray Toledo as a mere employee of the king. In fact, as the Conde de Oropesa, he was a member of the Spanish high nobility. In his rush to deal with the imposing figure of Toledo, Guaman Poma skips over the actual fourth viceroy, Diego de Zúñiga y Velasco, Conde de Nieva (1561–1564), and the interim rulers who served until 1570.

[207] In charge of congregating and settling (*reducidor y poblador*): As viceroy, Toledo energetically pursued the Spanish colonial policy of *reducción,* the congregation or consolidation of dispersed indigenous settlements into compact and more easily controlled Spanish-style rural towns. The policy was never successfully implemented, yet terrible social disruptions resulted from the attempt to impose the new model by uprooting traditional Andean dispersed settlements and resettling them into reconfigured political territories. The term *reducción* refers to the policy as well as to a consolidated settlement. As Guaman Poma hints in the next sentence, many *reducciones* failed to thrive as functioning towns because the Spanish laid them out in sites prone to flooding, avalanches, or other natural disasters.

[208] In the Andean agricultural system, indigenous communities exploited the varied microclimates up and down the Andean mountains by keeping fields under cultivation at different elevations, sometimes at great distances from one another. Living in *reducciones* forced Andeans to give up this "vertical" organization of farming.

◆ **He was received** in the city of Huamanga; from there, he continued to the city of Cusco. On the way, he stopped at Vilcashuaman, where he ascended the staircase up to the seat (*usno*) of the Inca, and thus he was received like the Inca himself by the noble lords.[209] He also commanded the oldest and foremost of the nobles—Don Alonso Naccha Huarcaya, from the pueblo of San Pedro de Queca[210] in the province of the Lucanas, Andamarcas, and Soras—to ascend to the summit of the *usno*.

He then went on to the city of Cusco, where he called up soldiers and drilled them for [an attack on] the city of Vilcabamba. They armed themselves against Topa Amaro Inca and his captains, Curi Paucar and Mana Cutana. To practice the drill, he mounted his rutting mare in the plaza of the hospital of Cusco alongside the soldiers and captains, whom he arrayed in good formation with many arms and harquebuses.

[The way to Vilcabamba] was very mountainous, with many monkeys, *wacamayas* (parrots), other birds, mountain lions, foxes, and deer. Deep in the mountains, many Indians were armed with slings and spears and with *waylla quipa* and *antara* [trumpets and panpipes]. A false Inca was being carried on his litter as they attacked Don Francisco de Toledo. [The Spaniards] waged battle against the Inca, capturing him and overthrowing the Indians. [It turned out that] it was merely a formation set up to simulate a battle. There was no battle, and the Inca did not defend himself. Rather, the Inca ran away, for he was only a boy and understood nothing. They captured him, alone, on the banks of the river. No Indians were with him.

◆ **Don Francisco de Toledo gave** orders that *corregidores* be dispatched to the provinces, causing great harm to the Indians of this kingdom. Because of the *corregidores,* the land will be lost. They have caused great harm, many quarrels, and terrible losses among the Indians. The land will be lost, the entire kingdom will become desolate and deserted, and the king will be very poor because of these *corregidores,* as well as the padres, the *encomenderos,* and the other Spaniards who rob the Indians of their estates—their lands, houses, croplands, pastures—and also of their wives and daughters. Whether they are married or still maidens, these women are already beginning to bear mestizos and *cholos*. Some clergymen have twenty children, and there is no remedy.

---

[209] Vilcashuaman, an important late Incaic administrative center about seventy miles north of Guaman Poma's home pueblo of Chipao, on the road to Huamanga. The *usnu* is a pyramidal structure with an imposing staircase and a double throne carved from a single large stone at top.

[210] San Pedro de Queca: a small pueblo about a mile from Chipao. One imagines that Guaman Poma must have known this noble personally.

**Don Francisco de Toledo decreed** in his ordinances that the so-called catechism boys should enter the *doctrina* at the age of four and leave at the age of six. He did not say "girls" or "maidens," only "boys." But the padres and *doctrina* priests pay no attention; they gather in the girls so that they can keep mistresses nearby, have dozens of children, multiply the numbers of little mestizos, and force unmarried women to work. They claim that they are taming [the young women] and making them into Christians. Because of this, the numbers of Indians have not multiplied, and will not multiply, in this kingdom.

**Don Francisco de Toledo issued** one decree that would be one of the holiest things that could be done in the service of God and His Majesty and for the welfare of the poor Indians, if only it were obeyed, if only the ordinances he decreed were carried out. He decreed that no Spanish citizens[211]— no *encomenderos* of Indians—should enter the Indians' pueblos, nor should any other Spaniards, mestizos, mulattos, or blacks. Rather, they should go live in their own cities. If they were married to Indian women, they should take the women with them. They should not live [in Indian pueblos] as overseers. This was to avoid causing harm and damage among the Indians, for [outsiders] would cause uprisings and spread their bad vices. The Spaniards would take on mistresses and give rise to a cursed line of mestizos. The Indians of this kingdom would not multiply. [The mestizo sons] would take wives and daughters by force; they would learn to be scoundrels; they would refuse to obey their noble lords, and would become idlers, thieves, *yanaconas,* and *bachilleres,*[212] and the women would become tremendous whores. They would pick up other distasteful habits and bad works, too.

Let it be understood: these are the things that would happen if many Spaniards were to live in the Indians' pueblos. As time went on, they would do great harm to His Majesty, because they would press him in the same way that the conquerors rebelled against the royal crown—Don Francisco Pizarro, Don Diego de Almagro (the elder and the younger alike), Gonzalo Pizarro, Francisco Hernández Girón, the old Carreño, and the other captains and soldiers. For the Indians have never rebelled, from the time of the conquest up until today, nor has any rumor of revolt been heard. They have been faithful, just as they kept faith with and were faithful towards the Incas in the old days. They were every bit as faithful towards the emperor-king Don Carlos of glorious memory, and towards our lord Don Philip II who is now in glory, and likewise towards His Sacred Majesty Don Philip III. We

---

[211] Citizen (*vecino*): see Glossary.

[212] *Bachilleres,* men with bachelor degrees, often priests; the word also had the connotation of "fast talker, windbag." Guaman Poma complains elsewhere about priests who falsely claim to have degrees.

Indians of this kingdom are faithful. We have given our faith to the crown ever since the conquest, and we have ratified it over and over. The Indians of this kingdom are faithful.

**Don Francisco de Toledo decreed** in his ordinances that no *corregidores, doctrina* priests, *encomenderos,* nor any Spaniards should employ the poor Indians in any type of labor. Instead, the Indians should work on their own estates, and pay the tribute that they are obliged to give. Young Indian men, old men and women past tributary age, widows, unmarried women, orphans, and catechism boys should work in their own fields and help increase their community treasuries (*sapsi*). But the *corregidores, doctrina* priests, and *encomenderos* should live from their salaries, and should engage in no commerce or contracts in this kingdom.

**Don Francisco de Toledo affirmed** the ordinances that he had excerpted and approved from among those of the ancient Indians (the *Wari Wiracocha Runa,* the *Wari Runa,* the *Purun Runa,* and the *Auca Pacha Runa,* and the *Incap Runa*)—the good laws that the Incas had upheld. The Inca had decreed that these same good laws be followed throughout the kingdom, though he added idolatrous matters and ceremonies such as the worship of idols (*wacas*).

Thus, Don Francisco de Toledo decreed that the Indians should follow their custom of eating together in the public plaza and celebrating there as well.[213] He also ordered [that the Indian pueblos appoint] justices of the peace, local magistrates, chief constables and minor constables, and town criers; executioners, jailers, field justices, and attorneys; *fiscales,* sextons, cantors, and master cantors.[214]

◆ **The first justices** of the peace were not obeyed or respected by the Indians, who called them *michoc Quilliscachi* [judges from the Quilliscachi Inca *ayllu*].[215] It is said that if two justices of the peace quarreled, the town

[213] Murra and Adorno (ms. p. 58, n. 2), citing Garcilaso de la Vega *(Los comentarios reales* [1609], book V, chapter xi), note that "every ten days, when the cycle of the Andean week came to an end, the ethnic lords would offer a meal to the people" in an act of "reciprocity and redistribution." Guaman Poma comments more than once on the old custom of providing public meals to all the members of the society, which he calls "an ancient law of God and holy good work of mercy" (ms. pp. 912–13).

[214] In Spanish, these are *alcalde, regidor, alguacil mayor y menor, pregonero, verdugo, alcaide y alcalde de campo, procurador, fiscal, sacristán, cantor,* and *maestro.* This list of the principal public offices for Indian officials under colonial rule parallels the list given in the "ordinances of the Inca," pp. 57–68. The first four offices formed the civil hierarchy, the next four made up the criminal justice system, and the final four formed the religious hierarchy of a colonial Indian pueblo.

[215] Guaman Poma states in the "ordinances of the Inca" that members of the Quilliscachi *ayllu* were promoted under Inca rule to serve as local magistrates, and he elsewhere mentions their reputation as "gossips and liars" (see footnotes 71 and 88).

crier would arrest them, give them a whipping at the public whipping post, and make them carry his chair and do other mean tasks. The greenhorns [*chapetones,* recently arrived Spaniards] would mock these justices and magistrates.

I shall explain why such things happened: it was because young and less respected men were named to be the justices of the peace, while old, honored men were named to be the town criers. The law of obedience that people followed was to obey old men, not youths. That was why they would rather obey an old man than a young man. What a fine law of God in this world! Therefore, they feared the honored old men as they would their own fathers and mothers—this is one of God's Ten Commandments, which the Indians kept in this kingdom without even realizing it.

◆ **In the time** of Don Francisco de Toledo—from the time of the Incas, through the time of emperor Don Carlos, up to the time of Don Francisco de Toledo—there were charitable people and humble Christians among both Spaniards and Indians—people who obeyed their fathers, mothers, king, prelates, justices, and nobles. There were no Dons or Doñas, and there was no world turned upside-down. Likewise, clothes from Castile and local clothing, as well as cattle and food, were worth nothing in those days.[216]

[Today,] greengrocers, shoemakers, tailors, and potters call themselves Dons and Doñas, licentiates, doctors, and everything imaginable. These are bad people, ungrateful to God and the king; why does the king allow them their freedom? A Jew, a Moor, a common laborer can beat his local lord, noble, or magistrate. [This is the same thing as] disobeying his father and mother in this life.

CAPTAIN MARTÍN García de Loyola went to conquer Topa Amaro Inca under orders from viceroy Don Francisco de Toledo, as his captain of the guard.[217] He caught Topa Amaro Inca and his captains, Cura Paucar, Mana Cutana, Atoc, Waca Mayta, and Rumi Sonco, together with other captains, *auquicunas,* and *ñustacunas,* and all the *mamacunas.* He led them captive to Cusco.

**He led Topa Amaro Inca** captive as the young crowned king (*inca*), the king and lord of this kingdom. Captain Martín García de Loyola led him

---

[216] That is, in the early conquest period, the Spaniards were generous in giving away clothing, food, and cattle in acts that were understood as traditional Andean reciprocity; in later years, these commodities came to represent wealth, which became the new standard of nobility. (I have transposed this sentence and the following for better sense.)

[217] The final campaign against Vilcabamba was launched in the spring of 1572 and returned to Cusco, with Topa Amaro and other leading Incas as captives, in September of that year. Topa Amaro was executed after a three-day show trial on September 24, 1572.

Captain García de Loyola leading him captive.

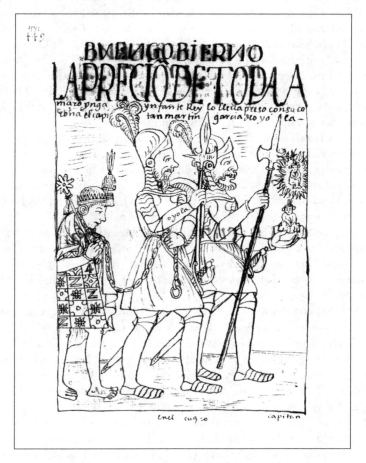

[Loyola leads the captive Inca while another Spaniard carries
his captured *wacas*.]

## In Cusco.

barefoot, his hands cuffed and his neck yoked to a golden chain. The other captain walked in front, carrying his sun god of pure gold and his idol of Wanacauri, along with all his arms, his captains, and the [royal] boys (*auquicunas*) and girls (*ñustacunas*). They forced them to walk down the street of citizen Diego de Silva, in whose house Don Francisco de Toledo was staying. [Toledo] peered out a window and saw everything: they were holding Topa Amaro Inca, Don Carlos Paullo Topa Inca, Don Alonso Atauchi, and all the other Incas of the city of Cusco captive.

◆ **Don Sebastián de Lartaun,** bishop of the city of Cusco,[218] knelt before viceroy Don Francisco de Toledo and begged for the life of Topa Amaro Inca. All the priests, canons, conquerors, citizens, and noble Indians of this kingdom begged alongside him. They even offered to give His Majesty large quantities of silver for the Inca's life. But there was no remedy, not even when the noblewomen of Cusco joined in.

◆ **Don Francisco de Toledo** was deeply angered by Topa Amaro, because he had been informed what the Inca had said. [The Inca] was only a boy, but he was quite right: when [Toledo] had called for him to come, he had said that an Inca, such as he, had no desire to meet with a steward. This caused such hatred in Toledo that, in his anger, he sentenced the Inca to death; he sentenced Topa Amaro Inca to be beheaded.

Oh, proud Christian! You have caused His Majesty's treasury to lose the millions that the city would have given, the hidden treasures of the Inca's ancestors! How many mines and riches has His Majesty lost simply because Don Francisco Toledo wanted to make himself into a lord and king! Do not be like him!

TOPA AMARO INCA WAS BEHEADED in accordance with the sentence handed down by Don Francisco de Toledo. He passed this sentence on the child king *(Inca)*, who died a baptized Christian, at the age of fifteen.[219]

His death was bewailed by all the ladies, nobles, and Indians in this kingdom. The whole city was filled with lamentation, and all the church bells tolled. All the noblemen, ladies, noble Indians, and clerics attended his burial; they accompanied him as he was buried in the principal church of the city of Cusco. Then Don Francisco de Toledo ceased [to rage].

**Before he was beheaded,** Topa Amaro Inca requested an appeal of his sentence, that he be granted life. He said he would be His Majesty's slave, or would give many millions in gold and silver—the hidden treasures of his

---

[218] Lartaun was bishop of Cusco from 1571 to 1583. Murra and Adorno note (ms. p. 452, n. 1) that Garcilaso, Murúa, and other later chroniclers relate similar stories of other clergymen (not Lartaun) begging Toledo to spare Topa Amaro's life.

[219] As the son of Manco Inca (1516–1544), and not, as Guaman Poma writes, his grandson, Topa Amaro must have been at least twenty-eight years old in 1572.

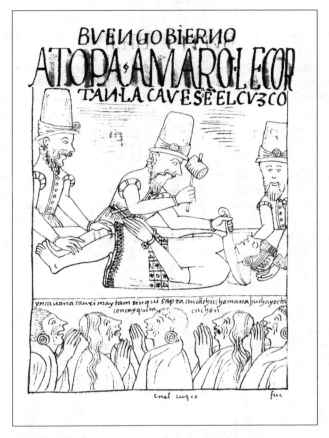

"*Inca Wanacauri,*[220] *maytam rinqui? Sapra aucanchiccho mana hucha- yocta concayquita cuchon?*" [Inca Wanacauri, where are you going? Is our wicked enemy cutting your blameless neck?]

### In Cusco.

---

[220] Guaman Poma explains this term (ms. p. 183): "They called the legitimate one *Inca Wanacauri*, which means *king.*" By using this title, he implies here, the people of Cusco were declaring Topa Amaro to be their legitimate ruler.

ancestors—or would show them where there were many mines and riches, and he said that he would serve for the rest of his life. But there was no remedy. He was sentenced; the royal child Topa Amaro Inca was executed, his head cut off. See here, Christian, the pride of Don Francisco de Toledo, which, beyond [breaking] the law, caused such losses in the service of God and His Majesty.

How could a king, a prince, a duke, a count, a marquis, or even a gentleman be sentenced to death by his own servant, a poor gentleman? The only name for this is rising up and yearning to be higher than the king. The only person who has the power to hear the cases of gentleman such as these and to pass sentence on them is the king himself. Not even his viceroy or his royal Audiencia can hear such cases. Rather, these cases must be passed to his own hands, so that, as the powerful lord, he might pardon or sentence his greatest vassal in the whole world. That is the law.

♦ **After Don Francisco de Toledo** had congregated, inspected, and settled the entire kingdom, he ordered a general inspection tour of its tributary Indians. The inspectors—Jerónimo de Silva, Rodrigo de Cantos, and the other general inspectors—were to inspect each province throughout the kingdom, just as they had in the first general inspection tour under Damián de la Bandera.[221] When the provinces were inspected, the nobles of these kingdoms hid their sons and grandsons, while the absent Indians[222]—very large numbers of them in each Indian pueblo—went uninspected. Each of them should have been inscribed as taxpayers to His Majesty, but they turned poor tributary Indians into noble *caciques*. In this way, the land has come to be destroyed and scorned, and His Majesty has lost his treasury.

*[Guaman Poma follows this criticism of Toledo's 1571 general inspection of Peru with his own proposal for a properly run inspection: he suggests reforming Spanish colonial rule by reinstating native Andean rulers. The king of Spain would rule in place of the Inca, having inherited his crown. A few selected Spanish officials would continue to serve in a bureaucratic function, but would have to subsist on their salaries, would have no access to Indian servants (either paid or forced), and would serve under the native Andean lords. Rules of succession*

[221] Jerónimo de Silva, a major *encomendero* in the Lima area who had conducted inspection tours (*visitas*) under Audiencia President Gasca in 1549 and General Inspector Bandera in 1557, inspected Jauja in 1571. Rodrigo Canto inspected Pachacamac in 1573.

[222] Absent Indians (*indios ausentes*): large numbers of tributary Indians left their home pueblos and wandered to other jurisdictions in colonial Peru in order to escape paying tribute, which was imposed only on Indians who were resident in their own pueblos. This was one of the ways in which the colonial tribute system exacerbated the social dislocations of post-conquest society.

*would be created to penalize Andean women rulers who married outside of the native nobility, because (according to Guaman Pomás expressed view) lineage flows from the man, not the woman. This view actually contradicts what we know of pre-conquest Andean society, which had been characterized by gender parallelism and separate lines of descent for women and men. Guaman Pomás proposal also envisions a slight Europeanization of the traditional Andean system of dual rulership: instead of two male co-rulers (the Capac Inca and his designated heir) and parallel female rulers (the Coyas), there would be one primary and one subordinate male ruler. In other ways, however, his "inspection tour" is an idealized portrait of pre-conquest Andean rulership.]*

THE GENERAL INSPECTION TOUR of the tributary Indians of this kingdom, composed by Don Felipe de Ayala, prince, the author of this chronicle, based on the ancient inspection tours of this kingdom as decreed by his ancestors Topa Inca Yupanqui, former king of this kingdom, and his grandfather *capac apo* Waman Chawa of the Yaro Willca–Allauca Wanaco lineage, the viceroy and second-in-command to the Inca, the most excellent lord of this kingdom.

The general inspection tour: *auca camayoc, puric wayna* (tributaries), *macho llucsic, uncoc, wañoc, sipas, iquima, tasque, waccha, casarasca.*[223]

♦ **The general inspectors,** or re-inspectors, of the tributary Indians should be cautioned to keep within the bounds of this order, by God's right and by the law and justice of this kingdom. If an inspector should infringe it, he shall be punished and his report nullified, in accordance with justice and the law.

To the natural lords,[224] proprietors, nobles (*curacas*), and petty authorities of each province and pueblo in this kingdom, their king and lord was *capac apo* Topa Inca Yupanqui, the son of the sun. His seat (called a *tiana*) was made of purest gold, and was a whole cubit high. He was the king (*Inca*) throughout this kingdom. Today, his title has passed on:

---

[223] A list of some of the census categories to be used in the inspection.

[224] Natural lords (*señores naturales*): here Guaman Poma bolsters his argument in favor of the Andean rulers by using a term from Aristotelian and Thomist natural law doctrine. Las Casas and other Spanish "defenders of the Indians" based their arguments on the principle that all people should be able to keep their own property and be ruled by their own laws, and that the "natural lords" of all territories should be secure in their rulership, so long as they have not waged wars of aggression against a "Christian lord." Viceroy Toledo countered with the argument that the Andean *curacas* were mere appointees of the tyrannical Incas, and therefore did not deserve the title of "natural lords." Guaman Poma prefers to defend the Andean rulers by emphasizing their "Christian" qualities, but here (and at only two other points in ms. pp. 573 and 917) he draws on natural law rhetoric in a calculated response to Toledo.

**In his place is our lord, His Sacred Catholic Majesty** king Don Philip III of Spain.

Throughout this kingdom, the Inca's second-in-command (*capac*) was *capac apo* Waman Chawa of the Yaro Willca–Allauca Wanoco *ayllu*. This most excellent lord had a *tiana* of the purest silver, a full cubit in height; he was the great lord of this kingdom.

Then came *apo* Waman Poma (*capac apo* Waman Chawa's younger brother), who was the lord of the *Chinchaysuyus,* rather like a duke. His *tiana* was made of tin, and was less than a cubit high. The same was true of *apo* Ninarua, *apo* Castilla Pari, and *apo* Mullo. These men are the only ones who should be called *capac apo* or *apo;* no one else should be given these titles.[225]

Even though the Incas did not directly descend from the *Wari Wiracocha,* the *Wari Runa,* the *Purun Runa,* or the *Auca Runa,* it was sufficient that they (my uncles, the Incas) had conquered this kingdom and had ruled it for 1,500 years.

This concludes the inspection of the kings.

A **wamanin apo** had a painted wooden *tiana,* one cubit high. *Wamanin* means "province" or "district." These lords are nobles; today there is only one [in each province].

**The lords called** *hunu apo* [lords of a myriad] serve today as seconds-in-command [to the *wamanin apo*]. In the time of the Incas, they were called *hunu auca camayoc* [masters of a myriad soldiers], and if the number of tributaries under one of them did not amount to one hundred thousand, he was not allowed to keep his title, his *tiana,* or his position as lord. They had plain wooden *tianas,* half a cubit high, and both the primary *caciques* and these seconds-in-command in each provinces had the fronts of their *tianas* painted.

There shall not be more than one second-in-command and one head lord [in each province]. There shall not be more than one, whether he is a legitimate heir, a natural son, or a bastard.[226] If there is no legitimate heir, may the natural son rule; if there is no natural heir, the bastard son shall govern.

---

[225] In other words, Guaman Poma argues, Peru should have a dual emperor: the king of Spain, who inherited the Inca imperial crown, and his "*segunda persona,*" the *capac apo* descendant of Waman Chawa. (He hints elsewhere that he himself deserves this title.) Under these dual rulers there should be the lords (*apo*) of the four sectors (*suyu*) of the empire. Ninarua, Castilla Pari, and Mullo were the hereditary lords of Andesuyu, Collasuyu, and Condesuyu, respectively. Guaman Poma mentions all three names in connection with Inca era rulers (ms. pp. 77 and 170), and later mentions Don Cristóbal Castilla Pari, Don Juan Mullo, Don Diego Mullo, and Don Pedro Ninarua as *caciques* under Spanish rule (ms. pp. 564 and 1089).

[226] See footnote 10 on the Spanish legal terms "legitimate," "natural," and "bastard."

If the governorship has passed to a legitimate daughter, a natural daughter, or a bastard daughter, then a noble or a petty tribute–paying authority shall govern, but he shall not neglect to pay his tribute and personal service.

Even if every Indian in a province dies, and there is not one Indian left, as long as one lord remains as the head and the other as the foot, they are still the lords over their lands, and they are lords over every Spaniard and black who might live in their territory. Since this right belongs to these lords by blood, lineage, and law, according to God and his law no one can take it away from them.

This is true even if it is an [unmarried] woman who inherits the right. If she [later] marries a noble Indian, her line and lordship become higher, and she deserves more honor. For it is the man who makes the lineage, not the woman. But if a woman, daughter, or sister, having become the lady of a great titled house, marries a tributary Indian (*mitayo*), she likewise becomes a tributary Indian woman of low estate like her husband. She will not pass her rights on to her children, according to justice. If she marries a black man (whether slave or free) who has received God's curse, she becomes a slave and a black woman like her husband. But he will have to take everything with him, including her lost honor. Any [non-Indian] man who marries an Indian woman—even if he is a black, a Jew, or a Moor—will have to take her to the cities and live there. If both the man and the woman belong to a noble [Andean] lineage, he will govern and be the lord in [her province]: he will gain the honor, merit, faculties, and preeminence that God gave her. If she marries a low-class Indian, she loses her merit and honor.[227]

The same is true among Spaniards. A marriage between a *mitayo* [tributary] Indian man and a *mitayo* Indian woman is pure, just like a marriage between a Jewish or Moorish man and a Jewish or Moorish woman. If both he and she are nobles, then the legitimate child of their marriage will be a son of God, and if it were possible, he should sit on a golden *tiana,* by God's right and by justice in this kingdom.

♦ **The noble *caciques*** and seconds-in-command are under the rule of the Inca (today, the king and prince of this kingdom), of the *capac apo* (most excellent lord), and of the lords (*apo*), as outlined above. These *caciques,* down to the level of the *chunca* and *pisca camachicoc* [authorities over ten and five households], are in charge of their jurisdictions. By law, no Spaniards—who are foreigners in this kingdom—should be resident in the *caciques'* jurisdictions, or take actual, bodily possession of them; this is especially true of new arrivals. A native, no matter from where, would be

---

[227] The sentences in this paragraph have been rearranged for the sake of clarity. The reference to "God's curse" apparently alludes to the racist interpretation of the curse on the descendants of Ham (Genesis 9: 20–27) as applying to Africans.

better than someone from Castile. [These *caciques*] may be called lords of the kingdom and proprietors of the Indies.

Therefore, anyone who enters one of these lords' jurisdictions, whether he be a Spaniard, a gentleman, an *hidalgo,* an *encomendero,* or a mestizo, a mulatto, a black, a slave, or an Indian who has recently arrived in that province, is the lord's subject and must obey him. The *cacique* is the natural lord there, because he is in the jurisdiction that was given to him by God, the king, and the laws of these kingdoms. If one of those people does not wish to become his subject, he is welcome to leave the jurisdiction. [But if the foreigner stays,] he must obey and serve, even if he has been decorated by His Majesty, because no one has revoked, or could revoke, the *cacique's* lordship, by God's law, which His Majesty the emperor Don Carlos confirmed and gave to the noble Indians of this kingdom.

*[Guaman Poma's model inspection continues (ms. pp. 457–59) with instructions for distinguishing between the hierarchical levels of native lordship, the kinds of thrones* (tiana) *each deserves, and how each should be compensated with a combination of cropland, cattle, personal service by their tributaries, and a royal salary. He then addresses the compensation due to Spanish colonial officials, proposes that they be overseen by an Indian official such as himself, and objects to the colonial term "tributary Indian."]*

**Overseeing [these local authorities],** the *corregidor* should have a salary. The priests and *encomenderos* likewise should be given salaries and nothing else; they should not enter among the Indians or have dealings with them, and they should employ no Indian man or woman in this kingdom.

**Overseeing all of them** shall be the administrator-protector and general deputy of each province[228] in this kingdom. He shall oversee each of these officials, in order to defend the commons (*sapsi*) and the poor Indians. His salary should be set at one seventh of [the produce of] the commons (*sapsi*) throughout this kingdom.

**Each married tributary** Indian should be inspected, together with his *chacra* [fields] and cattle. Then inspect the unmarried Indian men who pay half tribute—but do not say "tribute"; they should be called "tax-payers,"[229] for saying "tribute" implies that they are slaves—followed by adolescent boys, young boys, old men past [tributary age], sick men, old

---

[228] Guaman Poma elsewhere gives himself the title of "administrator-protector and deputy *corregidor* of the province of Lucanas" (ms. p. 369). In this paragraph, he proposes a reversal of colonial practice by placing Indian provincial officials over the heads of Spanish *corregidores, encomenderos,* and priests.

[229] Tax-payers: *pecheros,* the term for Spanish commoners. See Glossary.

women, unmarried women, adolescent girls, and young girls. This is the order in which they should be inspected in this kingdom, by law.

It would be very proper, would serve God and His Majesty, and would be good for public order, if His Majesty were to set up royal colleges for the sons of nobles, for blacks, and colleges for Indian commoners throughout the kingdom, so that Christianity and faith in God might advance in the world, and service to the royal crown might increase in the world.[230]

*[An illustration, ms. p. 460, depicts Toledo slumped forward in a Castilian armchair. The headline reads, "Don Francisco de Toledo died intestate in Castile, of vexation, because His Majesty did not grant him an audience."]*

DON FRANCISCO DE TOLEDO, viceroy, having completed all his business here in the kingdom of the Indians, returned to Castile. He hoped to enter [the palace] and kiss the hands of His Majesty king Don Philip II, but the gentleman-in-waiting paid him no attention; he did not allow him to enter. Facing this vexation, he went home, refused to eat, and sat down in a chair. While sitting there, he died intestate and took leave of this life. His life came to an end while he was wracked with sorrow at not seeing the face of his lord and king.[231]

In the harm [Toledo] did in this kingdom—to the Inca, to the Indian nobles, as well as to the conquerors of this kingdom—you can see, gentlemen, the pride of a poor underling. He yearned to rise up, and he did so, killing the king and lord of this kingdom, when the only one who should hear such a case is the king and lord himself; no one else may pass such a sentence and sign the death warrant for another lord and king. Thus, it was pride that killed Don Francisco de Toledo.

*[An illustration, ms. p. 462, depicts a Spaniard in sixteenth-century armor standing shoulder-to-shoulder with an Inca ruler in traditional dress. The heading reads, "Martín Arbieto and Don Tomás Topa Inca began the conquest of the Andesuyus." The caption reads, "In the Andes mountains."]*

MARTÍN [HURTADO DE] ARBIETO, Don Tomás Topa Inca Yupanqui, and Padre Gaspar de Zúñiga began the conquest of the *Andesuyus* and the *Chunchos*.[232] They conquered [the pueblo of] Manari Anti, and [its people]

---

[230] This paragraph is a late addition in the bottom margin.

[231] Toledo returned to Spain in 1581 and died in either 1582 or 1584.

[232] The reasons for telling this coda to the story of viceroy Toledo are, first, to reinforce the idea that Spanish Peru had not expanded beyond the Inca realm of Tawantinsuyu, despite attempts to conquer the "savage" (*chuncho*) mountainous jungles past Cusco; and second, to reintroduce the story of Guaman Poma's saintly half-brother, Martín de

obeyed the Christians, served them, and made peace with them. But after [the Spaniards] had fooled [those people] and made them Christians, they began to pressure them, mistreat them, and demand gold and silver from them. For example, they burned their noble *cacique* and lord (*capac apo*) Tampulla Apo Walpaco. Upon seeing this, all [the people of the pueblo] were enraged; they rose up in rebellion and killed all the Christians.

The author's brother, Padre Martín de Ayala, had entered with them, so that he could die a martyr in the service of God, but he then returned (as has been mentioned) to the hospital of the city of Cusco as a hermit. He brought with him the great blessing of an illness sent to him by God—an illness from the Andes. This saintly man, Padre Martín de Ayala, the hermit, gave thanks to God for this illness. Later he became a priest and said Mass. He died in the hospital of the city of Huamanga.

*[The section on "Good Government" continues with portraits and one-page histories of the next six viceroys of Peru (ms. pp. 464–75), followed by equally brief descriptions of the Spanish religious establishment in Peru (ms. pp. 476–87): the Church hierarchy, friars (Franciscan, Mercedarian, Dominican, and Augustinian), the "Holy Inquisition," Jesuits, hermits (ordinary Spaniards who fled city life for a life of contemplation and serving God), and nuns. Of these, he singles out the nuns, hermits, Franciscans, and Jesuits for praise:*

> *They call all men "brothers" and all women "sisters." They own nothing; they give everything in alms to the poor, like the Franciscan friars. If only the priests, the Dominicans, the Mercedarians, and the Augustinians acted like these padres of the Company of Jesus, who have no desire to return wealthy to Castile nor to build up their estates! Their wealth consists of souls! (ms. p. 483)*

*Perhaps surprisingly to modern readers, he also praises the "charitable and saintly" grand Inquisitor of Peru; this attitude is in character, however, for Indians were exempt from the colonial Inquisition, which targeted only Spaniards and the others (mestizos, mulattos, and blacks) in their social world. He also modestly proposes that a kind of vice-pope be appointed for Peru to rule there in the pope's stead, just as the viceroy rules in place of the Spanish king: "For the good government of God and of the Holy Mother Church, the second-in-command of the pope of Rome should reside in the city and court of Los Reyes de Lima—a cardinal who would oversee all the archbishops, bishops, religious orders, and monasteries in this kingdom" (ms. p. 477). He concludes this*

---

Ayala. I have found no sources for this story and little independent evidence about the events and characters in it. Arbieto led the expedition to capture Topa Amaro. Gaspar de Zúñiga was the name of the tenth viceroy of Peru, but could hardly be the padre mentioned here. If Don Tomás Topa Inca Yupanqui existed, he was presumably a Christianized descendant of the Inca royal family who had joined forces with the Spanish.

# The President and Magistrates of His Majesty's Audiencia and the Justices of the Royal Court, the Prosecutor, and the Chief Constable of This Kingdom.

[Postscript:] For good government, there should also be a learned advocate, two defenders [of the Indians] who shall share a salary, two attorneys, an interpreter, and another person fluent in the [Quechua] language who can draw up memoranda for the use of the advocate, the defenders, and [. . .] petitions, nor [. . .]

*The royal audiencia.*

*section with the following description of the Audiencia of Lima, the ruling body of colonial Peru.]*

AFTER HAVING COMPLETED their terms in office, none of these most Christian governors has ever been found to have favored the Indians.[233] Instead, they have all come to add more burdens on the Indians and to favor the citizens, the wealthy, and the mine owners. Not one of them, it seems, has written or reported on the harsh labor and misfortunes of the poor Indians. Yet the nobles are leading wretched lives, a great many Indians are dying in this kingdom, and the Indians are slowly disappearing. A new governor arrives and squeezes them with taxes and other obligations—he may even demand taxes for the church in Cusco. Then another governor comes and squeezes more, with forced labor for the *corregidores.* Then another comes and squeezes by sending the Indians to work in the mines, where they die. Then others come to favor the priests and the *doctrina* padres—through those kinds of favors, they destroy the Indians and expel them from their pueblos. Yet none of them write to His Holiness or to His Majesty about these things so that they might find a remedy. Every day brings more harm. Even the friars take away the Indians' estates and move into their houses and *chacras* (farms).

Not one president or magistrate of His Majesty's Audiencia has written to His Majesty, nor have the archbishop, the bishops, the prelates of the religious orders, the priests, or the padres of the Company of Jesus. Instead, even they force their way onto the Indians lands and *chacras.* There is no one who will stand up for the poor of Jesus Christ, unless He returns and comes back to the world to stand up for the poor. In that way the Indians will be favored, after all the harms and evils they have suffered in this kingdom, for everything has gone against the poor Indians. These people are sent from Castile to favor and help [the Indians], but instead they harm them when they arrive in this kingdom.

**For good government,** the most excellent viceroys should govern for a term of twelve years in this kingdom. They should also get to know the land, every city and province in it, and all the *corregidores,* the *encomenderos,* the padres and priests of *doctrinas,* and the citizens of its cities, for good government, justice, the punishing of bad deeds and the rewarding of

---

[233] The illustration of the Audiencia of Lima—the highest legislative, executive, and judicial body in colonial Peru—is not followed by the expected description of the Audiencia, but by a generalized complaint about the viceroys of Peru and the state of the Spanish colonial administration, which fails in every respect to live up to the promises of "good government." This indictment signals a transition from the chronicle format to the remainder of the book, in which Guaman Poma systematically critiques colonial society.

good Christians. As a servant of God and His Majesty, he should favor the poor. He should treat the gentlemen of this kingdom as gentlemen, the taxpaying commoners as taxpaying commoners, the natives as natives, and the foreigners as foreigners.

## PROLOGUE TO THE READER OF "HIS HOLINESS AND HIS MAJESTY" THAT YOU MIGHT SEE ALL THE THINGS THAT ARE DONE IN THE SERVICE OF GOD, THE HOLY MOTHER CHURCH, HIS HOLINESS, AND HIS MAJESTY

THE PURPOSE OF GOOD justice, public order, and Christianity in your kingdom of Peru in the Indies is to give relief and aid, for the sake of our Christianity, in the service of God, his blessed mother St. Mary, and all the saints and angels who are in Glory; and to preserve our holy Catholic faith, the Church of our holy father the pope of Rome, our lord and Catholic king, Don Philip III of glorious memory, and the state, life, and growth of many kingdoms and empires throughout the whole world. May this be in his royal service. God grant he enjoy this [book], for his holy service.

Here end the chapters on the conquest and on the good justice and good government that have been established in this kingdom, with all their Christianity. Yet the poor Indians are still persecuted and harassed, and have not found His Majesty's favor. Nor will there be a remedy for them, until His Majesty sends someone to remedy their troubles: this kingdom awaits him.

*492*

# THE PROVINCIAL *CORREGIDOR* OF THIS KINGDOM, AND HIS NOTARY[234]—CHAPTER ONE.

[The notary is writing:] "Don Diego de Avendano[235]

*In the provinces.*

[234] Notary, or scribe (*escribano*): a key functionary in the justice system of Spain and its empire. The notary's position in the Spanish legal system was lower than a lawyer's but much greater than that of a notary in the U.S. system. Notaries drew up legal documents, presented cases in court, kept records of wills and property deeds, and wrote the official records of magistrates such as the *corregidor*.

[235] The detail in the face and figure of the foppishly dressed *corregidor* makes one suspect this is an actual portrait. Don Diego de Avendaño may have been a descendent of Pedro de Avendaño, an *encomendero* of the *Lucanos Laramati* people in 1557 (see Steve Stern, *Peru's Indian Peoples and the Challenge of Spanish Conquest: Huamanga to 1640* [Madison, Wis.: University of Wisconsin Press, 1982], 31). He may also be the unnamed *corregidor* of the province of the Lucanas who is the villain in Guaman Poma's story of the heroic Indian noble Don Cristóbal de León a, pp. 171–73.

# PART 7.
## CONQUEST SOCIETY IN THE ANDES

*[This long section is a sustained critique of Spanish society in early seventeenth-century Peru. Guaman Poma begins by criticizing every level of the Spanish civil government in the provincial countryside, from high (the* corregidores *or provincial governors) to low (the deputy* corregidores, *local judges, and notaries). He continues with the key occupational groups and social types of Spaniards seen in the countryside: mine owners; the stewards* (mayordomos) *of Spanish estates and mines; merchants, travelers, and vagabonds. Religious figures come next:* encomenderos *(powerful Spaniards, placed here in the text because their claim over Indian lives and labor came from their promise to care for Indian souls), priests of Indian parishes, Indian lay religious leaders, and inspectors sent to the countryside by the bishop. A brief "history of the blacks" and a set of satirical dialogues and impassioned conclusions close out this part. Guaman Poma's aim throughout is to denounce the pervasive abuse and corruption of Spanish rule, while highlighting the rare cases of Spaniards who act justly, favor the poor, and refuse to meddle in Indian affairs.]*

## HISTORY OF THE *CORREGIDORES* OF THIS KINGDOM AND THEIR LIVES

491–528, selections

*[First, "The* Corregidores." *Outside of the capital Audiencia cities such as Lima and Quito, each province in Spanish America was governed by a magistrate called a* corregidor *(or, in some later provinces, an alcalde mayor). Like the viceroy himself, the* corregidor *was both judge and executive authority; his decisions could only be appealed to the Audiencia and the viceroy. A* corregidor *typically underwent a formal investigation and audit* (residencia) *at the end of his term, but until the* residencia *came, he had almost completely free rein to make money from his office in whatever way he saw fit. The scope of possible abuse made the* corregidor *the most visible target of village discontent and uprisings in colonial times.]*

◆ **THEY LIVE AS** absolute rulers with little fear of justice or of God, throughout the kingdom. One of them will extract thirty thousand pesos from a *corregimiento* and become rich before he leaves, harming the poor Indians and the nobles, scorning them, and taking away their offices and duties, in this kingdom.

**SINCE THE TIME** when these *corregidores* were created by decree of Don Francisco de Toledo [viceroy, 1569–1581], they have caused terrible damage to these kingdoms of Peru. By the time they finish their terms and leave their *corregimientos,* they amass fortunes of more than fifty thousand pesos, at the cost, and to the detriment, of the poor Indians throughout this kingdom. And there is no remedy: in this way, the Indians are coming to an end.

◆ **The *corregidores,*** claiming to defend the poor Indians of this kingdom from the damage done by the padres, the *doctrina* priests, the *encomenderos,* and the other Spaniards such as stewards, travelers, and judges in this kingdom, take and steal everything for themselves, without giving anything to the Indians.

◆ **The *corregidores*** get involved in commerce and trade and many other things, and for these purposes they take money from the community treasuries and the tribute collections, or they borrow money from the village priests. The noble *caciques* do not defend against this, because the *corregidores* befriend them and make them their *compadres;* the padres and the *corregidores* then praise them: "Oh, Don Pedro! What a good noble *cacique* you are!" They are friends in this kingdom. Other nobles are afraid that the *corregidor* will mistreat them, or will take away the ruling offices that God and His Majesty gave them, or will accuse them with false information, and so they keep quiet about what goes on and pretend not to notice.

◆ **The *corregidores,*** *doctrina* priests, *encomenderos,* stewards, and other Spaniards who go about among the Indians, all act as absolute lords with little fear of God and justice. They do terrible harm and damage to the poor nobles and Indians of this kingdom.

◆ **The *corregidores*** make money by robbing the poor Indians. Because they have favor at court and in the Audiencia, they can punish and destroy the poor Indians in the provinces, who must keep quiet.

◆ **The *corregidores*** who are honorable and Christian, and who fear God and His Majesty, earn their salary cleanly and are satisfied with it. They do not get into trouble by having too many friends, and they have no enemies. If there are no charges against them, their enemies have to keep quiet. Their purses fill with reales, they give good accounts of themselves to the Audiencia, and they deserve new assignments as *corregidores.*

◆ **Most *corregidores*** end up being harried with audits at the end of their terms, with debts, liabilities, and tremendous complaints, with large numbers of enemies, expenses, trials, and lawsuits. Petitions rain down on their heads. By the time they leave their *corregimientos,* they are naked and poor, because they are gambling, whoring, swaggering friends of the padres, priests, and *encomenderos.* They put on many banquets and invite all the Spaniards; they hire twenty deputy *corregidores.* But they are enemies of the noble *caciques* and the poor Indians, consuming the sweat of their brows and their labor. They are enemies of the poor. Yet God punishes the proud: He turned Luzbel into Lucifer, the prince of darkness.

*[Guaman Poma's indictment of the* corregidores *continues in the same vein for several pages. He accuses them of collaborating with* encomenderos, doctrina *priests, and the false* caciques *they hand-pick to replace true Andean nobles. These men plot to engage in commerce in Indian communities (breaking several royal decrees), to circumvent the laws decreed by the viceroy and the Audiencia, to corrupt their auditors, and to "harass the poor Indians and their noble* caciques, *punish them, abuse them, and take away their estates, in this kingdom." An illustration (ms. p. 495) shows a* corregidor *and an* encomendero *standing next to a table overflowing with trays full of reales and "fighting over money—which of them should get to keep more." From ms. p. 497:]*

◆ The *corregidores,* padres, and *encomenderos* despise the *ladino* Indians[236] who know how to read and write, especially if they know how to draw up petitions, because they fear these Indians will demand audits of all the injuries, harms, and damages they have caused. If they can, they banish these Indians from their pueblos in this kingdom.

◆ The *corregidor,* the *encomendero,* the padre, and the noble *cacique* punish and shame poor Indians who are innocent of any guilt or crime, and so the Indians, both men and women, absent themselves throughout the kingdom. Thus, if any Indian men or women should go absent through the fault of a *corregidor,* padre, *encomendero,* or noble *cacique,* [that official] should not be given the salary that he is usually paid in money and in kind, nor should he be served, and he should be charged. The Indian men and women should be counted every year or every other year, throughout this kingdom of Peru, and thus no Indian will go absent.

DON CRISTÓBAL DE León was harassed by the *corregidor* of the province of the Lucanas. This same Don Cristóbal, the son of Don García Mullo Wamani, second-in-command to Don Diego Luca of the Oma Pacha *ayllu* in the pueblo of San Pedro de Queca, was a disciple of the author of this book, who has had many other disciples, all of them nobles who became Christians, *ladino* [fluent in Spanish], and fond of defending the poor.[237]

---

[236] *Indios ladinos:* Indians who had become fluent in Spanish in addition to their own languages. See Rolena Adorno, "Images of *Indios Ladinos* in Early Colonial Peru," in Kenneth Andrien and Rolena Adorno, eds., *Transatlantic Encounters: Europeans and Andeans in the Sixteenth Century* (Berkeley: University of California Press, 1991), 232–70, and "The Indigenous Ethnographer: The *'Indio Ladino'* as Historian and Cultural Mediation," in Stuart Schwartz, ed., *Implicit Understandings: Observing, Reporting, and Reflecting on the Encounters between Europeans and Other Peoples in the Early Modern Era* (Cambridge: Cambridge University Press, 1994), 378–402.

[237] According to Murra and Adorno (ms. p. 499, n. 1 and n. 2), Don García Mullo Wamani and the three nobles mentioned at the end of the paragraph are all named in the 1586 report (*relación geográfica*) on the district of the Lucanas Andamarcas. Queca is about a mile from Guaman Poma's hometown of Chipao, Lucanas, and Guaman Poma returns to the case of Don Cristóbal several times in this book.

# THE *CORREGIDOR* IMPRISONS AND ABUSES DON CRISTÓBAL DE LEÓN, SECOND-IN-COMMAND, FOR DEFENDING THE INDIANS OF HIS PROVINCE.

[*Corregidor:*]
"*Warcuscayqui
galera-man
carcoscayqui.*
[I'll hang you,
I'll send you to
the galleys.]"

[Don Cristóbal:]
"*Runarayco cay
sepo-pi ñacarisac.*
[For my people
I shall suffer in
these stocks.]"

*In the provinces.*

This Indian turned out full of skill and spirit; even though the padres, priests, *corregidores,* and *encomenderos* persecuted him, Don Cristóbal de León defended himself. All his labor has been to defend the Indians, because he has refused to send Indians to convey wine from the plains to Cusco, nor has he consented to use the Indians in *rescates* [forced trading] as readily as those asses, Don Fernando Caquiamarca, Don Diego Luca, Don Juan Pillcone, and the other Lucanas and Soras. All of them, including their wives and daughters, spin yarn and weave cloth for the *corregidor,* and thus they do business with the *corregidor.*

Don Cristóbal went to complain about all this and to demand justice from the viceroy, but the *corregidor* arrested him, punished him, shamed him, and tried to have him banished to the galleys. He kept him imprisoned in the stocks, with shackles on his feet and handcuffs on his wrists. He did not let him speak even with his own wife, and he constantly threatened him and wrote lies about him to His Excellency, simply to take revenge on Don Cristóbal de León. He said that he would have him banished to the galley or would hang him.

Therefore, to avoid suffering such troubles, other nobles prefer not to defend the Indians from all their misfortunes. If this Indian were not a drunkard, he would be as good as any Spaniard in skills, spirit, and Christianity—he has so much brotherhood and public order, and he is so eager for his subjects to become rich. That was why he defended them from the *corregidor,* the padre, the *encomendero,* and the other Spaniards, deputy *corregidores,* and other thieves.

**ANOTHER *CORREGIDOR*** harassed Don Cristóbal and arrested him for refusing to give him Indians for transporting goods, spinning yarn, weaving cloth, and other kinds of commerce. To keep Don Cristóbal from complaining or sending messages, the *corregidor* kept him imprisoned day and night in stocks and shackles in his own bedroom, behind his bed canopy, so that he could not speak with anyone. Ass of a *corregidor!* That was how his predecessor, the former *corregidor,* had come out poor, in debt, and prosecuted. This *corregidor* and his wife did well because they were discreet. But it was his wife who governed; she did not allow him to harm any living soul, and so he managed to pull through without lawsuits or debts, because his wife knew more than her husband did. His predecessors, the former *corregidor* and his wife, were ruined, along with their notary. Things should be done for good, not for evil.

Fools of *corregidores!* Asses of *caciques!* In this world, God lives, as do his justice and the king. But let me tell Your Majesty: no matter what, Your Majesty should defend the nobles, for so much harm is being done to you by the *corregidores,* padres, *encomenderos,* mine owners, Spanish travelers,

## ANOTHER *CORREGIDOR* HARRASSES DON CRISTÓBAL DE LEÓN, ONCE MORE BECAUSE HE SPOKE UP IN FAVOR OF THE INDIANS.

[Don Cristóbal:] "For the sake of God, I will suffer these troubles."

[The sleeping *corregidor:*] "*Hina wañuy*

[I hope you die there, troublemaker!"]

*In the provinces.*

deputies, judges, church inspectors, stewards, brothers, the children of the padres, and all their servants.

Look at this poor man, Don Cristóbal de León: see how he was harassed and persecuted while they slept, stole, robbed, gambled, and ended up rich. The poor suffer terrible troubles. How many *corregidores,* while still alive, are already in hell? If they are all against the poor Indians of this kingdom, just see how persecuted the *caciques* and poor Indians of this kingdom must be! And there is no remedy.

**Another *corregidor*** and an inspector from the Holy Mother Church finally destroyed and banished poor Don Cristóbal de León in the year 1612. All the *corregidores,* padres, and priests of his pueblo took their revenge on this defender of God and His Majesty. First, they took revenge on charity; they took revenge on works of mercy; they took revenge on the Ten Commandments of God; and they took revenge on the defender of Jesus Christ, so that they could steal and rob from the poor and fornicate with their wives, daughters, and maidens. Because of all his service in favor of the poor of Jesus Christ, they took revenge on Don Cristóbal de León for defending them. And they took revenge on His Majesty, because the Indians belong to his royal crown.

*[A lengthy catalogue of abuses by the* corregidores *and suggested remedies follows. Guaman Poma accuses lascivious priests and* corregidores *of going on night rounds in Indian pueblos as an excuse to break into houses and "lift the women's blankets and look at their shame." He insists that Spanish* corregidores *and Indian justices of the peace ought to be considered equally "lords and justices of His Majesty; neither one has the advantage over the other," so they should treat each other with mutual respect. In actual practice, however, the* corregidores *slight Andean nobles and honor "low-class people" at their dinner tables:]*

♦ **The *corregidores,*** padres, Spaniards, and gentlemen, and the noble *caciques,* even though they are lords with titles passed down from their ancestors, sit at their tables to eat, converse, drink, and gamble with nosy people, scoundrels, highwaymen, thieves, liars, louts, drunks, Jews, and Moors, and with low-class people—*mitayo* Indians. They tell their secrets to them, and hold conversations with these mestizos, mulattos, and blacks. That is why there are so many Dons and Doñas in this life who are as empty as gourds.

*[Guaman Poma argues that, to preserve their honor,* corregidores *should only dine with other* corregidores *and their immediate employees; priests should eat with other priests, Indian nobles with other Indian nobles, and commoners with commoners. He couches part of his argument in terms of the Spanish racist ideology of purity of blood: "If the man is a commoner or a Jew and the woman*

## THE *CORREGIDOR* INVITES LOW-CLASS PEOPLE—*MITAYO* INDIANS, MESTIZOS, MULATTOS—TO EAT AT HIS TABLE.

Mestizo

[*Corregidor*:]" I make a toast to you, señor *curaca*."

Mulatto

[Tributary Indian, dressed as a *curaca*:] "Apo [Lord], your lordship, *noca* servis-*cayqui* [I am here to serve you]."

*In the provinces.*

*is from a gentleman's household of Old Christians, he will ruin all her relatives, lineages, and children, for they are of a miserable stock, worse than mestizos."
However, Guaman Poma takes this ideology in a different direction than the colonial elite:]*

Whether he is black, Spanish, or Indian, he deserves to be honored if he is a gentleman with a title passed down from his ancestral lineage. Honor such gentlemen, for in honoring them, you honor yourself. As the saying goes: "Honor good gentlemen that they may honor you. Do good to your fellow men, and you do good to yourself. Be charitable and God will provide for you. Be friendly and you will have many friends."

*[An illustration, ms. p. 512, shows the "very Christian and greatly learned cor-regidor Licentiate Gregorio López de Puga" giving a peso in alms to a poor Indian.]*

◆ **One *corregidor*,** named Gregorio López de Puga, was very Christian, a learned man, and a friend and servant of God, of the poor, and of His Majesty, who did justice righteously. He was so Christian that he was sent [to be the *corregidor* of the Lucanas] by viceroy Don García, Marquis of Cañete, because the *corregidor* of that province at the time was a man named Licentiate Cristóbal de Ovando. Ovando was such a "learned" man that he caused sheer destruction and great harm to the noble *caciques* and poor Indians. His Majesty had sent him to collect a state loan, but he took it and stole it for himself in that province. He was a great friend of the *encomenderos* and *doctrina* priests, and a great enemy of the noble *caciques* and poor Indians. So it was, at first. His friends—the *encomenderos,* the padres, and the Spaniards—persecuted him and incited the Indians; they made war on him behind his back. As a result, he died amid lawsuits, very poor, in debt, and persecuted.

Thus the new *corregidor,* Gregorio López de Puga, being a good man of letters and a wise man, sought to avoid such lawsuits, perdition, and dishonor, and so he asked me how he could pull through his term in the *corregimiento* with honor and without suits. So I took him by the hand, because he was a good, Christian, God-fearing man, and showed him what he had to do.

First of all, he should fear God, not err in doing justice, and pass sentence according to the merits of each case. He should favor the poor Indians. He should have the eyes of a lion, and bite with teeth and molars. He should not nod off or let himself be fooled. He should not befriend the priests and *encomenderos,* nor should he keep Spaniards or deputies. If some padre or *encomendero* should ask him to punish a noble *cacique* or a poor Indian, he should not do so; rather, he should favor the Indian, because the padres and *encomenderos* try to stir up lawsuits under cover of justice—he should take no counsel from them. Nor should he invite them to banquets or permit himself to be invited by them, and he should not confide his secrets (good or bad) to them, nor have any conversation with them, because they will become witnesses against the *corregidor*. But he should honor the noble *caciques* and love the Indians as much as he can, because the worst mortal enemy of the *corregidores* are the padres, *encomenderos,* and Spaniards, who get involved with the system of justice and use it to take revenge on the poor Indians.

This *corregidor* therefore was able to leave his office laughing at the padres and *encomenderos* and Spaniards. Even though they had kept urging the nobles and Indians of the province to file lawsuits, the Indians all said that Licentiate Puga was a saint. When he left the *corregimiento*, everyone cried, and the poor wept and wailed. This *corregidor* also profited quietly. He had no wife, children, servants, deputies, or notary; only his own person and his own table in the province.

**Why should the** *corregidor's* brother or father-in-law, or some other relative of the *corregidor,* the priest, or the *encomendero,* want to meddle and stay at his side? Because they want to rob alongside him, and eat at the expense of the Indians of this kingdom. And there is no remedy, and so the Indians of this kingdom absent themselves. . . .

◆ **The brothers, relatives,** and kinsmen of the *corregidor,* the priest, and the *encomendero* quickly enrich themselves. With the favor and help of [those officers], they become wild beasts, attacking the poor Indians and stealing their estates, cattle, food, and clothing, and fornicating with their maidens. They punish and harass them on their own account, and force them to work. Thus they become rich, but they never have to face an audit at the end of their terms. And there is no remedy in this kingdom.

*[Guaman Poma proposes a motto for the* corregidores, *to be painted on the doors to the town council hall below the royal coat of arms: "Fear God, be a good justice, and do not become involved in doing evil or harm" (illustration, ms. p. 515). He includes a sample notarized document from a* corregidor *(real or invented), Pedro de Torres of the pueblo of Huancayo, for exempting older Indian men and widowed Indian women from tribute, personal service, and threats to their property. He suggests a second motto, to be painted "in large letters" on the doors of inns below the initials of Jesus and Mary: "Christians: fear God and Justice, be not proud, and do not call the justices, that you be not punished" (illustration, ms. p. 517). After further criticism of men and women who attach themselves to the households of* corregidores *and other officials as interpreters, cooks, and servants, in order to be able to rob the Indians, Guaman Poma includes a model last will and testament for "the Indians of this*

*kingdom," showing how property is to be divided among heirs, or in the absence of direct heirs, left to "the community." He specifies that no official should interfere in drafting wills, and that no Spaniard, mulatto, or mestizo should be allowed to inherit land from an Indian.]*

*[The "Chapter on Corregidores" continues with a "Chapter on Notaries, Deputy Corregidores, and Judges," minor provincial officials whom Guaman Poma finds even more venal than the corregidores themselves. The general conclusion to this double chapter, from ms. pp. 527–28, follows:]*

## TO THE READERS OF "*CORREGIDORES,* DEPUTY *CORREGIDORES,* COMMISSIONER JUDGES, NOTARIES, AND SECRETARIES"

**CHRISTIAN READERS:** know that God's good justices—judges who are honorable—should want to get through their terms of office in the *corregimientos* without lawsuits. They should take with them, in good stead, the small amount that they have earned, but not all that they have stolen: let them leave behind everything except for their poverty, and not feel shamed. They should be able to look the viceroy and his Audiencia in the face and be honored. Those who do ill should be offered no other position in this kingdom. Judges will then keep to a clean path and have many friends, while their enemies will be mocked and will weep. You will come out laughing, as did the *corregidor* and judge Gregorio López de Puga—a licentiate, a brave judge, and a Christian, who was no *criollo*[238] but rather was born in Spain and studied in Salamanca. There had been so many lawsuits among the other *corregidores,* one *corregidor* against another, that he asked me (as a level-headed, wise, and well-read man) how he might get through his terms without such suits. I answered him in the way I have described above.

Here, then, is my advice, which you may take if you want to get through your term without lawsuits and leave your office with your purse filled with *reales* while the poor Indians mourn [your departure].

First of all, you should do your work as God ordained. Be a good Christian, fear God, and favor the poor of Jesus Christ.

Second, you should be a brave judge, and display justice and a lion's eyes and teeth to the Spaniards, *encomenderos,* padres, and *doctrina* priests.

Third, do not punish anyone without sufficient evidence, and never do so at the bidding of *encomenderos* or priests, and never do anything simply because the padres will it. If you were to do so, you would be ruined. Rather, they have always been terrible enemies, like knives, inciting the

---

[238] *Criollo* (creole): a person of any background who was born and raised in the colonial Americas.

Indians with the harm they cause and bringing up charges when *corregidores* are audited at the ends of their terms. Therefore, *corregidor,* tell each of them to go say their Masses and their prayers for the dead: "Say the Mass, toll the church bells, and take confession, as the Holy Council [of Trent] has ordained you do." If each one would stick to his own office and benefice, all would be well and he would be honored.

Fourth, you should avoid friendships with *encomenderos, padres, and other Spaniards,* and you should not keep deputies, judges, brothers, children, or notaries around, lest they use the *corregidor* as an excuse to rob and steal from the poor Indians.

Fifth, you should honor all your subjects—the noble *caciques* and lords of your district, the *camachicos* (petty authorities), the poor Indians, and the outsiders.[239] You should get along with the [Indian] justices of the peace and notaries, honor them in each pueblo, as His Majesty has decreed, and seat them at your table. When they are found guilty of civil or criminal crimes, you should punish them with love, charity, and on the basis of good information, and not shame them, even if they are poor, for in so doing you will serve God and His Majesty.

Sixth, you should keep the treasury so that not a single real is lost, and you should engage in no dealings, commerce, or *rescates* [forced trading], nor should you keep many *mitayos* or servants. Two Indians should be enough for you, one for the kitchen and stable and the other to serve as a *pongo,* who should be exempt.[240]

Seventh, read everything that has been set down and written in these chapters, the right and the wrong, in this *Chronicle,* so that you might punish the wrong in your own spirit and flesh first, and might honor what is right. Thus will God, His Majesty, and his royal crown be served.

So it was that this brave judge and *corregidor* was sent on to the city of Cusco with a second commission from His Excellency. All the poor Indians wept [at his departure] because of his good justice, while his enemies were mocked. Therefore all the Spaniards disliked him, to the point that a Spaniard killed him—it was not an Indian [who did it]. That Christian man met the end of his life in Cusco.

Look, Christian reader of *"Corregidores,* Judges, and Notaries": you should also do a bit more. When you arrive in any province, you should not allow Spaniards, mestizos, mulattos, or Indian women who have been

---

[239] Outsiders (forasteros): Indians who migrated from their home pueblos to avoid tribute obligations or to look for better opportunities in other Indian communities.

[240] *Pongo:* an Indian who worked for an overlord, such as a Spanish governor or estate owner, for one week a year without pay. Guaman Poma insists that, in exchange for this service, the *pongo* should be exempt from paying tribute.

mistresses of Spaniards or priests to live among the Indians; nor should you be a friend of the padre or the *encomendero*. You have to do a bit more if you wish to leave with your honor intact, be free of lawsuits, and have some money when you leave—just the little bit that you earned, for which you should give thanks to God. Then you will make the viceroy content, for through you he will relieve his conscience, and he will consider you a good judge, and for your merits he will give you other positions. You will be found in the books of government as a good judge. Therefore, leave off all your bad ways, and you shall be honored as a *corregidor*.

## THE MINE OWNERS                                   *529–560*

*[Guaman Poma moves from the consideration of colonial civil officers to a critique of Spaniards who make a living in and around the Indian communities of Peru: mine owners, stewards, traveling merchants, and other Spaniards who pass through the countryside. First is a short chapter on "Mine Owners" which opens with a graphic rebuke: mine owners "cruelly punish" the Indian caciques (viewed here as the "true lords" of lands that the mine owners have taken over and which they now rule despotically); they refuse to pay the Indians who are forced to travel long distances to work in their mines; they attack and rape the Indian women who are attracted to the mines to serve as cooks. But worst of all is simply having to work in the mines, especially the mercury mines of Huancavelica, in Guaman Poma's home territory. Mercury or quicksilver was the active ingredient in the processing of silver ore that gave Peru its wealth, and keeping a constant supply of the mineral was so important to the colony that the viceroys created a forced labor draft, bringing some 3,000 Indian tributaries from the surrounding region to the mine. Guaman Poma blames the labor draft for depopulating the Indian communities of the region.]*

*[An illustration, ms. p. 529, labeled "The corregidores and judges cruelly punish the noble caciques," shows five caciques being punished and tortured "in the mines" in ways described below, while a Spanish corregidor looks on with approval.]*

**THE QUICKSILVER MINES** of Huancavelica are where the poor Indians are so harshly punished, where they are tortured and so many Indians die; it is there that the noble *caciques* of this kingdom are finished off and tortured. The same is true in all the other mines: the silver mines of Potosí, the silver mines of Chocllo Cocha, the gold mines of Carabaya, and the other mines elsewhere in this kingdom. The owners and stewards of the mines, whether Spaniards, mestizos, or Indians, are such tyrants, with no fear of God or justice, because they are not audited and are not inspected twice a year. And thus there is no remedy.

**They hang one** noble *cacique* by his feet, and they seat another one on a llama and whip him. Others are bound, stark naked, to the whipping post, where they are punished and their hair is roughly shorn.[241] Still others are kept in the public jail in stocks and fetters, without being given any food or water or being allowed to provide their own. All of this abuse and shaming is done to them under the excuse that a few Indians are missing from the *mita* [forced labor draft]. These punishments are carried out against the lords of the land in this kingdom, who hold their titles by His Majesty. They are punished most cruelly, as if they were thieves or traitors. Because of these troubles, they have died in shame, and there is no remedy.

And they are not paid for the labor of traveling to and from the mines or for the time they spend at the mines. The Indians, under the pretext of mining chores, are made to spend their workdays herding cattle and conveying goods; they are sent off to the plains, and the Indians die. Some have to make *cumpis* [fine woven cloth]; others are ordered to weave coarse cloth; and others are turned into *rescate* [forced trading] traffickers—these Indians are not paid for their labor, and their work is kept hidden.

And [the mine owners] keep Indian cooking women in their residences; they use cooking as a pretext for taking concubines. They and their stewards force their way on some of the daughters of their Indian servants and deflower them, and they force their way on their servants' wives by sending their husbands off to the mines at night, or by sending them somewhere far away. And they oblige the Indians to accept corn or meat or *chicha* [corn beer] or cheese or bread at their own expense, and they deduct [the price] from their labor and their workdays. In this way, the Indians end up very poor and deep in debt, and they have no way to pay their tribute.

There is no remedy for all this, because any *corregidor,* governor, or judge who enters comes to an agreement with [the mine owners], and all [the owners] join forces in bribing him. When he sees the gold with his own eyes, he would rather tell them to kill all the poor Indians. Even the protector of the Indians is useless; he is, instead, against the Indians. He does not defend them against these torments from hell, nor does he warn Your Majesty or your royal Audiencia about the harms done to the poor Indians.

Your Majesty should know: where do the mine owners get the means to dress up all in silk and gold and silver, other than from the labor of the

---

[241] As elsewhere in the book, Guaman Poma uses the Spanish term *carnero* (ram, a male sheep) for the Andean llama; his illustration, ms. p. 541, shows clearly that the animal is a llama. In Spain, seating a bound prisoner on a ram and parading him or her naked through a town was the worst form of public humiliation, usually reserved for those found guilty of heresy or blasphemy. Shearing the hair was a punishment particularly aimed at Indians in both the Andes and Mexico, who felt it as a shameful affront.

poor Indians and from what they steal from Your Majesty? Therefore, it would be good that these mine owners be inspected every six months and audited and held to account, and that the mines be inspected. Because they whip the Indian women in their husbands' absence, and they also whip their husbands, their clothes hiked up and their shameful parts exposed—they whip them as if they were small children, on their bottoms; and they beat other Indians as if they were animals, horses, as if they were their black slaves; and they commit so many other offenses that it would take too long to write them all, which we leave to God and to your judges and justices.

Because of all these offenses, [the Indians] leave their pueblos to avoid going to the mines, where they would suffer torments and martyrdom. To avoid suffering the demonic pains and torments of that inferno, some flee the mines, while others flee the highway that would bring them to the mines, to keep from dying a sudden death. Those who go would rather die than live, and they beg to be finished off once and for all, because, when they get the quicksilver poisoning, they dry up like sticks, they get asthma, and they cannot live by day or by night. They last a year or two like that, and then they die.

Therefore, for my part, I recommend that Your Majesty have your governor and your Audiencia report to you, write to you, and inform you, so that some Christian might stand up for the poor of Jesus Christ, in order that this might be remedied and that all the ills and harm done in the mines of this kingdom might cease to grow.

*[Guaman Poma lists the mine owners' economic offenses: they do not pay the "Indian captains or the Indian servants" for their travel to the mines, and sometimes not for their work; they pay no compensation when an Indian worker dies or is permanently injured; they pay nothing for the service of the workers' wives and children, nor for the use of their ropes, bags, and llamas; they and their stewards take bribes from their friends to divert the* mita *[labor draft] workers from the mines for work as unpaid domestic servants. He lists the wages that the workers should receive: eight reales a day plus meals for work in the mercury mines; four reales a day plus food in the silver and gold mines. When an Indian called for* mita *labor hires a replacement worker, his replacement should be paid ten silver pesos for the two months of mandatory* mita *service. The whole process should be overseen by civil and ecclesiastical judges. He continues:]*

**When the Indians** who go to serve in the mines or plazas hold a fiesta with their dances, music, and songs (*taquíes, cachawa, haylle, harawi, pincollo*), no judge may prohibit them; because the poor celebrate so that they can work, and when they return to work they bring this happiness to console their spirits and their bodies. But the padres and *corregidores* hinder them, because they want [the Indians] to give them money and food.

**In the quicksilver mines,** the Indians who enter the tunnel of any mine should enter for one day, and should not enter again until they leave; the same should hold with each Indian who does *mita* service in the quicksilver ovens, until he completes his *mita*. In this way, he will not get quicksilver poisoning and will not die. If a mine owner allows any Indians to enter twice, he should be punished, deprived of his position, and have his mines and Indians taken away from him. In this way, the Indians will multiply and will not die so swiftly, nor will they come to an end.

**THE MINE OWNERS** send judges to the [Indian] pueblos, under the pretext that an Indian worker is missing, at the expense of the Indians and the *caciques*. Thus the judge commits foolish acts and eats at the expense of the Indians and the *caciques* and steals and robs from all the Indians in the province, whether they are guilty or not. He causes great harm, and at the end of it he is not audited. Everything that he takes from their farms, he takes by force, and he strips the noble *cacique*. And there is no remedy in this kingdom.

**The mine owners** do not pay attention to whether their Indians and people are Christians. Nor do they teach them the doctrine on Wednesdays and Fridays. Nor do they order them to confess before entering the mine tunnels. Nor do they order them to observe Sundays and fiestas. Nor do they order their wives and the old and young to attend Mass. Nor do they celebrate All Saints' Day or the requiem Mass for all those who have died in their mines and settlements, including the plaza servants and the workers in their sugar mills, pastures, fields, textile mills, sugar plantations, and vineyards—even their black slaves; they all ought to be listed on their rolls, having served [the mine owners], they should remember them for what they owe, and should have this obligation on their consciences. In order that this holy service might take place, the vicars and parish priests should demand it of all those who have mines, plazas, farms, cattle pastures, vineyards, sugar plantations, or textile mills. The citizens [wealthy Spaniards] should also have a very solemn Mass said for the souls of their Indians; in this way, God will be served in this kingdom.

**The Indians in the mines** and in the plazas, the Indian servants, should not have drunken fits or *taquies* or any kind of fiesta, nor should they take [their pay] in food, nor should it be offered to them. Because, when they go back to their pueblos, they go naked; they do not bring back half a real, or even a quarter-real, to pay their tribute or support their wives and children. In this way, they fall into debt and fall far behind in paying their

The mine owners send judges to rob the noble *caciques* and poor Indians in their pueblos.

### *On the mines.*

tribute. With their drunken fits, they serve the demons. Therefore, the justices should not allow this, and if they do allow it, they should be fined on each occasion one hundred pesos for the treasury.

*[Guaman Poma criticizes "Indian captains"—minor Indian officials in charge of rounding up* mita *workers for the mines in Huancavelica and Potosí—for abusing their ability to charge Indians for hiring replacement workers for the* mita, *accusing them of overcharging and ruining the Indians; instead, he proposes, the captains should personally have to make up the* mita *service of missing Indians. He also criticizes* mita *Indians for bringing their wives and daughters to the mines, and he concludes this chapter with another call for separation between the Indian and Spanish settlements.]*

**In the mines and plazas** of this kingdom, as soon as the *mita* is completed—once the required number of months of service are completed—all the Indians who have served, together with everyone who helped them, their children, wives, and brothers, should be sent away from the [Spanish] cities, towns, mines, and other settlements in this kingdom.

Likewise, the absent Indians, along with their wives and children—even if they are tradesmen, or rather *yanacona*, descendents of the *puma ranra* (highwaymen and thieves from the time of the Inca)—should be inspected, and no one else should be allowed to join them. All the others should be sent away from them; even these [*yanaconas*] should be kept half a league away from cities and towns, away from living among Spaniards. In this way, they will become Christian and will multiply; for only Spaniards, Spanish ladies, and blacks should live in the cities and towns, and no Indian woman or girl should enter them, under the penalties that Your Majesty has established. These penalties should be carried out, and notice should be served throughout the cities, towns, and mines of this kingdom.

539–560    **THE STEWARDS OF THIS KINGDOM: THE *ENCOMENDEROS'* STEWARDS FOR COLLECTING TRIBUTE; THE STEWARDS OF THE [SPANISH] RANCHES, FARMS, SUGAR PLANTATIONS, TEXTILE MILLS, SUGAR MILLS, ORCHARDS, THE MINES OF THE ANDES, AND COCA FARMS; HOUSE STEWARDS; AND THE STEWARDS OF *CORREGIDORES,* PADRES, AND OTHER RICH SPANIARDS**

*[The next group to be criticized are the stewards or overseers (mayordomos) of Spanish estates and mines. These were administrators (usually but not necessarily Spanish) who were hired by the owners of Spanish business undertakings, farms, and wealthy households in the Americas to handle their day-to-day operations.]*

THESE STEWARDS are absolute despots. First, because they are never audited. Second, because they are never inspected. Third, because they are never punished. Therefore, they wrong the poor Indians who are going about their day labor, their chores, and their work.

If a laborer loses ten llamas, the steward makes him pay for twenty llamas. He takes away all his pay. He refuses to give him any food. He makes his wife and children work; he should have to pay each of them for their work day, but he even makes them work at night, and to keep from paying them, he hides their work, or hides other things that he has in his possession, and so he gets away with not paying them.

These stewards keep company with other Spanish stewards. They and their companions all have mistresses; they rob the Indians, and they have crowds of little mestizo sons and daughters. They deflower the maidens—the daughters of Indian herders, cattlemen, and servants. Aside from this, they have dozens of whores, in their kitchens and in their workers' huts. In order to do all these things, they bribe the *corregidores,* judges, and *doctrina* priests, who therefore would indulge them even if they were to beat a poor Indian to death. There is no remedy: there is not even an inspector for these stewards in this kingdom.

♦ **The stewards make** their own justice; they arrest, punish, and imprison Indian men and women in their storerooms and houses. A steward will also demand a half dozen men and a half dozen women to work for him as *mitayos;* he will make them spin yarn, weave cloth, and work as bakers, *chicha* vendors, and store keepers, and he will have lots of *yanaconas* [male servants] and *chinas* [female servants]—servant boys, cooks, maids, butlers, and much pomp and circumstance. This makes [his employer,] the *encomendero, corregidor,* or padre, very happy: indeed, [the employer] will take the Indian women into his own house, and so turn them into tremendous whores. That is why the Indians do not multiply, and there is no remedy in this kingdom.

**It would be most** just if all the fields, corrals, and pastures that have been sold in His Majesty's name were returned and restituted, because they cannot in good conscience be taken from the natives, the legitimate proprietors of these fields. One *hanegada* of land might have sold for ten silver pesos, another for twenty, depending on the result of the auctions, but even if they had been sold for one hundred pesos, the purchasers have been more than repaid in crops and cattle, and thus the Spaniards should return these fields, corrals, and pastures to the Indians.[242]

---

[242] There had been a wave of land sales by the crown in the 1590s, to be followed by more in the 1620s and 1630s. (Technically, these were not land sales, but fees paid for legalized title to land, *composiciones de tierras*). The land affected was considered "idle,"

After the land is returned to the Indians, it will be worth much more to His Majesty, because the Indian man or woman to whom a field belonged, or the pueblo that has owned a communal field or pasture with proper titles since *ab initio,* since the time of Topa Inca Yupanqui, Wayna Capac Inca, and the Christian conquest, can let, lease, and rent the land to the Spaniards, mestizos, mulattos, blacks, *cholos, zambaigos*—all those who are tending towards a new stock and generation—and to the Indians who inherited no land. They can rent it, and [the renters] can pay a certain amount to the land owner, and the land owner can pay the fifth to His Majesty every year, in this kingdom.[243] His Majesty should name a salaried general judge, who would reside in the city of Los Reyes de Lima. If an Indian did not rent out his land, he would not need to pay this tax.

Therefore, they should not sell these lands to the Spaniards, unless [the buyer and the owner] agree among themselves to sell and alienate a piece of land. In this way, neither the Indians nor the Spaniards will be wronged; God and His Majesty will be served; and His Majesty will not lose his royal fifth in this kingdom of the Indies of Peru.

## CHAPTER OF THE WAYFARERS

*[Guaman Poma now moves from the loss of Indian land at the hands of the stewards to the loss of Indian autonomy through the presence of Spanish travelers and other outsiders in the countryside. To facilitate communications between the coast and the highland mining and agricultural districts, the Spanish turned the Inca way stations* (tampu) *into the inns known in Andean Spanish as* tambos. *Guaman Poma is particularly critical of Spanish behavior in these* tambos; *he again insists that Spaniards and other non-Indians should remain in their cities, and that Indians should remain in the pueblos. (The following two paragraphs, from the end of "The Stewards," belong thematically to this chapter.)]*

◆ *CHOLOS* **AND** *ZAMBAIGOS* should pay personal tax and tribute,[244] and they should take part in all the calls for personal service in this kingdom,

---

"vacant," or "abandoned," though the most frequently targeted fields were valuable ones lying close to Spanish markets in Lima, other Spanish towns, and the mines. A *hanegada* or *fanegada* is the amount of land that can be sown with a *fanega* (roughly 1.5 bushels) of grain, about seven or eight acres as figured in south-central Peru. See Stern, *Peru's Indian Peoples and the Challenge of Spanish Conquest,* p. 116.

[243] The fifth (*el quinto*): As an incentive for returning land to its rightful Indian owners, Guaman Poma proposes an annual tax on land rental equivalent to the 20 percent royal tax on gold and silver ore mined in the Spanish realms.

[244] *Cholo, zambaigo:* Guaman Poma nowhere defines these terms, though he always lists them together with each other and with the "mixed" racial groups, mestizos and mulattos.

because the *cholo* is pure Indian in every way—which should not be taken to mean that he is of titled noble stock—for he has nothing of the Spaniard about him. This is the fault and the sin of his father: it is a curse of God to have a son of ill fame in this world—mestizo, *cholo,* mulatto, or *zambaigo.* To be a good child of God, a son of Adam and his wife Eve, the servants of God, [one should be] pure Spanish, pure Indian, or pure black.

These people and their descendents—the mestizos and mulattos, as well as mestizas and mulatas, *cholas,* and *zambaigas*—should never be allowed to stay in the Indian pueblos; they should live in the [Spanish] cities, towns, and hamlets of this kingdom. The justices who allow [them to live in Indian pueblos] should be punished and pay a fine to His Majesty's treasury, in this kingdom.

◆ **AS SOON AS THE** Spanish wayfarers who travel along the royal highways reach a *tambo,* they—even the priests—angrily grab the Indians who work in the *tambo* and the local [Indian] magistrate, slapping the magistrate around and beating the Indians with sticks. They demand *mitayos* [forced laborers] and lots of *camarico* [gifts]: corn, potatoes, mutton, chicken, eggs, lard and bacon, peppers, salt, cabbage, lettuce, onion and garlic, cilantro, peppermint, tallow candles, *cocoba, chochoca, chuño* and quinoa, *chiche, chicha,* and *chusi* (blankets),[245] pots, water jugs, and rope for tying up their horses. They demand an Indian to serve as their *pongo,* another Indian to take their horses to pasture, another Indian to drive the horse train, and they keep the rest of the horses in the stable guarded by another Indian who serves them as *watacamayoc* [constable]. Then they demand ten loads of hay and a load of firewood, and they demand a cook.

The cost of all this adds up to twelve pesos a day, but the Spaniards feel they have clean consciences, as they say. Some of them will pay four reales; others will offer to barter in order to avoid paying anything. Then they leave with all their money. They demand horses and llamas, and load down the pack animals so much that they die along the road; then they make the poor Indians pay for the horses and llamas, while other Spaniards pick up

In other sources, *zambaigo* refers to a person of mixed Indian and black descent. In contemporary Peru, *cholo* usually refers to a person of Indian descent who has moved to a city and abandoned a rural Indian identity. By calling for these people to pay tribute and "personal service" (*servicio personal,* the forced labor that commoner Indians had to perform at the bidding of priests and other high-ranking Spaniards), Guaman Poma includes them in the category of "Indian commoner"; at the same time, by insisting that they live in Spanish cities and towns, he excludes them from the Indian community.

[245] *Cocoba,* a dish made with dried white potatoes; *chochoca,* dried corn; *chuño,* dried potatoes; quinoa, an Andean grain; *chiche,* shrimp and small fish; *chicha,* corn beer; *chusi,* blankets. Guaman Poma cleverly employs alliteration to imply that the Spanish travelers demanded every product imaginable.

SPANIARDS OF THE *TAMBOS*, AND CRIOLLOS,
MESTIZOS, MULATTOS, AND CRIOLLAS
AND MESTIZAS, AND CHRISTIAN
SPANIARDS FROM CASTILE.

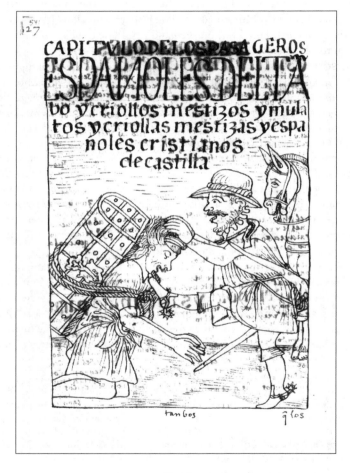

*Tambos.*

the loads and move on with them on their own horses. Others demand five or ten Indians and make them bear the loads as if they were horses; they drive them like pack animals, and do not pay them.

All of this should weigh on the consciences of the *corregidores* and justices, who ought to force the travelers to pay and should not allow them to demand pack horses and llamas or to pile their loads on the poor Indians of this kingdom. If the *corregidores* do not remedy this, it should be listed as a charge in the audit at the end of their terms, for His Majesty appoints them, and this is why they receive a salary.

◆ The *tamberos* in these kingdoms—the Spaniards who rent *tambos* from the Indians or from other people—have no right to those *tambos*. They demand Indians to work for them, and they each employ twenty tributary Indians in their *tambos*, but do not pay them. *Prostitutes — local*

In addition, each *tambero* keeps a half dozen Indian women as disreputable whores, and keeps other Indian women under the pretext that they are the wives of their *yanaconas*, or that they are *chinaconas* [female servants]. Some of them are married women. The *tamberos* take advantage of them and do great offense to the service of God. They demand *mitayas* [Indian women forced to give labor tribute] without regard to whether they are unmarried women, widows, or wives. In the *tambos*, these women are harmed, corrupted, and become tremendous whores. The women are not paid, but they are delighted to wear new clothes and colorful *chumpis* [sashes]. They paint their faces to become whores and scoundrels. Their own mothers instruct them and act as their procuresses. *offense to God*

Using the *mita* [labor draft] as a pretext, the *tamberos* force their *mitayos* to haul hay and firewood, and they send the young men off to the plains. In this way, being sent off on long errands, the husbands die, and the *tamberos* keep their wives as mistresses. Thus they sin and do great offense to the service of God.

They also take away the wives, daughters, and sisters of Indian travelers. They lock them up and take them by force, threatening their husbands, fathers, or brothers. They also steal their food and belongings, and do many other harmful things that will never be remedied, because they are never audited. Because of this, the Indians cannot multiply; they have no children, and they are disappearing.

**I decided to spend** a few days in some *tambos*, to see some Spaniards as I had seen the Indians. The most passable *tambo* was Tambo Quemado.[246]

---

[246] Located in or near the modern village of Tambo Quemado in the southeastern corner of Guaman Poma's home province of Lucanas Laramati, about ninety-five miles from Chipao. Guaman Poma mentions several pueblos from this area of the province, which connects Lucanas with the coastal highway to Lima.

I will first speak about certain Spaniards who have little conscience. A Spaniard or a padre will arrive at the *tambo.* He will pick up a truncheon and, without bothering to see whether the person he is talking to is a *cacique* or a magistrate, he will demand a *mitayo,* corn, eggs, chickens, hay, firewood, and other odds and ends, all at the expense of the Indians. Then, the next morning, he will leave without paying for any of it. Apart from this, he will take their blankets, or the gourds that they eat from, and he will demand horses and take Indians as his guides. Under the pretext of needing guides, he will make them haul his burdens, and he will force them to march on, pounding the poor Indians with a stick. So, see here, Christian: what does this bad man deserve but punishment for the harm he has done? It could also be said that His Majesty should not have ordered that [the *tambos*] be given to the Spaniards, because it is now on his royal conscience.

I will also say that, when I was at Tambo Quemado, a poor, sick Spaniard came by. It seemed to me that he was a hermit, so I went up to the Spaniard and saw that he was very poor and naked. He was leading by the reins a horse that was laden with a set of saddle packs. When he arrived, he asked the *tambero,* the *curaca,* and the magistrate whether he could beg for alms. He told them that he was very poor, old, and sick. He said that he was going on a pilgrimage in the service of the Mother of God, to the chapel of Our Lady of Copacabana, and that he was wearing his habit hidden under his clothes so that he could travel without having anyone find out. Thus, this good, saintly man begged for alms all through the pueblo, entering even the houses of the *curaca* and the magistrate. Truly I tell you that no one gave him so much as a wisp of hay, and nothing at all to eat. I myself sought out an Indian outsider—he was a shoemaker, and *ladino* [fluent in Spanish]. This Indian brought hay, firewood, and water for the poor man, while from the poor possessions that I had, I gave him food to eat and supplies for his journey. I told him, "Sir, these brothers of mine have no sense of charity unless it is beaten out of them. This is all the fault of their bad priest, who does not teach them Christianity; he only wants everything for himself." And the good man said, "It is the fault of the *corregidor,* because he does not allow *ladino* [Spanish-speaking] Indians to be magistrates. May God remedy it." Thus, the Indian who does not fear God also deserves to be punished, in this kingdom.

◆ **Many Dons and Doñas** pass through the *tambos.* In regard to the injuries that are done in the world, I will say a few appropriate words about this subject. It is astonishing that every man, woman, and priest should be entitled to call himself or herself Don and Doña, and that the priests should call themselves Licentiate, Bachelor, Master, or Doctor. Let them all purchase their titles from His Majesty and start calling themselves Don, Doña,

and Licentiate, and may they all be well examined by His Majesty's colle-
giate authorities in Spain, and let each of them have his titles—if, that is,
he is a son of a gentleman by legitimate descent or proprietary lineage that
comes to him by right. Because these people are robbing the noble [Indian]
lords and ladies of the grants that God and His Majesty have given them,
and which they have had from their ancestors.

It is only with the aim of harassing the Indians of this kingdom and taking away their estates that the Spaniards call themselves Don and Doña,
though they are petty merchants, Jews, and base people. Their parents used
to work in peddling, petty merchandise, tailoring, shoemaking, and other
very base manual crafts. Likewise, the Indian men and Indian women use
the Don to do great damage. The wives of mestizos and mulattos likewise
call themselves Doñas, so that the world is turning on its head. The *doctrina*
padres likewise call themselves Licentiates, using that title to claim that they
are great *apos* (lords), and to rob the poor Indians of this kingdom of everything they have, and to insult the truly learned, who have earned their titles
from His Majesty. Therefore, each of these people should be punished and
fined one hundred pesos for His Majesty's treasury and the expenses of justice; Indians, twenty pesos. Any justice should be able to impose these fines,
for the service of God and His Majesty and for the well-being and increase
of the poor Indians of this kingdom and throughout the world.

## VAGABOND SPANIARDS OF THIS KINGDOM

MANY SPANIARDS WANDER along the royal highways, passing through the
*tambos* and the Indian pueblos. These vagabonds are Jews and Moors.
When one enters a *tambo*, he sets the land into an uproar. Picking up a
stick, he beats the Indians badly, demanding, "Give me *mitayo!* Take that,
*mitayo!* Give me *camarico!* Take that, *camarico!*" They have no other
wealth. The richest of them has at most a black, a servant boy, and two
beasts of burden—one for him, the other for his saddlebags. He has one set
of clothes for the road and one other for the city. He eats and spends twelve
pesos worth a day, all at the Indians' expense, yet he says that he is a gentleman, an *apo*, a Doctor, and a Licentiate, and he leaves each *tambo* and
Indian pueblo without paying.

That is how he gets around the kingdom. He is such a big, strong man
that he refuses to get down off his horse to carry firewood, hay, or water, or
to serve another man, as he would in Castile, where those who have no
money do not leave their houses and their pueblos. That is why there are
highwaymen and vagabonds in Castile and in this kingdom.

In the time of the Incas, to keep such men from becoming rebels and
vagabonds and to make them very obedient in this kingdom, the noble
lords and poor Indians had to carry an insignia that took the place of a

"*Puri* [get moving], Indian dog!"

***Tambos.***

license from the Inca. Wherever they went with that insignia, when they approached the *corregidores* (*tocricoc*) and judges (*michoc*), they would be asked, "*Ima ñacac runam canqui? Pacta iscay sonco runa canquiman?* [What cursed man are you? Might you be a traitor?]" They would reply, "*Incap capacpa siminwan unanchanwanmi purini.* [I walk with the word and the insignia of the Capac Inca.]" In this way they accounted for themselves to the *corregidores* (*tocricoc*) and the magistrates *(Equeco, Quemequero)* of those days.

So that they might be recognized and honored, the Spaniards in this kingdom should wear their licenses on their chests wherever they go. Each of them, whether he be a taxpaying commoner, an hidalgo, a gentleman, a Jew, a Moor, a mestizo, a mulatto, or a black, should account for himself and show his license to the *corregidor,* or, where there is no *corregidor,* to the local magistrate or the magistrate of the *tambo.* Those who carry no license should be arrested, have their belongings sequestered, and be brought before the *corregidor* of the district. Those who do carry licenses from His Majesty or from his government or council should be allowed to pass on, after first giving a surety that they will pay the Indians by their own hands. Priests should likewise carry licenses from their prelates; otherwise, any justice of the Holy Mother Church or of His Majesty should be able to arrest them in this kingdom. In this way, God and His Majesty will be served.

**Why, in Castile,** should there be any Spanish highwaymen, thieves, and vagabonds? There, they have no one to fool and rob so that they can eat for free, without working, as they do in this kingdom, where they eat, rob, and are served for free. They rob and plunder the poor Indians along the royal highway and in the *tambos* of this kingdom, taking their belongings as well as their lands, wives, and daughters. Therefore there are many more highwaymen in this kingdom than there are in Castile. . . .

*[The chapter on "The Wayfarers" transitions into a sequence of short chapters on what can only be called Guaman Poma's stereotypes of Spanish, mulatto, mestizo, and* criollo *men and women as lazy, greedy, and proud. In one extended scene, he imagines a conversation among the members of a Spanish family in Peru as they discuss how their children can enrich them by becoming priests and cheating the Indians. He again makes unfavorable comparisons between the charitable Spaniards of Castile and the corrupt Spaniards of Peru.]*

◆ **SPANISH MEN AND WOMEN,** as well as Indians and blacks, who are very large and fat are slack, fainthearted good-for-nothings. They are great gluttons who drink the best wine and *chicha.* Therefore they have large behinds, walk little, are not good soldiers, have no judgment, and are lazy. The blacks are bad slaves and idlers. Those who have large faces and heads

## SPANIARDS: ON THE BUILD AND HEIGHT OF MEN AND WOMEN.

[The Botero-sized man and woman are not as innocent as they might appear at first glance. The man is making an obscene gesture with his right hand and holding his phallic sword hilt with his left. The woman's left hand hovers over her genitals, and in her right she holds a rose, a sign of accepting the man's solicitation.]

*Sizes.*

are fools, dolts, and frauds, as well as stubborn, stingy, and greedy—the men and the women alike.

If they are wide in body, whether they are large or small (but especially if they are small), they leap about like monkeys, are big-boned, have very wide palms, and are red-faced and curly-haired. If they have the eye of a traitor or traitoress, beware of them. If they have an honorable eye, that is the sign of a good friend; all the worse for their enemies, for they can lay a person low with a single punch. Some of them do good works, but in mestizos and mulattos, [this build] is a good sign for sending them to the galleys, because they will never serve God or king. *body types*

Men who are tall and lean as sardines, and women with thin legs, are slack, excessively amorous, and wracked with jealousy.

Men and women of middling height, with good builds, good faces, and large eyes, are spirited, wise, and learned. They always use their understanding to serve God and His Majesty. These gentlemen run the world. They are hard-working, charitable, just, and do good works. The man should have little beard, and the woman should have large eyes, a small mouth, a narrow foot, and an ant's waist. If one of these men has a broad chest and a wide back, and broad palms and feet, he is a thief, a highwayman, and a ruffian who fears neither God nor His justice.

If the man is small in body, lean, and thin, he is a gentleman, and the woman is a lady. The man runs lightly and quick as a deer, and is hardworking, spirited, loving, rich, and very knowledgeable; a doctor or licentiate who lives by his skill. These people run the world; they are Christian, both men and women—Spaniard, Indian, or black, in this world.

**These Spaniards and their servants,** who travel the world in this kingdom, should not pass through the cities and pueblos between the eve of a major religious holiday or Sunday and the following day, under penalty of paying twelve pesos to the church. Spaniards should be the first to enter the church, so that the natives might learn. By these means, God and Christianity will be served, and the Indians will increase in this kingdom.

**What the Spanish Christians imagine** when they have many children. They endeavor to imagine everything plated in silver and gold, and that they will have riches. They think of it day and night, both husband and wife.

The husband tells his wife, "Señora, don't you know, I am constantly thinking that all our children should study; because, whether they learn their letters well or badly, they shall become priests."

The wife replies, "How well thought and well stated, dear señor, light of my eyes! For God has given us all these children so we can make money and get rich. Our son Yaquito will be a little priest, and so will Francisquillo, because then they will make money and send us Indian men and women to serve us, and lots of gifts besides—partridges, hens, eggs, fruit, corn, potatoes, even the plants that the Indians eat. And they will send us little servant girls and boys, Indian wards. For, my señor, wouldn't it be good if Alonsito were an Augustinian friar, and Martinillo a Dominican, and Gonzalico a Mercedarian? Dear God, we can really use all the gifts our children will bring us!"

"Señora, wouldn't it be good if Alonsito became a Franciscan friar, and Martinillo joined the Company of Jesus?"

"No, señor, because those are the orders that do not remember their fathers and mothers. They are poor orders; their members become saints and don't make money, so they wouldn't have anything to give us."

The children reply: "Father, dear mother, it would be better to serve God by getting married, having children, building up a household, and working, not by robbing the poor Indians with little fear of God. Rather than being a priest, it would be better to be a Franciscan friar."

"Hush, children, you know nothing. You are being foolish. Lots of priests enrich their fathers and mothers and their brothers, and they are rich with silver and bars of gold. I see them go back to Castile with more than fifty thousand pesos—I have seen it with my own eyes. Likewise, many others get a parish and have little mestizo sons and daughters. Your mother would raise your children, and when they grow up they would serve in the house. That's better than buying blacks to serve in the house. So don't go around brooding over it, all you have to do is become *doctrina* priests and get rich, and you'll see how much treasure you'll have."

"Señor, can a priest be rich? I have heard that the first priest was Jesus Christ, and he was the poorest of all. Then, his apostle St. Peter was very poor, and he even left behind the poor possessions he had to follow Jesus Christ. So, they weren't rich."

"Haven't I told you to hush, little fools? For you know nothing. See here, if the bishop were to take everything away and give it to the church, and if he were to add up the salaries and Masses and offerings and give it all to the church and the people, that would be bad, just like what the friars do. And if he were to order them not to be rich and follow the law of God, that would be something else; then no one would want to be a priest, and nobody would call himself a proprietor."[247]

"Dear father, dear mother, now I say that we will become priests—only priests, not friars. Tomorrow, let's have a solemn festivity on that spot over there and let's sing in this manner:

---

[247] Proprietor (*propietario*): in this context, the term refers to a priest who has title to a parish. Elsewhere, Guaman Poma argues that parish priests should not call themselves *propietarios,* because the only legitimate property owners in Peru are the Indians.

"How well said, dear Lord,
How well said, dear Lord,
By singing the requiem Mass
We'll get rich, we'll get rich.

"What a good idea my father has: let's get rich.
What a good idea my mother has: let's get rich.

"And we'll take a boat to Spain,
We'll get rich,
For in Spain we will be rich,
In the world we will be rich."

**The grants that His Majesty** should bestow should necessarily be these: when some gentleman or hidalgo is a great servant of His Majesty and of his royal crown, then that gentleman himself, or his son, grandson, great-grandson, brothers, or close relatives should be given a grant—even if [the relative] is a baby at the breast, a sick man, a cripple, an old man who can no longer get around, or a woman. The deserving person should be given some government office, such as a *corregimiento* or an administrative post, if he deserves it, whether he is Spanish, Indian, or black, so that he can eat and make a living. The child and the old man should be governed by some other charitable and learned Christian, and should communicate with him. This law and decree should not be neglected, throughout the world and the kingdom of Christianity, in the service of God and His Majesty. If one of these men should rise up against the royal crown, he should not be given a perpetual post, because God punishes such pride as He did Lucifer; thus, that man should lose everything.

**Mulattos and mestizos** should not be allowed to carry defensive arms, because they enter among the Indian natives and get drunk, worse than the Indians do, and then they kill each other. They are haughty towards their uncles,[248] and they dislike the Indians and are bad Christians, enemies of the Indians. Thus, they should have to prove with twelve witnesses that they are good Christians and sons of gentlemen before they are allowed to carry arms and keep their titles. If they are the sons of a gentleman, an hidalgo, or an Old Christian, let them prove it and purchase a license from His Majesty, and so they will each have their titles, even if they are mestizos. Despite all this, if one of them is a commoner and a taxpayer, he should be recognized as such. Even if he marries the daughter of a noble, he should be

---

[248] Guaman Poma imagines that all mestizos and mulattos are the offspring of Spanish men and Indian or black women (as indeed most were in the early years of colonization). The uncles of these mestizos and mulattoes, then, would be Indian men—their mothers' brothers and male cousins.

expelled straight away from the Indian pueblos, because of the scandals to which [mestizos] give rise, and for being a bad stock in this kingdom.

### *CRIOLLOS*[249]

◆ **THE** *CRIOLLOS* who are raised on the milk of Indian or black women, or that of mestizas or mulatas, are fierce and proud, lazy, lying, gambling, greedy, uncharitable, wretched, sly, and enemies of the poor Indians and the Spaniards. Thus, *criollos* are like mestizos, yet they are worse than mestizos, because they have never been seen to do any service, nor has it been written anywhere that they have ever served God or His Majesty anywhere in this kingdom or in all Castile.

◆ **The** *criollos* **are** worse than mestizos, mulattos, and blacks, but the mestizos are even worse for their Indian uncles, aunts, mothers, brothers and sisters, cousins, and relatives. They are extremely fierce and proud, and they assault the poor Indians on the highways and rob them of their belongings. They go about attacking and stealing all over the kingdom, and they give a lot of anguish to the *corregidores*. If they were allowed to live among the Indians in this kingdom, they would destroy and provoke the Indian pueblos of this kingdom.

◆ **The Spaniards** and Spanish ladies these days wear a new kind of clothes. The clothes, customs, and obedience that they used to have were different in this kingdom. Thus, the first Indians were taught by the good Christians of old, and the Indians of these times are being taught by these, the bad Christians. Hence everything is going to waste throughout the kingdom. Indian tributaries become Dons and Doñas, and they wear a new kind of clothes, and they all give in to drunkenness, the Indian men and women alike. Indian women no longer like Indian men, only Spaniards, and they become tremendous whores and give birth only to mestizos, a bad stock in this kingdom.

### *CRIOLLAS*

◆ **THE** *CRIOLLAS* who are raised on the milk of Indian women are worse than mestizas or mulatas: lazy, lying, deceptive, scheming, greedy women who do not tell the truth. They are enemies of the poor Indians, and have no charity or good works among the poor.

But the mestizas are much worse for the Indian women, for their aunts and uncles, and for their mothers and nursemaids, because they are against

---

[249] *Criollo* (creole): a man born and raised in the colonial Americas. *Criollos* (and *criollas*, creole women) can be of any ethnic or racial background, but here Guaman Poma is refering specifically to Peruvian-born Spaniards.

*In the pueblos.*

# THE PROUD *CRIOLLA*, MESTIZA, OR MULATTA OF THIS KINGDOM.

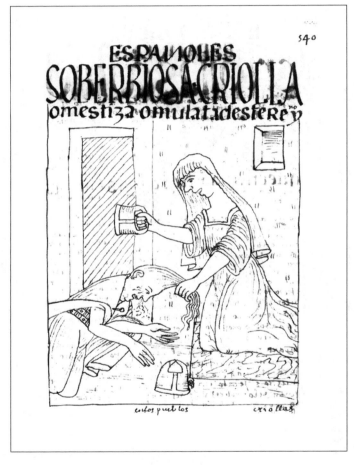

*In the pueblos.*

their fellows, the poor Indians. It is from them that the Indian women learn to be scoundrels and disobedient. They fear neither God nor justice. Because they see all the mestiza's wickedness, they become the worst Indian whores in this kingdom, and there is no remedy.

♦ **Even in the smallest hamlet,** as long as it has a half dozen Spaniards, mestizos, or mulattos, it would be very just and useful for there to be a deputy *corregidor* with his own notary, or a notary named by the crown or town council. This judge should not be appointed by the local *corregidor,* but should be given his title by His Majesty and his government. But if there is an aggrieved party, they may appeal their case to the jurisdiction of the *corregimiento,* for this is proper in the service of God and His Majesty. The priest of the closest parish [to the small hamlet] shall administer the sacrament; if there is sufficient income, the hamlet may have its own priest, who should not be called a vicar, but a parish priest.[250] The vicars should stay in the provincial capital cities and towns.

To this effect, every [Spanish] town, hamlet, and city should rent fields to the Indians every year. To rent them out, they should have common property (*sapsi*), such as vineyards, sugar plantations, textile mills, croplands, cattle, clothing, rental income, and sugar mills. May they grow throughout the kingdom, for the service of God and His Majesty. From this common property, they will pay their royal fifth, excise tax, personal tax, tithes, and first fruits,[251] and will make loans, in case of need, to His Majesty for the defense of our holy Catholic faith—all this for the service of God and His Majesty, the welfare of the poor Indians of this kingdom and throughout the world, and the Christianity, public order, and multiplication of the Indians.

*[Guaman Poma added a set of additional prescriptions for reforming Spanish behavior in Peru as marginal postscripts to ms. pp. 547–55. These follow.]*

Every loaf of bread should be marked with a cross in the center, and    547
Christians should keep a cross in the center of their dining table. If they do

---

[250] Vicar (*vicario*): the parish priest (*cura*) of a large rural parish would typically hire assistant priests (*vicarios*) to serve outlying communities. This type of *vicario* is the lowest position in the church hierarchy; however, the word *vicario* was also used for one of the highest positions, the *vicario general* or vicar-general, the title of a judge in ecclesiastical courts. Guaman Poma here accuses lowly rural assistant priests of abusing the title of "vicar" to act like vicars-general, who should only be appointed in the large Spanish cities and towns.

[251] These taxes (in Spanish, *quinto real, alcabala, pecho, diezmos, primicias*) were the main sources of royal and church income. Guaman Poma's proposal here is, in essence, to Andeanize the Spanish settlements by making them adopt the Andean practice of keeping *sapsi* (common property, worked in common) to pay for public administration.

not do this, they should be punished in this world by the Holy Office [of the Inquisition], and should forfeit their bread, so that God our Lord may thereby be served in the world.

549    Such Spaniards, Indians, blacks, and women should not be given loans or other business dealings if they have bad habits, especially if they are liars, gossips, gamblers, drunks, smokers, whoremongers, jealous, haughty, or miserly. Nor should they be given offices, nor trusted with prisoners, nor collect alms [. . .].

550    Neither these Spaniards nor other persons should be made soldiers or paid by our lord the king, wasting His Majesty's royal treasury, until they reach the age of thirty, forty, or fifty; from the age of thirty on, they can be well employed in the service of God our Lord and the royal crown in this world.

551    *Criollo* Spaniards and mestizos should retire to their houses at six in the evening; Castilian Spaniards should retire at seven. They should not be allowed to remain alone in the countryside and farms, because they might prove to be treacherous highwaymen, for they are bad people, disobedient towards their lord and king, and should be punished by justice in the world.

553    Spaniards, mestizos, [Spanish] ladies, mestizas, black [men and] women, mulattos, and mulatas should not be allowed to wear Indians' clothes, nor should Indian men and women be allowed to wear Spaniards' clothes, because under such pretexts they do great offense to God, do not serve His Majesty, and lack all obedience to law. This should be seriously punished by the justices.

555    When Spaniards, Indians, and blacks go on local religious processions, the women should walk in one part of the procession and the men should walk in another, and they should not talk with each other, because they only go on processions and accompany the sacrament so that they can act like scoundrels. This should be punished by all the justices in the world, in this kingdom, in Lima.

*[An illustration, ms. p. 556, shows an elegant noble Spanish couple, wearing old-fashioned clothing and holding rosaries, under the heading: "Spaniards from Castile, Christians."]*

## CASTILE

◆ **THE SPANISH MEN AND WOMEN** who were born in Castile have much more honor and have learned the doctrine well. They have complete Christian faith and are filled with hope and charity, love for their fellows, and keep God's justice and writings. Thus, they follow the Ten Commandments of God and the Holy Mother Church, and all the good works of mercy. They listen lovingly, charitably, and humbly to the holy gospel.

They would rather be poor than rich, and they are hard workers and friends of everyone. That is why, although all things may be as burnt chaff, everything from Castile is valuable. It is impossible to put so much Christianity, works of mercy, alms, deeds, and service to God and His Majesty into writing. See here, Christian: who among you in this kingdom has offered, or been obliged, to go to war in Castile and conquer the Moors in service of God and His Majesty, or send an armada there? I don't see any of you doing anything in this land; instead, you are all against the poor of Jesus Christ. Instead, the poor people who come from Castile do charity and help the Indians in this kingdom with love. That is what Christian women are like. All they do is work and give alms, while they never give rise to anger among the poor Indians, for they well know that God and His Majesty gave the land to the Indians of this kingdom. This is the greatness of Castile and the Old Christians.

*[An illustration, ms. p. 558, shows a crucifix on the conceptual right-hand side of the panel and the Spanish coat of arms on the left, under the heading, "The Holy Catholic Faith and the Royal arms and royal crown fill the world and this kingdom. May they be placed over everything." The chapter ends with a declaration of faith in Catholicism and the mission of Castile in the world, with an implicit argument that Peru should be considered an equal partner with Spain. The general conclusion to the series of chapters that began with "Mine Owners" follows.]*

## TO THE CHRISTIAN READER OF *"TAMBEROS,* INN KEEPERS, SPANISH WAYFARERS AND TRAVELERS, LADIES, MINE OWNERS, STEWARDS, SPANISH TRAVELERS, MULE DRIVERS, TRAVELING MERCHANTS, PEDDLERS, TRADERS, MERCHANTS, AND SHOPKEEPERS IN THIS KINGDOM"

*from 559*

READ THIS CHAPTER, and may it restrain you. Do not be proud, as you normally are, as when you arrive at the *tambos* and grab His Majesty's local magistrates by the hair and they, like barbarians, give in. Even if you were marched through the streets and given one hundred lashes as just punishment, even after all that you would still have your pride, like that great, handsome angel, Luzbel, who became Lucifer, the great devil, and lost heaven through his pride. When you arrive at the poor Indians' farms, you immediately steal their cattle, food, sacks, wool, rope, meat jerky, and corn. If you can manage it, you take their money as well, and force them to work for free. In the *tambos,* you refuse to pay them for their labor, their sweat, their days of work, and their food and other goods. In all this, you have no fear of God or justice. On the highways, you are such absolute lords that you beat your *mitayo* Indians like beasts of burden, and you load them down like animals and force them to march ahead of you. You favor each other when you do these things. There is no justice for the Indian, for you always find the cursed enemy of God and of the poor of Jesus Christ at your door—the *corregidor*. He would rather punish the poor than you.

Consider now how Christian the Indians are, and how they fear God, the king, and justice. If they were to go to your land and kingdom, and there take away your wives, daughters, belongings, and labor; and if, on top of that, they were to load you down with burdens like pack horses, drive you along the road with sticks, and beat you like pigs, what would you do then? All this would eat you alive and would leave you unhappy. You would put the blame—and the punishment that awaits in hell—for all this on the *corregidores* and the magistrates, for taking you and tying you up and giving you a thousand lashes for your pride. Why do you drive your horse along, then? With all the wrong you do through your sins, you have come here to kill yourselves. The judge punishes the poor man with beatings. The proud man is the one who should die for his pride, just as proud demons have always died.

Therefore, Christian reader, reform yourselves and serve God. Be humble, pay your fellow men, and do not die intestate because of your sins and your pride. Do not be punished, as when Don García, the marquis and viceroy, ordered a gentleman to be hanged for killing a poor Indian: the viceroy refused to eat until he had seen the gentleman hanged, because he had killed one of the poor of Jesus Christ. Therefore, reform yourselves.

## *561–573*    CHAPTER OF THE *ENCOMENDEROS:* THE *ENCOMENDEROS* OF INDIANS IN THIS KINGDOM, SOME OF THEM BEING GOOD CHRISTIANS, FRIENDS OF GOD AND OF THE POOR, AND OTHERS BEING THEIR ENEMIES: EACH IN THEIR OWN CHAPTER SHALL DECLARE THEIR HISTORIES, LIVES, AND CHRISTIANITY

*[The next group to come under criticism are the* encomenderos, *the highest ranking members of Spanish colonial society. Drawn largely from the ranks of leading conquerors and their descendents, or from wealthy Spaniards with good connections in the royal or viceregal court, these men were given the* encomienda *or "trust" of caring for the spiritual needs of a group of Indians (usually an entire province under a native lord or* curaca). *In exchange for the spiritual burden they were undertaking, they were allowed a certain amount of tribute from "their" Indians. In the early years, this tribute was in the form of both agricultural products and forced, unpaid labor. By the 1540s, legal restrictions attempted to suppress the use of forced labor tribute, but the* encomenderos *rebelled against the "New Laws" and continued their former practices for*

*many more generations. To undercut the rationale for having encomenderos, Guaman Poma argues that the native lords of the Andes are more noble than the encomenderos; that they believe fully in Catholic doctrine and accept the king of Spain as their own; and that "there was no conquest," as he has previously insisted.]*

THE *ENCOMENDEROS* of this kingdom, who have received grants of Indi-     563
ans from His Majesty, use the fact that these grants name them *encomenderos* and conquerors as a pretext to do great harm—first of all, to the Indians and lords of these kingdoms who are often more noble than some of the *encomenderos* themselves. For [the Indian lords] are not Jews or Moors, but rather Christians by blood and lineage, who have faith in God and know that there is one true God. . . . The Indians of this kingdom recognize and obey all the viceroys, judges, and justices of God, and they hold His Majesty to be their lord and *encomendero*.

The *encomenderos* go around playing cards and gambling and holding many feasts and banquets. They dress in silks and spend very liberally, since it costs them none of their own sweat or labor; instead, they demand money from the poor Indians, and it does not pain them that it comes from the poor Indians' labor. They do not even pray to God for the poor Indians, nor for the health of our lord the king, nor for the pope's health, and they do not remember the labor of the poor Indians in this kingdom. This is why God punished them and their children in this kingdom.

For some *encomenderos,* citizens, Spaniards, and soldiers are the sons or grandsons of men who were traitors against the royal crown in the time of the battle of Quito [. . .] and other battles. They were traitors, because what they did once they did for all time; [their treachery] was investigated, examined, and declared with flying banners. [. . .]

These *encomenderos* cannot call themselves *encomenderos* of Indians nor conquerors by dint of justice, because they were not the conquerors of the Indians; rather, the Indians willingly made peace with the royal crown without rising up against it, as the primary princes, lords, and great nobles of this kingdom went to the port of Tumbes to meet the arriving Christians, messengers of the Catholic emperor-king Don Carlos. [. . .] Thus, the four parts of this kingdom went to make peace and kiss the hands and feet of our lord the emperor-king Don Carlos of glorious memory. It would have been enough if only His Excellency Don Martín de Ayala had gone to make peace and serve the royal crown for all of Peru, for he was a great lord (*capac apo*), the second-in-command of the Inca, and his viceroy for these kingdoms. Therefore, we have no *encomenderos* or conquerors; instead, we belong to the royal crown of His Majesty, in the service of God and his royal crown.

**No *corregidor* should** be selected or given a grant to be an *encomendero;* nor should any judges, tradesmen, rich men or their sons, or mine owners be named as such, for they already have been given grants from His Majesty that allow them to eat; instead, the poor men and gentlemen who have served His Majesty should be given the means to eat through these grants. For it is more beneficial that the poor be allowed to eat than the rich, in order that everyone might eat and might serve God and His Majesty throughout the world and this kingdom. And this man should be a proven gentleman: not a Jew or a Moor, but an Old Christian and a servant of God and His Majesty, a gentleman, an hidalgo, and a charitable and learned man with no self-interest in this kingdom.

The ***encomenderos, corregidores,*** and padres cannot be store owners, neither by themselves nor with a partner; nor can they be merchants, farmers, livestock owners, by themselves nor with partners. If they should be found to be such, [their businesses] should be taken from them, and the Indians and poor Spanish soldiers who have no salaries, rental income, mines, or other estates should be allowed to earn a living. Thus, the world and this kingdom should be left to the poor. And priests should not be allowed to have [an estate worth] more than five hundred [pesos],[252] and if they do have more, it should be taken from them. [. . .]

573 **TO THE READERS OF "*ENCOMENDEROS* OF THE INDIANS OF THIS KINGDOM"**

**SEE, CHRISTIAN READERS:** read these chapters and place your hands on your chests and hearts and speak first attentively with God. Give Him infinite thanks, and remember above all the king who has graciously given you the grant of eating for free, without owing anything, taking the food away from the natural lords and great nobles of this kingdom. You say that you are conquerors, but you carried out this conquest with two words that you learned to say: "*Ama mancha, noca Inca* [No be afraid, I am Inca]." You said no more than this; it cost you nothing, for the only battles and uprisings were among yourselves, you traitors. You yearned to be kings, in place of the one who, as a Catholic Christian, has given you food to eat without any right of your own. Without considering everything, you have gone behind his back to injure the poor Indians so badly.

The first conquerors did recognize and consider this, and they feared God and His Majesty, whom they obeyed and honored. They sat to eat with the nobles, and gave them all the cloth and clothing they could want. If there was a frost and the crops were lost, they pardoned the poor Indians in this

---

[252] See ms. p. 700: "priests should not have an estate to support them worth more than five hundred pesos, and if a priest has more, it should be donated to the Holy Church."

kingdom. Thus, Captain Cárdenas left a large legacy of Castilian sheep to the community property (*sapsi*) in Chocorvos, Yauyos, and Huilcancho, which today have more than 50,000 sheep. Captain Peña was a saintly man who loved his Indians; though he left them little inheritance, he did put many communities in good order, and as a result the Jauja valley is now rich. The *encomendero* of the Lucanas, Don Pedro de Córdoba of the Order of Santiago, left nothing to the Indians, but he did decree that the province of the Lucanas should restore all of the Indians' community property (*sapsi*) and appoint an administrator. In this way, he favored them against the harms and injuries of the *corregidor* and the priest. His son was Christian as well; Don Andrés de Córdoba favored the poor. The citizens of Cusco, Charca, Arequipa, Lima, and Quito also favored the poor, while others abused them.

See, Christian reader: endeavor to favor the poor of Jesus Christ and thereby serve God and His Majesty. Give alms, contribute to community property, favor your poor Indians and defend them from the *corregidor* and the *doctrina* priest. Do not use your favoring them as a cover for robbing them of their poor possessions. Fear God and justice, and tell your Indians that they belong to God and the royal crown: "Both you and I belong to His Majesty." Teach them in this way, open their eyes to deceptions, and do not deceive them with lies. In this way, you will serve God and gain heaven, God will aid you, and the king will thank you.

## CHAPTER ONE OF THE *DOCTRINA* PADRES OF THIS KINGDOM OF PERU

*from*
*574–674*

*[The next chapter, on parish priests, is by far the longest in the book, at 101 pages. This length reflects the importance of the priests in the colonial government. For most Indians in early seventeenth-century Peru, the civil authorities—*corregidores *and* encomenderos*—were distant and often inaccessible figures, who left the everyday running of their enterprises to deputies (*tenientes*) and stewards (*mayordomos*). The* doctrina *priest was the face of colonial rule. Guaman Poma's indictment (ms. pp. 576–626) charges that the* doctrina *priests: (1) were arrogant, disregarding the examples of humility set by the fathers of the church; (2) ruled their parishes as absolute tyrants; (3) forced their parishioners to work for them without pay, sometimes in sweatshop conditions; (4) freely used women Indians as mistresses, giving rise to a generation of "little mestizos" and threatening the future of the Indians; (5) meted out cruel punishments to any parishioners who opposed their abusive rule; (6) gambled, dueled, and drank with other Spaniards, mestizos, and disreputable Indians; (7) did not learn Indian languages properly, and used the little language skill*

*they had to preach self-serving sermons (of which he gives several examples, in the priests' broken Quechua).*

*Guaman Poma then lays out his view of the proper behavior for priests, and takes time to praise certain priests, Franciscans, hermits, nuns, and Jesuits for keeping true to their calling (ms. pp. 627–56). Other friars, however, such as Augustinians, Dominicans, and Mercedarians, have the same vices as the average parish priest (ms. pp. 657–63). The chapter concludes with Guaman Poma's reflections on justice and the proper role of priests.]*

576–580  ◆ **THE PRIESTS AND PADRES,** who stand in for God and his saints—the cleric St. Peter, the Mercedarian friar of Our Lady of Mercy, the lord St. Francis, St. Dominic, St. Augustine, and the hermits St. Paul, the first hermit, and St. Anthony—do not do as those blessed souls did. Instead, they tend towards greed for silver, clothes, the things of the world, the sins of the flesh, and appetites and wrongs that cannot be put into writing, though the good reader will immediately know that they are well worth exemplary punishments. They should be punished by the Holy Inquisition, and the blame for this state should be laid to their prelates and superiors. Their sins harm the Spaniards, and even more so the New Christians, who are the Indians and blacks. How can a priest who has a dozen children set a good example for the Indians of this kingdom?

◆ **The *doctrina* padres and priests** are very bad-tempered, despotic, and proud, and they are filled with disdain, which causes the Indians to keep away from them in fear. These priests forget that our Lord Jesus Christ made himself poor and humble, so that he might attract the poor sinners, gather them in, and bring them into his holy church, and from there bring them to His kingdom of heaven.

◆ **The *doctrina* padres and priests** keep their siblings, children, or relatives with them, or some other Spaniard, mestizo, or mulatto, or they keep slave men or women, or many Indian servants—*yanaconas* and *chinaconas* (cooks). In so doing, they greatly increase the wrongs and robberies of the poor Indians in this kingdom.

◆ **The *doctrina* padres** trade and do business, in their own persons and through others, causing great damage; and they do not pay. With the pretext of paying [their debts], they employ many Indians, and there is no remedy, throughout the kingdom.

◆ **The padres and priests oversee** the making of cloth—*cumpi* and *awasca* for women, and *chumpi*—to sell, claiming that the cloth is for their prelates. They tell their managers to order the poor Indians to make the cloth, employing them without paying them anything at all, throughout the kingdom.

◆ The *doctrina* **padres and priests** employ [Indians], making them weave cloth (*awasca*) for sacks, tents, bed covers, tablecloths, *chumpis, winchas,* laces, ropes, and other things, which they sell and trade without paying for them. To do this, they punish the nobles, the magistrates, and the lay religious leaders. Because of all this labor, people leave [their pueblos] throughout the kingdom.

◆ The *doctrina* **padres and priests** in this kingdom—each and every one of them—employ Indians as *mitayos*. Two Indians in the kitchen, another in the stable, another as gardener, another as doorman, another in the kitchen, more *mitayos* to chop firewood, carry hay, herd cattle, and to serve as traders, messengers, field hands, chicken guards, goatherds, shepherds, cowherds, horse *camayo* [keeper], and swineherds. They also employ the Indian men and women in other irrelevant tasks, and for this reason [the Indians] leave their houses.

◆ The *doctrina* **padres and priests** keep ten mules in their stables, along with others that belong to their friends, and fatten them all at the expense of the harsh labor of Indian men and unmarried women. Some priests keep whole herds of cows, up to a thousand head, or flocks of goats or sheep, or large numbers of pigs, horses, or local sheep [llamas], 100 or 200 chickens, capons, and rabbits; and they have fields for the managers of each herd, along with corrals and houses, all employing the poor Indians, who do not get paid. But if one of them loses an animal, he is charged 100 [reales] for it, yet he is never paid or given anything to eat. Because of such harsh labor, people leave.

◆ The **padres and priests** in this kingdom each keep four unmarried women as *mitayas* (cooks) in their kitchens, along with a head cook who prepares the food, not to mention many beautiful unmarried women kept in the house as *mitayas*. They also each keep more than eight young men and others as stable boys, stewards, and much pomp and circumstance, all at the expense of the Indians. These *yanaconas* and their wives eat up a bushel and a half of food every day, and they do not pay for it. The Indian women give birth to mestizos, and they become scoundrels and whores in this kingdom.

◆ The *doctrina* **padres and priests** in this kingdom demand Indians and llamas to transport wine, peppers, coca, and corn. Some priests send their cargo on the backs of the Indians, bringing wine from the plains and coca from the mountainous lowlands. The Indians, being from the high mountains, die of fevers and chills when they enter the hot country. And if the Indian breaks [what he is carrying], he is forced to pay for it.

◆ The *doctrina* **padres** compel widows and unmarried women to spin and weave, accusing them of having lovers as an excuse for making them work without pay. In this way, the Indian women become whores, and

# PADRES: FORCING THE INDIAN WOMEN TO WEAVE CLOTH BY ACCUSING THEM OF HAVING LOVERS— THEY BEAT THEM AND DO NOT PAY.

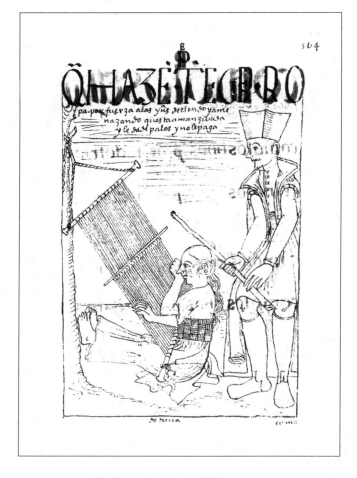

*In the* doctrina.

there is no remedy. They no longer wish to get married, because they are following the padre or another Spaniard. Thus the Indians do not multiply in this kingdom, but only mestizos and mestizas, and there is no remedy.

◆ The *doctrina* **padres and priests** in each pueblo take and keep the treasuries of their churches, religious brotherhoods, and hospitals, claiming to help them while spending [their funds]: this calls out for punishment. They are abetted by the *corregidor* or the inspector in making these demands, and under these pretexts they rob the Indians of their treasuries and common property.

◆ The *doctrina* **padres and priests** in this kingdom keep the offerings and alms given at the Masses for the dead. They demand six [pesos] for singing the High Mass, when the set fee is three; for Low Mass, they demand four, when the set fee is one. Some charge as much as ten or twenty and do not even say the Mass. They charge four reales for an offering for the dead, when such alms are supposed to be voluntary. These things call out for restitution: they should return their belongings to the poor Indians, and such padres should be punished in this kingdom. There is no remedy.

◆ The *doctrina* **padres** demand five pesos for wedding ceremonies and four pesos for baptisms, paying no attention to the fact that His Majesty has given them a salary. This calls out for restitution and punishment.

◆ The *doctrina* **padres** eat at no cost to themselves, refusing to pay for their wheat, corn, potatoes, mutton, chicken, eggs, bacon, lard, tallow candles, peppers, salt, *tamos, cawi, chochoca, chuño,* quinoa, beans, lima beans, chickpeas, fava beans, fish, shrimp, lettuce, cabbages, garlic, onion, cilantro, parsley, peppermint, and other condiments, dishes, and fruits, as well as firewood and hay. They pay nothing for all this, even though the expense adds up to a dozen pesos a day; sometimes they pay four reales to salve their consciences. And there is no remedy, nor is there any favor for the poor Indians of this kingdom. Thus, the Indians leave and depopulate their pueblos, because of such hard labor.

◆ The *doctrina* **padres** refuse to follow the decrees set out by the Holy Council [of Trent] and His Majesty's ordinances and royal stipulations, even though these state that they are not to keep unmarried women, married women, widows, old women, young women, or girls in their houses and kitchens, nor are they to gather them in under the pretext of teaching them doctrine, because of the damage and quarrels. The Indians will cease to multiply and will come to an end, bringing an end to their estates and their service to God and His Majesty. Instead, [the laws] state that [girls] should serve their mothers and fathers, and should come to the aid of their communities (*sapsi*) in every province. There is no remedy. Therefore, the numbers of mestizos and *cholos* multiply in this kingdom.

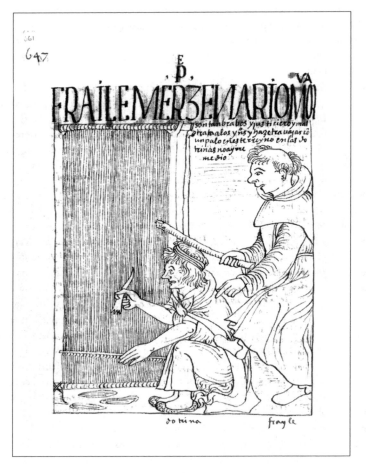

They are so fierce and exacting; they mistreat the Indians and beat them to make them work in the *doctrinas* of this kingdom. There is no remedy.

### *In the* doctrina.

◆ The *doctrina* **padres** come to ruin because they meddle beyond their station in matters of ecclesiastic and secular justice, acting as vicars general when they are mere parish priests. They pretend that they are the *corregidores* and that they have the offices of magistrate and noble *cacique,* issuing and overturning decrees. In this way they become involved in lawsuits, drawing up petitions and notes in their own hand, setting bad examples for their pueblos, and being destructive towards the noble *caciques, corregidores,* and *encomenderos.* And there is no remedy. They act as absolute despots, and thereby destroy the Indians of this kingdom.

◆ **Padre Juan Bautista Albadán** was the priest of San Cristóbal de Pampachiri.[253] He was a despotic, cruel padre. The things that this man did cannot be written. When one Indian from the pueblo, named Diego Carwas, did not give him a sheep, he took him and strapped him to a crossbeam like the cross of St. Andrew. He tied him there naked and began to burn him with a tallow candle, putting the flame on his backside and his shameful parts, lighting many candles and abusing him, opening his backside with his hands. They said that this priest did many other things that cannot be written, but God should know of them, and that he did many other harmful and wicked things. Thus, he tortured the "painters," as they were known there. He did this because the unmarried daughters of Don Juan Wacrau had complained that Padre Albadán would take off their clothes and stare at their backsides and vulvas, and would stick his fingers in their backsides and give them four slaps. He would do this every morning to each of the girls. The governor, Don León Apawasco, defended [Don Juan] from all this, so Padre Albadán testified against him, claiming that the governor was hiding Indians from the inspectors. In this way, he forced [the governor] into exile, and Apawasco died from this grief.

Therefore, padres, look and see whether you do not all deserve to have the Holy Office [of the Inquisition] punish you for your pride. You do these things under the pretext of claiming to be proprietors, making young maidens enter your *doctrinas.* These troubles and griefs are killing the bishops of this kingdom, because you are punishing us cruelly.

## MERCEDARIAN FRIARS

661–663

**THIS FRIAR, MURÚA,** was the prefect of the pueblo of Yanaca in the province of the Aymaraes.[254] He was terribly destructive to the Indians, causing

---

[253] In the province of Andahuaylas, just east of Guaman Poma's home province of Lucanas Laramati.

[254] Guaman Poma was apparently a close collaborator with the Mercedarian friar and chronicler Martín de Murúa in the 1580s and 1590s, before a falling out between the two in 1604–1606. See Adorno, *Guaman Poma* (2000), pp. xx and liv–lv; and Juan Ossio,

harm, damage, and troubles. He gathered together the unmarried women to spin yarn, to weave cloth, to make *cumpi, awasca,* tents, tablecloths, *wasca* [rope], blankets, and sacks, to dye wool, and to mix *chicha.* He imposed punishments on the Indians of the pueblo, on the outsider Indians, on the community treasury of the Indians, and on unmarried Indian women, boys, and girls. He would bear witness against them in order to rob them, saying that he was thereby serving his prelate, who would therefore never remove him from [his post as parish priest of] the *doctrina,* and threatening to whip them to death. He caused them such trouble and punishments that the Indians left and the pueblos became depopulated, so that the Indians owed the *encomendero* ten thousand pesos in uncollected tribute.

This friar was also the *corregidor's* deputy judge. He would steal married women and the Indian men's daughters and sisters, and he would tell them that, even if he were removed from the *doctrina,* he would still go home to the friary to eat and sleep.

**This friar Murúa** was the *doctrina* priest of the pueblos of Pocohuanca, Pacica, and Pichihua.[255] He was padre, *corregidor,* vicar, magistrate, and executioner with his own hands. He disciplined, punished, and did justice as if he were the church inspector. Under these pretexts, he gathered in all the maidens and passed judgments, making and unmaking decrees.

He had one tributary Indian whom he called Don Hernando, whose daughter he kept in his kitchen. He favored this Hernando on account of his daughter, which stirred up everyone in the pueblo. Hernando made himself a *curaca,* like it or not, and he was always named pueblo magistrate. He took away one Indian woman's property and beat her to death, and he forced two pregnant Indian women to move, because that was what the padre wanted. Even though he performed idolatry, [Murúa] let it pass; out of fear of the padre, the *corregidor* did not wish to do justice. Captain Alonso de Medina, the *corregidor,* began the case against Hernando, asking his [Indian] district magistrate, Don Domingo Conespaniura, to collect evidence, review it, and do justice, together with the town council notary. Therefore, Don Domingo reviewed the case and sentenced Hernando to fifty lashes, removal from office, and banishment [from the pueblo] for having turned idolater, having beaten the Indian woman to death, and having moved her children. He passed sentence and banished him without fear of Padre Murúa.

---

"Tras la huella de Fray Martín de Murúa," paper presented at the Primer Congreso Internacional de Peruanistas en el Extranjero, Harvard University, 29 April 1999 (www.fas.harvard.edu/~icop/juanossio.html).

[255] Small communities near Yanaca in the province of Aymaraes.

When the padre found out about this business, he went to see the *corregidor* and argued with him, threatening to write to the Audiencia because of the way the *corregidor* had favored his district magistrate, and telling the *corregidor* to take away the magistrate's staff of office and banish him. But the *corregidor* was afraid to take away Don Domingo's staff of office. The notary, Andrés González de Vargas, told the *corregidor*, "See here, señor *corregidor*, just do what the padre tells you to do. Let's not go up against the padres or the *encomenderos*, because we didn't come here to favor the Indians. Even if we were to hang a half dozen Indians and skin them, tomorrow or the next day we'll be leaving this place. Let's take a good pile of reales with us, and not get mixed up in problems. If you don't do what the padre told you to do, señor *corregidor*, then I want to leave this post."

The saintly *corregidor* was so Christian and God-fearing that he told the notary, "God go with you, and good riddance, because the king pays me to favor the poor and do justice for them."

Nevertheless, the notary and the priest together defeated him, and so the priest was able to take away Don Domingo's staff of office as judge and punish him. He punished him to take revenge for what he had done to the Indian Hernando, his father-in-law. He went together with another friar to punish him, and the foolish, blockheaded magistrate was frightened and let himself be defeated.

For this and many other reasons, it is not good for friars to be *doctrina* priests; rather, they should stay in their friaries. For priests are the ones who belong to the order of the apostles, teaching doctrine. See how much harm one friar did to this magistrate, who was a *curaca* over five hundred Indians in his band. What I have written here is a matter of mockery, and if I were to write this friar's entire life, I would not finish writing it in a year. No Christian in the world would believe how free the friars are to roam outside their friaries in this kingdom.

*[Guaman Poma ends the chapter with a series of proposals for reforming the colonial church:*

*(1) He criticizes the fees that priests exact from their parishioners for saying Mass on feast days such as All Saints, when they charge "each Indian, whether or not they have dead family members," arbitrary and outrageous fees such as five pesos, a small llama, a bushel of potatoes, or three pounds of good wool. Instead, priests should be limited to the moderate fees prescribed by the Council of Trent—no more than "one half-real per Indian male and one ear of corn per Indian female." (ms. pp. 664–65)*

*(2) Indian sextons (sacristanes)* should call their *ayllus to Mass with a series of twenty peals of the church bells. Minor officials will no longer go*

*through the pueblo calling people to Mass, which Guaman Poma sees as an excuse for their entering houses to "rob and fornicate." But, when all the parishioners are in the church, the officials should make the rounds of the pueblo so that they can catch those who ignore the tolling bells and punish them. He concludes: "In this way, their Christianity will be reformed, and they will know that the bells are calling them as Christians. For the Indians have already been Christians for fifty or one hundred years; the old people—the people of the Incas—are dying out, and the people now are the children of baptized Christians; they are now Old Christians."*[256] *(ms. pp. 666–67)*

*(3) Indian pueblos should meet in council to consider complaints raised against the priest, and should forward those complaints to a regional vicar general for judgment. While the complaint is under investigation, the priest should be removed from office, with pay, and a replacement appointed. (ms. pp. 668–69)*

*(4) Monasteries and friaries should not be allowed to serve as places of refuge for people who have been convicted of heinous crimes and sentenced to death. (ms. pp. 669–70)*

*(5) The friaries should be inspected annually, and the prelates who head them should be able to prove "that they are noble people, gentlemen and hidalgos, Old Christians," and should have to pass an examination in letters, for "without good blood and without letters, they cannot rule or govern the letters of God and the laws of these kingdoms." (ms. pp. 670–71)*

*Guaman Poma's concluding proposal follows. Here he criticizes the common Spanish usage by which priests of Indian parishes called themselves* propietarios *(proprietors or owners) of the parish benefice, and he ties his critique of priests back to his views on the legitimacy of Spanish rule.]*

671–74   **All the *doctrina* padres** are foreigners—that is, in the language of the Indians, *mitmac*—from Castile, so they cannot call themselves proprietors, even if they are sons of Spaniards, unless they are also sons of Indians. Thus, the *doctrina* padres of this kingdom are in no way proprietors; they are mere interim priests, because the Indians alone are the legitimate proprietors

---

[256] In Spain, "Old Christian" was a racialized term used to distinguish those with "purity of blood" from the "New Christians," those descended in any degree from Jews or Muslims. In the Americas, the Spanish authorities considered all Indians (even those born after many generations of Spanish rule and Catholic indoctrination) to be "new to the faith," and they used this classification to deny Indians access to the priesthood and other honors. The idea that Indians had become "Old Christians" was thus a serious, though futile, claim.

whom God planted in this kingdom. If an Indian should happen to go to Spain, he would be a foreigner (*mitmac*) in Spain. Therefore, by God and by justice, there are no Spanish proprietors in this kingdom; even if a Spaniard is born in this kingdom, he is still a son of foreigners (*mitmacpa churin, mitmacpa wawaynin*).

The king alone is a proprietor and a legitimate Inca king, because when Wascar was the Inca king, his brother Atawalpa, the bastard Inca king, killed him. Don Francisco Pizarro sentenced Atawalpa for his guilt, and he died and left his crown to the emperor-king. Afterwards, the conquerors in their greed and lowness tried to become kings and rose up. The emperor-king defended himself against them all, labored, and won this land; thus, he is the proprietor and legitimate Inca king. Therefore, there are no other proprietors anywhere in the kingdom other than the noble Indian princes. Even if a mestizo or a mulatto is a proprietor on his mother's side, it must be known what band (*ayllu*) he belongs to, and he must reside in the cities.

*[An illustration, ms. p. 672, shows the coat of arms of the bishops of Peru.]*

## PROLOGUE

### TO THE READERS OF "THE PADRES OF THIS KINGDOM"

**THE ONLY THING** you must do, Christian padres, is commend yourselves to God.

The second thing is to read these chapters, and cease being fierce. Humble yourselves before your prelates; do not be despotic lords; do not meddle in doing justice when that is not your place; do not enter into government, nor give orders from a post of justice or of the noble *caciques* and magistrates. Do not go beyond the Holy Council [of Trent], beyond all that was decreed by God in the Ten Commandments, the Holy Gospel, and the good works of mercy, and beyond all His Majesty's decrees. Do not go beyond the Testaments.

Be satisfied with your salary and altar fees. Pay what you owe for your food. You must pay for hay, firewood, other products, and the labor of the *mitayos*.

Do not introduce the living soul of a woman into your consecrated house without pondering that you are a priest. Do not let your other sins be known in public, for you are setting a bad example for Christians.

Do not fight with everyone in the pueblo, nor with any poor Indian man or woman, as you do, taking up arms—a sword—against laymen soldiers and attacking them like highwaymen on the open roads, taking away the Indians' estates and stealing their women, their daughters, and everything they own, even though you have never been charged with these crimes.

Fear no man, but only God, the pope, His Majesty, and your prelates.

If any person should complain about all the harm you have caused, or if they should abuse you and beat you, you should accept their blows, and any judge who might favor you would be foolish, because the person who begins something should pay for it.

For you, being a priest is a pretext for insolence. You do not look to see if someone is rich or poor. As a result, when you end up in a quarrel over the evils you have done, you immediately claim that your opponents are bad Christians and soldiers or bad Indians.

On this occasion, let me reply to His Lordship [the bishop], and let me say:

I beg Your Lordship be pleased to hear my plea for justice, that Your Lordship might discover the truth. Send us the reverend padres from the Company of Jesus, or the reverend friars and padres from the Order of St. Francis (but from no other religious order), for six months. If we are wrong, and we end up quarreling with these saintly religious men, these servants of Jesus Christ, then punish us. Otherwise, Your Lordship will discover the whole truth, will do service to God and justice to us, and will favor the poor Indians. Your Lordship may see the crimes and the insolence with which [the priest] treats the Spaniards; what might he not do with my Indians, helpless and poor as they are?

In this way, Your Lordship will no longer have to bear the hardship of hearing so many complaints, will well establish the punishment of rebels and evil men, and will favor the poor of Jesus Christ. Your Lordship should send the inspectors on tours of inspection with this list of charges.

Under express threat of excommunication, order the padres and priests that you assign to the parishes to paint Your Lordship's coat of arms on their doors on the main street as soon as they arrive, and below the coat of arms, to write in letters large enough to be read by every Christian and padre who faces them, these words: "Leave off all business dealings, and act as a priest. Any woman who enters the padre's house shall be excommunicated and punished by all His Majesty's justices." If the priest does not put up this sign, he should be fined one hundred pesos each time he is charged, and he should be punished. Through these means, he will be restrained, will mend his ways, will show less pride and lust, and will humble himself in obedience to the Holy Council of this kingdom. Let him not take away the Indians' estates, saying that they gave them to him during confession, for a confession must not be revealed; instead, what is in their testaments must be fulfilled.

These coats of arms and signs should be placed in every city, town, hamlet, and pueblo, both large and small, throughout this kingdom, as examples, so that people might keep the signs in their sight. The letters should be very large, so that the padres themselves will read them; the Indian men and women will take them as an example; the Indian women who lead bad lives, the *fiscales,* and the sextons will learn to fear the hands of justice; and the *mitayas* and married, unmarried, and widowed Indian women and Indian maidens and girls will have no excuse for entering the house of any padre in this kingdom.

In this way, Your Lordship will live long and enjoy good health and life, without so many quarrels and complaints in this kingdom. That is why the illustrious bishops have died in this kingdom. If Your Lordship wishes to keep his health, hear not the petitions of a padre who is being sent to prison, but rather let him rest there, for that is justice.

## THE CHURCH

*[The chapter on priests is followed by one on the Church. The Indian lay officials (fiscales, cantors, sextons, stewards, choirmasters, and artisans) who ran rural parishes on a day-to-day basis, often with little interference from the nominal parish priests, are covered in ms. pp. 675–88. One of the final subchapters within the chapter on the Church (ms. pp. 689–705) covers pastoral inspectors (visitadores), beginning with a description of Cristóbal de Albornoz, for whom Guaman Poma worked in the 1570s and whom he admired for his honesty.]*

CRISTÓBAL DE ALBORNOZ, general inspector for the Holy Church: this   *689–691* man was a fierce judge.[257] He cruelly punished the padres and proud men; he punished the demons, the *wacas* (idols) of the Indians, breaking and burning them; he made the Indian sorcerers, both men and women, wear the penitential cap;[258] and he punished the false sorcerers: *taqui oncoy,*

---

[257] Cristóbal de Albornoz is best known for his efforts at "extirpating idolatries" in Peru, particularly during his tour as *visitador* in the provinces of Soras and Lucanas in 1568–1570 when an Andean religious revival movement known as *Taki Unquy* ("dancing sickness") advocated a return to the old forms of worship and a rejection of all that was Christian and European. The available evidence seems to confirm Guaman Poma's claim to have accompanied Albornoz on this *visita,* and it is likely that this experience taught Guaman Poma much of what he knew both about the Huamanga region and about Catholic orthodoxy (Adorno, *Guaman Poma* [2000], xlv–lvi). See also Luis Millones and Sara Castro-Klaren, *El Retorno de las huacas: Estudios y documentos sobre el Taki Onqoy, siglo XVI* (Lima: Instituto de Estudios Peruanos, 1990), which contains documents by Albornoz; Sara Castro-Klaren, "Dancing and the Sacred in the Andes: From the Taqui-Oncoy to Rasu-Niti," in Stephen Greenblatt, ed., *New World Encounters* (Berkeley: University of California Press, 1993); and Ranulfo Cavero Carrasco, *Los dioses vencidos: Una lectura antropológica del Taki Onqoy* (Ayacucho, Peru: Universidad Nacional de San Cristóbal de Huamanga, 2001).

[258] Penitential cap (*coroza*): as in the illustration, on p. 222. Wearing a *coroza* and a rope around the neck while carrying a candle in a public procession were penitences imposed by the church on those convicted of witchcraft.

# FIRST CHAPTER OF INSPECTORS:
## CRISTÓBAL DE ALBORNOZ,
## GENERAL INSPECTOR FOR THE
## HOLY MOTHER CHURCH, GOOD JUSTICE.

*Judge.*

*illapa, chuqui illa, waca wilca, sara illa, llama illa, chirapa, pacha mama, pucyo yaycusca, waca wilca macascan, oncoycuna sara urmachisca, papa urmachisca, ayapchasca.*[259] This fierce judge punished all these things. He took no bribes; nor did he rob, nor travel with pomp and circumstance. He was a simple, saintly man who feared God, and thus he did everything in the service of God in this kingdom.

Don Juan Cocha Quispe, the *fiscal* [lay religious leader], was a low-ranking *Quichihua* Indian.[260] By order of Cristóbal de Albornoz, he destroyed all the *wacas* (idols), hiding his own, and thereby he reached the rank of *curaca*. But he took large bribes, and in this way he ended up very rich, while the judge ended up poor. Hence, he became the *curaca* (head noble) whom all the *Quichihua* and *mitmac* [outsider] Indians obeyed, and even today his sons continue in the rulership of that *ayllu, Quichihua.*

**The inspectors should** take away any arms, whether defensive or offensive, that the priest or any of His Majesty's justices might have. The inspector should take away the arms, or, if [the priests] carry them after being warned, he should punish them, because carrying such arms frightens the Indians; apart from this, the priests bear very powerful arms by the fact of being anointed and consecrated by God. Even if they are hermits, they are servants of Jesus Christ, and they are blessed in this world by good works.

**When the inspectors** banish the parish priests from the *doctrinas* in this kingdom, they move to the nearest [Spanish] city or town, and they return to walk around in the Indian pueblo demanding *camaricos* and *mitayos* (food and servants) for free, threatening the nobles and the Indians, telling them that they are going to move back to the *doctrina* as soon as their six months of banishment are over, and that they will then whip [the Indians] to death for not sending them chickens and eggs and partridges and fruit. [The priests] order them to herd their cattle, and tell the sextons and *fiscales* and young men to come serve them; if they do not serve them, the priests write to the *corregidor* and his deputy to have them punished. In this way,

---

[259] A list of common "superstitions," as the religious practices of the Andes were seen by orthodox Catholics. In order: *Taki Unquy* ("dancing sickness"); lightning (a manifestation of divine power); precious *illa* (a stone found near the point of a lightning strike, thought to embody the power of lightning and used as a "power object"); sacred *waqa;* corn *illa* and llama *illa* (two types of stone "power objects"); rainbow; Mother Earth (a sacred personification of the earth); entering a spring (some springs were thought to cause disease); hitting a sacred *waqa;* sicknesses (caused by) dropping corn; by dropping potatoes; by the presence of a dead body.

[260] That is, an Indian of the *Quichihua ayllu.* Guaman Poma elsewhere uses the same spelling (*quichiua*) for the Quechua language. It is debated whether the Spanish took the name of the language from this *ayllu* (who spoke a language closely related to the Quechua of Cusco) or if the similarity between the two names is merely coincidental.

each of them favors himself and helps himself and robs the poor Indians in this kingdom.

**The inspectors cannot** grant titles, nor choose vicars nor judges nor preachers nor licentiates; instead, only His Majesty can do so—or, in his name, His Lordship the bishop; because the inspectors take bribes and name ten vicars—mere children—in one province, to the great harm of the Indians. Each vicar destroys and acts childish; this is foolishness, and harms the province.

**The inspectors charge** fifteen pesos for each parish church, when they ought to charge two pesos for each church and one peso for each religious brotherhood in this kingdom.

**The inspectors travel** with such pomp and circumstance and extravagance that they keep the Indians in the pueblos and do not allow them to go to the mines and plazas and *tambos* and *chacras* (fields) [in order to earn money] for their tribute. The Indians are perishing in this kingdom.

694    [. . .] There is no justice in this kingdom of the Indies: it is all in Castile. There is nothing but sorrow for the poor Indians, punishment and shaming.[. . .] May Jesus Christ come and redeem it.

Regarding this, let me say that a certain Padre Peralta, from the *doctrina* of San Pedro de Queca, felt hatred and enmity toward an Indian second-in-command named Don Cristóbal de León, because the padre traded, and made [León] work, and locked all the young women [in his house].[261] He even took [León's] daughter, and stole other things from his estate, and put him to work at other jobs, and did not allow him to defend the Indians, as he was obliged to do as their second-in-command. I will not write down this padre's entire life and crimes, for it would take too long; the charges against him will suffice. This León wrote down several charges in his own handwriting, to plead for justice from His Lordship. A mestiza woman and her brother warned the padre; he then came after [León] with two men, arrested him, took away all his documents, trussed him up as a prisoner, and turned him over to another cheat, the *corregidor* Toledo—who was his friend, because the padre had loaned the *corregidor* two thousand pesos. Therefore, between the two of them they kept the prisoner in discomfort, trying lawsuits against him, so that León would die under false testimony.

It was then that an inspector came, another *criollo* cheat from Huamanga. His Lordship had sent him to inspect the padre, but he did not inspect him; instead, he inspected Don Cristóbal de León and the Indians, which is quite the contrary. They kept him closely imprisoned in fetters and stocks in his opponent's house, in order to make Padre Peralta happy, and

---

261 Guaman Poma has already written about his "disciple," Don Cristóbal; see pp. 169–73.

they paid no attention to the charges that León had leveled. In addition to this, the inspector sequestered his entire estate and sold it off cheaply to his own friends, leaving [León] with nothing. Aside from this, the padre burnt down his house and everything he owned.

In addition, when León found himself in this predicament, punished and naked, he said, "Inspector, sir, if His Lordship sent you to inspect the *doctrina* padres, why have you inspected me and destroyed my entire estate? I have been told that you were bribed. I am going to appeal all this before His Lordship, and I want to appear personally as the aggrieved party, together with my Indians."

Then, in anger and hatred, [the inspector] sentenced him and punished him and left him naked and took testimony against him, just as they had done to Don García Portocarrero before they beheaded him in Huamanga. So this is another Huamanga. He did not want to banish [León] to Cusco or to Lima, lest he might appear before His Majesty or before His Lordship.

In addition, because the padre had the inspector's favor, he punished the Indians who brought food to [León], hanging them from the whipping post and harming them in other ways.

Therefore, a *doctrina* padre cannot be a judge—especially if he is from Huamanga. [This inspector] should be punished: because he did not punish the padre; because he punished the Indian when he was not allowed to do so; because he inspected [León's] estates; and because he gave the padre free rein by not allowing [León's] appeal. He tried to act like a second bishop and head of the church, because he permitted the padre to burn down [León's] house, and he did not make him pay restitution for it, excommunicate him, throw him out of the *doctrina,* and send him as a prisoner to His Lordship's higher court. For these reasons, inspectors should be named in Spain by the hand of His Holiness and His Majesty, for the well-being of the noble Indians.

**The inspectors use a very great deal of food** at the expense of the Indi- *696–697* ans. They think that they do it at the expense of the padres, but all the expense goes to the poor Indians of this kingdom.

**The inspectors come with great ceremony** and pomp and circumstance, and they bring many people and pack animals and throngs that disturb the land. In this way they bother and give trouble to the Indians, and the Indians become afraid to draw near them to ask for justice. Thus these judges come in vain to this kingdom.

**The inspectors become very enraged** when the padres, the noble *caciques,* the poor Indians, and the outsider Indians do not bribe them or give them gifts of silver, clothing, silverware, *cumpi* textiles, or other gifts and bribes of food and services at the expense of the poor Indians. And, without paying for it, they mistreat and pass sentences with high fines against the padres as well and the poor Indians of this kingdom.

◆ **Some inspectors are very quick-tempered,** proud, and impetuous. In this way they ride roughshod over the padres and the Indians, who are afraid of them; so there is no justice, because they are the serpents, and they do not try to favor the poor. God save us from such ills.

◆ **The inspectors can be bribed:** inspectors, for a thousand pesos; notaries, for five hundred pesos; legal counsels, for one hundred pesos; and interpreters, for fifty pesos. With all this, the poor Indians of this kingdom cannot attain justice, and therefore the *doctrina* padres become arrogant.

**Because the [priests] have** the inspectors' favor, after the inspection is over, they order any Indian men and women who complained to be whipped cruelly, for having asked for justice before the inspector of this kingdom. Therefore, the Indians run away in this kingdom.

**Because all the judges and inspectors** are bribed by the *doctrina* padres, for that reason they severely punish and shame any Indians who ask for justice. As this is the inspector's business, there is no remedy; rather, the harm done to the Indians of this kingdom grows and grows. Because of all these troubles, they run away and the land becomes depopulated.

**No *doctrina* priest** should be chosen as an inspector or judge; rather, an inspector must necessarily be a canon, an archdeacon, or His Lordship [the bishop] himself or his vicar general; or else a distinguished man, a servant of Jesus Christ, a man of letters, a doctor or licentiate who has passed his examinations, a rich man who has never in his life been the priest of a *doctrina;* or one of the reverend padres of the Company of Jesus. He should have justice, love, and charity, and should do things in the right way, punishing the proud priest and favoring the Indians, and he should bring Christian officers with him without carrying away bribes, and he should bring a protector [of the Indians] on his inspections throughout this kingdom.

**The inspectors come** for no other reason than to steal, and they do no justice. As much money as they can take for themselves, they do take, and they do not punish the stewards, sextons, and *fiscales* [lay church officials] for spending and wasting the property of the church, the religious brotherhoods, and the [community] fields, croplands, and cattle; instead, they favor them, as long as they bribe and pay the inspectors and their notaries, throughout this kingdom.

705    **The inspectors who** do inspections should try the priests, the former inspectors, and all the past priests, if they find any cause or complaints or damage done. They should try the former priests as well, even if they left office one hundred years ago, because they sometimes join forces with the *corregidor,* the *encomendero,* and the *caciques,* and the poor Indians languish on their account, because the priests take everything they own. To keep

their wicked tricks from being discovered, the priests usually order the town criers to announce that the cost of the *mita* should be paid after the inspector's departure, under penalty of punishments, fines, and banishment. Facing these penalties, the poor Indians of this kingdom decline to press for justice, and if any Indian man or woman ever complains, [the priest] immediately picks up a sword or a knife, as if he were ready to kill the Indian, and he beats and punishes him. Therefore it is very just that the priest of the *doctrina* should not appear during the pastoral inspection and judgment, but rather that he remain in the city and the bishopric, or however His Lordship [the bishop] prefers. If the Indians demand it, it should be seen that there is no complaint from any living soul, not even from a child; and it should be clear that the priest has used his office as a priest and not as a judge, and that he has treated the Indians with love, charity, sermons, and the teaching of Christianity, throughout the world and in this kingdom.

*[The subchapter on church inspectors is followed, curiously, by Guaman Poma's suggestion for a standardized list of prices for foods and services, which he suggests should be imposed throughout the kingdom (ms. pp. 705–7). Perhaps he includes the price list here because he feels that the church inspectors are the only Spanish officials who might be trusted to enforce his price list, given that "the viceroys and the presidents and judges of the* Audiencia *have never reached every pueblo, nor can they reach them all or know all the harm that is done in this kingdom." The chapter closes with an allegorical reflection on the problems faced by the Indians within the colonial regime.]*

◆ **The Indians fear** the *corregidores* because they are worse than serpents.    *708–716*
They eat people, because they eat their livelihoods and their entrails and take away their property like fierce animals. They are the strongest of all; they beat and rob all the others in this kingdom, and there is no remedy.

**The Indians fear** the *encomendero* because he is the lion. When he grabs his prey he never lets go; with his claws, being such a fierce animal, he never pardons the poor man and never feels grateful to him, as a wild beast in this kingdom, and there is no remedy.

**The Indians fear** the *doctrina* priests because they are wily foxes. They are licentiates who know more than foxes about hunting the Indians, catching them, and stealing their estates, their women, and their daughters, for they are wily men of letters, licentiates, and *bachilleres*. That is why they call themselves men of letters; the good fox is a doctor, a man of letters.[262]

---

[262] Man of letters (*letrado*): any man with a post-elementary education, a rare status at the time. (No women were allowed to pursue higher education, so there were no "*letradas*.") Licentiate (*licenciado*): a man with a university degree roughly equivalent to a B.A., usually employed as a lawyer. *Bachiller:* a man with a baccalaureate, most often a

# Six Ravenous Animals Feared by the Poor Indians in This Kingdom.

Serpent—
*Corregidor*

Lion—
*encomendero*

Mouse—
noble *cacique*

Tiger—
Spaniards
of the
*tambos*

Fox—
*doctrina* padre

Cat—
notary

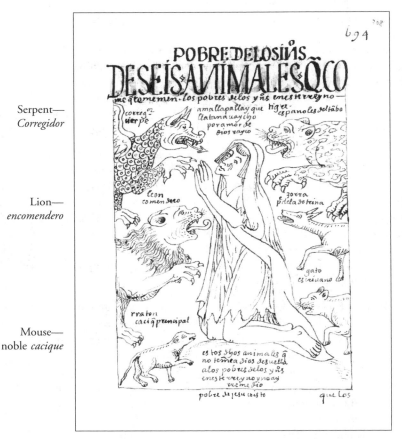

[Indian, in center:]
*Ama llapallayque llatanawaycho,* por amor de dios-*rayco.*
["Don't all of you strip me naked, for the love of God."]

These animals, which have no fear of God, skin the poor
Indians in this kingdom. There is no remedy.

***The poor of Jesus Christ.***

And thus in this kingdom they destroy the poor Indians, and there is no remedy.

**The Indians fear** the notary because he is a hunting cat. He stalks and works and grabs and does not let the poor mouse move. Thus, he stalks the poor Indians' estates until he grabs them, and once he grabs them, he does not allow them to wriggle. He is quick to grab them, and there is no remedy for the poor Indians.

**The Indians fear** the Spaniards of the *tambos,* travelers who fear neither God nor justice, because they are tigers, fierce animals. As soon as one reaches the *tambo,* it is: "Give me this, *mitaya!* Take that, *mitayo!* Give me comforts and services!" He takes ten pesos worth and uses it up and does not pay for it. He does not care whether he is dealing with an *alcalde,* a noble *cacique,* or a poor Indian; he beats him badly, and takes everything he has, and walks off with it, the same in the pueblos as in the countryside. He is worse than the other animals, and there is no remedy for the poor Indians.

**The poor Indians fear** the noble *caciques*—for low Indians turn themselves into *caciques,* and five out of ten Indian petty authorities turn themselves into noble *curacas*—because they are mice. They steal from the Indians' estates by day and by night; without anyone noticing it, they steal and rob. They demand extra tribute (*ricachicos*), *isancas* [baskets], fruit, money, and other foods. They spend as much of the common property (*sapsi*) as they can, which means that they spend more than any other animal, because they are at it day and night, and there is no remedy for the poor Indians of this kingdom.

Thus, between the serpent, the lion, the tiger, the fox, the cat, and the mouse, these six animals who eat the poor Indian leave him no room to move; between them all, they skin him, and he cannot move. Among these thieves, they help one another and protect each other. If the noble *cacique* defends this poor Indian, the others all eat him and kill him. Therefore, the noble *cacique* is not supposed to know about civil or criminal law, because the others would be his mortal enemies in this kingdom.

*[An illustration, ms. p. 710, shows "His Lordship Don Sebastián de Mendoza,*[263] *bishop of the great city and capital of Cusco: very Christian, righteous, fond of favoring the poor Indians and nobles of this kingdom." The next page is addressed to the bishop, who headed the diocese of Cusco from 1609 to 1618.]*

---

priest; also slang for a fast-talker or charlatan. *Doctor:* a man with a doctorate (usually a priest, not a medical practitioner, few of whom had doctorates).

[263] His actual name was Fernando Mendoza González, and he was a member of the Jesuit, not the Theatine order, as Guaman Poma mistakenly writes.

**May God keep His Lordship,** increase his health and his life, and give him more understanding and grace, so that he might do justice and favor the poor of Jesus Christ.

While I was thinking, after so many years of hoping for a remedy and writing this *Chronicle and Welfare of the Natives* in service of God and His Majesty, I saw that, on this occasion, His Majesty had decreed a most saintly thing in the service of God, by naming a bishop from the order of the Company of Jesus, a Theatine padre, who has begun and will finish his rule with good justice, and who is now punishing the proud and despotic padres who break the law. Oh, what good justice comes from this good house! A saintly man: as he is beginning with rigorous justice, so will he finish. He will establish Christianity here!

It seems to me that the bad and disobedient priests must wish him ill, with all their wrath, pride, and lust, and with their selfishness for controlling estates, meddling in justice, and calling themselves proprietors, which is as much as to call themselves rival bishops. That is why no one should be chosen as a *doctrina* priest, no matter what favors he is owed, until he is past fifty years of age. If he is a young man who has given up the vices that have been described here, and he behaves like a parish priest, then, based on this, he should be granted the post even if he is only a child; however, he should not be called a proprietor but an interim priest, and he should put down a deposit as security. In no other way should any *doctrina* be given out.

Because of all the damage that has been caused and all the favors that the priests have enjoyed, His Majesty should appoint a general inspector, who shall reside in the city of Los Reyes [de Lima]. From there, let him send four inspectors to the four parts of this kingdom, that they might visit the entire Holy Church, for the sake of good justice.

His Majesty should decree, for the conservation and growth of the service of God and of his royal crown, that before confirming any bishop, archbishop, prelate, commissioner, dean, canon, president, judge, general inspector, or other high official in his office, they must first take the vows and the habits of the Company of Jesus or of the Franciscan order, and they must remain in that religious orders for several months.

For the conservation of souls, they should also have a place of study in these orders of the Company of Jesus and of St. Francis. They should run a charitable school, a place of study for the sons of the noble *caciques,* the seconds-in-command, and the Indians, both rich and poor. They should teach these children in the place of study, that they might turn out good Christian sons, for the good government, public order, and Christianity of this kingdom.

*[Guaman Poma insists that the men chosen to be the bishops and archbishops of Peru must be honorable, learned, noble, humble, and Old Christians. They*

*must be willing and able to arrest immoral priests and appoint interim replace-
ments. The priors and provincials of the friaries of Peru should likewise be able
to arrest and punish their friars. Finally, the head of the "Holy Inquisition"
should oversee the entire church.*

*An illustration, ms. p. 713, shows Guaman Poma's proposed "Cardinal of All
the Oriental Indies of Peru, Second-in-Command of His Holiness" seated on a
throne, with an archbishop at his right hand and a bishop at his left. The text
on the next ms. p. calls on King Philip III to appoint this "lieutenant of the
Holy Father, the pope in Rome" to serve as "a Cardinal over all the church, the
archbishops, bishops, honorary bishops, and prelates" in the Indies, including
Peru, the Caribbean, Mexico, and even "Great China." In this way, "the Holy
Mother Church of Rome will be filled in this kingdom, and the friars in their
friaries."]*

## PROLOGUE TO THE READER OF "THE REVEREND-IN-CHRIST ARCHBISHOP, BISHOPS, CATHEDRAL CHAPTERS (*SEDE VACANTE*), HIS LORDSHIP THE INQUISITOR, HIS LORDSHIP OF THE HOLY CRUSADE; AND THE REVEREND PRELATES AND GENERAL INSPECTORS OF THE HOLY CHURCH IN THESE KINGDOMS AND JURISDICTIONS"

MAY YOUR LORDSHIP read this book and chronicle, and the chapters it
contains, and may you carry out justice. What is written here was not done
to cause harm or damage, but to serve God and good justice, so that bad
Christians and proud men might mend their ways. Your Lordship should
know that, had I set out to write about each padre or Spaniard separately,
there would not have been enough paper; therefore, I have talked about all
of them together. Your Lordship should keep a copy of this book, to see to
your justice. It is right that every church inspector carry a copy of this book
and follow it when taking accounts, doing inspections, and meting out
punishments. Each vicar should have another copy of the book, and the
*doctrina* padres should each have another copy, so that they can confess the
Indians and learn the language, and to restrain their consciences and their
pride with this book.

To this end, Your Lordship should impose the penalty of high excommunication in this kingdom, for the service of God and good Christianity,
and for good public order in this kingdom. In this way, the proud will be
humbled, will serve God, and will obey Your Lordship throughout the
kingdom.

I, the author Don Felipe Guaman Poma de Ayala, say that the Christian
reader will be shocked and amazed to read this book, chronicle, and chapter, and will ask who taught me all this and how I came to know so much.

Let me tell you, it has cost me thirty years of hard work, if I am not mistaken; but at the very least, twenty years of labor and privation. Leaving my houses, children, and possessions behind, I have labored, entering in among the poor and serving God and His Majesty, learning the languages and how to read and write, and serving the learned, those who know nothing, and those who know many things. I educated myself in palaces, in the seat of good government, and in the *Audiencia;* I have served the viceroys, the *Audiencia* president and judges, the court magistrates, the very illustrious-in-Christ bishops, and the illustrious commissioners. I have dealt with padres, *corregidores, encomenderos,* and inspectors, serving as their interpreter.

I have had conversations with and asked questions of the poor Spaniards, poor Indians, and poor blacks, whom I have seen with the inspectors of the holy church, the general inspectors of tributary Indians, and the re-inspectors of land titles. I dealt with them as a poor man myself, and so they disclosed their poverty to me, and the priests their pride. If I were to write down all that has happened to me in this way, all the troubles I have suffered in the pueblos from the pride of the padres, *corregidores, encomenderos,* and noble *caciques,* and the way they persecute the poor of Jesus Christ—at times it makes you want to cry, and at other times it makes you laugh and feel pity for them. Thus, I have seen all this with my own eyes, for the remedy of the poor and in the service of God and His Majesty. I have seen so many things, it is shocking.

Now, you may say that I am against the padres, *corregidores, encomenderos,* [. . .], and noble *caciques.*[264]

*[Guaman Poma responds that he writes what he does to serve God and king, and in fear of retribution from God, who destroyed Sodom in biblical times and "six pueblos" in the time of the Incas.]*

There are many saints in the world whom we do not know, and it is because of the prayers of these blessed people that God does not punish us. It frightens me to see that God's servants are so loose and free, and are masters of bad living. God forgive us!

Do not get angry, Christian readers, when you read this book. Read it well, and use it to restrain yourselves.

Certainly there are some *corregidores,* padres, *encomenderos,* Spaniards, noble *caciques,* and poor Indians who are servants of Jesus Christ. There are some padres who have served for thirty years in a single *doctrina,* and in the cities there are very saintly padres. Good men will laugh at this book; bad men will get angry, will be aggrieved by it, and will want to kill me. Yet I

---

[264] A corner at the top of ms. p. 716 is torn off, leaving this paragraph incomplete.

say to you, Christian readers, that you have never had a brother who so desires the salvation of your souls and consciences, who has done so much to free you in this world from the troubles, sorrows, and sins, and who has honored you so well. If you take this book and read it word by word, you will sit down and weep with your soul, and you will see what is bad and what is not bad. Freed from the bad things, you will talk freely with your lord and prelate, and you will be honored. You will have a place in the world, with the great and the small; you will speak with the pope and the king, and they will hold you in their eyes and in their souls. Repay me then with your prayers.

## THE BLACKS                                          717–725

*[A short chapter on "The Blacks" rounds out Guaman Poma's systematic account of colonial Spanish society. To the modern reader, this chapter seems to display a contradictory mixture of heartfelt sympathy for the plight of enslaved Africans and rank prejudice against those same people, who are viewed through the stereotypes imposed by the cruel regime that abuses them. One key to this paradox is the fact that Guaman Poma lived in a world where slavery was naturalized and questioned by no one. A more immediate key is the fact that, as he does with Spaniards, Guaman Poma draws a sharp distinction between the "good, Christian" blacks born in Africa (or Guinea, as West Africa was known at the time) and the lazy, immoral "criollo blacks" born in Peru. Many blacks in colonial Peru had been born in Spain, in the Americas, or in Peru itself to parents of African descent (some enslaved, some free) who had lived in the Spanish-speaking world for generations.*

*What both African and criollo blacks had in common was a position at the bottom of the Spanish social ladder. Nevertheless, they were on that ladder, and were part of the Spanish-speaking world. This is the final key to Guaman Poma's contradictory attitude. In contrast to the blacks, the Indians of colonial Peru formed a world apart. While the "Spanish" cities of Peru were evenly divided between black and Spanish populations, almost all of the Indians who made up the vast majority of the overall population lived in increasingly ruralized pueblos, set aside from the Spanish world and held in disdain by all the members of that world.]*

*[An illustration, ms. p. 717, shows a "black Christian man and woman," dressed in Spanish-style clothes and kneeling in prayer before an image of the Virgin. A marginal note, addressed to the king of Spain, argues that the people of "the king of Guinea are strong and can defeat the Great Turk and subjugate him, in the service of God and your royal crown, helping you with arms and food."]*

HUMBLE, CHRISTIAN, and well-married blacks: when the untutored blacks[265] from Guinea take their faith in Jesus Christ and in Christianity, they become faithful, believe in God, keep the commandments and the saintly good works, and serve and obey their masters. They are quick to believe the faith. They work. They are charitable and loving towards their fellow men. Untutored blacks make good slaves, for San Juan Buenaventura was one of them.[266] The Spaniards say that untutored blacks are worthless, but they do not know what they are saying: what they need to do is to teach them with love, courtesy, and doctrine. One of these untutored blacks is worth two black *criollos;* the untutored ones turn out to be saints.

♦ **The black *criollo* men and women** are charlatans, troublemakers, liars, thieves, robbers, highwaymen, gamblers, drunks, smokers, and tricksters. With their bad way of living, their sheer wickedness, and their talking back, they are the death of their masters. They can be holding the rosary in their hands, and all they are thinking of is how they are going to steal something. They learn nothing from sermons, from preaching, from lashes, nor from being sprinkled with hot bacon grease. The more they are punished, the more wicked they become, and there is no remedy, whether the black *criollo* is a man or a woman. That is why God punishes them, and they kill each other when they are getting drunk or gambling. These scoundrels teach their wicked ways to the untutored blacks.

The Indians from the *yungas* [tropical lowlands] who serve as *yanaconas* and *chinaconas* [male and female Indian servants] are blacks and worse than blacks; they pick up all the blacks' vices in this kingdom.

♦ **All blacks should be married:** in the first place, in service to God and His Majesty. Second, so that they can multiply and have children to bless heaven. Third, to increase their masters' estates, that God may be served.

Let me explain the reason why this does not happen: there are many men and women who hinder their marriages and the service of God. These people should be excommunicated and heavily punished, because, when [two blacks] are married, they sell the husband to someone else, and in that way

---

[265] Untutored blacks, *bozales:* the pejorative but standard term for enslaved Africans in the Spanish empire. *Bozal* later took on even more pejorative meanings—"dumb, wild, savage"—but Guaman Poma uses it in its earlier sense, "unskilled, untutored." The Spanish social hierarchy made a sharp distinction between *bozales* (blacks born in Africa) and *negros criollos* (blacks born in the Americas, who therefore grew up in a Spanish world). Guaman Poma also applies the term *bozales* to Indians seen as unsophisticated.

[266] San Juan Buenaventura: referring not to the thirteenth-century Italian St. Bonaventure but to an enslaved African named after him—perhaps a member of the Lima religious brotherhood made up of Africans from Bioho (Equatorial Guinea) and dedicated to San Juan de Buenaventura.

[the blacks] cannot serve God. They should be living in the same house, well married, serving God. If not, they should be together every night; or [the wife] should be free two days a week, to go serve her husband and give him what he needs. Likewise, the black man should have another two days [a week] to go serve his wife, if the two of them cannot be together. That way, God is served. If their masters or mistresses refuse to give their permission, they should be excommunicated and punished. If the husband runs away to see his wife, he should be free and not be punished; rather, justice should favor him and give him permission eight days out of every month to make a life in the service of God.

Likewise, none of the sons or daughters of a house should be sold and taken away from their mothers, fathers, and relatives, because then there would be no one to mourn for them, either in life or in death.

They should be freely allowed to plant crops for themselves, if they wish, and to have small ranches, raise chickens, and build up property by their sweat and labor, as well as to learn how to read and write, and [to learn] the doctrine, Christianity, public order, and honor. They should be taught the doctrine, and if they should turn out to be thieves, scoundrels, drunks, coca-chewers, tobacco-smokers, frauds, and gossips, they should be punished and burnt until they reform and become good. Because the master who coddles them will be carried off by the devil and punished by God for having bad slaves, while God will carry off the masters of good slaves, just as he will carry off the good slaves themselves, from this life.

**One *criollo* black** used to say about his master: "This owner of mine doesn't like me. He's a terrible scoundrel, he fornicates with his *comadres* and wastes his fortune on poor children. He's miserly; he neither eats nor drinks, but he loves eating for free. He ought to be drawn and quartered."

See here, Christians, how you place your trust in your slaves, who seek your deaths and endeavor to control your lives and deaths. I understood this black very well. This black slave was saying these things because [his master] did not let him steal, get drunk, run around with whores, smoke tobacco, or gamble on any games. If he had been allowed to continue these vices, he would have said, "Oh, what a saintly master I have!" Therefore, black slaves are not to be trusted. It is a great gift to keep them in jangling irons.

Another time, there was a conversation among a group of blacks, all laden with irons, who were arguing with each other. One said to the other, "You're laden with irons because you're a scoundrel, a drunk, and a smoker." The other one replied, "And you, because you're a perfect thief and a runaway; that's why you're laden with irons."

Therefore, when a black man or woman is a scoundrel, it is a saintly matter, and very much in the service of God, His Majesty, and the good of their souls and their flesh, to chain them with irons. There is no reason to whip them or abuse them; they would pay no attention to it. Irons will tame them. Why should you threaten them, when threats yield no results and they will just run away to the countryside? A good punishment is a good set of irons: they will tame any scoundrel. This I state in the service of God and His Majesty.

◆ **THE GOOD, CHRISTIAN BLACKS** have such patience, when they are married and serving God, for their wicked Spanish masters. The worst are the [Spanish] women, who, with little fear of God or justice, mistreat them and demand daily payments from them—eight reales, or twelve reales, plus another four reales for tribute. They give them nothing to eat or to wear, so [the blacks] are left naked. But, because they are slaves, they keep quiet and pretend not to notice, and only commend themselves to God. Poor people. There is no justice, and that is why they flee these masters.

◆ **Black men and women** turn bad and teach themselves to be notorious thieves, highwaymen, and bad Christians—some, because they are not given what they need to live; others, because they are never punished or taught the doctrine; still others, because their masters mistreat them for no reason, punish them cruelly, give them no food, demand money from them, and make them work without eating. After working from early in the morning, they are only called in for breakfast at twelve noon, and are fed only once a day. Anyone who works so hard has to eat breakfast, lunch, and dinner. They also give them no dainties to eat, and no meat; yet they are also flesh and blood, Christians who desire to eat appetizing food and dainties. This is the reason why they run away and steal. Their masters should be punished on this account, for the justice of the poor.

◆ **In the cities, towns, and hamlets,** as well as in the sugar plantations, vineyards, and fields, wherever there are ten blacks, they should have their justice of the peace, local magistrate, and royal notary. Wherever there are more than ten, they should also have a chief constable and minor constable, a defender, a town crier, and a jailer. These officers of justice should carry defensive arms—sword, halberd, and coat of mail—as should the blacks of gentlemen, of hidalgos, and of noble *caciques,* those who stand by their sides and who stand watch in the fields. No others should be allowed to carry [weapons], not even a small knife, in this kingdom, because great harm could result. These officials should be blacks or mulattos, whether slave or emancipated, for our Lord Jesus Christ also died that there might be God and justice and public order and Christianity among them.

After being elected justice of the peace or chosen as officials, they should be given permission to take two days a week to administer justice and Christian law; on Wednesdays and Fridays every week, they should go to the town hall to sit in judgment.

# How the Good Black Men and Women Bear with such Patience and Love for Jesus Christ the Wickedness of Their Master, Who Has no Charity nor Love for His Fellow Men.

*Pride.*

♦ **Black or mulatto men and women** slaves and captives may not be punished by their masters and mistresses for civil or criminal sins or for any crime; nor may they, their wives, or their children be punished if they have committed no crime. Only their own justices of the peace [may punish them], and all the other justices of God and His Majesty, who must first investigate the crime, and then punish them in accordance with it. If it happens to be a matter of value, they must first conduct an investigation at the expense of [the slave's] master, and then punish [the slave] as an example to others, following Christian law in the world and in this kingdom.

♦ **Some black men and women** in the cities, towns, and hamlets become, through their vices, tremendous thieves and highwaymen—even the women—because of the reasons I will describe.

First, because they are not fed three times a day—breakfast, lunch, and dinner—and are not given clothes and shoes to wear; because of this, they become thieves. The blame in this belongs to their masters, who should be fined for His Majesty's treasury and to cover the expenses of justice.

Second, they become tremendous drunkards.

Third, they become tremendous gamblers, loafers, and idlers, and therefore go in for stealing other people's property.

Fourth, they get the vice of being tobacco-smokers.

Fifth, the men become whoremongers and the women become great whores; they mount with Spaniards and make a living this way, stealing from their masters or other people. They deserve to be punished as an example to others.

♦ **They may be pardoned** the first time from being hanged for thievery, and their guilt may be punished by cutting off an ear. The second time, they should be hanged. Otherwise, the master of the black or mulatto man or woman should pay the fine for the crime to His Majesty's treasury and to cover the expenses of justice, and to the person to whom it is owed. If [the slave] is freed, his master should keep him in irons, which is in service of God, and not take them off until he dies. This is right and proper, according to the law, justice, Christianity, and good order, for the reform of the wicked and as an example to everyone in the world.

♦ **THE BLACKS** of the *corregidores* and *encomenderos* are very brazen; they force their way on Indian women, whether married or maidens, and their masters allow them. Under this pretext, they have many mulatto children, boys and girls. And to pay the Indian women, they steal money for food from their masters, and they demand many Indian men and women *mitayos,* as well as food, all to give to the Indian whores. Yet their masters do not punish them; instead, they favor them. This is why the Indian women become scoundrels just like the blacks of the *corregidores,* the

## HOW THE BLACK *CRIOLLO* MEN STEAL MONEY FROM THEIR MASTERS TO DECEIVE THE INDIAN WHORES, AND THE BLACK *CRIOLLA* WOMEN STEAL TO SERVE THEIR SPANISH AND BLACK LOVERS.

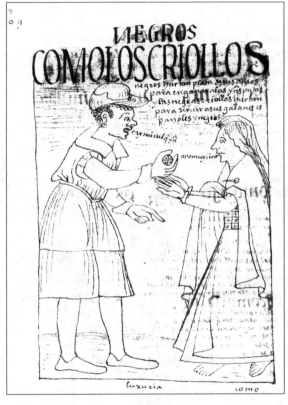

"*Caymi culqui, india.*"

[Here's some money, Indian.]

"*Apo, muy señor.*"

[Lord, dear sir.]

*Lust.*

*encomenderos,* and the *doctrina* padres in this kingdom. And there is no remedy, and therefore the Indians are coming to an end.

◆ **If a mulatta woman** gives birth to a mulatto-quarteroon, or a *zambaigo* [part Indian] quarteroon, so that the child has all the look of a Spaniard, with just an ear's worth of black stock, then by the laws of justice, the gentleman is free, as a gentleman; the taxpaying commoner [is free], as a commoner; the Indian, as an Indian commoner; the [Indian] noble, as a noble; the prince, as a prince.[267]

But the child of a mulatto man and a black woman is a complete slave. The child of a Spanish or Indian man and a black woman is a complete slave, because the child is one half captive black, properly figured. If they want to free this stock, they should notify the authorities and free one half, and the other half is theirs, for this is the sheer law.[268] The child of a captive mulatta woman and a mulatto man is a complete captive: this is sheer justice and Christian law.

◆ **Blacks should not** be brought to Indian pueblos by any *corregidor, encomendero,* padre, or noble *cacique,* unless the black man is married to his equal, a black woman. If he is married to an Indian woman, they should be expelled from the province, under penalty of one hundred pesos for the king's treasury.

The black, mulatto, and *zambaigo* men and women should be gathered into their houses at four in the morning, and they should not live by themselves in the countryside, even if they are free, because they are bad people, [. . .] who fear neither God nor justice; they are thieves and [. . .].[269]

## PROLOGUE TO THE CHRISTIAN READER OF "THE BLACK SLAVE MEN AND WOMEN"

MY BROTHERS, YOU should know one thing: that our Lord Jesus Christ suffered more hard work, though he was the living God, than you, who are poor sinners, ever will. Bear it all with patience, and forgive those who do you harm and evil; bear them with patience. Saintly men, whoever is like you shall be amassing treasures daily in heaven, more than you can know. With all this, hold to the true God and keep his faith and commandments.

---

[267] In other words, the child would take the status of the father. Guaman Poma's proposal here contradicts Spanish law, which held that the child of an enslaved woman was a slave, regardless of the father's status, while the child of a free woman was always free.

[268] It was relatively common for people to free their enslaved relatives, or themselves, by paying an established price, but here Guaman Poma proposes that the child of an enslaved woman and a free man could be freed by paying for only the mother's half of the child.

[269] These lines are a late marginal addition and are cut off at the end.

Suffer as our Lord suffered. Together with the prophets, call out to the Lord with hymns and tears, just as king David sang His praises. For, if a king could call out singing and weeping to God, what should we sinners do? Call out with our tears, of course. It is thus, with tears in your voices, that the Lord will hear you, will send comfort to your hearts, will regale you, and will promise you the prize, the crown of heaven, which is so much better than gold and lilies and precious stones and jewels that not even the angel of heaven could describe it or think it. He would not dare to describe it or portray it: a hundred thousand times more resplendent than the sun, the place where we will gather together in heaven, as God promised us, for ever and ever.

The poor blacks are turned into tributaries, with little fear of God. [Their masters] demand tribute from them every month—twenty pesos from the black women, and the same amount from the men. If they do not pay, they are brutally whipped. Faced with such labor and harassment, they leave and become runaways, and they may rise up. God forbid [. . .].[270]

## WICKED REPRIMANDS

726–727

*[Guaman Poma concludes his account of Spanish society in Peru with a series of short didactical chapters. The first three are composed of satirical dialogues; the fourth chapter provides a counterpoint by highlighting the virtues of a few just people in various walks of life. The first set of satirical dialogues, "Wicked Reprimands," shows how* corregidores, encomenderos, *and priests used their positions of power (and their knowledge of Quechua) to bully "their"* caciques *into acquiescing to their schemes.]*

THE WICKED REPRIMANDS of the *corregidor,* and the threats he makes to the Indians in this kingdom. This is what he says: "*Cam runacuna allilla uyariway. Rey-pa* corregidor-*ninmi cani. Rey-tam mañacune alli colquita tarinaypac. Allilla simiyta uyariway.* Tiniente alcalde mayor-*pa camachiscanta ruranqui, puchucananpac, mana cayta ruranqui, carcuscayqui curaca cayniquimanta. Cayta ruray cay* provincia-*pi.*"

This is what it means: "You *caciques* and petty authorities, listen well to me. I am the king's *corregidor,* for I requested this grant from the king so that I could make good money. Listen well to my words: obey my deputy *alcalde mayor;* whatever he commands, you must carry it out (spinning, weaving, carrying wine to Cusco);[271] if you do not do all this, I swear I will

---

[270] These lines are a late marginal addition and are cut off at the end.

[271] Spinning, weaving, carrying wine to Cusco: the Quechua says only "completing the task." Otherwise, Guaman Poma's Spanish translation follows his Quechua closely.

throw you out of your *cacicazgos* [rulerships]. Therefore, do these things in this province."

With this wicked reprimand and threat, he then orders that a cup of wine be given to the poor *cacique,* and the *cacique* invites thirty or forty Indians to serve [the *corregidor*] as porters. In this way, there is a shortage of Indians in the mines, and unpaid tribute, and all the Indians leave their pueblos in this kingdom.

**The wicked reprimands** of the *encomendero,* and the threats he makes to the Indians in this kingdom. This is what he says: "*Say curacacuna, yayaquita* comendedor-*niquita chapacniquita alli uyariway. Allilla causasun,* padre corregidor-*mantapas aswan allin cani. Yayaypa* conquistador-*pa runanmi canqui. Chinata* muchachu-*ta yanaconata,* estancia-*ta alli pircanqui, wasita ruranqui, michecta camachinqui. Tambo runata cari warmita yanapachiqui. Mana cayta ruraptiquica, warcoscayqui, causacta pampascayqui, curaca cayniquimanta carcosqayqui. Runaymi canqui.*"

After this threat, he gives the poor *cacique* a little drink of wine, and then he gives the poor *cacique* some clothing. This is what he said to threaten him:

"You *curacas,* you should listen well to me, your padre and *encomendero* <and your guardian>.[272] Let us live well, for I am better than the priest and the *corregidor.* You were the people of my father the conqueror, so you should give me *china* [servant girls] and *yanacona* (boys) so that you can build good walls on my farms and build me houses and send me Indians to be herders, shepherds. Likewise, you will send me Indian men and women for the *tambo,* to help run it. If you do not do all these things, I will hang you, I will bury you alive, and I will throw you out of your *cacicazgo.* This I order you, because you are my Indians."

Just see how these *encomenderos* issue threats and wicked reprimands, so that everyone is against the noble *caciques,* their mortal enemies. Therefore, it would be proper to remove the *corregidores,* padres, *encomenderos,* and judges of this kingdom from cases in which their mortal enemies, the nobles of this kingdom, are accused of civil or criminal sins.

**The wicked reprimands** of the padre, and the threats he makes to the Indians in this kingdom. [. . .][273] This is what the padre says:

"Sons, I want to inform you, slowly, that here in this pueblo, you *caciques* and I, the padre, have to live together forever, until we die; we will live, we will wear clothes, <we will acquire property>, and we will sin with women,

---

[272] "Your guardian" (*chapacniquita*) is in the Quechua only. Guaman Poma's Spanish follows his Quechua quite closely otherwise.

[273] The omitted Quechua version is essentially identical to the Spanish (except for one phrase from the Quechua, added in angled brackets).

but nobody will find out anything. I am your padre-proprietor. Even if you were to sue me, you would not throw me out or beat me. Now, the *corregidor*, the Spaniards, and the *encomenderos* are easily thrown out of the land; all you do is tell them, 'Go on, get out of this land,' and they quickly leave the land. But you know, the king gave me this *doctrina*, so what can the bishop do to me? Therefore, sons, do not have conversations here in our pueblo with Spaniards, or with *ladino* [Spanish-speaking] Indians who can read and write, educated Indians. Do not keep your Indians around, because they will learn of the sins we commit with women, and also of the *rescates* [forced trading] that you do and that I do; they will learn everything, and will file a complaint about us. Never allow your Indians to have conversations with Spaniards, because they will talk with them about our wrongs. Therefore, it would be best if you threw them all out of our pueblo."

See, Christian, the wicked reprimand and bad example of this priest: he does not want there to be Christians or public order, and therefore he does not like for there to be schools or for anyone to learn how to read and write. He wants them to be idolatrous infidels; the Indians of this kingdom will never become Christians if those who are supposed to sing the gospel take it away instead and hinder them so that they cannot understand it and serve God and His Majesty. This does great harm to the poor Indians of this kingdom. Therefore, [the priests] are against the Christian *caciques* and *ladino* Indians of this kingdom.

The wicked reprimands of the false *caciques*, who are created by the viceroys and the royal *Audiencia* and favored by the *corregidores, encomenderos*, padres, notaries, and defenders. Tributary Indians become nobles; being low people, they sell the poor Indians and claim that they are serving them. When the Indians talk back, they punish them.[274]

## CHATS AND CONVERSATIONS AMONG OFFICE-SEEKERS

728–731

*[In his second series of satirical dialogues, Guaman Poma imagines the calculations and deal-making that he supposes must go on among men and women at all levels of colonial society, beginning with the "office-seekers"—Spaniards seeking official posts and fantasizing about the money they will wring from their positions. In these dialogues, he continues all the way down the social scale to the "captive black slaves" from Africa and the "Indian whores" escaping the poverty of the countryside. He carefully captures the language and speech patterns of each group along the way.]*

---

[274] This paragraph is a late marginal addition.

**AMONG THE CORREGIDORES** of this kingdom, this is what they say:

"Señor, I am seeking an office as a *corregidor* in which I might make ten or twelve thousand pesos."

"Señor, how could you possibly make so much money, if the salary is just one thousand pesos a year?"

"Señor, I will set up a business. It will have to be done well, not badly. I'll come in there and stick it to the nobles as far as I can manage. They'll have to find me silver from under the earth. Otherwise, I'll take as much money as I want from the community treasury, the church funds, the hospital. Or, otherwise, I'll borrow from the *doctrina* padres. Besides, all the Indians in the province will have to come in on my *rescates*."

"Señor, if you can do all this, you will turn out rich. But be careful, señor; it is better to do it well, not badly, so that no one will level complaints against you when you are audited [at the end of your term]."

"Señor, whoever comes after me will do as much and more if he has good luck. So there's no reason to fear the audit or the guarantor; all I have to do is shut my mouth, close my eyes, and drive the Indians hard. Since one term has nothing to do with the next, I don't know what might come, and I have no fear."

**Chat and conversation** of the office-seekers, among the *encomenderos* of this kingdom. This is what they say:

"Señor Don Alejandro Farfán, how many stewards do you keep among the Indians you have?"

"Señor, I keep one Spanish steward to collect the tribute; as you know, he has to pay me double. And on my cattle ranches, I keep another Spaniard for the cows and mares, and another Spaniard for the sheep and goats. And another Spaniard for the croplands."

"And, señor, how can you maintain four Spaniards?"

"Señor, they can figure out how to make their living. All the pueblos serve them, and they earn double."

"Señor, can the Indians manage with all that?"

"Señor, yes, they can; but if not, let it finish them off. What do I care? They're my Indians. If [my stewards] are supposed to charge them one sheep, they'll charge them two. I keep quiet and make believe that I don't notice. If we didn't do all this, we would not have enough to buy our clothes or to gamble."

"Señor, what if they don't do all this?"

"Señor, I'll hang and bury one of my Indian nobles, or I'll send him to a Spaniard or a black who'll beat him to death. I'll pay for it, and that will put a stop to it."

**Chat and conversation** of the office-seekers, among the *doctrina* padres of this kingdom. This is what they say:

"Señor, they say that you had gone to see His Lordship the bishop, and that His Lordship was very fierce and had gone about punishing [priests] cruelly, and that he was a Theatine. Because of this, many padres have tried to leave for other dioceses. If he is a Theatine, he does not forgive. If that is true, then how can we become rich? If he were like the ecclesiastic bishop, Don Sebastián, or like Don Antonio de Raya, or if he were like Don Fray Gregorio de Montalvo, then he would turn in favor of the padres, and the Indians would be afraid to complain." [275]

"Señor, let me reply to all this. I had heard the same news, so I went by myself to find out about it from His Lordship. He is a very saintly man—humble, very Christian, and not overly dour. Even though he asked me whether I was doing well in the *doctrina* and whether they were good Indians there, I answered him in a couple of words: first, that they were terrible drunkards, and that the hardest work for me was forcing them to come to catechism and to Mass. He told me that I should go straight back to the *doctrina,* and that he would send an inspector to see how things were and to do justice. Señor, I left a message with the secretary and officials that, if any Indian happened to go there to complain, they should contradict him, and I would serve them. Señor, I haven't had any more trouble."

"Señor, he does not sound very strict, then."

"No, señor. In fact, they say that the head inspector is a *doctrina* priest, just like us. There's nothing to fear. And his officers are satisfied with a little bit of money."

"Señor, we have to get busy and find some cash. Otherwise, we'll die."

"Even if we spend a thousand pesos, the Indians will pay us. So let's keep still, waiting for the chief inspector like a pregnant woman: after she gives birth, she's free. Likewise, as soon as the inspection is over, we'll be free."

"Well, señor, I'm afraid for you, because you beat and mistreated Don Francisco Auqui Quia, the governor, and Don Pedro Poma."

"Señor, I'm not afraid of them any more. I already bribed them with a jug of wine. Besides, the *corregidor,* for his part, and the *encomendero* have threatened them and told them that, if they complain, they'll skin them alive with whippings. So, we'll get by."

**Chat and conversation** among the soldiers who wander through this kingdom. This is what they say:

"Señor, soldier, what should we do? We're poor."

---

[275] The men mentioned were the bishops of Cusco during Guaman Poma's adult life: Sebastián Lartaun (1570–1583), Gregorio de Montalvo (1587–1592), Antonio de Raya (1594–1606), and Fernando Mendoza González (1608–1618), the bishop at the time this book was written, whom Guaman Poma mistakenly identified as a Theatine (he was actually a member of the closely related Jesuit order).

"Señor, what we can do is: we're gamblers, so we can use that to get as far as Potosí, win or lose. In the *tambos* we'll eat for free and gamble for the reales that the priests earn by singing, and the money the *corregidores* earn by sleeping and eating. And we'll gamble with the *encomenderos,* who earn their money by strolling around."

"Señor, you and I have trades—I'm a blacksmith, and you're a carpenter. Shouldn't we work?"

"Señor, that would be impossible, because it's better to be a constable, a jailer, or a church assistant, in the city or out on an inspection tour. With that kind of trade, we can steal at our ease and gamble in the *tambos.* We'll say that we're the *corregidor's* brother, and that way we won't have to pay. We'll spend our lives doing that, and we'll never get audited. If we can't do that, then we'll rob some rich man and hotfoot it somewhere far away, where God might help us. We'll live the life in this kingdom, like we could never do in Castile. It's better to die here in this kingdom."

**Chat and conversation** among the ladies and maidens of this kingdom. This is what they say:

"My señora, I don't know what we shall do to get through this life."

"Señora, you should know that we can manage it very well. Let's find a half dozen Indian *chinas* [serving girls], and another half dozen mestizas, and dress them up. When the young fellows see them, they'll all gather together and come here, bringing money for us and for the mestizas and Indian *chinas.* That way, without having to work, we'll eat, dress up, and have a good life in this city. It's better to do this than to get married, it seems to me."

**Chat and conversation** among the poor tributary Indians of this kingdom. This is what they say:

"Señor, we Indians are so poor. What should we do?"

"Señor, let's make ourselves *caciques* by force. Let's put on capes and jackets, buy a horse, and have breakfast with the *corregidor* and the padre. Whenever they demand Indians or order something done, we'll give them what they want right away. That way, they'll make us justices of the peace, and we'll eat at the expense of the poor Indians."

"Señor, we're so persecuted. First, by the Spanish mine owners; then, by the Spaniards of the *tambo,* the *encomenderos* and their stewards, the estates, the *corregidores,* the deputy *corregidor,* the notaries; and by the padre and his brothers; and by the *caciques,* justices of the peace, *curacas,* and petty authorities—we're under such strain. Let's just leave and abandon the pueblo, because it would be better for us to run away to other pueblos. There we could rest, and our wives and children could rest from the labor that the padre and his assistants force on us. So let's leave."

**Chat and conversation** among the captive black slaves of this kingdom. This is what they say:

"No good, Fra'ci'co. What we going to do? Your master so wicked, my master so wicked. Always saying, 'Give me money, take this,' beating you, breaking your head, not giving tobacco, *chicha,* food to eat."

"So, what we do?"

"Look, Fra'ci'co, my friend, you go one way, I take off another, and we head straight to hills. We'll take black woman there and camp out. We kill Indian, Spaniard. If we caught, only die once. There we sleep, eat, smoke tobacco, bring wine, *chicha.* Just drunk all the time, and that all. Fra'ci'co, let's go."

**Chat and conversation** among the Indian whores, sitting in a circle.[276]

They say: "Sister, dear, let's go to Cusco, to Potosí, to Huamanga, to the mines, to Lima, to [. . .]. The Spaniards and the blacks will give us money. Perhaps we'll die with the adulterers, with the Spaniards."

They say: "Sister, friend, let's go to the cities, to Lima. Sister, let's not die. There, even if we die with the Spaniards, it won't be with the Indian *mitayos.*"

## QUESTIONS ABOUT DEALINGS AND COMMERCE    732–740

*[The last set of dialogues depict everyone in the colonial world, from top to bottom, as busy concocting crooked deals to advance their personal interests.]*

**THE QUESTION ABOUT** dealings and commerce for the *corregidores,* which a man who plans to become a *corregidor* puts to a former *corregidor* in this kingdom. In the city of Los Reyes de Lima, the question is as follows:

"Señor, do me the honor of telling me, since you were the *corregidor* of such-and-such province, what is it that I should do? What dealings or commerce should I go into? I have already been selected as the *corregidor* of Collao, or of Andahuallas, or of Lucanas. Señor, what kind of dealings or commerce can I keep in that province?"

"Señor, I will tell you that the best dealings are in making clothes, trafficking coca or wine, making *chicha,* having wine shops, and baking bread—but don't let any Indians sell bread or bake it. Also, take all the wool and livestock from the community and from the Indians. Also, you can remove any money you find in the community treasury, then hurry up and hire ten deputies. If you can, keep one deputy in each pueblo, or at the

---

[276] This dialogue is a late addition on the bottom margin of ms. p. 731; some letters are lost at the edges, and the translation is partly conjectural. The first paragraph is in Quechua; the second is a loose Spanish translation.

least one *alcalde mayor,* so that they can stay there and serve as your stewards and dealers. Padre Alonso de Bobadilla and Padre Melchor de Preste are rich men; they have thirty or fifty thousand pesos that they could loan you for *rescates* and commerce. The *encomendero* and his stewards will also loan you money, but you have to know how to manage them: if they say 'she sells,' you say 'she sells.' If they say 'seashells,' you say 'seashells,' and then stop. Make your fortune, and keep your mouth closed. If you don't do what they tell you to do, they will destroy you."

"Señor, what will all the padres say?"

"The padres also have dealings and commerce of their own. They have all the maidens, and they make them work, spinning and weaving. They do that under the pretext of running the *doctrina,* and they deflower them all, and each one of them has twenty little mestizo children, so they have no reason to talk."

"Señor, what will the noble *caciques* say?"

"Señor, the nobles, Don Juan and Don Pedro, are *ladinos* [fluent in Spanish]; they know how to read and write, and they are not noble *caciques* but rather *mitayo* Indians. I kicked out the ones who were [*caciques*], and I put these two in their place so that [the people] will work for me and fear me. You should do the same. You should find yourself a couple of little *ladinos,* even if they are troublesome charlatans and rogues, and make one of them your *alcalde mayor* right away. Make them your *compadres* and seat them at your table. What they want to do is drink until they fall down. Invite them to a jug of wine—it costs very little, and with that, they'll be happy and keep quiet. As for the rest, punish and threaten them. That way, they'll keep quiet, and so you will end up rich, with fifty thousand pesos from being the *corregidor.*"

**The question for the deputy** *corregidores* of this kingdom is as follows:

"Señor, the *corregidor* keeps me to serve him as his deputy in the province of the Soras, so that I will force them to sell to him and make him a fortune. I make them run a shop for him. I make the *mitayos* in the *tambo* work—spinning, weaving, and doing other *rescates.* And a *chicha* shop, and a bakery."

"Señor, won't the *caciques* say anything about it?"

"Señor, I'd give a thousand lashes to anyone who talked back to me."

"But if you work for someone else, how can you thrive and eat and dress well?"

"Señor, that is why I take the best for myself. That is why I make them work day and night. I want to make more of myself and take advantage, so I tell them, 'Brothers, see here, you're all working for the *corregidor,* who's the viceroy's brother. Even if you raise trouble with the law, you won't kick him out. But if you don't work, I'll punish you, and he'll punish you, and he'll throw you out of your *cacicazgo.*"

With such threats as these, and with so many deputies, the provinces are being destroyed, and everything the Indians have is being stolen. No one should be allowed to name deputies or *alcaldes mayores* except for His Majesty and his governing royal council, in the world and in this kingdom.

**The question for the notaries,** whom the *corregidores* keep in the provinces to draw up contracts in this kingdom, is as follows:

"Señor *corregidor,* you should know that we ought to enter that province with harshness and fierceness and much pomp and circumstance, and then start making a fortune right away. I'll take charge. I'll tell all the nobles that you have friends in the *Audiencia,* and that you are the brother of one of the *Audiencia* judges, and that you're a licentiate, a man of letters, and that your name is Don Diego de Miserly. That way, they'll all start working for you, and maybe they'll work for me, too. We'll take all the king's gold from the community treasuries."

"Señor, what if they condemn me and complain about me during the audit [at the end of my term]? What should I say?"

"Señor, I won't be audited, so if the Indians ask to have you audited, this is what I'll tell them:[277] 'Brothers, *curacas,* this señor *corregidor* is the son of a great lord. I am his brother. Don't fall behind with people, with workers. Who knows if the señor *corregidor* won't hang you. Since I am a notary, I will help you out. But you must help me with your llamas, your baskets, and your ropes.'—'Very good, señor. You are my lord, notary. You will help us greatly. I, the *curaca,* will order these things done.' Señor, this is how the notaries have their way in this kingdom and fool the Indians."

**The question for the sons** of *encomenderos,* so that they can hire and keep Indian servants, cattle, and croplands among the Indians in this kingdom, is as follows:

"Señores, see here: I am the *encomendero's* son.[278] 'See here, *curaca,* if you do not listen to me, I will hang one of you. I am your lord. I will bury you alive. Give me, *mita* me, some *muchachos, chinas, yanaconas,* and herders for my cows, sheep, and goats.' Señor, with this threat I will demand Indian servants.

"Besides, señor, I am a miner. As a miner, I can get away with letting my cattle graze on my Indians' land. I'm telling you, my father was a first

---

[277] The imagined conversation with the *curaca* is in Quechua, with a few Spanish words (señor, *corregidor,* notary, work, help) thrown in.

[278] The short speech that follows is in Quechua, again with Spanish loan words. *"Mita me"* means "give me the work that you owe me (according to Andean rules of reciprocity)," but the use of the term by the *encomendero's* son takes it out of its original Andean context: he has done nothing for the Indians that he should be able to demand a *mita* in return.

conqueror,[279] so I can skin my Indians. So my Indians have to serve me, and they have to do *mita* for me, and give me *camarico* [gifts]. And if I can collect extra tribute, or else give the Indian noble a thousand lashes, he'll have to live with it. That way, he'll know who the *encomendero* is. Señor, this tribute won't be sent to Cusco or to Potosí. We'll make money at the Indians' expense. This way, we'll be rich."

"May it come to pass."

**The question for the stewards** whom the *encomenderos* hire to make contracts and *rescates* among the Indians in this kingdom. This is what they ask among themselves:

"Señor, they've asked me to be their steward, to collect the tribute from their grant."

"Oh, how wonderful, señor! You'll be another *encomendero!* But be quick about stuffing your purse."

"Señor, they've hired me to be the steward of the estate."

"Señor, that's even better. If you're quick about selling the cattle and hiring the Indians to do *rescates* and making them work, it'll all be for you. That's better than being the *encomendero.*"

"Señor, what other dealings can I have? And commerce, and being partners with the *encomendero* and the *corregidor* and the padre and the noble *caciques?*"

"Señor, it seems to me that you should go in for commerce, and have lots of *mitayos.* When it's time to collect tribute, you should collect extra food, corn, chickens, clothes, and sheep. Make them bring you extra, and pay them on the cheap. If it's worth four pesos, give them one or two. And don't pay the *mitayos* at all for doing *mita* for the *encomendero.* As for food, firewood, and hay, there's no reason to pay for them, because [the Indians] are obliged to bring those things. But you should keep the *cacique* happy: offer him a drink from time to time, because the wine will satisfy him. If the *encomendero* comes, feed him at your expense, because the *mita* Indians give you everything. And give him the tributary taxes in cash; you can later go and collect as much as you want [from the Indians]."

"Señor, what about the padre? How can we keep him happy?"

"Señor, your wife will know how to keep the padre happy, as well as the deputy, the *corregidor,* and so on. Women know how to live well and make money, so she'll give Indian women to the deputy, the *alcalde,* and the padre on her own account, to be their *chinaconas,* serving girls. With all this, you'll be more than an *encomendero.* Just steal as much as you can get

---

[279] In early Spanish America, the first conquerors in any given area formed the highest-ranking local elite.

away with, and you'll come off rich, and then get richer, and then you can move to one of the cities in this kingdom."

**The question that the mine owners** ask among themselves, about getting deals and commerce and making something off of the Indians in this kingdom, is as follows:

"Señor, do you think I should arrange with His Majesty to run a gold, or silver, or quicksilver mine? Tell me, what kind of money could I make from a mine?"

"Señor, you should know that if [His Majesty] gives you thirty Indians, you should use them as Indians for running commerce and *rescates*. If the Indian loses [the merchandise], make him pay four times over. You should also keep an Indian woman to make *chicha,* and one to bake bread. Send some to the lowlands, and if an Indian dies, make them pay you for it. They'll never audit you! Build houses, keep cattle, and don't ever pay the Indians—just take their labor. That way, you'll end up rich. What you should do, if you can, is pay all the Indians in *chicha.* Let that Indian woman of yours, Doña Firfilera, give it to them. When it's pay time, give it to them all in food; that way, all the cash will end up in your hands."

"Señor, won't the poor Indians have to pay their tribute? Shouldn't they bring the money to their wives and children?"

"Señor, what should we care about that? Even if the devil carries them off, so long as you have reales in your house, what do you care about that? Let's get rich during the days we have to live in this life. Let's have money, and then we'll be done."

**The question for judges** who would like to benefit a bit and have dealings and commerce among the Indians. This is the question they ask among themselves in this kingdom:

"Señor, I'm being sent to be a judge in the provinces."

"I advise you to spend no money. Eat at the Indians' expense, and be sure to take advantage of cattle on the Indians' ranchlands. As for your salary, collect as much as you can, because you'll never be audited, and you can punish the noble *caciques* severely so that they'll give you whatever you want out of fear. You'll keep your staff of office for a few days, because, after all, you have the favor of the *Audiencia.*"

**The question that the *doctrina* padres** ask each other, about having dealings and commerce among the Indians in this kingdom, is as follows:

"Señor, you are an old hand in this kingdom; please tell me what I need to do to make money."

"Let me tell you that, no matter which *doctrina* you are sent to, you must make your entrance with authority and ferocity. Tell everyone that you are a gentleman, a licentiate, a man of letters, and an *apo.* Do not talk with the Indians; show authority and fierceness. Find the wiliest of them and whip him raw, and throw him out of the pueblo if you can get away with it. Gather in all the unmarried women and place them in the *doctrina,* and do the same with the young men. Make them spin and weave cloth and take care of your goats, sheep, pigs, and chickens. You'll want to have fields sown with corn, wheat, and potatoes. Make the commoners work in your dealings and commerce. Push them as hard as you can, and punish them. Make your fortune as quick as you can, and then move to a city where you can stroll and eat at your leisure. Also, when you arrive, you should preach this little sermon to the Indians:[280] 'My children, I come to this *doctrina.* I am the son of a great lord. I am not padre for no reason. You come well to Mass at the *doctrina.* Make good offerings for the spirits on All Saints Day. Bring good money, all the good llamas. Do *mita* well. Help me, your padre. If you do not listen to my words, I will kill you, I will hang you. Not even the viceroy could do anything to me, the padre. *Curacas, alcaldes,* witches, sorcerers: know me well. I am the great lord padre.'"

"Señor, are the Indians that untutored, that they can be told such things in their pueblos?"

"Yes, señor, they are that fainthearted and powerless. Take Don Diego Carwas[281] and Don Alonso Chancawilca, a couple of little *ladinos:* just scare them once, and they'll cower and run away. You should know that you ought to bring a Spaniard—one of your brothers or friends—to spend a night. Pay him a half dozen pesos and get him to whip them raw. After that, they'll pay you a thousand pesos. To keep them from complaining the next day, greet them and give them a little bit of wine to drink. That will tame them; they'll be afraid of you, and won't complain about anything you do. After that, you'll want to do justice. You'll govern and meddle in everything. All the Indians will bring their complaints to you, as the justice. You'll set up your court and punish the *alcaldes* and nobles; then the Indian men and women will be under your control. If one of them is a friend of yours, make him the *alcalde,* or the *fiscal,* or the sexton, or the cantor. You can toss out the governor."

"Señor, what will the *corregidor* say?"

"Señor, the *corregidor* is a great thief and worse, so you have no need to worry."

"Señor, I am afraid of the general inspector—it hurts even if he charges a fine of just half a real, because if he comes to get us for one complaint, he'll leave with a hundred."

---

[280] The sermon is in Quechua, with several religious and government terms left in Spanish (*doctrina,* father, Mass, offering, All Saints Day, spirits, viceroy, *alcalde,* sorcerers). It shows only a basic understanding of Quechua grammar.

[281] Carwas was mentioned in an earlier anecdote (p. 213, ms. p. 580) about the abuse of native officials by priests.

"Señor, what you have to do is, when you know that the general inspector is going to come, flatter your enemies and make them your friends. So long as they're not Spanish, you have no reason to fear the drunken Indians. Then, give presents to everybody when the time comes, and pretend to be nice and docile in the meanwhile; don't meddle in anything until the storm and the fury have blown over."

"Señor, what should I do after the inspector arrives?"

"Señor, you should do this: first, send him a little something under the table, like a little gift of 500 pesos hidden in a letter. Second, kiss up to him: receive him in another pueblo, bring him to your house, keep him very comfortable there—wash his feet for him. Third, give 500 pesos to his notary, and 200 to his legal counsel and his interpreter. Go ahead and give generously, because it will all be at the Indians' expense. When all is said and done, you'll have lost 2,000 pesos, but you'll get back 12,000. You're the proprietor of it all, by order of His Majesty, so what should you care? Even if you were to kill a half dozen Indians and steal all their property and wives and sons and daughters, it's just a matter of spending, because the inspector doesn't come to do anything but rob and take bribes. He'd sooner punish the Indian who complained about you. If we were interim padres, then we'd be sorry, but now we're proprietors, as good as bishops, and with no overhead. That's the best thing we have going in this kingdom."

**The question that the inspectors** ask each other, when they try to have dealings and commerce and make some money from the *doctrina* padres and noble Indians and poor people of this kingdom, is as follows:

"Señor, they've appointed me to be the general inspector for the Holy Mother Church in the provinces of Lucanas, Andahuaylas, and Vilcashuaman. And you?"

"Señor, I've been appointed to the provinces of Collao, Canas, Pacajes, and Canches. Yours is better than mine."

"Señor, please tell me, what kind of money can I make in these provinces with some little deals?"

"Señor, let me tell you what you should do. You should do as follows: when you are on the inspection tour, don't touch the servants of His Lordship [the bishop], of the vicar general, of the dean of the cathedral, or of the canons, or any of their friends. Even if they are guilty of a crime, don't touch them; rather, honor them. Don't fine them or demand bribes from them, either, because they will write about it, and things will go badly for you. As for the Indians and their religious brotherhoods, take as much money as you can get from them. Fine all the Indians and all the priests who aren't in favor; skin them alive. You should come in with bluster and ferocity and wrath and pomp, and act with severity. You should not care at all, because, first, you will never be audited or asked for accounts, and you are passing through quickly. Also, if you act like a little saint, you will end up very poor, and so will your secretary and officers; let the money flow so that none of them will complain. If the *doctrina* padre gives a bribe, you had better punish the Indian who complained about him, collecting information only because the padre is serving you. For he will keep you happy; what profit could you get from the Indian? After he is punished, the Indian will remain an Indian, while you will collect your money and leave. Now, if you were going to be audited, or if you had to find a guarantor, then you would be sorry. But as things are, you should do as much business as you can off of the inspection that you were appointed to do. Just remember this piece of advice: act as finicky as a little saint, and tell your secretary and your legal counsel to take the bribes. That way, you'll come out rich from your inspection tour, and soon you'll be strolling in the city."

*741–751*

## SENTENCES PASSED BY THE CHRISTIANS
## THE SENTENCES ON THE INDICTMENTS OF
## THIS *CHRONICLE,* BY THE NOBLE CHRISTIAN
## GENTLEMEN OF THIS KINGDOM

*[In counterpoint to the preceding sets of satirical dialogues, these "Sentences" give examples of virtuous people from every walk of life. Guaman Poma implies that, rare as such people may be, they effectively pass judgment on their immoral colleagues by living virtuous lives. Throughout this chapter, Guaman Poma uses the word* capítulos *("chapters") in its secondary meaning of "indictments" or "list of charges." We see here that many of the "chapters" in his book are likewise meant to be charges in an indictment of the colonial system. The "sentences" that he describes in this chapter are not literal judicial sentences passed on indictment charges in a court of law, but rather the living examples given by rightous gentlemen from various stations: through their just actions, they have passed judgment on the criminal activities of their counterparts. In the general conclusion to this set of didactic chapters, Guaman Poma declares that this book is itself such a "sentence" on the immorality of colonial society.]*

**THE FIRST GENTLEMAN:** Don Pedro de Córdoba y Guzmán of the Order of Santiago, Lance Captain–Major of the city of Los Reyes de Lima, *encomendero* of the *Lucanas* Indians, was a very great and saintly man, most Christian.[282] He pronounced this sentence: that no *encomendero* should go

---

[282] Pedro de Córdoba y Guzmán (mentioned earlier on p. 207, ms. p. 573) came to Peru in 1556 with his uncle, the newly named viceroy Andrés Hurtado de Mendoza, and was given the *encomienda* of the Lucanas.

to the Indian pueblos, nor should his wife, children, or stewards. They should stay in the city, where they can serve God and His Majesty.

This Christian man shared his salary with his Indians in his *encomienda,* and he forgave half the food tribute that they owed him. He never entered the *encomienda* territory, nor did he ever wish to have a steward; instead, he hired an Indian, Don Diego Chachapoya,[283] and so he kept no Spaniard [on Indian land]. They say that his son, Don Rodrigo, once stayed [on the *encomienda*], and because of that, Don Pedro sent him to serve as captain of the army in Chile.[284]

This gentleman strongly defended [the Indians] from the *corregidores,* from the *doctrina* padres, and from other Spaniards, and he did not like having deputies. He gave many alms, was charitable, and had no bluster. He was a plain and simple man, and fond of having conversations with the poor. He called everyone "son." He had no estate or croplands, because he did not want to occupy the poor Indians. He did not demand *camaricos* [gifts], *mitayos* [Indian laborers], *isancas* [baskets], fruit, *yanaconas* [male Indian servants], *chinaconas* [female Indian servants], or Indians to work in *rescates* or commerce. If any Indian brought him a present that was worth one real, he would give the Indian eight reales.

Look at this sentence, Christians, citizens, *encomenderos:* it is the sentence of a saintly man who grieved for the poor Indians when he saw their troubles. Therefore he put this sentence into effect, that through it His Majesty might fill the world and this kingdom with justice.

**The sentence that** Captain Cárdenas, citizen of the city of Huamanga, pronounced for his Indians in his *encomienda* of the Chocorbos, Santiago, Huaytara, Vilcancho, and Yauyos, where the Indians today have five thousand Castilian sheep:[285] although this gentleman had five sons, he left [his estate] to everyone, as if they were all his children, dividing it among his Indians. He will truly be in heaven, for he loved the poor so well. He also divided [his estate] among the nobles, for their part. That is why they are rich today. What a good, Christian sentence, which should serve as an example and punishment for wicked people, so that His Majesty and his justices should carry out this sentence!

**The sentence of** the gentleman Hernando Palomina, *encomendero* of the

---

[283] Guaman Poma frequently states his opinion that the *Chachapoyas* (early Spanish allies against the Incas) had all become *yanaconas,* personal servants to the Spanish.

[284] Distant, poor, and inhospitable in Guaman Poma's time, Chile was considered a good place to banish unruly subordinates.

[285] Cárdenas is mentioned together with Córdoba on ms. p. 573; on that page, the Indians are said to have fifty thousand sheep. Murra and Adorno (ms. p. 573, n. 2) identify him as Francisco de Cárdenas, one of the founders of Huamanga.

*Soras* Indians and citizen of the city of Huamanga: though he gave them nothing, it was nevertheless a great work of alms and charity for the poor Indians that he never left the city to go among the Indians in his *encomienda;* nor did he wish for his brothers or sons to enter there and disturb his Indians; nor did he wish to have a steward who would occupy the Indians. He would send the tribute that they gave him to the *corregidor.* He never demanded *mitayos* or gifts (*camaricos*) from the poor Indians. What a good sentence, what good charity for his fellow men, to exempt the poor Indians from the indictments mentioned and from skinning them alive! He is very rich, because he does not gamble and play trumps: a noble gentleman. His Majesty shall see this sentence and shall do justice and make amends for the poor of God in this kingdom.

**The sentence of** Captain Alonso de Medina, *corregidor* and chief magistrate of the *encomienda* territory and province of the Aymaraes, a most Christian man: he had no more than one old Indian who served him; he had no servants, no serving boys, no sons, no wife, and no brother, nor did he demand anything at all—no food, no *mita* service, not even a chicken or eggs. He never ate more than a bowl of meat. He had no dealings or contracts. He did not gamble, and showed no pomp or pride. He helped the poor. Therefore, the Spaniards hated him. He was a servant of viceroy Count Don Carlos Monterrey [1604–1606]. This most Christian man began to whip the thieving *encomenderos,* Spaniards, and *doctrina* padres. Because he had no dealings, and therefore had nothing to fear even if they threatened him, they had no complaints that they could write to the viceroy or the *Audiencia.* His sentence should stand as an example and punishment to the wicked *corregidores,* whereby His Majesty shall see it and do justice through this sentence against the indictments that have been drawn up.

**The sentence of** the *corregidor* of the province of the Lucanas, Gregorio López de Puga:[286] this was a greatly learned man, a licentiate, and very Christian. He passed sentence as a learned man, for he never meddled in matters that did not pertain to his jurisdiction. He had no dealings, and he demanded nothing. He went alone. They even say he did not hire a notary; instead, he did justice alone. He returned much to the Indians, and he honored the nobles. He threw the Spaniards, deputies, mestizos, and mulattos out of the *corregimiento,* and he punished the vagabond Spaniards.

He passed sentence and made judgements on these indictments, based on which His Majesty shall pass sentence and make judgements in favor of the poor of this kingdom, by passing the sentences of these two gentlemen, these Christian *corregidores,* and saying that the king, in discharging his royal conscience, had sent them to do justice, not to rob people or set them

---

[286] Also mentioned earlier (p. 175, ms. pp. 512–14 and 527).

to labor; to honor the good and punish the wicked; to favor the poor and encourage the nobles to favor their vassals; to give alms, charity, and love to the widows, the orphans, and the persecuted; to help them, as God decreed in his commandments and gospel, as declared by the holy prophets, the servants of Jesus Christ, captain of God and His Majesty. In this way, you have passed sentence on these indictments.

These gentlemen should be life-long *corregidores:* their good works make them proprietors, and as such they pass sentence on the indictments mentioned in this kingdom. Therefore, a *corregidor* should have no wife or children, and should be sixty years of age, for the good government of administering justice in the *corregimientos,* and should be a judge or notary in this kingdom, so that His Majesty may rely on good sentences being passed throughout the kingdom.

**The sentence of** Padre Juan López de Quintanilla, judge and general inspector of the Holy Mother Church for the jurisdiction (*sede vacante*) and cathedral chapter of Cusco:[287] when this most Christian commissioner was doing his inspections, he did not go about with bluster, pomp, or crowds of people, but only with his notary and his legal counsel. He never took bribes. In some places, he received no comfortable treatment when he arrived, but he suffered in silence, and he returned many times for the sake of the poor Indians. He would sooner give alms, charity, and love.

He ordered the town criers to announce that he had not come to the pueblos to inspect the Indians but rather the churches, the church decorations, the padre's house, and the padre himself—[to investigate] whether [the priest] was robbing and doing harm to the poor Indian men and women. That was why God, the pope, and the king (as the patron of the Holy Church) had sent him. "Therefore, do not be afraid, poor people!"

Thereupon, one proud padre—being a sheer scoundrel, or a bad Christian, disobedient to God and the Holy Mother Church of Rome—fled his *doctrina,* leaving word that everyone in the pueblo should disappear and flee, and that no one should give him water or food, and that they should lock him in the church. And so the Indians did; they fled and hid.

Just look at the pride and disobedience that the priests show towards their prelates and judges! What will they do towards laymen, when they are so impudent, so despotic, without God, without pope, without king? Not even the pope or the king are so free, because they obey God, the Ten Commandments, and the gospel and law of God.

---

[287] *Sede vacante:* there was no bishop in Cusco from July 1606 to January 1609; at the time, Guaman Poma's home region of Huamanga still belonged to this diocese. López is highlighted in a section (ms. pp. 695–96) omitted in this translation.

Oh, what a good sentence by the judge-inspector, to pass sentence with his humility, love, charity, patience, and poverty: he sentenced the padre, not the poor Indians, and he did not do it for the money. This Christian was a greatly learned man, for he passed judgment with justice, and was victorious. He should be a model for inspectors throughout the world, who should punish the rebellious padres, and not punish the poor Indians or go after the padres' purses and reales, as other inspectors do when they show favor to criminal padres while punishing and shaming poor Indians like Don Cristóbal de León: they sell all [the poor Indians'] property, burn and destroy their houses, and banish them to the galleys. This judge was victorious over [such inspectors]; he sentenced and judged them. His Holiness the Pope in Rome and His Majesty, patron of the Holy Mother Church, should see this, and pass sentence on these indictments, and bring justice.

**The sentence of** the vicar general of the province of the Andamarcas, Soras, and Lucanas, as a very Christian judge and learned man: Padre Diego Beltrán de Saravia, the parish priest of Santa María de Peña de Francia de Vilcabamba de Suntuto, was the vicar general of the same province, and he resided in the center and capital of the province.[288] He was a most Christian priest. He passed sentence with his Christianity and the love, charity, humility, and favor he showed the poor Indians of the province.

This padre defended [the poor Indians] from the *corregidor,* the deputies, the *encomenderos,* the judges, the Spaniards, and the stewards, fending off their injuries, labors, and harassment. This Christian padre put up so many defenses, they cannot all be written down. He spent his estate in defending the poor. Therefore, he died a poor man in his parish house. He served for thirty-five years.

In addition, he never demanded *mitayos,* and never had a [female] cook, nor did he ever allow one in his house during his life. He only had one *mitayo* and one servant boy, and he hired lame Indians to be his *fiscal* and sextons. He had only one mule. He never meddled in the testaments of Indians after they died, and he had no *rescates.* He never gathered girls or maidens in the *doctrina;* he only allowed boys, from the age of six. He had no children of his own. He was more than sixty years old. Indian women were never seen entering his house, not even the kitchen, and he whipped the Indian women who did enter. He never invited the Spaniard or the *corregidor* to eat from the property of the poor. He did not have dealings or keep croplands and cattle. He never meddled in administering justice. He did not punish; he did not go around taking notes on the Indians; he did

---

[288] Suntunto was Guaman Poma's birth pueblo. Guaman Poma paints a much less charitable picture of this priest on p. 308 (ms. p. 944), accusing him of leading the successful legal suit to expel Guaman Poma from the province in 1600.

not do the rounds of houses day and night. He allowed the poor to work in their fields, go out to make money for their tribute payments, and run their own *rescates*. He distributed the church offerings as alms among the poor.

This was a saintly man, parish priest, and vicar general, who passed sentences in a most Christian way. He could have been a bishop and an inspector for the Holy Mother Church. Oh, what good sentences! With these, the Indians never left their pueblos, because they were not squeezed or punished by these sentences: may His Holiness the Pope in Rome and His Majesty pass sentence in the indictments that have been brought in favor of the Indians.

**The sentence of** Padre Bachiller Avendaño, the *doctrina* and parish priest of the pueblo of Nombre de Jesús de Pucyulla: this padre remained in his *doctrina* for twenty years and died there. He was very Christian. The Indians never complained about him. He never demanded *mitayos* or *camarico* [gifts], and he never brought in Spaniards or his brothers or kin; he kept them all away from him. He only had one ten-year-old serving boy, who served him in the kitchen, making his dinner. And he had only one mule. In one day he would only eat one chicken for dinner and one pullet for supper. He refused all business. He did not let *mitayas* or maidens into his house, nor did he call them to *doctrina;* instead, he gathered in the boys from the age of six years. He never punished or meddled in doing justice, nor did he have dealings and commerce. He was a most Christian man; he was quicker to give alms to the poor than to the rich Spaniards. He never made the rounds of the houses by day or night, and he did not wander the streets. He used his office very honorably. He confessed the girls and maidens, even the old women; he confessed all the Indians by himself, without hiring [an assistant]. He did not want to be a vicar or a judge, so as not to do ill to the poor Indians.

This Christian passed sentence: he said that padres should be subject to their prelates, and that they should not be ordained when they are boys, but rather at the age of fifty; nor should they meddle in justice, nor have dealings, nor have women or servants. This was his sentence and his judgment: may His Holiness the Pope of Rome and His Majesty pass sentence on these indictments and complaints.

**The sentence of** Padre Martín de Ayala, parish priest and benefice holder of the hospital for the poor Indians of Jesus Christ, the patients in the hospital of the city of Huamanga: this Padre Martín de Ayala was mestizo, the son of an important gentleman and the grandson of Topa Inca Yupanqui, the lord and king of this kingdom, but he was a very saintly man. As such, he passed sentence on the mestizos and *criollos* of this kingdom with his humility, charity, love of God, penitence, alms, holy works, and service to God and His Majesty. From the age of seven, he entered into the service of

God in the hospital of the city of Cusco. He received a hermit's habit, and from there he became an ordained priest. He died serving God at the age of forty. But he performed many miracles. His sentence deserves to be remembered and pronounced by the pope of Rome and by His Majesty in answer to the indictments.

**The sentence of** Juan García de la Vega, mine owner for His Majesty in the Villa Rica de Oropesa de Huancavelica, the quicksilver mines: this gentleman was mestizo, the son of Juan de la Vega, an Old Christian and a very charitable servant of God and His Majesty who gave and made loans to His Majesty. He did not wish to see the noble *caciques* and Indians punished, hanged by the feet, or shamed, nor did he consent to having their work and their day wages taken away. He gave them food and drink from his house at no charge, and so God gave him a large fortune. He did not like for his stewards to pay his Indian workers; he himself gave them encouragement, with love and charity, so that the Indians would work in the mines. He comforted and defended his Indians from the bad Christians and from the *corregidor,* in the distribution of Indians and in the royal storehouse. When they heard "Juan García," they all wanted to be his Indians: they all jumped up and down, and even pulled out their hair, because they were dying to go with Juan García. But when they heard "Sotomayor" and "Contreras," they all ran off, hid, and pretended to be dead, not to go with them.[289]

Here you see, Christian mine owners, how Juan García has sentenced you with his love, charity, service to God and His Majesty, and favor for the poor. He has passed sentence on the indictments, giving an example of service to God and His Majesty and the good of the poor Indians in all the mines of this kingdom, gold, silver, and quicksilver. The sentence is passed, signed, and carried out.

**The sentence of** Pero Sánchez, a native of Valladolid in Spain, a poor man and Old Christian who traveled through the *tambos* of this kingdom: he passed sentence with his humility, meekness, charity, and love for God and fellow man. He never demanded *mitayos* or any kind of comfort. When he bought food, he first paid the Indians with his own hands, and only then received the food; and with all that, he still said "please, by the love of God." He called the Indians "my brothers, children of Adam." It happened one day that he found no *mitayo* Indian; he gave thanks to God, and did not go to their houses to seek them out, nor did he allow the Indians to carry him. He would shout out loud: "Christians, come and be comforted by the love of God!"

---

[289] Murra and Adorno note (ms. p. 748, n. 1) that Juan de Sotomayor and Pedro de Contreras were major mine owners in Huancavelica in the 1580s. Stern, *Peru's Indian Peoples* (p. 230, n. 18), cites a source dated 1607 that confirms the respective reputations of Juan García de la Vega (described as a mestizo) and Sotomayor.

See, Christian, what a good sentence this Christian traveler through the *tambos* decreed. After all, he was born in Castile; if he were *criollo* or mestizo, he would not have passed such a sentence in the *tambos* of this kingdom. He passed this sentence so that His Majesty and his justice would sentence and judge these indictments in this kingdom. Judge and record it, finally.

**The sentence of** Alonso Hernández Coronado, a resident in the city of Huamanga: he was one of the elders, an Old Christian and one of the very wise men. He was more learned than the learned in his spirit. He was filled with faith in Jesus Christ, love, charity, and good works of mercy. He served God and His Majesty, was properly married, and his sons were well instructed in the doctrine. He hoped that all his sons would become priests.

He taught his sons doctrine, saying: "Even if you become priests, sons, I want to say a few words to you. My sons, do not waver from the path, nor fall behind in your letters. Strive to learn more, and if you do find out more, even so you should continue to ask questions of your elders, the learned, and the wise. Even if he doesn't know his letters, an old man knows more than a young man, for God has given him wisdom, truth, and teaching.

"I will tell you more, my sons. The creator is God the Father: he it is who has given you wisdom, life, and sustenance. The mother is the Holy Mother Church, which is all the wise men in the world. Trying to take on the justices and your king is like trying to embrace the sky with your hands. Therefore, do not take on your prelate and lord.

"So I tell you, my sons: how goodly it seems when each one is in his station: the pope on his pontifical throne, the king with his crown, the gentleman on his horse, the hidalgo with his excise tax, the taxpaying commoner with his personal tax, the Jew as Jew, the Old Christian as Old Christian. I command you, my sons, do not pass beyond the credo in God the Father to other business."

This was the sentence that he passed as a faithful Christian; a good sentence. Much good may this judicious sentence do for Christians.

**The sentence of** the most excellent lord Don Martín Guaman Mallqui de Ayala, the second-in-command of his father-in-law Topa Inca Yupanqui and his viceroy in this kingdom, the author's father, who resides in the royal crown province of the Andamarcas: this prince passed sentence as a gentleman and lord of this kingdom, who served God in his holy house for thirty years, bringing out servants, cleaning the house, and buying food for the poor people in the hospital. He also served His Majesty in the battle of Collao de Huarina Pampa, in the clash with Gonzalo Pizarro, where he won the name of Ayala while serving His Majesty. He served in Chupas

Pampa, Huaraco Urco, and in Huamanga in the clash with Don Diego de Almagro the Younger, where he served His Majesty. He served in the battle of Huatacocha, in the clash with Francisco Hernández Girón, who was overthrown and sent fleeing to Jauja, where the *Wanca* Indians captured him unarmed.

He was a most Christian, charitable, alms-giving man. He was married to his wife, Doña Juana Coya, the younger and legitimate daughter of Topa Inca, former lord and king of this kingdom. Thus, he was a great lord, like the most excellent Duke of Alba in Castile. He was the first to give the sign of peace to the ambassador of the emperor-king, and he gave the peace to all the Christians in this kingdom. He greatly favored his vassals. He passed sentence with his humility and charity, by serving God and His Majesty and by doing good works and giving alms: a good sentence, worthy of memory, whereby His Majesty and his justice should pass sentence on the indictments leveled against the nobles of this kingdom.

**The sentence of** a poor tributary Indian from the pueblo of San Felipe Santiago Uchucmarca:[290] this Indian petty authority passed sentence with his poverty, humility, charity, and love of neighbor; a most Christian man. He was always the *alcalde* in his pueblo. This poor man was poisoned by quicksilver in the mines of Huancavelica. He would raise his hands to God, bending his knees, and say: "Take me quickly, Lord, from this life, as soon as possible, because the burdens on me are so great." Because he hired [a replacement worker to serve in his place] in the mines, he paid tribute, and he served in the *tambo,* serving the Spaniards, the *encomendero,* the *corregidor,* the padre, the judge, the stewards, and their brothers, wives, children, servants, and slaves, and the noble Indians. In serving them, with their trafficking and *rescates,* and in giving them food and comforts—everything contained in these indictments—this Christian man passed sentence with his poverty, giving an example whereby His Majesty and his justice should pass sentence for the good of the poor Indians of this kingdom.

**The sentence of** the saintly black man San Juan Buenaventura, along with all the reverend Jesuit and Franciscan padres and the hermits: they all passed sentence—the saintly black man, with his humility, charity, and love of the poor; and they had no pride and made penitence, gave alms, and often scoured their flesh. He passed sentence in his flesh and in the lives of the blacks, to serve as an example in the world; sentence should be passed on these indictments leveled in the world.

---

[290] In the southeastern corner of Lucanas province, near Tambo Quemado. It is known today as Uchuymarca.

## PROLOGUE TO THE READERS OF "YOU MEN WHO SEEK OFFICES AND BENEFICES, *CORREGIMIENTOS,* AND GOVERNMENT IN THE WORLD AND IN THIS KINGDOM"

YET YOU SEEK them to do evil and steal money, and you are not sated—you Christian readers who might read these sentences—with all the harm and evil that has been done in the world and in this kingdom.

These Christians have been sentenced and judged, and thus I hold this book of the *First Chronicle,* this sentence, to be finished and decreed, in the service of God and His Majesty, for the good of our fellow men, and for the government and good justice of this kingdom. Therefore, Christian reader, you should see that, from the beginning, God is God and shall be God forever and ever—in heaven, on earth, and in hell, He is one true God: likewise, the most holy pope, second-in-command of God, and our lord and king, the monarch of the world, shall pass sentence and decree justice for whoever is in the right according to justice and the law, by the ordinances of the world; and for this kingdom, they shall keep this *Chronicle* in the archive of the world as it is in heaven, in the cathedral of Rome as a memorial, and in the capital of our Christianity, our Spain, where His Royal Catholic Majesty resides, may God keep him, in Spain, the capital of the world.

## THE GOOD NOBLE SHOULD BE EXAMINED IN SPANISH WRITING AND LANGUAGE.

He should know how to draw up a petition, a questionnaire, and a lawsuit; and he should not be a drunk, a coca-chewer, a gambler, or a liar in this kingdom.

[On the document being written by the noble:] "For the first half of the year, Pedro N. paid eighty pesos."

### *In this kingdom.*

# PART 8.
# ANDEAN SOCIETY UNDER SPANISH RULE

*[The last major section of the book, on post-conquest Andean society, brings us full circle to the subject of the first long part, which dealt with Andean society under Inca rule. This section is divided into three chapters: "The Nobles," "The Indian Justices," and "The Indians." The first of these comments on the descendents of the Inca and high Andean nobles under Spanish rule; the second catalogs the lower-ranking local indigenous officials who administered Indian pueblos; the third covers the bulk of the indigenous population, kept segregated in Guaman Poma's writing from the nobles just as he wished to keep them separated in everyday social life. Together, the nobles and the local officials comprised the colonial system of indirect rule over the commoner majority. Guaman Poma uses these chapters to advocate for the honor, respect, and salaries (to be paid by the crown) that he felt were due to Indian rulers in exchange for their dutiful fulfillment of their responsibilities. He also insists on their need to act morally (no drinking wine or chewing coca), and to dress in ways that distinguish them from each other according to their place in the hierarchy, from Spaniards, and from commoner Indians. He specifies that only the nobles with authority over one thousand or more tributaries should be allowed to use the honorific title "Don," and he complains bitterly of the petty authorities who pass themselves off to uncaring Spaniards as high-ranking* curacas. *The charges of abuse by Spaniards in collusion with Indian authorities, leveled throughout the book and repeated here, are attributed to these "false* caciques.*"]*

## THE NOBLES

*from pages 752–805*

*[In the selections from "The Nobles" presented here, Guaman Poma advocates for a wealthy and honored indigenous nobility as the key to a revived Andean world, and he insists on the importance of strictly maintaining social distinctions between noble and commoner, between men and women, between Spaniard and Indian. He justifies his call for a wealthy neo-Incan nobility by arguing that the true Andean nobles are "Christians" who safeguard the welfare of the poor. To this end, he calls for all nobles to become literate and fluent in Spanish, the better to defend their people.]*

THE NOBLE *CACIQUES* should be examined in the language of Castile and in the common language of Quechua. They should prove that they were raised without *chicha* [corn beer] and have never tasted wine in their lives

*784–785*

263

nor gambled. To this end, they should be raised as Christians and *ladinos* [fluent in Spanish], and, if at all possible, should learn Latin, reading, writing, and arithmetic, and should be able to arrange petitions and questionnaires for the defense of their own persons and of their Indians and vassal subjects, the poor of Jesus Christ. They should be good Christians: humble, charitable, witty, gentle towards good people, and fierce towards the evil. They should have both honey and bile. They should be men of verve and high spirits, for that is what is needed, that they not fear the devil nor the *corregidores, encomenderos,* padres, or Spaniards, but rather fear only God and His Majesty. If a *cacique* does not have high spirits or the other qualities mentioned, another more spirited man should govern and should share half of the *cacique's* salary, together with all his other perquisites and the services of his Indians.

**The noble *caciques*** and all the Indians should own a great deal of property, in order to serve God Our Lord and His Majesty and the poor Indians. They should hire each other, and should pay each other with their own hands. If they serve and reform, may they find favor and own male and female slaves, without causing harm to the Indians; and if they can, may the nobles and the Indians in this kingdom own riches that they can leave for their souls and for their heirs, or for the poor, or for their communities and their children, in their wills.

**The noble *caciques,*** being Christians—as are their wives and children—should keep very clean and should dress like Spaniards from [the proceeds of] their estates, without robbing or stealing from the poor Indians, and they should behave with great Christianity, in order that their Indian subjects might follow them in their orderliness, cleanliness, and service of God and His Majesty. Likewise, the poor Indians should observe cleanliness throughout the kingdom—some better than others—and should not be harassed by the *corregidor,* the padre, or the judge in this kingdom.

800–803    **HOW GOODLY THEY APPEAR,** each in their own clothing: the noble *cacique* as noble *cacique,* the Indian man as Indian man, the noblewoman as lady, and the Indian woman as Indian woman, each dressed so that they may be recognized, respected, and honored. If they are sheer drunkards and coca-chewers, [the nobles] are not honored, even if they do dress in their natural style. They should wear blouses[291] and should wear their hair over their ears in such a way as to differentiate themselves from the Indians and appear as noble *caciques* and lords of the land. If they wear whiskers like cooked shrimp, they will look like mestizos, *cholos,* people of bad stock, mulattos, *zambaigos.*

---

[291] Guaman Poma, like the Spanish chroniclers of his day, distinguished between the Incaic wide-sleeved, tailless blouse (*camiseta*) and the Spanish men's shirt (*camisa*).

# HOW GOODLY APPEAR THE NOBLE IN HIS CLOTHING, AND THE INDIAN IN HIS CLOTHING, RESPECTIVELY.

*In this kingdom.*

Likewise, no Indian should wear whiskers, but rather only his own natural style.

A Spaniard without whiskers looks like an old whore, his face a mask. The Spaniard is honored by his beard. If he had long hair like the Indian he would appear savage, a wild animal. Wearing his true Spaniard's clothing, bearded, and with cropped hair, he is honored in the world.[. . .]

**The noble *caciques*** who marry their daughters to *mitayo* Indians lose the honor and preeminence that a noble *cacique* has in this kingdom, if the [son-in-law] is a low tributary, a taxpayer to His Majesty. But if he is a noble, he enjoys the privileges granted by the emperor-king. When a man marries a *mitaya* Indian woman, his children and his descendents are mestizos, but at least the man makes the stock. But if the woman—whether a legitimate daughter, a natural child, or a bastard[292]—Doña Francisca, Doña Juana—marries a *mitayo* Indian or a slave, then she is a slave and a *mitaya*. She has taken the title of Doña that was granted to her by the emperor Don Carlos and thrown it in the river; she has carried it down and drowned it, so that now it is lost, never to return. If it dies, it dies once and for all, as if she had submerged the "Doña" in the depths of the sea. The cause of this, and the blame for it, lies with her father and mother and all her relatives. She can no longer call herself "Doña," even if she is Spanish; she and all her stock and offspring have lost the honor of the "Don," and are now erased, low, degraded—especially her children, and even more so the grandchildren who descend from her, when they should have risen higher in the honor of the world.

Thus, with honor one serves God; for the patriarchs, the prophets, the Mother of God, and God himself wished for good stock and honor. All the saints were of good stock and honorable, while Judas Iscariot was of bad stock. Bad stock can never give rise to saints or good people in this world. So it is that, in this life, market women, tavern women, and bakery women call themselves Doña Fulana, and the punks, scoundrels, thieves, highwaymen, drunks, Jews, Moors, and taxpaying commoners call themselves Don Fulano. To call oneself "Don," one must be an Old Christian, a gentleman, and of good blood, and the title should have been granted by His Majesty. All judges should enforce this rule in this kingdom, and should punish the Indians and Spaniards alike [who pretend to be "Dons"], in the world. [. . .]

---

[292] See footnote 10 on the terms "legitimate," "natural," and "bastard." Guaman Poma's use of these terms may conflate Spanish and Andean lineage customs, but his view of descent as presented here—that lineage is determined in a unitary way by the male line only—is in line with Spanish views, and contrasts with Andean ideas of dual descent along both male and female lines.

The noble *caciques* should be honored in these kingdoms. Their sons and brothers—legitimate, natural, or bastard—should not gather with the common Indians in the plaza on any day when the Indians are being counted, during the feast days; instead, they should be counted in the church or the cemetery every year. They should be saying their rosaries or reciting their prayers or reading their books every Sunday and feast day of the year, while the common people pray. And the outsider Indians should gather with them in the cemetery, so that the *alcalde* might recognize them, in this kingdom.

The noble Indian ladies should be honored as the wives of noble *caciques,* [as should] the daughters and sisters of these titled Doñas—legitimate, natural, or bastard—so long as they do not marry low Indians and tributaries, or Spaniards, mestizos, blacks, or mulattos. If one should marry a low man, she should be listed with the common Indians. Each of these Doñas should sit on her own low seat, and the outsider women should sit beside them. Each of them should say her rosary or recite her prayers; they should all be praying or reading the lives of the saints, as Christian women, and they should not fall short. If they have serving girls, the padre and the *alcalde* should not disturb them; the servants should stay with the ladies to pray, and the ladies should teach them to be Christian women and become pure and Christian.

## THE INDIAN JUSTICES AND TOWN COUNCILS

*selected from 806–833*

*[In these selections from "The Indian Justices," Guaman Poma broadens his call for Spanish literacy among the Andean nobility to encompass the ranks of the indigenous local government. Indian officials, he says, must be fluent in both written and spoken Spanish and Quechua in order to navigate the colonial system to the benefit of their people. His position here and in the previous chapter could be called conservative, in that he favors reestablishing the pre-colonial status hierarchy, but it is a radical position when viewed against the backdrop of his literate Spanish contemporaries, who inveighed in reports and chronicles against duplicitous* indios ladinos—*bilingual Indians who manipulated the colonial justice system in their own favor (as the Spanish commentators alleged), or in favor of the Indians (as Guaman Poma hoped).]*

THE NOTARY of the town council, or the notary public, or His Majesty's royal notary:    *828–831*

The community should pay twelve pesos, twelve half-*hanegas* [of corn or potatoes], and twelve llamas each year to the notary public of their province, who should reside, together with the noble *cacique* and the administrator, in the head pueblo of that province.

# The Town Council Notary
## (*Quilqaycamayoc*) Appointed
## by His Majesty.

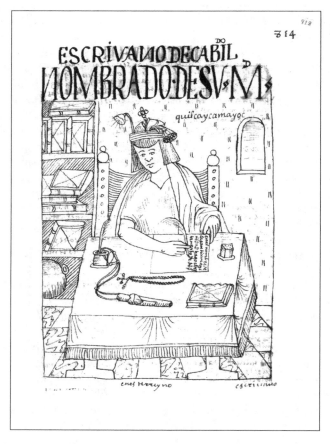

[On the document being written by the notary:] "In the name of the Holy Trinity, I draw up the last will and testament of Don Pedro."

### *In this kingdom.*

Every pueblo should have its appointed notary, who should be exempt from paying tribute and other obligations, throughout this kingdom, so that the ordinances of God and His Majesty may be carried out. Even the smallest of pueblos should have its notary, and his testimony should be deemed as valid as that of a royal notary public. In order that he might certify, authorize, and give testimony for their excellencies the viceroys, the royal *Audiencia,* and His Majesty's justices, and so that he might have no fear of the *corregidor,* his deputy, the civil and church judges, the church inspectors, or the *encomenderos,* he should be given all the faculties of a judicial secretary.

Hence, he should record all the tribute, such as silver, cloth, corn, wheat, chickens, llamas, and anything else that might be assessed. Together with the noble *cacique* and the authorities of the pueblo, the notary should collect it from the tributaries—not from Indian women, only Indian men— and note it down every six months in the tribute book; he should also note down all the troubling incidents caused by the *corregidores* with their dealings, *rescates, ricachicos,* and *mitayos,* taking everything from food to firewood and hay every day; and he should note down how many Spaniards, servants, and maids there are, with their names.

Likewise, [he should note down] all the damage that the *doctrina* padres and priests cause and all the services they demand, how many Indian men and women, and the names of their companions, servants, maids, and cooks; everything from food to firewood and hay they use every day; and how much they collect for all the alms, offerings, prayers for the dead, high Masses, low Masses, Masses for the dead or for health or for alms that they offer every day, and whether or not they say Mass on Sundays and feast days. Also, who supplies the priest with wax, incense, and soap; and how many days *mita* service lasts in each pueblo, and whether people shirk their obligations and errands. He should also inspect the kitchen, stables, and house of the *corregidor* and the padre in order to note it all down. If they go out to do the rounds of the pueblo, and if they steal from the rich or the poor, he should write it all down. The *alcaldes* should do the same, noting down even the firewood, hay, salt, stew, straw, and all the other little things that are never set down; it all adds up to money.

*[Guaman Poma continues to specify which details the notary should record, from abuses by the* corregidor *and the details of* mita *service to a catalogue of the property, including individual trees, of the community and its nobles and commoners.]*

**Testaments should be drawn up** without calling any [witnesses]; instead, the testator should unburden his conscience and declare everything by his own free will, without being disturbed by anyone, and he should leave his possessions or estate to whomever he wishes, by his free will. But he should declare his legitimate sons and daughters and their ages, his natural sons and daughters, and his bastard sons and daughters. If he leaves his possessions or his ruling title to his bastard son [instead of] his natural son or legitimate son, he should do so because his legitimate son never gave him a pitcher of water in his life, but instead beat him, while the bastard son served him like a black slave and fulfilled what God ordained in the Ten Commandments: if he loved and honored his father and his mother, then everything should be left to him. The one who did not obey the commandment should be punished by God and by his father. In this way, he will not be disturbed. When his testament is complete, he should have the noble *cacique* and the protector of the province sign it.

The notary should keep a copy [of the testament] in a separate book, and return the original to its owner. He should make copies of all the commandments, decrees, and edicts, and return the originals, throughout the kingdom, so that its laws and justice might be obeyed.

**All judges, both civil** and ecclesiastic, in these kingdoms should accept the petitions, memoranda, questionnaires, notices, and letters that the Indians present to them, even if they are written in Indian languages; they should respond [to them], even if only in a short note at the bottom of the page, and with their response they should return them for the sake of their right and justice. Even if the judge is an Indian *alcalde,* he should never deliver judgments by word, but rather should do so with letters. In order that the *corregidor* may have it on record, if a judgment comes by word, he should refuse to hear it and should ask for it in writing; thus His Majesty will see and approve it. He should not tear them up, and should not hide them, and should not allow [the *alcalde*] to seek out a lawyer; instead, he should receive petitions whether they are well done or badly done.

This [refusing petitions and accepting verbal judgments] is the cause of much harm, and because of it [the Indians] will never attain justice nor achieve it. His Majesty knows nothing about this. As a service, I informed His Excellency Don Luis de Velasco, the viceroy, who set a fine of one hundred silver pesos on every *corregidor,* to insure that the Indians would draw up petitions and give them to him, so that justice would be carried out over them in this kingdom.

*selected
from
834–922*

## THE INDIANS

*[The commoners, who made up the vast majority of the population of early seventeenth-century Peru, are the subject of the final chapter in this part. The title of the chapter is "The Christian Indians," or more simply, "Indios," a word that Guaman Poma always tries to avoid using in reference to anyone but commoners, resisting the Spanish tendency to stamp the native Andean nobility with the*

*"Indian" label. His basic purpose in this chapter is to highlight the Christianity of the Andean Indians. The extended texts of untranslated Quechua Christian prayers in this chapter (not included here), among the longest examples of the language in the book, are meant to provide graphic evidence of a vigorous, Andean Christianity. Guaman Poma argues that, because of their Christianity and orderliness, the Indians should be allowed to work and worship on their own, without Spanish interference. He gives several examples of the knowledge and wisdom of the Andean past, as well as of the decadence of Indians under Spanish rule; in his argument, Andeans were more Christian before the Spanish arrived than after. As he puts it in his introduction to the chapter (ms. p. 834): "If the* doctrina *padres and priests, the* corregidores, *the* encomenderos, *and the Spaniards would leave them alone, there would be saints and great, Christian learned men among them; those people hinder them with their business dealings. What they have learned, they have learned by force in this kingdom: Christianity and public order." The following brief selections provide a sampling of the themes treated in this chapter.]*

THE LAW AND ORDER that the Indians follow and have followed since the first Indian whom God placed in this New World, from *Wari Wiracocha Runa, Wari Runa, Purun Runa, Auca Runa,* and *Incap Runa* until today— the law of mercy and of helping one another, rich and poor alike, to work the fields and grow all sorts of crops together in community, which is generally called *yupanacuy, mincay, yapuyta, quillayta, carpayta, tarpuyta, patata chacrata llamata wasita larcata, puchucayta, cochopayta, yupanacuyta, corayta, corpa macayta, chacmayta, minca sitan hila collina taqui, satana taqui wira anca*[293]—is a custom of Christians. No other generation in the world has had such a law and order, such a work of mercy to benefit the old, the infirm, and the orphan. They help one another so that everyone may have food to eat, without any interest in money, unlike the Spaniards who always demand pay and day wages. If someone does *minca,*[294] he has

856–857

---

[293] This is a list of terms for communal and reciprocal work (*yupanakuy, minkay*) and for agricultural tasks and celebrations that are carried out communally (plowing, planting, irrigating, pruning, fertilizing, digging ditches, building houses, herding llamas).

[294] *Minka* is a system for calling on neighbors and kin to help with agricultural tasks. There is a presumption that the person who "*minka*s" others to do work, such as plowing and planting a field, will reciprocate in kind when called on. In the meantime, however, the person calling for *minka* labor soothes any potential inequalities by providing food for the workers. The Spanish understood *minka* as hiring day labor, and soon shifted to paying their "*minca*" workers with day wages instead of food and drink, a cultural misunderstanding that reinforced their position of social superiority and led to resentment among the colonized Indians. See Catherine Allen, *The Hold Life Has: Coca and Cultural Identity in an Andean Communityy,* 2d ed. (Washington: Smithsonian Institution Press, 2002), 72–3, for modern examples of *minka.*

the obligation to give breakfast and drink; at midday, dinner and drink; and in the evening, supper and drink. He has this obligation on that same day. This holy work is called *corpachay.* Thus, this Christian law should not be hindered. During the planting season, the padres and *doctrina* priests, the judges and inspectors of the Holy Church, and the *corregidores* of this kingdom should not stop this law of *minca.*

870–877    **CRIOLLOS AND CRIOLLAS,** Indian men and women born into this life during the time of Spanish Christians, all of whom are as follows:

If they were Christians and followed the commandments and gospel of God and all that the Holy Church in Rome and His Majesty ordain; if they obeyed their fathers and mothers, their elders, the justices, and the noble *caciques;* if they worked with their labor; if they were polished, clean, honorable, and rich: then that would be a holy thing, in the service of God and His Majesty and the welfare of themselves and their souls—the Indians of this kingdom.

◆ **When *Criollo* and *Criolla*** Indian men and women become *yanaconas* and *chinaconas* [male and female servants to Spaniards], they become very lazy gamblers and thieves who do nothing but get drunk, enjoy themselves, play mandolins, and sing. They remember neither God nor king nor duty of any kind nor anything good or bad that they do. They have no humility, charity, or doctrine; rather, they have only pride, like treacherous scoundrels. They attack treacherously with knives and with daggers and with clubs and with stones, and the only cure for it is when they kill each other and die drunk. They refuse to carry burdens.[295] Both the men and the women wear [Spanish] clothes, and there is no cure for it. They go about like highwaymen, ruffians, and gypsies from Castile. Under the pretext of seeking adventure, they light out for other places, which is very harmful to the other poor Indians. The good Indians are picking up this custom of following the Spaniards' bad example. In the past, this did not happen in this kingdom.

Therefore, the *yanaconas*—or if they are not *yanaconas,* the tributary men and women from the *Chachapoyas* and *Cañaris*[296]—should pay four times one hundred silver pesos every year, and the women should pay twenty silver pesos, if they do not return to their congregated settlements and pueblos, and they should fulfill all their personal service duties. The noble *caciques* should charge them this fine without exception, and should lead them as prisoners to their pueblos. Any Spaniard who hinders this, or any Spanish lady, should pay two hundred pesos for His Majesty's treasury. Any

---

[295] Guaman Poma phrases this as an untranslatable pun: "*ni tray hato sino gato.*"

[296] Early allies of the Spanish who developed a reputation for being *yanaconas.* See Glossary.

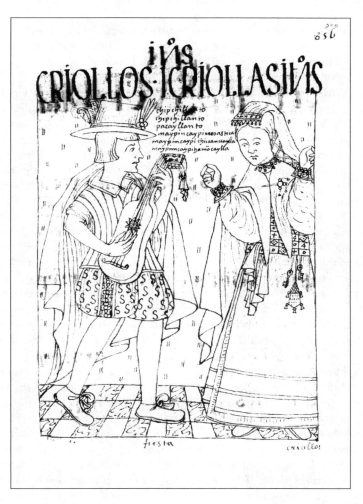

Fiesta.

| | |
|---|---|
| *Chipchi llanto,* | [Light and shadows, |
| *Chipchi llanto,* | Light and shadows, |
| *Pacay llanto.* | hiding shadows. |
| *Maypin? Caypi rosas tica.* | Where? Here: the roses. |
| *Maypin? Capi chiccn waylla.* | Where? Here: the wide pastures. |
| *Maypin? Caypi hamancaylla.* | Where? Here: the calla lilies.] |

**Fiesta.**

*corregidor* who hinders it or who does not deliver justice should be fined five hundred pesos and be punished when the audit is done in this kingdom, in the service of God and His Majesty.

◆ **The *marca camayocs*** (local authorities), *pampa camayocs* [field supervisors], and *quipucamayocs* (warehouse supervisors) take and steal from the poor Indians in their absence. Entering their houses, they take their money and food and steal their llamas, and there is no remedy.

◆ **When an Indian becomes a *bachiller*** [an educated man, or a charlatan], he immediately makes himself into a noble *cacique* or an authority of the *ayllu,* even though he has no title and has no right, and a gang of Indian scoundrels gathers around him. These people openly rob and steal, going house to house to rob the poor Indians in this kingdom, especially poor Indian women, of all they can carry. They steal all their possessions, and the *corregidor* is aware [of the robbery], because they steal things under the pretext of sending the Indians to do their *mita* service in this kingdom.

◆ **The Indians have learned** the very worst, when they should instead have been learning the best from the Christians, who teach them the worst things of all. And there is no remedy for them, because the world is lost. Even though they teach from the gospel, the teachers themselves do not believe in it. When [the Indians] are asked who taught them so much wickedness and disobedience, they reply that the *wiracochas* [Spaniards] taught them, because they covet silver, gold, and clothing, and are thieves, buggers, whores, and disobedient to God and their king. Lust, pride, avarice, gluttony, envy, sloth: they brought all these to this kingdom. This is their reply.

◆ **The Indians of the past** were much more Christian. Even though they were infidels, they followed the commandments of God and the good works of mercy; except for their idolatries, they were Christian. But in these days they do not want to follow [the commandments] at all, though they should follow them better, since they know how to read and write and are being taught the gospel and laws of God. As they are learning from bad teachers, the pupils do not turn out well, but rather according to the kind of teachers they have. When a padre keeps all the unmarried girls closed up in his house, some of them to scratch his belly and others to rub it, given that they see this, how could they become good Christians? And when there are so many little mestizos, the offspring of padres?

◆ **In this life** there are more drunks among the Indians than in the past. In the time of the Inca, there were none, nor were there any before that time, because of the good justice that existed then. If a man ever became difficult or spoke badly or grumbled or blasphemed or turned his face against his wife or fought with another man or with his wife, the Inca would soon order that justice be carried out on him. He killed drunks, and the penalty was death for being a drunk in this kingdom. Thus, there were never any drunks.

♦ **In these times,** killers and drunks are pardoned, and therefore the numbers of drunks and of sins grow, and they are not reformed. Nor are the drunks punished, not even when the justices encounter them. Among the drunks, they honor each other and offer each other toasts in this kingdom, which they should not do. It is right that drunks and coca-chewers should be punished as soon as they are seen, without the need for any other evidence, no sooner than an Indian man or woman is found drunk.

THE INDIANS IN THIS kingdom should be permitted by the *corregidor,* the padre, the inspector of the Holy Mother Church, and the judges, not to be detained in fiestas or the *doctrina* at planting time. On Sundays, Mass should be said before God's day dawns; by six in the morning, it should be over. On Wednesdays and Fridays, they should hold *doctrina* in their *chacras* (farms), because even before dawn the birds are already in the crops, destroying them. These fields should be guarded, because God and His Majesty are served through crops and food, and when the Indians eat and have enough food they do not abandon their pueblos. When the work is plowing virgin fields (which they call *chacmay mita*), once the proper time has passed, it is too late to plow. In order to plow fields for planting (which they call *yapuy pacha*) and to sow them (*tarpuy pacha, chacmay pacha*), if they do not sow the field at the proper day and time, if they are a minute too late, the crops are lost. And, from planting time until the crops are ripe, the fields of corn, potatoes, and other products must be guarded from cattle, foxes, deer, skunks, birds, partridges, parrots, and thieves. To this end, the Inca kept guards in the fields (they were called *arariwa parian*) and *pachacas* (farmers).[297] "Guard the corn, the potatoes, the llamas well from the foxes and pumas. Guard the corn as well from the llamas, foxes, deer, skunks, thrushes, small birds, partridges, tinamous, parrots, and human thieves." Thus, this rule should be followed in this kingdom, for the service of God and His Majesty.

**All the Indians** in this kingdom should obey everything that the Holy Mother Church ordains, and whatever the prelates, curates, and priests ordain: the Ten Commandments, the gospel, and the law of God, as they are ordained, and they should not pass them, neither more nor less. Those who pass them by should be punished and burned in this kingdom.

**All the Indians** of this kingdom should obey everything that His Majesty's justices ordain, and for the sake of justice the *corregidor,* the *alcaldes mayores,* and the *alcaldes ordinarios* should be obeyed; they should be

---

[297] The saying that follows is quoted in untranslated Quechua.

## FARMER ♦ *ARARIWA PARIAN* [SPARROW GUARD].

*Working.*

obeyed by Spaniards, blacks, and Indians. If they do not obey, they should be punished severely and publicly shamed. Thus, God and His Majesty will be served. But the justices should not be wrathful, rash, or hostile in this kingdom.[. . .]

AMONG THE INDIANS, even the most Christian of them—even if he knows how to read and write, wears a rosary, dresses like a Spaniard with a ruffled collar, and seems like a saint—when drunk will speak with the demons and worship the *wacas* (idols), the sun, and the *pacaricos: oncoycunamanta wanocmantapas pacaricoc, warachicoc, cusmallicoc, wacachicoc* [he performs the *paqariku* ritual for illness or death, the *warachiku* and *kusmalliku* coming-of-age ritual, and the *waqachiku* death rituals], and other sorceries. If the Indians would perform their fiestas without getting drunk, chewing coca leaves, or committing idolatry, those would be Christian fiestas. Dances (*taquies*), *haylles, cachiwas,* and *harawis* [victory songs, rounds, and love songs] would be fine if they were Christian. But as an eye witness, which I admit I have been, once they are drunk they commit idolatry and fornicate with their sisters, mothers, and married women. And when the women are drunk, they go out on their own and they themselves seek out men, paying no attention to whether those men are their own fathers or brothers.

*[Guaman Poma repeats his approval of the Inca's penalties for drunkenness, including the death penalty for repeat offenders.]*

THE INDIAN PHILOSOPHER-ASTROLOGERS know the hours, weeks, days, months, and years, for planting and harvesting the crops every year. One named Juan Yunpa, from the pueblo of Uchucmarca in the province of Lucana, held the title of philosophy; he was familiar with the stars, the course of the sun's path, the hours, months, and years, [. . .] and the path of the sun's course in summer and winter. From the month in which it begins, on one day in January, the philosopher says, the sun sits on its seat, up in that high degree, and from there it reigns, rules, and exercises power. Likewise, in the month of August, on St. John the Baptist's day, it sits on a different seat.[298] After arriving on this seat, its seat on the second day does not stir from the spot. On this, its main day, the sun rests, reigns, and rules from that degree. On the third day it "prepares for its journey" by stirring a very short minute—that is why they say that it is preparing for its journey. From that degree, it begins traveling every day, without rest, about half an

*897–899*

---

[298] Guaman Poma treats the months of the European calendar as translations of the Andean lunar months, leading here to some inaccuracy. The summer solstice (of the southern hemisphere) is in December, not January; St. John's Day (traditionally celebrated in Europe as the summer solstice) falls on June 24, not in August.

AN ASTROLOGER-POET WHO KNOWS ABOUT
THE PATH OF THE SUN, THE MOON, THE
ECLIPSES, THE STARS, AND THE COMETS; THE
HOURS, DAYS, MONTHS, AND YEARS; AND
ABOUT THE FOUR WINDS OF THE WORLD, IN
ORDER TO SOW CROPS, SINCE THE OLD DAYS.

*Astrologer.*

hour towards the left hand, heading towards the Northern Sea beyond the
mountains, during the six months beginning with the first month, January
(*Capac Raymi Camay Quilla*), through February (*Paucar Waray Hatun
Pocoy Quilla*), March (*Pacha Pocoy Quilla*), April (*Inca Raymi Camay
Quilla*), May (*Atun Cusqui Aymoray Quilla*), June (*Haucay Cusqui Quilla*),
and July (*Chacra Conacuy Quilla*).[299]

From this month of August it begins again, from the main seat to the second main seat. These two seats are very much in its power. Every month, the
sun has its own seat, at a different degree of sky, and the moon follows after
it as its wife and the queen of the stars; it follows the man, which points to
the sundial of the months of the year: August (*Chacra Yapuy Quilla*), September (*Coya Raymi Quilla*), October (*Uma Raymi Quilla*), November (*Aya
Marcay Quilla*), and December (*Capac Inti Raymi Quilla*).[300]

All the months are completed in the course of the path of the sun, which
begins over again in January. In that month, the sun sits in its seat, as has
been said, and so it goes every year. To learn the hours and minutes, the
astrologer says that the sun's rays and its sunlight point [in given direc-
tions]. Very early in the morning, as its light passes through a window, one
should see where it lands. Otherwise, one should watch to see from behind
which mountain it comes, rises, returns, and sits, for that point and the
path of the sun never err. From this, they can tell what time is right for
sowing fields early and late, for planting, for shearing the wool of the
alpacas, and which crops, foods, and fruits should be eaten or not, because
of the illnesses, risks, and dangers that come with each month.

Some look to see when the sun comes out from behind the mountain
peaks and ravines. They say that in the month of January the day is very
long and the night is short, and in August, the day is short and the night
long. They say that the moon is in a lower degree of the sky and the sun in
a very high degree, and that the moon is the wife and lady of the sun. The
sun is pictured as if it had whiskers, like men, and therefore they say they
"want to shave the sun's beard, the croplands" (*intip chacranta suncayta
tirasac*).[301]

---

[299] These names for Andean lunar months can be respectively translated as: major festival of creation month; flower time great harvest month; harvest time month; Inca
festival of creation month; great plowing and harvest month; rest and harvest month;
field distribution month.

[300] Respectively: field plowing month; festival of the Coya month; head festival month;
procession for the dead month; major festival of the sun month. The need to intercalate
"leap months" in the lunar calendar in order to stay in step with the solstices is probably
what leads Guaman Poma to place the southern winter solstice in the month of
"August."

[301] The Quechua translates as, "I will pull out the sun's fields, my beard."

Therefore they called the moon *Coya Raymi* and the sun *Inti Raymi*. During an eclipse of the moon, they called out loud, they shouted, "*Quilla mama, ama uncuychu, ama wañuchu. Cosanchicca, olconchicca macacoctacmi, anyacoctacmi* [Mother Moon, do not be ill, do not die. Our husbands, our males, are contending, are fighting]." These cries were shouted by the Indian women.

The philosophers say that in the stars they recognize [constellations of] men, women, llamas with their offspring, partridges, a hunter and a herder, a grinding stone, a mountain lion, a deer. From the comets, they learn what is going to happen, both the good signs and the bad: *cuyllorcuna, chasca cuyllor, oncoy cuyllor, casa cuyllor, pacari cuyllor, wara wara* [the stars, the evening star, the "stars of illness," the "stars of frost," the morning star, the Pleiades].

This Indian philosopher, Juan Yunpa, was more than one hundred and fifty years old. He had good eyes, teeth, and molars—he was not missing any of them, and he ate better than a young man. And he was a good Christian. All that he lacked was writing and reading.

915–22    **The Indian surgeons, barbers, and licentiates** who heal and bleed, and who know and understand about medicines, illnesses, sores, the herbs that are used to heal, and the medicines and purges in these kingdoms, are as good at healing as any doctor or licentiate of medicine. They say that all illnesses result from two things that men have: heat and cold, in any illness.[302] Likewise, the devout women physicians who heal, help women give birth, and cure dislocations. They even say that tobacco is a wonderful medicine; but for the morning chill, one smoke is good, and for the head and sight, a little bit of snuff is good. Do not use more than that, however, because it will cook your liver, and for heat, or a fever, it is a pestilential fire: one dies right away from using it. Thus the first people lived long lives, more than two hundred years. I will write no more about medical doctors, for theirs is another art and another labor in this kingdom.

◆ **In this kingdom** there are three generations [lineages] of Indians, which are: the *yunga* [lowland] Indians; the Indians from the sierra [the central mountains in the Cusco-Huamanga area]; and Indians from the mountains [the "wild" area north and east of Cusco]—the *Chunchos, Antis, Chirihuanays, Ancahuallo,* and *Warmi Auca.* They each have their own bands, dress, and generations, their own words, different stocks (*ayllus*).

---

[302] Heat and cold: this is the Galenic theory of medicine that was the standard in Europe at the time. Perhaps Andean medicine was based on an equivalent theory; or perhaps either Guaman Poma or the Andean healers themselves had reinterpreted Andean medicine in view of the prestigious foreign theory. Earlier (ms. p. 840), Guaman Poma defends native healers against charges of sorcery and idolatry. In his view, they are professionals and equal to their Spanish counterparts.

Each dress style has its own types of clothes. They differ in their words, foods, pastimes, dances (*taquíes*), and music. They also differ in their faces and bodies, throughout this kingdom.

The *Chachapoyas* and *Chunchos* are very white, like Spaniards. The *Yunga* Indians and the *Huanoco, Huayllas, Chiccay, Cajatambo, Wanca, Changa, Aymara, Cañari, Quispillacta, Huayro, Parinacocha, Pacage, Andamarca,* and *Lucana* are somewhat white, and gentlemen. The *Inca, Yunga, Yauyo, Chaclla, Picoy, Cayanpi, Angara, Cana, Tanquihua, Quichihua, Cusco Conde, Ariquipa Conde, Colla, Pacaje, Cana, Tanquihua, Callahuaya, Charca,* and *Chuhui*—all these Indians and their women are somewhat dark and tall in height. And the *Huancavilcas, Pomatambos, Poquina Collas, Chinchay Cocha, Quito, Cunti Cullahua, Huachimi, Yunga, Oro Colla,* and *Poquina Colla* Indians are very dark, very ugly in stature, wide, untutored, like blacks from Guinea, very wicked in [nature] and ugly in deeds, untutored, dirty, lazy, thieving, lying, like *waylla* [plains] Indians, throughout this kingdom.

THE AUTHOR WANDERED IN THE WORLD, poor, among the other poor Indians, to be able to see the world, attain [knowledge], and write this book and chronicle in service to God and His Majesty and for the good of the poor Indians of this kingdom. He labored for thirty years, leaving his pueblo, houses, and property behind, and taking to dressing in sackcloth, like the poorest of men. In this way the author attained the poverty he wished to have, in order to see and attain what there was in the world.

I tell you truly that God became man and true God, and poor. For, if He had come with all His majesty and light, no one could have drawn close to Him. "What might the true God do to me?" Therefore, He ordained that He come in poverty, so that the poor and the sinners might draw close and talk with Him. Thus, He decreed that His apostles and saints should be poor, humble, and charitable.

Who are the apostles and saints? They are the priests and padres, who are spread around all the pueblos of men in this world: they should be the apostles of Jesus Christ our Lord, doing the works of Jesus Christ. But that is not what they do; instead, they seek treasure and coins—for such things they are apostles.

Therefore, as I have said, I chose hard work and poverty, in order to attain [knowledge] and serve God and His Majesty. Why should I have lacked food and clothing in the world? For I have had grants from His Majesty since the days of my lord the emperor-king, may God keep him in His glory. My father, Don Martín de Ayala, the second-in-command of the Inca and his viceroy, won honor and lordship when he was the ambassador of the legitimate Wascar Inca, king of Peru. After that, my father, Don

Martín de Ayala, won again in the service of His Majesty, during the rebellion of Don Diego de Almagro and the rebellion of Gonzalo Pizarro, serving His Majesty, helping Captain Don Luis de Ávalos de Ayala. Later, he served once more in the rebellion of Francisco Hernández Girón, whom he destroyed when [Girón] was captured by the Indians of Jauja. Later still, when viceroy Don Francisco de Toledo named him captain of Vilcabamba and he flushed out the Inca Topa Amaro, he was granted a coat of arms and a salary, which were later confirmed by Viceroy Marquis Don García and by Don Luis de Velasco. Apart from all this, he had his rights as a natural lord and the second-in-command of His Majesty the Inca, and now of His Majesty of this kingdom.

But if I had come in bearing all this authority, the poor would not have drawn close to me, nor would anyone have wanted to harm the poor in my presence, as they always do. Since they do not recognize me, however, and they see me as poor, they steal the property and the wives and daughters of the poor in my presence, with little fear of God and justice. I tell you truly, by counting on my poverty, by introducing myself as a poor man among all those animals who devour the poor, they also devoured me, just as they devour the poor.

To vouch for this, it seemed best to write as someone who passes sentence based on what he sees with his own eyes of how these things have proceeded. First, about me: for this reason I made myself poor, moving among the other poor people, because that was what I had to do for what had to be done. As is known, the poor are scorned by the rich and the proud who are above them, and who seem to think that where the poor man is, there is no God and no justice. Yet they should clearly know through their faith that, wherever the poor be, there is Jesus Christ himself, and where God is, there is justice.

Therefore, Christians, do not scorn the poor of Jesus Christ. For you to see how you persecute these poor people, and so that truth may be made known, I shall tell the story of the poverty I experienced in my own person, and my troubles and misfortunes. What more might they do to the faint-hearted, powerless, foolish, unreasoning Indians? For the Spaniards steal their estates, their pueblos, their boundaries, and, beyond these, their possessions and the wives, sons, and daughters that God gave them. They are being driven hard, burdened like horses. They are also being made into slaves, for when they are called "tributaries," that is clearly another way of calling them slaves. This is why they do not multiply and cannot multiply.

The charge is that the Inca does not defend them. Who is the Inca? The Catholic king, as I have declared in other writings. For they have no one to defend them but the king, whose own people they are, and who through his labor won them and defends them, as I have said.

I would like to tell you of the labors I suffered while I was passing as a poor man. What happened was that I had a bit of property, which I entrusted to some Spaniards to safeguard for me; they immediately spent it and lost it all for me. (I said to myself that Spaniards are bad Christians and greedy people who cannot be trusted, whether they give you documents or not.) This happened to me with a rich man named Miguel Palomino.[303] He borrowed two hundred silver pesos from me, giving me a document. When I asked for the money, he refused and would not repay me. I took the case to the justices, but they all turn in the rich man's favor—the justice, the notary, the defender, all alike. The attorney and the defender told me to draw up petitions, but they brought me more perditions than petitions, and the attorneys-at-law were more like attorneys-at-larceny,[304] and the justices were more like sticks of wood. And this, while I was suing in defense of land that had come to me by right, just title, and possession since God made the earth, since the time of the Incas, since the conquest.

Knowing the truth, His Majesty and his whole *Audiencia* ruled and viewed and reviewed [my title to the land], and the viceroy had confirmed it, and had seen the land, in the valley of Santa Catalina de Chupas, where Don Diego de Almagro the Younger had battled against the royal crown.[305]

*[Guaman Poma lists, at length, settlements that had upheld his right to the land.]*

With things in this state, a deputy *corregidor* named Pedro de Rivera, citizen of Huamanga and a man who neither understands letters nor knows how to write, ignoring the decree in which His Majesty ordered him to go in person, sent a pair of notaries to do harm.[306]

See, then, oh God, how they favor your poor. This is what they did to me; what will they do to other poor people, who know nothing? I am in

---

[303] Miguel Palomino: according to Murra and Adorno (ms. p. 918, n. 1), the *alguacil mayor* of Huamanga in 1586; probably a member of the wealthy and powerful Palomino family of Huamanga.

[304] *Los procuradores son más proculadrones,* a favorite pun of Guaman Poma's.

[305] The Guaman lands in Santa Catalina de Chupas (a valley just south of the city of Huamanga) were in litigation from 1587 to at least 1600, when Guaman Poma's participation in the case was settled, brutally for him, with a ruling that he was not a native lord but an impostor, and an order that he be given two hundred lashes and banished from the province. This intensely humiliating experience was very likely what precipitated his work on this book. (See Adorno, *Guaman Poma* [2000], pp. xxv–xxxvi; and the Introduction to this translation.)

[306] Guaman Poma stops far short of revealing the shameful outcome of the case.

shock. Now, I say that the poorest ones are the Spaniards, because of what God and justice demand of them. What lashes, what punishments that wooden judge deserves! That is why no poor man can ever attain justice, because the rich have them all, as I have seen with my own eyes.

I will say more: after I gave up on trusting the Spaniards, I came to trust in the noble *caciques,* saying, "These are my brothers and kin." But I have seen too many of them replaced by drunkards, gamblers, coca-chewers. That is why the tribute collections are not to be trusted. There are so many arrears and expenses in the way they collect them; they collect the tribute and spend even more from the community funds (*sapsi*) and the estates of the poor Indians, which they take by force.

Turning aside from them, I began to converse with the priests and padres, saying, "These are saints, here in God's stead." I left a box full of clothes, shirts, felt, and other things with a padre named Francisco Caballeros. I had barely walked away when he broke the box open, took out my things, and spent it all immediately. It is lost to this day. Elsewhere, I suffered another misfortune when another padre, named Don Martín de Artiaga, took two horses from me by force. At the time, they were worth fifty pesos each, a total of one hundred pesos. He also took other smaller items that were also worth money. When I asked to have them back, he replied, "I already spent them on saying Masses."

So, having had such bad experiences with the padres, I resolved to trust in the poor Indians the next time I had to leave a bundle of things. In the pueblo of Santiago de Quirahuara, I left a locked box full of my impoverished possessions and other small items in the house of a poor Indian. In my absence, the padre of that pueblo—a very rich man—took the box, opened it, and spent everything. Later I wrote to ask for it back. He replied that he thought I was dead, and he had spent it on Masses. He filled his letter with threats.

See here, Christian, how much harm and damage was done to me as a poor man. What will they do to other poor people who know nothing, who are even poorer, and who have no one's favor?

Then the padres say, "Oh, what bad doctrine!" How could they not be rich, when they do all these things? You will say that the defenders have been hired at the king's expense to defend [the poor Indians]; but they would rather rob, steal, and advise each other. And there is no remedy.

The noble *curacas* do the same things. So do the *alcaldes* and *fiscales*. All of them steal, act proudly, and are enemies of the poor and fond of taking away their estates. Even more so, the mestizos, mulattos, *criollos,* and Spaniards, who even abuse the Indians in my presence.

See, Christian, all that was done to me—a Mercedarian friar named Murúa even tried to take my wife in the pueblo of Yanaca—all this damage, harm, and ill. And they do not want to see any *ladino* Indians who speak Castilian: they are frightened, and they order me to leave their pueblos. They aim for everyone to be fools, asses, so they can finish stealing everything they own—estates, wives, daughters. So, if a good noble *cacique* tries to defend them, they immediately try to toss him out with lawsuits and lies. But a *cacique* who wants to skin himself and rob the Indians so he can give it all to the Spaniards is a fine old Don Juan, an honorable *cacique.* This is why the Spaniards, *corregidores,* padres, *encomenderos,* deputies, stewards, vicars, and judges are the mortal enemies of the noble *caciques.* And this is why it is not right that they should try civil and criminal cases against the nobles, administrators, and seconds-in-command in this kingdom; only the king, and a judge whom he shall send, [should hear such cases] throughout this kingdom, because this would be in service of God and His Majesty, and would favor the poor Indians of this kingdom.

**The Indians who are poisoned** by quicksilver, or ill, and who hire other Indians [to work in their places] in the mines, should pay them seven silver pesos and four reales, and in food, one *hanega* of corn, and for meat or jerky, one silver peso and four reales—neither more nor less.[307] If they do pay more, both the hired Indian and the one who hired him should be punished. Because, in good conscience, [the hired Indian] should not be paid so much, which is more than half [of the *mita* Indian's wage for working in the mines], and when an Indian earns thirty-seven silver pesos and four reales for two months of work and labor, that is too much.

Those who are fit should not be allowed to hire [replacement workers]; only those with quicksilver poisoning should, because if they were to return to the mines, they would die right away. Therefore, an Indian with quicksilver poisoning should not be allowed to work, nor is it right to fool him. What he should pay for everything should be set at a fixed rate of fifteen [pesos]. The same should be done in all the mines of this kingdom.

**The Indians, blacks, and Spaniards** who are criminals, felons, arrogant, killers, thieves, and highwaymen in this kingdom should from this day

---

[307] These are wages for the standard two-month period of the *mita,* forced labor in mines or Spanish estates that was imposed on all tributary Indians. By the early 1600s, the colonial *mita* was monetized, bureaucratized, and completely divorced from the Andean *mita* system of reciprocal labor obligations from which it took its name. See Stern, *Peru's Indian Peoples* (pp. 149 and 197–200) on the monetized *mita,* hiring replacement Indians for *mita* service, and the reality of low wages, indebtedness, and long periods of service for *mita* workers. Guaman Poma here proposes a system that would retain monetary compensation but remove the market pressures that pushed replacement workers' wages above what the *mita* workers were paid.

forth be punished and banished to the quicksilver mines, sent into the tunnels to extract metals, wearing irons on their feet that are stamped "slaves of His Majesty." There they should be given food to eat and plenty of water, and they should never cease working and extracting metals.

It is much better in the mines than in the galleys. In the mines, they will purge their crimes and do penance, and they will die serving God and His Majesty. Thus, it is not right for them to be hanged.

A Spaniard who pays five thousand pesos for this work should be freed and allowed to go, but only after paying the full amount, not one real less, for his arrogance and sin.

The Indians, mestizos, mulattos, and blacks should not be pardoned or allowed to go free. Let them commend themselves to God, do penance there, and give their souls to God.

Those who commit other crimes should also be sent to the mine tunnels, for the appropriate number of months, days, weeks, or years, throughout this kingdom, with their food supplied by His Majesty.

**All the Spaniards who wish** to remain on the land should pay tribute. They, too, must pay tribute—gentlemen being free to pay only the *alcabala* [excise tax]—and obey the law that presently applies to the Indians of this kingdom: to serve God, be subject to the king, and not think otherwise, because this will take away their desire to eat in this kingdom. [This law should be enforced] by all of His Majesty's justices.

**The Indian petty authorities** in each pueblo should not meddle in any other pueblo, even if one of their *ayllus* (bands) is located there; instead, the authority of the other pueblo should be in charge. For this has been the cause of great harm and robberies, because, under the pretext of collecting tribute, [petty authorities] go [into neighboring pueblos] to take a great deal of money, clothing, and food, and there they stay, getting drunk at the expense of the poor Indians, and there is no remedy.

Likewise, the inspectors or re-inspectors of Indian tributaries should inspect no other pueblos, only their own pueblo and its authority. Only the noble *cacique* and the administrator should be in charge of the whole province. If he sends [an inspector], or if he comes to the Indians, he should be punished by the *alcaldes* or by the *corregidor*. And if the authority consents to having the authority from another pueblo sent into his, he should be punished. Thus, each one should look after his own pueblo, whether it has many Indians or few Indians, according to the laws of this kingdom.

No Indians should be allowed to carry arms, and those who have been granted [this privilege] should have it taken away, so that they never rise up, or do something foolish when they are drunk; only the noble *caciques* and seconds-in-command should have and bear arms. In addition, no Spaniard should ever be allowed, under any condition, to live among the

Indians, so that the land will not rise up at the insistence of some Spaniard in this kingdom.[308]

## PROLOGUE: CHRISTIAN READERS OF "THE GOOD CHRISTIAN INDIAN MEN AND INDIAN WOMEN"

GIVE ALL YOU THANKS to God our Lord for the great good He has given you: health, life, and honor, trades, crafts, and means of support, food and drink, rest and relaxation, feast days and work days in this world; and later, in the next life, glory for the good and punishment in hell for the wicked. Therefore, do not neglect to go forward in serving God the Creator: fear Him, honor Him, and keep the Ten Commandments, the holy gospel of God, the five commandments of the Holy Mother Church, and the good works of mercy. In addition to this, keep as your advocate, that she may pray for you, Our Lady Advocate St. Mary, ever-virgin Mother of God of Peña de Francia, together with all the saints and angels—prophets, martyrs, confessors, apostles, evangelists—and all the female saints—St. Anne, the mother of Our Lady, virgins, martyrs—that they may help bring you to the glory of the Lord, eternal father. May all the world shout aloud—and you much more so, Indian men and women—shout out loud with the prophets, as the prophet said: "Oh Lord, how long shall I shout and you will not hear me? Oh Lord, how long shall I cry out and you will not reply?" Say this together with them, crying and wailing with your hearts, your spirits, and your mouths, tongues, and eyes. Never cease to wail with the prophets, who will help you.

And may all the world respond to me, "Amen, Jesus." And you, brothers and sisters, Indian men and Indian women of this kingdom, respond to me, "Amen, Jesus."

---

[308] This paragraph is a late marginal addition. In Spain and indeed most of Europe at the time, only nobles were allowed the right or privilege to bear arms—mainly swords and long knives. In Spanish America, this right was extended to all Spaniards and to the Indian nobility. Indian commoners, blacks, and people of mixed lineage were not allowed to keep arms unless they received a specific exemption.

*The world, for giving thanks to God.*

# PART 9.
## CONCLUSIONS AND APPENDICES

*[A set of concluding chapters and appendices round out the* Chronicle. *In the first conclusion, "Considerations," Guaman Poma uses the didactic format of Catholic moral treatises, but he addresses his "Christian readers" as if he were a prosecuting attorney delivering his final summation of the case against Spanish rule in Peru. The second conclusion, "His Majesty Questions, the Author Replies," reframes the arguments of the book and presents them directly to the Spanish king as answers in an imagined dialogue. The first appendix (omitted here), a comprehensive geographical description of Spanish South America, situates the book in space, in much the same way that the first part of the book places it in world historical time. The second appendix (also omitted) describes the agricultural labors associated with each month of the year, reprising for the colonial era the information that Guaman Poma gave for Inca times in "The Months of the Year." The final chapter of the book, "From the World, the Author Returns," an autobiographical account of the hardships that the author endured to get his book to the king, draws on the concepts of virtue through suffering and of the duty to bear witness in order to lend authority to the work.]*

## CHAPTER ONE OF CONSIDERATIONS    923–973

CONSIDER, CHRISTIAN, first your service to God; then your service to His Majesty; then to your fellow men. Then consider all the harm and evil you are doing in foreign lands, and then consider how you are not serving God nor the Virgin Mary nor his saints or angels; then consider how you rob people here and there, and that you are proud, self-serving people who do not keep the commandments of God nor those of the Holy Mother Church of Rome. You know that heaven and hell exist, yet you proceed unjustly: consider all these things, for the good of your soul.

### CHAPTER ONE OF CONSIDERATIONS: THINGS YOU SHOULD CONSIDER DEEPLY IN YOUR HEART AND SPIRIT

CONSIDER, CHRISTIAN:

◆ God created heaven and the whole world, and all that exists there—even fish, animals, worms, butterflies, snails, ants, crickets, mosquitoes, and everything that exists there. Likewise, our father Adam and our mother Eve, the first people.

◆ They came to an end, punished by God with the waters of the Flood. Noah was left in the Ark with his six married sons.

◆ God sent one of the offspring sons to the Indies, to the New World of this kingdom. He was a *wiracocha* (Spaniard).[309] That was why the first Indian was called *Wari Wiracocha Runa.* The second was *Wari Runa,* the third was *Purun Runa,* the fourth was *Auca Runa,* and the fifth was *Incap Runa.*[310]

The sixth was *Pachacuti Runa* [the people of the World Upside Down]— when Challco Chima Inca, Quis Quis Inca, and Awa Panti Inca were the captains; when Topa Cusiwalpa Wascar was the legitimate Inca, and was opposed by his brother Atawalpa, the bastard Inca: *Aucanacuscan Pacha, Cutiscan Pacha* [the warring era, the overthrown era].

The seventh was Christian Conquest *Runa:* Don Francisco Pizarro, Don Diego de Almagro, and Don Luis de Ávalos de Ayala: *Conquistascan Pacha* [the Conquered era]. These were the *Runa* of queen Doña Juana of Castile and Emperor Don Carlos's era.[311]

The eighth was in the Christian era: the era of those who became enemies, turned against our king, and rebeled; of the traitors Francisco Pizarro, his brother Gonzalo Pizarro, Don Diego de Almagro the Elder, his mestizo son Don Diego de Almagro the Younger, and Francisco Hernández Girón; the *Auca Tucuscan Pacha Runa* [the people of the era of those who became enemies].

The ninth: that of making good Christians and good justice; of *capac apo* (emperor-king) Don Carlos; his son, king Don Philip II; and his son, king Don Philip III, may he live long for our sake and guard our Christian well-being with his powerful lordship.

The tenth: our Christianity triumphs and increases.

*Cayta yuyaycunqui soncoyqui animayquipi* (this you should consider in your heart and in your spirit), Christian.

**Consider that the first Indians,** the *Wari Wiracocha Runa,* and the second people, the *Wari Runa* (some say that the latter were giants), the third people, the *Purun Runa,* and the fourth, the *Auca Runa,* were people of little understanding, yet they were not idolaters. The Spaniards were also people

---

[309] *Wiracocha:* the early colonial Quechua term for Spaniard; see Glossary. Spaniard (*español*): as previously noted, Guaman Poma counted anyone who was not a native Andean as a "Spaniard," much as Europeans considered all the peoples of the Americas "Indians."

[310] *Runa* means "man, person, people." These are the types or "generations" of people who lived in the Andes throughout the succeeding *pachas* (worlds or eras). These and the following sentences summarize the history of the "ages of Indians" that Guaman Poma has covered in his book.

[311] Up to this point, most of the Quechua phrases in this section are followed by Spanish glosses or interspersed with Spanish; the next three sentences are written in Quechua without translations.

of little understanding, but from the very earliest times they were heathen idolaters, just as the Indians from the age of the Inca on were idolaters.

Those first Indians had a shadowy knowledge of the Creator.

◆ They called out to Him: *"Ticse Caylla Wiracocha Dios, maypim canqui? Hanac pachapicho? Uco pachapicho? Ticse caylla pachapicho, Runa Camac, allpamanta llutac, cay pacha imaymanatapas rurac?"* So that you might consider it, this is what they said: "Oh my Spaniard-God, creator of men and of the world, where are you? In heaven or on earth, at the ends of the earth or in hell? Creator of the men from the earth, and of this world and of all things, creator of all things."[312] With these words, the ancient Indians knelt and prayed, raising their hands and looking up at heaven, until the fourth age of the world, the age called that of the *Auca Runa*. You must consider everything that has been said here, Christian.

**Consider that the Indians** in the time of the Incas committed idolatry like the heathens, worshipping the sun as the father of the Inca, the moon as his mother, and the stars as his brothers and sisters, along with their *waca willca* (idol), Wana Cauri, and the place from which it emerged, Pacaritambo. Thus the Inca ordered everyone throughout his kingdom to worship all the *waca willca* (idols and demons); all the Indians of this kingdom worshiped them.

Despite all this, they kept all of God's commandments and his good works of mercy in this kingdom—things that the Christians themselves do not keep, even today. You, Christian, should consider that the bad priests are the cause of this.

**Consider: when wise men** compose and write books in the service of God, even if they write them in the form of fables, some are good for serving God, and some are good for reforming people's lives, or for entertainment, or for the good of the body in this world. These are the holy doctors of the Church, illuminated by the Holy Spirit, who has given them this grace. Even if these men have died, they should be called doctors of God and of the holy Church, or of law, or of medicine: men such as the right reverend Fray Luis de Granada, who has done great works to advance the

---

[312] Guaman Poma's Spanish gloss follows his Quechua rather closely. My translation of the Quechua is: "Foundational, nearby Wiracocha-God, where are you? In the upper world? In the lower world? In the foundational, nearby world, oh creator of people, who molded them from earth, who made this world and all that exists?" In the Quechua version, he appends the Spanish word *dios* (God) to *Wiracocha,* probably as a gloss, but in the Spanish version he translates *Wiracocha* as *español* (Spaniard). His Quechua uses standard seventeenth-century translations for the Catholic concepts of heaven (*hanaq pacha,* "upper world, sky") and hell (*uku pacha,* "lower world, interior of the earth"), as well as standard epithets for *Wiracocha: tiqsi* (foundation) and *qaylla* (nearby, present), which are also applied to the world.

service of God;[313] the reverend Fray Domingo, who wrote the vocabulary
and grammar of the Indians, on which he worked for so many years before
he was able publish it;[314] Fray Pedro de Oré of the order of St. Francis;[315]
and many other holy doctors and lawyers, teachers and learned men. These
men deserve such titles; but others, who have not gone so far as to write the
letters A, B, C, want to call themselves learned: no, they are asses and
frauds, and they should sign their names "Don Drunkard" and "Doña
Blockhead."

The Christian readers should consider all these things.

♦ **The first Indians,** though they were idolaters since [the time of] the
Incas, had faith in and kept the commandments of their gods; they obeyed
the law and did good works. They had kings and great lords, captains and
justices and all the government, full faith in the royal crown and His Majesty the Inca, conserving this among themselves.

**Consider the matter** of this life: while there are so many good friars and
justices, everyone is rebelling against the faith in Jesus Christ and the laws
of the king and of their great lords because they have such bad teachers. In
this way the Christians lose their souls in this life: you must consider this,
Christian.

**Consider how the poor Indians** have so many Inca kings. In the old
days, they had only one Inca king, but in this present life there are many
Incas. The *corregidor* is an Inca, his dozen deputies are Incas, the *corregidor's*
brother or son, the *corregidor's* wife, and all of his servants—even the black
slaves—are Incas, and all his relatives and notaries are Incas. The *encomendero* and his brothers or sons and servants, his stewards, his mestizo and
mulatto servants,[316] his blacks, and his wife, his *yanaconas* [male Indian ser-
vants] and *chinaconas* [female Indian servants] and cooks: all are Incas. And
his parents and brothers and stewards; his *yanaconas,* cooks, and friends;
even the sextons and guardians of his chapels and his cantors: all are Incas.

---

[313] Luis de Granada (1504–1588): a Spanish Dominican whose popular books of medi-
tations, *Memorial de la vida christiana* (*A Memorial of a Christian Life,* Rouen, 1586),
served as Guaman Poma's model for this chapter of "considerations" or items for medita-
tion. See Adorno, *Guaman Poma* (2000), and Murra and Adorno (ms. p. 923, n. 1).

[314] Domingo de Santo Tomás (1499–1570) published the first grammar and the first
lexicon of Quechua, *Grammática o arte de la lengua general de los indios de los reynos del
Perú* and *Lexicon o vocabulario de la lengua general del Perú* (Valladolid, 1560).

[315] According to Murra and Adorno (ms. p. 926, n. 2), the reference is to Luis Jerónimo
de Oré (1554–1629), a Franciscan born in Guaman Poma's home province of Huamanga and famed for his command of Quechua, who wrote a number of histories and
books of evangelization between 1598 and 1619.

[316] Mestizo: someone with both Spanish and Indian ancestry; mulatto: someone with
both Spanish and African ancestry.

## HOLY WORKS OF MERCY CARRIED OUT BY THE INDIANS OF THIS KINGDOM TOWARD THEIR FELLOW MEN.

And thus they eat in the public square, giving food to the poor, to the sick, and to the pilgrims, following the ancient law and the law of God with their good works of mercy: *Corpachanqui* [You give them shelter.].

*Holy works of mercy.*

All the above-mentioned do great damage and harm to the Indians of this kingdom. You must consider all these Incas.

**Consider how many struggles** the Indians have in this life. In the time of the Incas they did not have so many; but the mestizos and Spaniards have taught them to lie and steal, because they want to get their handful of coins and their *camaricos* and their *mitayos*[317] and their presents; they take these things by force from the poor Indians: consider this.

**Consider that the Indians** have already taken up the Spaniards' habit of gambling and borrowing, and that some Indians owe 1,000 pesos, or 500, or 200—something that the Indians of this kingdom never did in the time of the Inca. You must consider how the Spanish taught them this vice.

**Then you must consider** that all the world is God's, and therefore Castile belongs to the Spanish, the Indies belong to the Indians, and Guinea [Africa] belongs to the blacks. Each of these are the legitimate proprietors, and not only by law.

◆ St. Paul wrote that after ten years one had possession and could be called Roman. How fine might this law be: because, if one Spaniard goes into [the land of] another Spaniard, even of a Jew or a Moor, they are all Spaniards; he is not meddling with any other nation, for they are all Spaniards from Castile. By the law of Castile, they do not belong to any other generation, and according to the Indians' reckoning, they are held to be, and by law should be called, "foreigners," or, in the language of the Indians, *mitmac Castillamanta samoc* (*mitmacs* who came from Castile).[318]

The Indians are the natural owners of this kingdom, while Spaniards born in Spain are foreigners (*mitmacs*) here in this kingdom. Each is the legitimate proprietor and possessor of his own kingdom—not by the king, but by God and by God's justice. He made the world with all its lands, and He planted each seed in them: the Spaniard in Castile, the Indian in the Indies, the black in Guinea. Therefore, so long as Indians have no idolatry, and so long as they have Christianity and chapels, even if there are only two Indians, they should take turns being the local magistrate each year, so that among them they might have God, justice, and king, who has entered as the proprietor and legitimate lord. For he is the Inca and the king, and no other Spaniard or priest needs to enter, because the

---

[317] *Camarico:* tribute, or contributions; *mitayo:* Indians performing communal labor (originally, for the good of their community). These were old Andean social institutions that the Spanish settlers twisted into mechanisms for extracting money and labor from the Indians.

[318] Guaman Poma refers to Spaniards in Peru by the term for Incaic imperial settlers. Like the Spanish in colonized Peru, the Incas' *mitmaqkuna* were privileged foreigners who retained their own distinctive clothing, language, and laws when they settled among restive communities.

Inca was the proprietor and the legitimate king; therefore, that is what the king himself is now, for the crown won it. Then poor[319] Don Francisco Pizarro, Don Diego de Almagro, Gonzalo Pizarro, Carvajal, and Francisco Hernández Girón took it, but [the king] defended it against them. It cost him great trouble; he lost it, and with great trouble he won it back. Therefore he, the king, is the legitimate proprietor.

And thus, even if he gives a land grant to a priest or a Spaniard, and they get title to some fields from the king, they are not proprietors. They therefore owe obedience to the noble lords and justices—both lords and ladies—who are the legitimate proprietors of the land, so all the Spanish men, Spanish women, mestizos, mulattos, and blacks, should serve and honor them.

In this way they would serve God and His Majesty, in accordance with Christian law and the law of every native in his own kingdom throughout the world and Christendom. You must consider, Christian, this law of God.

**You must consider** that in the time of the Incas, and later, during the conquest, both Indian men and women and Spaniards were very obedient. They had great faith in God and great loyalty, and were filled with charity and humility. They raised their sons and daughters with strict punishments and good doctrine. They wore no capes or hats up to the age of twenty, until their beards came in, and were very obedient to God, their mothers and fathers, and the king. They obeyed the elderly men and women; they called their elders "father," "mother," and "brother," and called those younger than they "sons." They were very respectful, full of humility, and were well born and well raised. In this way, the Indians soon took up their faith in God with all their hearts and souls.

But the people of this life are lost. This is the fault of their fathers and mothers, whom God will have to punish on account of their sons and cast them to hell.

**Consider that there is no justice** in this life. Everything is self-interest and a fondness for rising up and taking the lives of others and killing one another. If some gentleman were to take a stand and raise the royal banner to defend the city for the royal crown and fight for even a few moments, if he were to give even a bit of an effort in the service of God and His Majesty, that would be a great service and an honor for his city that would live in the world's memory. But when the world's memory is of affronts, trickery, and

---

[319] Poor (*los pobres de*): one assumes that Guaman Poma is being sarcastic here. On the many other occasions when he uses the phrase, he is expressing pity for a victim (*los pobres de los indios,* "the poor Indians," and *los pobres de Jesucristo,* "the poor of Jesus Christ").

# HUMILITY, OBEDIENCE, AND SERVICE TO GOD AND TO ONE'S FATHER AND MOTHER, AND TO HIS MAJESTY.

Among the men and women in the old time of the conquest, to the age of twenty, Spaniards and Indians wore no cape or hat, and the Indians of this kingdom kept the good example of Cajetan of Rome.[320]

*Example of Cajetan.*

---

[320] Guaman Poma has "Caton de Roma," but Murra and Adorno note (ms. p. 930, n. 1) that he is actually referring to Cajetan (Cayetano or Gaetano, 1480–1547), a pious Italian monk who founded the order of Theatines or Congregation of Clerks Regular at Rome. He was canonized in 1671.

wickedness, the sign for that is infamy and dishonor. Such acts should be buried deep and hidden far from sight. But what a saint is the poor gentleman who was martyred as a Christian and not an infidel: he is one of the true saints, and his place is in heaven.

*[As an example of such a "saint," Guaman Poma tells the story of Don García de Solís Portocarrera, "a noble knight of the order of Santiago and the former* corregidor *and chief justice of the city of Huamanga and the mines of Huancavelica," who was arrested and executed on false charges, but who went to the executioner's block with prayers on his lips rather than rash words for his accusers.]*

**When it comes to** the Indians' public order and Christianity, they should be left alone and not bothered with so much trouble and mistreatment, robbing them of their estates and other things, and taking away their wives and daughters—things that are never done in the promised land of Christianity.

So that you might see that the Indians are Christians and that they have faith: they maintain chapels, altars, and shrines on their farms (*chacras*), and they keep images, decorations, banners, and many candles and wax tapers; they also have majordomos and officers of the religious brotherhood, along with simple lay members and brothers—twenty-four altogether. On feast days, they have lots of dances (*haylles* and *taquies*), all at the Indians' expense, to honor the feast day. Because the Spaniards and citizens have viewed with envy the fact that the brotherhood has an estate worth fifty thousand pesos, they go after the Indians. They have no call to do this. If these Indians were citizens and *encomenderos* of Indians, and if they had incomes like the citizens, I believe there would be much more Christianity and public order. Yet they say that the Indians are barbarians and that they are not Christians. Things are just the opposite of what the avaricious Spaniards of this kingdom say. This you must consider, Christian.

**Consider that the poor Indians** in this life never attain justice, because everyone is self-interested, and everyone steals and robs from the Indians of this kingdom. Consider this.

**Consider how the *corregidores*** mistreat and rob the Indians, as do [the *corregidores*'] wives, brothers, and relatives, as well as their notaries, deputies and servants in this kingdom. Consider.

**Consider how the *doctrina* priests** mistreat them and steal, as do their brothers, children,[321] and servants, and even their cooks, throughout this kingdom. You must consider this.

---

[321] Guaman Poma has frequently accused rural priests of breaking their vows of celibacy and having illegitimate children by Indian mothers.

A religious brotherhood with twenty-four Indian brothers
and sisters dedicated to this holy order

Santa María
de Peña de
Francia, 1613

*Christianity.*

Consider how the *encomenderos* mistreat them and steal and rob, as do their wives, stewards, brothers, children, the wives of their stewards, their relatives, and their servants, using tribute collection as their pretext; they help themselves, demanding gifts, *mitayos,* and *camaricos* in this kingdom. You must consider this injustice.

Consider how His Majesty's mine owners and their stewards rob and mistreat them, with the pretext that they say they are serving His Majesty. They punish and mistreat their Indian servants and their wives and children in this kingdom. Consider the harm they do.

Consider how the Spanish wayfarers steal and rob them: travelers who reach the *tambos* and pueblos, and who beat the poor Indians, the pueblo officials, and their *mitayos.* These Christians forcibly load them down as if they were horses and beasts of burden, using force in this kingdom. You must consider this.

Consider how the judges, investigators, and secretaries rob and steal from [the Indians], under the pretext that they are protecting the mines and plazas[322] to which [the Indians] have been sent by the *corregidores* and district magistrates. They strip naked the poor Indians, the noble *caciques,* and the other rulers in this kingdom. Consider this.

Consider how the Indians are robbed and deprived of their estates, of their labor, and of everything they have, by those same noble *caciques,* seconds-in-command, and petty authorities: the *curacas* of *waranca* [1,000 households], of *pisca pachaca* [500 households], of *pisca chunca* [50 households], of *chunca* [10 households], of *pisca* [5 households]; the justices of the peace, petty authorities, aldermen, chief constables, lower constables, jailer, and town crier; for all are against the poor Indians in this kingdom. Consider.

Consider how the *alcaldes mayores,* the *alcaldes* of mines and plazas, and the *alcaldes* of fields and *tambos* all rob and steal from the poor Indians. These steal more than anyone else in the kingdom. You must consider this mistreatment in your heart and soul.

Consider how the major and minor *fiscales* of the Church, and the sextons, cantors, stewards, and members and officers of religious brotherhoods

---

[322] Mines and plazas: in colonial Peru, all able-bodied Indian commoners were expected to take turns fulfilling the forced labor draft (*mita*). Some were sent by the *mita* to work in the silver and mercury mines, but others were sent to the public squares of Spanish colonial cities, where Spanish residents selected them as day laborers or seasonal workers to toil on their estates and in their houses. The "*indios de las minas*" and the "*indios de la plaza*" were supposed to receive a fixed wage for their labor, but as Guaman Poma complains here, Spanish officials and others were ready to step in and relieve them of their already insufficient pay.

all rob and steal from [the Indians]. In this kingdom, they rob and steal from the Indians. Consider this burden on the poor.

**Consider how the Indians** and the poor parishioners of the *doctrinas* are stolen from and robbed by the pastoral inspectors and the officers of the Holy Mother Church. The notaries, the *fiscales,* and the curates themselves in each pueblo rob the Indian men and women, with the pretext of the pastoral visits that they perform in this kingdom. Consider.

**Consider how tax collectors**—the stewards and officers of the royal crown of His Majesty; the treasurers and the judges—rob and steal everything they can from the Indians, with the pretext of collecting taxes and tribute in this kingdom. Consider this deeply.

◆ **The *corregidores*** are the mortal enemies of Indian men, and the priests of the *doctrinas* are the mortal enemies of Indian women, and even more so, of the noble *caciques.* All the Spaniards are against the poor Indians of this kingdom. You must consider this very deeply.

**Consider that the poor** of Jesus Christ—the blind, the crippled, the sick, the old men, the old women, the widows, the orphans—suffer many troubles in this life, and there are no alms for them. There are no Christians and no saints here: they are all up in heaven. And so, there is no charity. That is why these poor people suffer from troubles, hunger, and thirst, cold, punishment, and persecution in this kingdom. Consider.

**Consider that the noble** *caciques,* and the other Indians who make themselves into petty authorities in this kingdom, hold back all the land in and around the pueblos. Whether they are agricultural fields, pastures, or corrals, they are too much to own, and the fields are lost because the petty authorities do not cultivate them. They keep the Indians from cultivating them, saying that the fields belong to them, and they demand to be paid rent, renting out the fields and taking advantage of them, while they do not give those fields to the heirs who inherited them. Therefore, in places such as gorges (*waycos*), *pucyos* [springs], and rivers, where they can get water for irrigation, the fields are lost and broken and overrun with brush, and the terraces fall down. Everything that the first Indians did—the *Wari Wiracocha Runa,* the *Wari Runa,* the *Purun Runa,* and the *Auca Runa*—everything they worked so hard on, breaking the virgin soil, is being lost. In some parts, they say, those first Indians would sift the earth to remove the little pebbles, which is why there are still piles of pebbles around; these are the pebbles they removed by sifting them out. They created all the terraces by hand. Even if the land was flat, they made an effort to straighten it up, at the cost of meals and hard work. So it is not right for the fields to be lost, for if they are not cultivated, they will be lost forever. All the worse for the poor heirs; and so God loses their service, and His Majesty loses his royal fifth.

♦ The Spanish *corregidores* and padres mistreat the poor Indian men and women in this kingdom. They are in the Indian's land, yet they do not take that into consideration, and they fear neither God nor His Majesty's justice.

*Pride.*

The *doctrina* padres are overjoyed to see them lose their lands, because then the padres plant them, under the pretext that they are for the *doctrina*. Then, they throw the Indians off their fields and pay them nothing. For their part, the *corregidores* also throw them off; in fact, the *encomenderos* do even more to throw them off, because they force their way onto the fields and places, the gorges and agricultural lands and pastures, and they do great damage there, setting their goats, sheep, cows, and mares to graze. And they pay nothing to the poor Indians; nor do they pay the tithe nor the first fruits;[323] nor do they pay His Majesty the royal fifth, nor the sales tax, nor the tribute, which are all his by right.

And so, in this kingdom it would be very just if everyone could eat and sustain himself and plant his fields—Indians as well as Spaniards, mestizos, mulattos, and emancipated blacks. The *encomenderos,* priests, *corregidores,* and their brothers, sons, and relatives should not be allowed to interfere. If a man is a native Indian, he should not have to pay to work the fields; but if he is an outsider Indian or a Spaniard, he should pay the owner of the field—except that he should not pay him in *chicha,* wine, or coca leaves, but rather in silver, so that the owner can pay his tribute and taxes, and have money to support his wife and children; while the rent for mines should be paid in corn, wheat, clothes, or cattle.

And the fields, *moya*s [orchards], pastures, and corrals should never be sold by any means; nor should they be left to the priest by the owner's testament, but rather to the community, if he has no heir. And if [the owner] should commit some minor offense, the Indians should be able to throw him off of his fields, but neither the priest nor the *corregidor* nor the *encomendero* should be able to throw him off.

The priest should not have Indian mistresses, nor Indian men or boys as servants, on his fields. If he does, the *corregidor* should throw the priest off those fields.

In this way, the fields of this kingdom will be very advantageous to the service of God and His Majesty. Consider this: this whole kingdom would be filled with Christians, in every [Spanish] town and hamlet and [Indian] pueblo.

**Consider the good** public order, law, and justice that the Indians once had: the king and his council, the justices, the princes, the nobles, the gentlemen of this kingdom. The king was the *capac*—for example, Topa Inca Yupanqui. The princes were the *auquicuna*. There were high lords, *capac*

---

[323] Tithe, first fruits (*primicias*): church taxes paid to the parish priest. Non-European food products, such as corn and potatoes, were exempt from these taxes, but Spaniards were supposed to pay them on the Spanish products (wheat, wool, cattle) that they produced on their farms.

And the good slaves bear it patiently by the love of God. They do not give them clothes to wear or food to eat, and they do not consider that God created them and died for them as He did for the Spaniards.

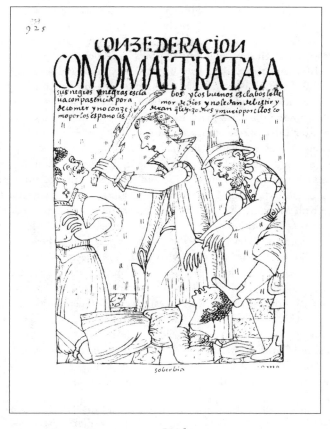

*Pride.*

*apo,* such as Waman Chawa of the Allauca Wanaco–Yaro Willka lineage. The noble lords were the *Wamanin apo.* The lord of a district was the *apo;* his deputies were the *curacas.* The petty authorities and gentlemen were the *waranca curaca,* the *pisca pachaca camachicoc,* the *pachaca camachicoc,* the *pisca chunca camachicoc,* the *chunca camachicoc,* and the *pisca camachicoc.* The *Coya* was the queen; the *ñusta* was the princess; *palla,* lady; *capac warmi,* Her Excellency; *curaca warmi,* high lady; *allicac warmi,* lady.[324]

◆ **The good and Christian** blacks bear such patience. Though they be married and serving God, their wicked, proud Spanish masters and mistresses, who fear neither God nor justice, mistreat them and demand their day's work, and give them nothing to eat and nothing to wear, leaving them naked. Since they find themselves enslaved, they keep quiet and commend themselves to God and the Virgin Mary and to all the saints and angels in heaven in this kingdom. You must consider this, Christian.

**Consider that there are many black Christians,** and that from them have come such saints as San Juan de Buenaventura. Yet from them there also come the very bad, disobedient, lying thieves, assailants, drunks, and gamblers among the black men and women in this kingdom. Consider.

**Consider how black men and women** become bad and learn to be notorious thieves, assailants, and bad Christians—some, because they are never punished and are not placed in the leg irons that tame rogues, and because they are not taught doctrine and there is no justice among them; others, because their masters and mistresses mistreat them without reason and punish them cruelly, giving them no food for breakfast, the midday meal, or supper, and giving them no clothes to eat. Yet they demand a lot of silver from the blacks out of their daily wages,[325] and they make them work without eating from daybreak to dusk. Some feed them, out of sheer miserliness, once a day at twelve noon, and they call that breakfast; and so they die. Anyone who works needs to eat three times a day to keep working for long. And they never give them treats or meat. The poor black men and women in this kingdom are also Christians, and they, too, have an appetite for eating. Consider that you are becoming lost.

**Consider that these blacks** should not be able to bear offensive or defensive arms. Not even captive mulattos should be allowed to bear knives or cudgels. Before a mulatto, mestizo, or Spaniard can bear arms, he should

---

[324] These are titles that Guaman Poma has explained earlier in the book. (See pp. 3, 64, 156–60.) Here he lists them together in order to emphasize the complexity and comprehensiveness of native Andean government.

[325] Enslaved blacks in colonial Peru were rarely put to work in plantation agriculture; rather, those who were not employed as domestic servants or as foremen in mines or on farms were often sent out to find daily wage labor, and forced to turn over their wages to their masters.

first get permission from His Majesty. In the same way, Spaniards should not bear arms until they reach the age of twenty, and the young man should be given his weapon and his license to bear it by His Majesty's governors, who would give him those arms only for use in self-defense, in the service of God and His Majesty, and for the defense of our Holy Catholic faith of Christianity in this kingdom and in the world and throughout Christendom. This permission should come from His Majesty, and no one should be able to carry arms without a license, or after losing it. But blacks are rough men; they cannot be trusted. They are slaves: they want to live and to die at the same time. They are drunks, gamblers, thieves, and assailants. Thus they cannot be given arms, unless the arms are given to them by some great lord or judge or inspector or noble *cacique* in this kingdom; in that case, they may bear arms and halberds and be their lords' and masters' halberdiers.

And the Spaniards should not give licenses to bear arms to any men who are insane or foolish, nor to any man who is rash, nor to a man laden with debt, nor to a man jealous of his wife, nor to a perjurer, nor to a gambler, drunk, or thief, nor to a man who fears neither God nor justice nor priests nor the tonsured monks and hermits. All those mentioned should lose their arms, as should the noble *cacique* or second-in-command who proves to be a drunk, coca-chewer, and gambler. Neither they, nor their slaves or Indians on their behalf, should bear arms. If they are free of these things, they should freely bear arms, as should their brothers, sons, grandsons, great-grandsons, and descendents. To this end, they deserve licenses in accordance with the law and the grace of the emperor-king, who made Don Juan, Don Pedro, and Don Francisco gentlemen, throughout the kingdom. Consider this good public order and Christianity.

**Consider that in the world** there should be public order and Christianity in the great cities such as Lima. There should be four justices of the peace, forming a city council. And in the [Spanish] towns, such as Ica, there should be two justices of the peace, even if they are blacks or mulattos; if they are slaves, they should be emancipated by the Christian's law and the justice of God and His Majesty throughout the world. There should be justices of the peace, aldermen, a chief constable, lower constables, a jailer, a town crier, a notary for the town council, a *fiscal* of the church, and a town clerk among them. Likewise, Spanish and Indian quadroons are free men, by the king, whether [their father] is a gentleman, a commoner, a noble *cacique,* or an Indian commoner; if he is a pure mulatto, he is a slave.[326] All of these should be able to serve as notaries, justices, constables. Consider.

---

[326] Guaman Poma refers here to his legal theory about the children of enslaved mulatta women and free men; see p. 238 (ms. p. 724).

◆ **There are notorious** thieves and gamblers, ruffians, assailants, and liars in this kingdom, worse than the blacks and Spaniards in Castile. In the time of the Incas, people had no doors or strongboxes or locks and keys; they closed their houses with two little sticks. Today, however, there are tremendous thieves who force open locks and steal and rob from the Indians, just like the Spanish do, and worse than the blacks. In this life, the Indians who have no jobs and do no work want to have things, and all they understand is dressing well, drinking, and gambling at cards among themselves and with the Spaniards and blacks in this kingdom. Consider.

**Consider how lazy** the Indian men and women are in this life: they are idle *yanaconas* and *chinaconas,* because that is what the Spanish men and women teach them, taking them on as *yanaconas* (serving lads) and *chinaconas* (maids, cooks, baking women, and caretakers). In this way they are lost; they become tremendous whores, and give birth to mestizos; and thus, the pueblos are depopulated, the Indians come to an end, and the mestizos multiply. His Majesty fruitlessly loses in this kingdom. Consider this.

**Consider how the Indians** flee the Mass and the *doctrina* church and the sermons, because the priest of the *doctrina* is so cruel. He punishes them, treats them with force, and takes away their estates and their daughters, and thus they flee him. Yet when they see a priest from the Company of Jesus, or a Franciscan friar, or a hermit, they rejoice and do confession. Consider this hardship on the poor.

**Consider how the Indians** of this kingdom live in bad marriages. In the time of the Incas, there were no adulterers, whores, or bad wives; but today there are, for the following reasons: first, because that is what they see among the Spanish; second, because the women become tremendous drunkards and eat dainty food, and in that way lust is kindled in them; third, because they see the Spanish *corregidor,* priest, and *encomendero* living with mistresses, and they want to do the same; fourth, because [the Spanish] fornicate with the Indians' wives and virgin daughters by force, and there is no remedy. Thus the Indian women become tremendous whores, and afterwards that is what they remain, and there is no punishment. Consider this.

**Consider the clothes, customs, and dress** of the Indians and of the Spaniards, of the ancients and of those of this life, and the public order and Christianity that there is now, especially among the youngest Indians recently; and how they are New Christians, yet they have the advantage over the Old Christians, and will continue to have the advantage if they are left alone and taught. Consider this.

**Consider, Your Majesty,** all of the preceding indictments,[327] and, having

---

[327] Indictments: *capítulos,* which means both "list of charges" (referring to Guaman Poma's accusations in this chapter) and "chapters" (referring to all the chapters in the book).

[Man dressed as an Indian noble:] *Pachac cullqui.*

["Here's a hundred pesos"]

[Devil:] *"Alli suwaconqui. Noca yanapas-cayqui."* ["You'll be a good thief. I'll help you."]

*Thief*—**Suwa.**

considered them very carefully, once again consider the poor Indians of this kingdom. Consider the noble *caciques,* such as Don Cristóbal de León.[328] He was thrown out, dispossessed, punished, and humiliated because he favored, aided, and defended the poor Indians of his province. The priest, *corregidor,* and *encomendero* became his mortal enemies; what they most desired was that he be hanged or thrown to the galleys. The priests of his province persecuted him, and so he was punished and expeled from the province by the pastoral inspector of the Holy Mother Church at that time. The same inspector audited the priest of the province; even though the priest had done terrible damage, he ruled that he was a good teacher of doctrine and left him free. Not counting bribes, he got two thousand pesos from Don Cristóbal de León and sentenced him to a life of exile—which was what the priest and the *encomendero* and the others in the province had wanted. This happened in 1611.

Let me speak about this, so that Your Majesty may learn of it and consider it, and so that it be written as it truly was. All *corregidores* and their deputies, all Spaniards and priests, all self-interested *doctrina* padres and pastoral inspectors of the Holy Church, all judges and *encomenderos* are mortal enemies, because what the noble *caciques* of this kingdom should do is defend the poor Indians—their estates, their food, their persons, and especially their wives and daughters. Yet, when I was in this province, governing and defending the town called Concepción de Huaylla Pampa Apcara from all these fierce animals who fear neither God nor justice—the *corregidor* at the time was Don Antonio Monroy, and the provincial vicar was the priest Licentiate Alonso Rota—the great paper-pusher Diego Beltrán de Saravia, Hernán Rodríguez de Piñeda, and all the other priests for the *Lucanos* and *Soras* in that province got together, formed a town council, and named a notary to draw up a report and a criminal case. They went after my life, turning over every last bit of straw to take criminal revenge on me and throw me out of the province, so that they could go on despoiling it and taking the daughters of the poor Indians.[329] They did all this in order to humiliate me, though I was completely innocent; they mistreated me, harassed me, imprisoned me in the public jail, and ordered me never to set foot in that province. They act in this same way with all the other noble *caciques* in this, your kingdom of Peru. In this way, the noble lords come to an end, and the poor Indians run away, and the land is depopulated. Where the general rolls once listed a hundred Indian tributaries, today there are not even ten; and they, their cattle, and their

---

[328] His story is told on pp. 169–73 and 222–23 (ms. pp. 498–502 and 694).

[329] Guaman Poma was banished from his home province in 1600 (Adorno, *Guaman Poma* [2000], p. xxxvi).

estates are coming to an end, as I have told Your Majesty, that you may consider this.

Thus [the priests] deflower all the maidens, taking them for themselves until they begin to get old, under the pretext of teaching them the doctrine; once the women are old, past fifty years, and will never again in their lives bear children, they toss them off, leaving the Indian women crippled, ugly, sickly, lame, and limping. Thus the Indians do not multiply and will not multiply; instead, mestizos multiply and go about dressed as Indians. For this reason, Your Majesty should order a suspension of all civil and criminal court cases. Instead, the *Audiencia* itself, or a judge whom Your Majesty yourself might select, should hear these cases, sitting in residence in Los Reyes de Lima; and the opposing sides should appear in person before him, for the service of God and of your royal crown, and for the good of the poor of Jesus Christ. Your Majesty should submit this provision to the court of your kingdom, where your viceroy presides, and should command all the noble *caciques* of your kingdom to defend their Indians. In this way, Your Majesty will serve God and the welfare and increase of the Indians of this kingdom. Consider all this, Your Majesty, for the good of the Indians.

**Consider how things** such as clothes from Castile and from this land, and the cattle from Castile and from this land, and the food from Castile and from this land cost very little in the time of the conquest, because the Spanish ate only their native food, and the Indians likewise. It disgusted each of them to eat the other's food or wear their clothes. Now everyone wants to dress and eat better, and so everything costs too much in this kingdom, both the Spaniards' things and the Indians'. Consider.

*[An illustration, ms. p. 946, depicts "Santa María Peña de Francia," who leads a crowd of saints in kneeling in prayer to the risen Christ (who holds the cross with his pierced hands). The caption entreats the Christian reader to contemplate Mary's prayers to her son "for the world and for the sinners," and to have devotion in her.]*

**Santa María de Peña de Francia,** Mother of God, prays always for the sinners of the world. Consider: God does not punish us, despite all our evils, our disobedience, and our sins, both mortal and venial, on account of the prayers of the Virgin Mary and all the saints and angels in heaven, and all the holy men and women who are in this world—holy priests, clerics, friars, and hermits, and others who do not wear any habit; the holy men and women of this world. God our Lord and Savior and Creator holds us in his holy hand. Consider all this, in the world and in this kingdom.

Thus, everyone should feel a great obligation to serve him on his feast days and sabbaths throughout the world. The Mass should be a work of alms and charity for the Virgin Mary, to honor and serve her. The priests should not keep the alms; the alms should be for the candle wax and the lamp oil, for the Virgin Mary in this world. Consider this service to God.

**Consider, Your Majesty,** how a person who has an estate with cattle and sheep[330]—herds which he has built up through hard labor, and for which he grieves, because they have cost him his work and his labor—will not want them to die or to fall sick or to perish. If they should perish, what means will he have to support his children and grandchildren? He will want to increase his herds and become rich and grow greater for his memory's sake, and will want his cattle to be hale and healthy and fat, and to multiply so that he might live from this estate and this wealth of sheep, which God has given him, making him a man, and his father and grandfather [before him]. Because of these sheep, he has owned many kingdoms with this estate. God will later hold him to account for them, too, because God gave them to him; thus, he will be sure to come to the aid of these poor sheep.

Here you see, Your Majesty, what you must consider: for people perish in the quicksilver mines, and those who remain alive are poisoned with quicksilver until they are not worth a straw. If you do not come to their aid, Your Majesty and your royal crown shall perish; this must grieve you. The mine owners do not grieve and do not care. Nor do I wish for the mines to close; rather, they should increase, and there should be more mines and wealth. Your Majesty should give the word, and I will send Indians off to work the land, and I will give orders so that fewer will die and the quicksilver will be mined more easily. But Your Majesty must communicate with me. I will accompany you and render my opinion, as a prince of the Indians and a deputy of Your Majesty in this kingdom, a servant of your royal crown, and a Catholic Christian, who would serve in all the mines of this kingdom in the service of God, of Your Majesty, of our Holy Catholic faith and Christianity, and of the welfare of the Indians in this kingdom. Consider, Your Majesty.

**Consider that the poor sinners** of the world should be shown favor. This is very proper; it serves God, good justice, and Christian law. God has always been merciful, the friend of the poor. Sinners are always poor. Thus, Our Savior Jesus Christ came down from heaven to the world, was made flesh in the Virgin Mary, became God and man, and was martyred, spilling his precious blood and dying on the cross. And so it is, whether the poor

---

[330] Sheep (*ovejas*): Guaman Poma usually uses this word to refer to llamas and alpacas, because that is how the first Spanish conquerors described these woolly Andean cattle (which are actually camelids). In this passage, he no doubt also enjoyed the biblical resonance of the image of the shepherd's concern for his sheep.

sinner is guilty or not. For we have seen that these impetuous judges—and, let us add, these proud and foolish madmen who fear neither God nor his justice—humiliate, hang, behead, shoot with arrows, and garrote poor men who did not deserve death. For example, what Don Francisco de Toledo did when he beheaded the Inca king: though he was a mere soldier, he killed the king out of pride. Or what happened to the gentleman Don García de Solís Portocarrera, who died, though guiltless. Or the prince Don Melchor Carlos Inca, who was sent into exile, though guiltless. Or other princes, who are left to wander naked, though guiltless. Or other poor people who have died, who knows how, such as what happened to the mine owner Juan García de la Vega. Yet what remedy can an accused man look for from all this, if his enemy is an impassioned, mad, foolish, drunken, or self-interested man, and his notary is no different? Such men should not be allowed to pass sentence, nor should the cases on which they pass sentence be allowed to stand. A good, Christian judge should take up the case, retry it, and pass sentence on it anew. The bad man should not be consulted; rather, the good man should be consulted in the courtroom. Three people should be consulted—first, the justice; second, the accused; third, the plaintiff—so that one might not be harmed as the other was. All the poor people in the world should follow this order, and if the judges overstep it, they should be punished—and the notaries, more so. Consider, judge.

**Consider how the Spaniards** will go to hell over half a real. The same will happen to the Indians now, for this greed has arisen in the time of the Spanish—in the time of the Incas, there was no such greed for gold and silver. Therefore there are many thieves in this life, Indians as well as blacks, and especially the Spaniards, who skin the poor Indians, robbing and stealing from them. Not only this: they also take their wives and daughters, especially the priests. You must consider this lewdness of the world.

**Consider how God** and man died for the sinners of the world: *yuyaycuy imanam Dios wañurcan huchasipa runaraycu, cay pachapi cacpac* [consider how God died because of the sinners, for the sake of those who are here in this world].

Jesus Christ died for the world and for men. He underwent torment and martyrdom, and rose into heaven after being resurrected. In this life he was poor and persecuted; afterwards, on Judgment Day, he will return in majesty and glory. By his right hand, he will lead his blessed mother, St. Mary, and all the saints and angels, and will bring presents, garlands, and jewels to pay the poor who have been disdained. And at his left hand, hell will open up its maw to swallow the bad, disobedient, and proud sinners. Torments, fire, whippings, gall, punishments, humiliations, and tortures without glory await the bad sinners; and with them, all the demons, serpents,

## GOD DIED FOR THE WORLD AND FOR THE POOR SINNERS, THE CHILDREN OF ADAM AND EVE.

*He was crucified for the sins.*

scorpions, snakes, worms, and bad spirits more frightening than have ever been seen, for the punishment of all. They will assume flesh and blood from heaven and from hell; they will clothe themselves to go wherever God commands them, forevermore. Consider, Christian.

**Consider with deep attention** that God, too, has a mortal enemy who does not want to show Him his eyes. Consider, Christian, how deeply he hates Him, if he does not even look at Him with his eyes. You will ask, Christian, who is this enemy? The enemy is pride. There is nothing in the world or in heaven today as bad as the first sin that was committed against God: it was the pride of that lovely, handsome one, and of all his followers. You should see how they fell from heaven to the world, and continued on into deepest hell, where they are punished with perpetual fire for their pride.

Now consider that gentleman, Don Francisco de Toledo, the viceroy, whose pride made him want to be higher than the king, even though he was merely the king's viceroy. For in the world, the pope is the pope, ruling in the place of God; the emperors and kings, whether Spanish or Indian or black, are kings. The dukes, counts, marquises, and gentlemen descend from these kings; they were also kings at one time, and belonged to the great house—not like the gentlemen over here in this kingdom, who are all gentlemen by hook or by crook. They pay a handful of coins and draw up documents that say they are gentlemen; how is anyone to know whether they are stained with a bit of Jew, Moor, Turk, or Englishman? It would be so much better if they could say, "I am an Old Christian." A good documentary proof is valid if one of them brings it from his house and homeland in Spain, signed by His Majesty or by the royal council: that would be a true gentleman. As I have stated, a good gentleman in this world should be honored and deferred to and given way to. Even if you hold office or a position from His Majesty—even if you are a doctor or a lawyer—you should not desire to be higher than you are by blood and by lineage. However poor he might be, a gentleman who serves God and His Majesty deserves honor, preeminence, and authority.

Avoid being proud, Christian, by considering how Don Francisco de Toledo sentenced the king and heir Topa Amaro Inca to be beheaded, even though, by all rights, he should never have been subject to such a sentence any more than any of the other gentlemen mentioned above; not even if he had risen in rebellion should he have been scourged or shamed. Rather, [Toledo] should have knelt before him to offer him water and bread, and should have allowed him to bathe. Keeping him imprisoned until he could be handed over to His Majesty, [Toledo] should have provided him with pages and a butler to wait at his table and good food and great honor. Oh, Don Francisco de Toledo! With all your skill and your understanding of the law, you desired to be more than the king, and you executed justice on the king of Peru! If His Majesty had then sent a judge here, you would have been beheaded on the same scaffold; but he did not wish to do so. Since the king was so Christian, he left you to your sins, and in punishment for your pride, you beheaded yourself, Don Francisco de Toledo. God alone knows where you are now.

See, Christian, where pride leads. It is just as in the case of the gentleman Don García: a gentleman of His Majesty, he was beheaded after a trial without being given his right of appeal. Oh, poor gentleman, to fall into the hands of his own vassals! All this is what pride brings. Because they are lawyers or doctors, they presumptuously think they know everything. Poor people! You considered yourselves judges and justices, with the authority to sentence him to beheading and quartering, to being tortured and humiliated in the streets, and to being given one hundred lashes. Rather, you should weep in your soul and your conscience, quiver in your heart and spirit, and tremble in your flesh.

Come here, Christian! Consider that if you were sentenced to everything mentioned here, it should not grieve you; even in such a case, you should not be proud. Rather, you should yield yourself to His Majesty's hands and to his royal council.

Come here! Consider your body: your feet cannot rule over your head; your hands cannot tell your head what to do; not even your heart, which is greater, can do so. Without your head, you are worth nothing. Likewise, without God, a Christian is worth nothing. Without the pope and the Holy Mother Church, a Christian is worth nothing. Without the king, a body is worthy nothing. Thus, the head is the king and none other. Therefore, you should let him be the head; do not try to be another Don Francisco de Toledo or some other lawyer. The *doctrina* padres, the judges, and the inspectors are also trying to be like bishops. Anyone who appeals to His Excellency the bishop to find someone guilty or innocent should be ignored, because a foot cannot tell the head what to do; that is worthy of punishment. For example, poor Don Cristóbal de León made an appeal, and it was rejected and not accepted. Oh, poor Don León! For defending your Indians, you were humiliated, punished, exiled, and burdened with chains.

Look at the judge's pride: priests who are merely the pastors of *doctrinas* turn themselves into the judges and justices of the Indians. Consider their pride.

**Your soul must consider** that in heaven, in the world, and in hell there is only one God, Father, Son, and Holy Spirit. You must also consider that you were made for that great city in heaven, where God and the Virgin Mary and all the saints and angels are; you should go there, because for that you were made. And you must consider that hell was made for the bad, the proud, and the disobedient towards their Creator. Consider this.

Water of Life
*(Causay uno);*
*Hanac pacha*
[upper world]

*Waccha runa diospa simin wacaychacpa hanac pacha diospa llactan.*
[For the poor who kept the word of God, the upper-world city of God.]

**City of God for men.**

**Consider that the priests** should be very retiring: they should not wander the streets day and night—especially not the friars. Yet they leave their monasteries and just stroll around the world, causing disturbances, like soldiers. Their prelates are to blame for this; they should punish them and assign them heavy penances. Even if they are just lay brothers, they should not be allowed out of the monastery unaccompanied, and they should ask their prelate's permission. Thus, they should rightly be inspected by the general inspector of the holy Church.

You should learn and consider the reason why the *doctrina* padres are held in little veneration or esteem here. It is because they wander the streets day and night, rambling and strolling like men of the world, assailants, or thieves; as if they had in mind some sin of lust, envy, or pride. A very retiring and humble priest is known as a saint. Everyone comes to see such priests, bringing alms; and the sinners adhere more to them than to the gadabouts who disobey God and God's justice. This is why they assumed the habit and consecrated themselves. The same is true of married and unmarried men chosen by God in the world and in this kingdom. All the saintly priests, saintly married men, and saintly maidens and virgins and other sinners in the world, when they repent of their sins and return to Jesus Christ, are as good saints as any. They all belong to heaven; to the city of heaven. Consider the greatness of heaven.

**Here you must consider** the greatness of the good of heaven that awaits us: rise with your spirits, my brothers, up to this noble region, and look at it closely.[331]

What will it be like to see the loveliness of that sovereign city, those walls and doors of precious stones, those fountains flowing with the waters of life?

What will it be like to see nine choirs of angels, arranged in their hierarchies, all so lovely, so glorious, so well arranged, so resplendent?

What will it be like to see those ranks and thrones of virgins and confessors, of hermit monks and martyrs, of evangelical apostles, patriarchs, and prophets?

What will it be like to see the Most Sacred Holy Virgin, our advocate, exalted above all the choirs of angels?

What will it be like to see the most sacred humanity of Jesus Christ our Lord, sitting on the right hand of the Father, advocating for us and interceding on our behalf?

---

[331] According to Murra and Adorno (ms. p. 954, n. 1), Guaman Poma copies the first five of the six questions that follow directly from Fray Luis de Granada's *Memorial de la vida cristiana*.

What will it be like, above all, to see the most beatific and glorious Holiest Trinity: Father, Son, and Holy Spirit, one true God, in whom is placed all the faith of the true Christian, and whom he must consider and believe in, as a Catholic Christian?

**Consider that the Spanish nation** was Jewish: even though they had a different law, they had the same letters, dress, clothing, face, beards, and greed.[332] Though [the Spaniards] were gentiles and made different sacrifices, the Jews knew God very well and followed the law of Moses and the commandments. The Indians had none of this, neither their law nor their costume nor their faces nor their letters. Consider this.

**Consider how there are terrible** thieves among Christians in this time, because they learn from the Spanish Christians: they see how the *corregidores,* the priests, the *encomenderos,* the Spanish travelers in the *tambos,* and the justices rob and steal, and they give the lessons and primers in vice that the bad Christians in this kingdom give them. Thus is Christianity going to ruin in this kingdom. Consider this, Christian of the world.

**Here you must consider** the multitude of punishments that Divine Scripture signifies for us when it says that in hell there will be hunger and thirst and weeping and gnashing of teeth and double-edged blades, spirits created to exact vengeance, serpents and worms and scorpions and hammers and agencies and bile and stormy spirits and other such things, through which it figures the multitude and the shocking terribleness of the torments of that place. The inner and outer darkness of bodies and souls there will also be so thick that it could be felt by touch. There will be cold and fire that can never be extinguished to punish bodies and souls forever. To all this must be added the torment of that perpetual destroyer, the worm of conscience, so often mentioned in Scripture, which speaks of the worm. These worms will never end and never die, and their fire will never be extinguished. This worm is the rabid malice and fruitless repentance that evil people will always have there, and which will never come to an end,[333] not as long as God is God and world without end. Consider this punishment.

**Consider how** the Indian men and women in this life bear with such patience the evils of the Spaniards, priests, and *corregidores,* the mestizos,

---

[332] As has been noted, Guaman Poma applied the term "Spanish" to cover all Europeans, much as Europeans referred to all the peoples of the Americas as "Indians." From this point of view, the Spaniards, who had adopted the Jewish bible as their own Old Testament, were descendents of the Jews; their scriptures were the same, they all wore beards (unlike Indians), and in European art they were drawn wearing what Guaman Poma saw as the same clothes and features. His view here is a reversal of a contemporary European theory of the origin of Indians from one of the lost tribes of the Jews.

[333] According to Murra and Adorno (ms. p. 956, n. 1), the paragraph up to this point is copied from Granada's *Memorial.*

The Prince
of Darkness

The avariciou
man—the
ungrateful—
lust—pride

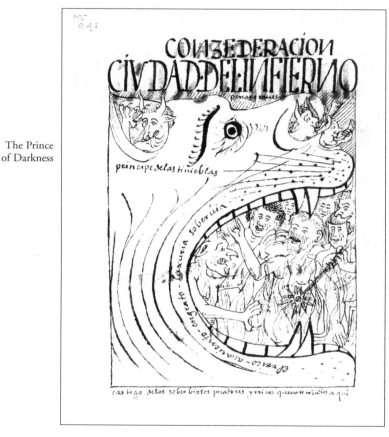

*Punishment of the proud sinners and rich men*
*who do not fear God.*

mulattos, and blacks, and the *yanaconas* and *chinaconas,* who rip out the lives and the entrails of the Indians. Consider.

**Consider the citizens** who have *encomiendas* of Indians, who out of sheer miserliness will send a quarter-real's worth of cheese to a noble *cacique* along with a letter. One of them will send an Indian to carry the letter nine leagues without paying him, and will demand that all the noble *caciques* come to visit him and to see him. The *corregidores,* the judges, the *doctrina* padres, and the inspectors of the Holy Mother Church act in the same way.

Consider the hearts of these people, what they are thinking. They do not really want to see the noble *caciques;* they just want [the *caciques*] to bring them presents of silver, gold, clothes, fruits, and other things, and they desire to see them so that they can demand their fortunes and Indians to use as carriers and miners. And the *doctrina* padres tell the Indians that they cannot go home to their pueblos without getting permission. Why should an Indian have to ask permission of a padre or a *corregidor* or an *encomendero,* if he is free? Rather, he should ask his noble *cacique* for permission, for he is his lord.

The Indian says to the padre, "With your *licencia,* I am going to my pueblo to work my fields and pay my *tasa.*"[334]

The padre says to him, "*Hijo,* go with my *licencia.* When you are there, make them sow fields for me. The *solteras* take good care of my *cabras, ovejas,* llamas, and chickens; see that they finish the job. Make them weave *sobrecamas.* Send me one hundred partridges, eggs, chickens, a *hanega* of potatoes, and a *hanega* of corn. That is all. Don't fail, or I'll *castigar* you. I'm the *padre* and the *propietario,* so *servir* me well."[335]

Consider, Christian, how miserly he is, tricking the Indians with a quarter-real of cheese when he is so rich. Why should he come to see you or to ask for your permission, when he does not owe it to you? You only want the Indians to come ask for your permission so that you can rob them. Consider this contemptible act towards free Christians, the poor men of God.

**Consider the most grievous** and painful punishment for Spanish men and women who are bad Christians: it would be to seize all their goods and banish them to Spain for ever and ever, or to Chile.[336] There could be no better punishment for them.

---

[334] He speaks in Quechua, translated here into English, with Spanish loan words left untranslated: *licencia,* permission; *tasa,* tribute.

[335] The priest answers in Quechua with many Spanish words: *hijo,* son; *solteras,* unmarried women; *cabras,* goats; *ovejas,* sheep; *sobrecamas,* blankets; *hanega,* a dry measure, 1.5 bushels; *castigar,* punish; *padre,* priest; *propietario,* proprietor; *servir,* serve.

[336] Chile: the farthest outpost of colonial Spanish South America.

And consider the great punishment and purgatory for the proud evil men who disobey God and His commandments—the murderers, traitors, assailants, thieves, and sorcerers. From this day forth, there should be no hangings of Spaniards, mestizos, mulattos, blacks, or Indians. They should be banished to the tunnels of the quicksilver mines forever, chained in irons, to mine for metal, and there they should give up their souls to God and serve His Majesty as slaves. This is the saintly sentence and penalty and consideration that may save the souls of the evil-doers of the world, in service to God and His Majesty.

**Consider the great harm** that the Indians receive from being charged the tithe.[337] The Indians of this kingdom have been granted relief from paying the tithe by His Holiness the Pope in Rome; yet the Spanish collect it from them for the following things: First, they pay their tithes from the labor and sweat of the Indians of this kingdom for all Spanish food and produce. Second, the *encomenderos* are paid by the sweat of the Indians, through their tribute in food, produce, grains, cattle, and clothing in this kingdom. Third, by the sweat of the Indians His Majesty pays the priests their salaries for the church, and [the priests] can leave the Holy Church with them. This was why the Indians were relieved from paying the tithe, because they have done so much other service. No Christendom in the world has served the Holy Church in Rome as much as this one. And you must consider this about these poor Indians and their labors.

**Consider that, in some pueblos,** they dug irrigation canals from the rivers, wells, lakes, or ponds. In the old times they would dig these canals, putting in so much labor that, if they had to be paid, it would have cost ten or twelve thousand pesos, or twenty thousand pesos. Before there was an Inca, since there were so many Indians and they had but one king and lord, they broke the land, dug the canals, and created all the raised-platform fields, which they called *patachacra* [raised fields] and *larca* [canals]. They dug them with the greatest skill in the world, doing it by hand, without tools; it seems as if each Indian placed one stone, and that was enough, so many people were there.

Thus, all the land throughout the kingdom became fields for sowing grain, even the land in the *yungas* [hot country], in the sandy deserts, and in the wicked mountains of this kingdom. The bridges, rivers, canals, lakes,

---

[337] The tithe (*diezmo*) was a ten percent tax on agricultural production, used to support the church. There was general agreement that the Indians of Spanish America, already faced with tribute and labor obligations to support *encomenderos* and priests, should be exempt from paying tithes on native foods such as corn and potatoes that they grew for their own sustenance. The first church councils of Mexico and Peru ruled, however, that Indians had to tithe what they grew to sell, particularly European products such as wheat, cows, and sheep.

ponds, and swamps were dug by the orders of the first kings and lords of the kingdoms. Later on, the Inca lords and kings ordered that they maintain the custom and law that none of these irrigation canals should be shifted. The corn fields and even the cattle pastures were irrigated in the mountain heights and in the ravines, and it is known that such a thing would never have been possible if the canals had not been built by so many people.

Thus, a penalty and a sentence without possibility of appeal was set: that no person should damage or remove a single stone, and no cattle should enter the canals. This law and ordinance was followed, in the service of God and of His Majesty and for the good of the commonwealth of this kingdom. Having seen this holy order and law, Don Francisco de Toledo ordered that it be kept, and His Majesty confirmed it.

Yet this law has not been kept, and so all the corn fields are being lost for lack of water. Because of this, the Indians lose their estates, His Majesty loses his royal fifth, and the Holy Mother Church loses the tithes that are owed her. And so, at this time, the Spaniards are releasing their animals and mule trains and cattle, and their goats and sheep cross over and do great damage. They take the water and break open the canals, which could never be put straight by any amount of money, and they only leave the smallest amount of water for the poor Indians; and so, the Indians are leaving their pueblos.

On account of this, in every pueblo there should be an irrigation judge (called a *sillquiwa*) who would distribute the water, mete out fines and punishments, and eject the cattle from the canals and corn fields; such things should be punished without fail. In this way, God and His Majesty will be served, as will the welfare of the communities and the welfare of the poor Indians of this kingdom. This law and ordinance should be kept and should be considered in this kingdom, for the good of the poor and the rich in the world.

**Consider closely in your spirit and heart** that a Christian who gives alms, and the person who receives alms, are two things. The good man is the glory, the bad man is the vainglory of the world: neither God nor the world rejoice in him; rather, the demons of hell rejoice, for some men are terrible misers, avaricious men who want neither glory nor vainglory. They are so miserly, they live off of *mita* and *moti patasca* [labor tribute and boiled hominy]. They are saving everything for hell, so their sins will weigh them down more heavily.

For others, it is vainglory to keep around their houses rich people, gamblers, starched, lazy thieves, and others who have estates: they feed these people and spend their household money, and in doing so they say they are giving alms. Again, others give alms to friars, clerics, and those who have all their hands, feet, and eyes—young men who could pick up a shovel, lazy men, and a few young women who could roll up their sleeves and get to work, but who give birth to children from different stocks. When they are heavy with child, they say that they are poor. Even if such people are given alms, it is vainglory to give alms to a priest. The priest gives the alms to whores.

This is not giving alms, nor does God receive these alms. The alms that God receives are those that go to those who are blind in both eyes, the lame and crippled, the sick, old people of eighty years, orphan-poor widows, those who have ten children, prisoners who have been banished into exile (for, even if they are gentlemen, they are prisoners and far from home), a few poor Franciscan padres, Jesuit friars, hermits, and the men and women who beg alms for some poor cripple or sick man. These are the alms that have been well employed, which God receives in his eyes, as the saints clearly taught us, and God Jesus Christ taught us through his gospel and his works of mercy: the saints begged for alms for the poor people in the world. Yet they make banquets and feasts, as I have said, for rich men and women, spending money on them, and then they praise themselves, saying that they have given alms. The vainglory of the world! This becomes the habit of the Indians, who do not want to eat in the public square as was their custom and a work of mercy and the law of this kingdom in the service of God. Consider, Christian.

**It should be considered** that there are a few Spanish women and Spanish men—not mestizos, quadroons, *criollos,* or mulattos, but Spaniards born in Castile—that there are men and women so holy that there is not enough paper to write about their Christianity, who love the poor Indians well, because they well know how hard they had to work in Castile, where nobody helps them. What a difference from this kingdom! And so, with this, when they see an Indian man or woman fall ill, they feed them with their own hands, with love and charity. What fine alms and charity, what works of mercy! May their smoke rise to heaven and fill the whole heaven with these saintly works, and may the Most Holy Trinity and the Virgin Mary and all the saints and angels receive them, to the welfare of these Christians in this kingdom, the best of Spain. No higher alms and charity can be written: a consideration for going to heaven.

**Consider that in this kingdom** the justices rob the honest poor, something that does not happen in Castile nor in the world. Thus, they arrest a poor Spaniard, mestizo, mulatto, or Indian on account of a single word from his enemy or from some self-interested Spaniard. It happens in this way: say a Spaniard borrowed a bit of cash so that he could gamble, or pay for whores, or eat. So as not to work, he wants to steal. If the poor man does not give him some of his cash, or will not lend it to him, he demands a loan, or he tries to make the poor man serve him or be his servant, or he tries to fornicate with [the poor man's] wife or daughter or sister. Under these pretexts, he draws up testimony [against the poor man], with the advice of the priest and the *corregidor,* and thus the man is arrested, and they take away his paltry possessions and rob him with the help of the notary, and there is no remedy.

Therefore it is very just and proper that, following law and equity, justice should be blind, as she is depicted, and should hold a scale in which she weighs things, and a sword in her right hand with which she cuts and delivers justice. She doesn't look at whether one is rich or poor; instead, she deals justly with all, for justice is God. And so, if one is seen stealing and killing, he should not be allowed to testify and condemn; instead, eyewitnesses should condemn him, and henceforth they should swear an oath on a consecrated altar. If they swear with temerity, they are perjurers and should be condemned. The judge cannot pass sentence on this; rather, his opponent should ask for it, and should take great vengeance. But first, justice must treat the accused with charity and mercy, and must give him a good defense attorney and guardian. And the accuser must accuse him with witnesses; if he accuses him without witnesses, he should be punished and banished and fined. If justice finds that he has no legitimate excuse, he should pay the fines and court costs and damages and losses, and he should take refuge from the civil or criminal court in the church. No one in the world should be allowed to remove him from the sanctuary in this kingdom, according to the law of God and of His Majesty throughout Christendom. Consider this.

**Consider God, Christian judges,** when you have to punish or (even worse) shame a gentleman or an hidalgo, or even a Jew or a black or an Indian, or even an infidel; for our Lord Jesus Christ died to redeem all men, and spilled his blood. Therefore, you must have charity and justice. In your sentences, endeavor to avoid shaming and torturing, hanging, shooting, quartering, and other penalties and punishments, in accordance with law and justice; such sentences must be meted out in keeping with [the prisoner's] age and guilt. The first thing the judge must learn is whether [the prisoner] is a gentleman or a noble, for nobles may not be tormented with any kind of torture, according to law.[338] And he must learn whether [the prisoner] is a child of twelve, or a man of twenty years or more. Torture and death sentences may be imposed [on men] up to the age of fifty—if [a man] is one day past fifty, his hour is past: that makes him an old man. From that age up to seventy, he should not be tortured

---

[338] This was true in regard to Spanish gentlemen (*caballeros*), who were subject to different laws and more lenient penalties than commoners. Guaman Poma's innovation is to put indigenous nobles (*principales*) into the same category as their Spanish counterparts.

nor sentenced to death. And if the accused confessed after being through torture, justice may no longer hang him nor punish him, for he has already gone through his martyrdom. Nor can he be banished to be a galley slave if he is already lame, ill, an old man, or a boy; rather, he should be a slave in the hospitals and monasteries. Also, torture should not go beyond what is called for in law; if the judge and notary let it go beyond that, and if their opponent dies, they should pay the same penalty to make amends: as an example to proud judges, they should be punished.

The same law that applies to gentlemen should likewise apply to women: they should not be given any form of torture, nor imprisoned in jail, but rather [be jailed] in their houses or in the house of a noblewoman.

Yet some judges let themselves be carried away when they hold the staff of justice. Whether the prisoner is guilty or not, they want to ride roughshod and create destruction and scandal, especially among the poor who have no money and find themselves beaten by law and ordinances and justice. Such judges deserve punishment, for they have not feared God and His justice—God, who created them and redeemed them, and who gave them the Ten Commandments. They were proud, and feared not justice nor His Majesty. They were proud like Luzbel, yet Lucifer was punished with all his soldier minions; they should likewise be punished. If the judge does not punish them, God shall punish them in hell, world without end. Consider this, judge.

**You must consider** the great majesty of the Inca Topa Inca Yupanqui, king of Peru, and of Wayna Capac Inca. For, having read in all the histories and chronicles of the world of all the kings, princes, and emperors of the world—the Christians, the Great Turk, the king of China, the emperors of Rome and all of Christendom, and of the Jews, and the kings of Guinea—I have found none with such great majesty. [All the others] were lesser; none have ever had such great majesty or been such great kings with such high crowns as my grandfather, the king Topa Inca Yupanqui, and Wayna Capac—the Incas, whose majesty was extremely great.

Consider: if any king were to see another king or great lord, he would immediately kill him or have him killed, and then would dethrone him and rule alone. Yet the Inca kept four kings, for the four parts of this kingdom. The greatest of them was the *capac apo* himself; he made Waman Chawa of the Allauca Wanoco–Yaro Willca lineage his second-in-command and viceroy. Once he had given them the crown, his sons and grandsons never took it away from them; such was the case with my most honorable great-grandfather. Likewise, the three princes were crowned to accompany and increase the grandeur of His Royal Majesty the Inca, who ordered that he be crowned with the crown of his ancestors. In this way, the Inca king gave himself authority and rose up higher, and because of the majesty of the Inca, no one could talk to him nor communicate with him nor laugh with him, nor could he feast with gentlemen nor with commoners, nor could he ever cry; rather, His Majesty the Inca was always contented. He would eat and drink and offer toasts, [but he did not] toast the common people; instead, he honored the kings who were his ancestors. With this, he expanded his city and his kingdom, and his majesty was greater and greater.

Secondly: no king in any city, town, or countryside, had a throne in the public square like the Inca's.

Thirdly: throughout the kingdom he kept all the roads clean, divided into day's travels, with inns all set up so that they even had dispensaries, and measured league by league and marked along the way.

Fourth: he ate shellfish that were brought to him live from a thousand leagues away, *mullo* from the city of Tumi.[339]

Fifth: he kept the chiefs of the naked *Chuncho* Indians, who eat human flesh, for the memory and the greatness of the world.

Consider the greatness of the Inca king, who, though he was barbarian, was descended in the woman's line from the lady Mama Waco, the *Coya* or queen, [a line] that had governed this kingdom for fifteen hundred years.

Thus, considering that my grandfather, for the greatness of the world, had been the monarch of all the people created by God in the four parts of the world, the monarch should be the king Don Philip III, may God prolong his life, to provide for the government of the world and the defense of our holy Catholic faith in the service of God.[340]

[To serve as his] first [viceroy], I offer one of my sons, a prince of this kingdom, a grandson and great-grandson of Topa Inca Yupanqui, the tenth king, a great wise man who established laws; he should keep the prince in his court for the memory and greatness of the world.

The second [viceroy should be] a prince of the black king of Guinea.

---

[339] *Mullu* is the Spondylus or thorny oyster; in South America, it is found only along the warm Pacific coast of Ecuador, but it was traded far to the south and into the high Andes as a highly valued luxury item and a symbol of royalty. The "city of Tumi" is Tumibamba (Tumi Pampa), which the Spanish conquered and then refounded as Cuenca, Ecuador; it is nearly 1,000 miles from Cusco.

[340] Guaman Poma consistently argues that the king of Spain has inherited the position of Inca ruler. Here he argues that the king should act as an Inca, and reconfigure his empire as a neo-Tawantinsuyu, dividing it into four parts with a subordinate king in each part. His description of how the kings should arrange themselves when they travel together recalls Guaman Poma's drawings of the Inca ruler and the heads of the four *suyu* of Tawantinsuyu. Significantly, he notes the lowered position of Peru in his proposed scheme by placing the "king of the Indies" on the monarch's left hand (the position once occupied by the lord of Collasuyu) rather than on his more honorable right hand.

The third [viceroy should be a prince] of the king of the Christians of Rome or some other kingdom of the world.

The fourth [viceroy should be] the king of the Moors of the Great Turk.

All four shall be crowned, with their scepters and fleece. In the center of these four parts of the world shall be the majesty and monarch of the world, king Don Philip, may God save his high crown. He represents the monarch of the world, and the four kings mentioned represent his lower, equal crowns. Whenever His Majesty, the monarch, goes out on foot, they should all go out on foot; whenever he goes on horseback, they should go on horseback with their mantels: on his right hand, the Christian king; behind him, the Moorish king; on his left hand, the king of the Indies; behind him, the black king of Guinea. In this way, he will represent the monarch of the world, for no king nor emperor could equal this monarch; for the king is the king of his jurisdiction, and the emperor is the emperor of his jurisdiction, but the monarch has no jurisdiction: he holds under his hand the worlds of these crowned kings. They should be salaried employees of his court, for the greatness of the universal world of all nations and kinds of people: the Indians, blacks, Christian Spaniards, Turks, Jews, and Moors of the world. A consideration for the greatness of His Majesty the king.

**Consider that the Indians** were not so barbarous nor fainthearted; rather, they had laws even before the first Inca. Afterwards, they had laws and Inca kings, princes and captains general. And then came the first king, the *capac apo* Manco Capac, who had as his viceroy and second-in-command the *capac apo* Waman Chawa of the Yaro Wilka–Allauca Wanoco lineage, the *incap rantin* [stand-in for the Inca]. He also had an adviser (*Inca rantin rimac*), a council (*tawantinsuyu camachic*), provincial *corregidores* (*tocricoc*), magistrates (*queme quero*), and judges (*runa taripac*). He also had constables (*watacamayoc*), town criers (*llacta camayoc, runa cayaricoc*), executioners (*runa sinac muchochic*), secretaries (*incap quipocnin*), and an accountant (*tawantinsuyu quipoc taripaspa*). The Indians thus had good public policy, laws, ordinances, justice, and sacrifices in this kingdom. Consider.

**Consider that these Indians** are so good, humble, and Christian, that if they did not have the vices of getting drunk on *chicha* and wine, chewing coca, and being as lazy as they are, they would be saints. If all of you in your land were Indians as over here; if you were laden like horses with burdens, and beaten with sticks to make you carry them as if you were beasts of burden; if they called you "horse, dog, pig, bastard, devil"; and if, on top of this, they were to take your wives and daughters and estates, your fields (*chacras*) and farms, with little fear of God or justice—consider these evils!—what would you say, Christians? I think you would eat them alive, and even so you would not be satisfied. And that is what all of you are like, laymen and churchmen alike, except for the reverend padres of St. Francis, the Jesuit padres, the hermit padres, and the holy lay sisters; and that is why I say that they are saints and do not meddle in matters of justice. All the baptized are also saints. You are Old Christians, yet you commit so many evils that if [the Indians] do not eat you alive, it is because they have been so well taught and corrected since the days of their ancestors, raised with a great deal of justice, fearing God and His justice, and fearing His Majesty, their lord and king. That is why they allow evil to be done to them, for if all the Indians were to rise up against you, they would eat you alive. They have been so abused that they would rise up against the Spaniards. So many have died for their sins that even an Indian woman would beat you with sticks in this kingdom. Therefore, fear God and His justice. Consider this.

**Consider that Don Francisco de Toledo,** the viceroy, ordered the depopulation and congregation of the pueblos of this kingdom.[341] Ever since, the Indians of this kingdom have died and have been dying out for the following reasons:

First, because the Indians were separated from pueblos founded in sites and locations selected by their wise nobles—their doctors, licentiates, and philosophers—where the climates and soils and water had been approved by the first Incas so that the people would multiply.

Where there were once ten thousand people—men of soldierly age, not counting women, old men, or children—today there are not ten tributary Indians who could be called *auca camayoc* [warriors, men of fighting age].

The new sites are sometimes set in damp lands that cause pestilence; that is why this has happened. Because of this, illnesses enter, borne in by that air. In some places, the sea air comes in, bearing pestilence and stench. In other places, the cause is the sun or the moon or the planets, which aim their force on those places.

All of these things are causes, as I have said. As for the rest, for the most part the Indians are killed by their drunkenness, by the grape juice, the wine, the *chicha,* and the coca, as well as the quicksilver. Having it in their mouths all day long, they swallow the dust with their coca, and thus their hearts are stopped by this dust and the coca, and they die, poisoned by quicksilver. As I have said, in the time of the Incas there was no drunkenness. The coming of Don Francisco to this kingdom has done great damage to the Indians. Consider.

**You should consider** that Don Francisco de Toledo, the viceroy, ordered one good thing in his ordinances, a good work of compassion in the service of God our Lord and of His Majesty: that the Indians should not have to

---

[341] Congregation: see footnote p. 207 on the infamous *reducciones* of Indian pueblos.

bear the tribute that they owe out of their pueblos, but should leave it there, and that the *encomenderos* should convey the spices, food, and other tributary items at their own expense.

Therefore, the local magistrate should have the tribute collected—the cash, corn, potatoes, wheat, chickens, sheep, and clothing that are due every six months, on Christmas and Midsummer Day. For this purpose, he should have a warehouse with a key and a strongbox for the cash and spices that are taxed; elsewhere, the magistrate should collect the tax from the Indians at the expense of the *corregidor,* the noble *cacique,* and the noble's second-in-command (that is, the *curaca* and the *camachicoc*) whose subjects they are.

Then, a week after Midsummer Day or Christmas, in each pueblo without exception, the *corregidor,* his notary or secretary, or some noble *cacique* who has some skill and knows how to read and write, should collect the taxes and distribute them to each salaried person: first, to the noble *cacique* and his second-in-command, and to the rest who earn salaries; then to the *doctrina* padre; then to the *encomendero;* then to the *corregidor.* Each of these people should carry [his share] from each pueblo without being given Indians to carry it, nor employing any Indians; they should carry them with mule trains and blacks, without demanding *mitayos* or *camaricos.* The warehouse and the Indian who guards it should be hired in the pueblo, day and night; the magistrate should pay them directly into their hands from the same taxes: one real each, for the house and for the Indian. The one who keeps watch over the cattle that are collected as tax should be paid one real, even if there is just one llama; and the one who keeps watch over the chickens should be paid another real.

If the noble *cacique,* the *corregidor,* the padre, and the *encomendero* do not carry off their portions, they should pay the Indian guard and the warehouse a prorated amount. And if they are not quick to do so, after the week of Midsummer Day or Christmas the *corregidor* must pay everything, because it is his responsibility and his own fault, for that is what His Majesty pays him to do. If anyone should use Indians to convey their tribute out of the pueblos or elsewhere, they should be fined, and the tribute should be taken from them and handed over to His Majesty, throughout this kingdom. Consider.

**Consider that Don Francisco de Toledo,** the viceroy, gave one order that was a very saintly thing, in the service of God and of His Majesty. It was an order that the Incas' council had enacted as law in this kingdom, one which Don Francisco de Toledo wished to have as well. Thus, he wanted the great Indian lords and nobles to be his subjects, to recognize the majesty of the king, and to be obedient and subject to the royal crown, so that the land and the great lords would not rise in rebellion.

◆ There was one great lord who, because he was so fat, refused to join in; he asked for permission to be excused, and this *capac apo,* Cullic Chawa, was always given leave. They say that this lord would eat every kind of food in a single meal—half a *hanega* of bread, meat, spices, and fruit—and that he would drink with the sun. He would fill a gigantic earthen jar for the sun, and then he would drink one *mate* while the sun drank the other from the jar. Since Cullic Chawa was such a big lord, he rose up against the royal crown of the Inca, together with *capac apo* Wari Callo from Hatun Colla. But [after they were defeated,] they were made into drums, so that their bellies were beaten like drums; these were called the *runa tinya* [people drums].

This is why [all colonial officials] should be subject to the royal crown of His Majesty the King Don Philip, may God grant him long life and give him more dominions and kingdoms. Thus, Don Francisco de Toledo ordered the citizens of each city—the *encomenderos* of Indians—to gather every month in the court in the city of Los Reyes de Lima, for the service of God and of His Majesty. Every two months, the citizen *encomenderos* of Indians should come to stay, all the way from the city of Nuevo Reino [de Bogotá] down to the city of Charca, including the whole kingdom of this Peru and its districts, the Eastern and Western Indies. Nor should they send their brothers or some hired hand; instead, they themselves must go in person, so that they may offer themselves to the service of God and of His Majesty's crown. They should appear in the city of Los Reyes de Lima, as has been stated, in the royal court and His Majesty's council, and should not send a judge there at the citizen's expense to spend a few days drawing a salary. In this way, the *encomenderos* will be made subjects and obedient throughout this kingdom of Peru. Consider obedience.

**Consider the Indians** who serve in the quicksilver, silver, and gold mines, and the Indians who serve in the plazas. The poor Indians should not go to work in those mines without being allowed to hear Mass and keep the great holidays and feast days of the year, as set by the Holy Mother Church in Rome, which are the greatest days of the year: the Birth of the Lord, Ash Wednesday, Palm Sunday, Holy Thursday, Easter of the Resurrection of the Lord, and Corpus Christi. They are forced to miss Mass on these days, and cannot even keep the holidays unless they do it on the road. It could not matter much to these Indians if they have to serve one or two weeks longer because they hear Mass and celebrate Easter and the holidays of God in the world. Thus, if the *corregidor,* padre, or noble *caciques* do not order this, they should be excommunicated and fined by the Holy Mother Church in this kingdom. Consider, Christian, this service of God in the world.

**You should consider** that the inspectors of the Holy Mother Church act as if they are bishops. They inspect the bad priests of the *doctrinas* and take bribes of two thousand pesos, and then they declare that they are free and have no fines to pay; that they are good priests—even though they have robbed, and have a dozen children, and have taken all the Indians' young women, and many other such harmful things. And there is no remedy. The cause of all this is that the inspector calls himself the proprietor and another bishop, just as the *doctrina* padre does. Therefore, there should be interim priests, and they should have to put up bonds, even if they are only to be in the *doctrina* for one day. Likewise, the inspector should give a guaranteed bond so that his inspection shall be straight and he might judge properly. Consider, judge.

**Consideration by the author.** Truly it is well to consider and believe, as a faithful and Catholic Christian, that God has everything. First: charity, love, and justice. He gives health to the spirit and the body, food and riches. The three persons are one true God, all of the same weight, all equal. He made heaven, first, for those who are good; the world, to multiply; and hell, to punish the wicked. Thus, he punished Luzbel, who had been such a great and beautiful angel, together with all his minions; and the wicked angels fell from heaven, like the sands of the sea and many more, according to the guilt they deserved. The first ones entered hell with their prince of darkness, to receive the worst punishments. Others stayed behind in the world, among men, to hinder our journey to heaven and trick us into sin; still others remained in the air, becoming imps.

After this, you should consider that God made the first man and woman, and brought their souls from heaven, and infused them with [their souls], making them the emperors and rulers of the world.

Consider that this first man had so much majesty that the sun, the moon, and the stars served him; and on earth, the wind, water, fish, animals, and fruit trees. Only one tree was he given that he was commanded not to eat; it was given to him so that he might be obedient to God who created him. He broke this commandment, given by God, and so he was deprived, removed from that paradise, and banished to this vale of tears, where we, his children, suffer toil and will continue to suffer until Judgment Day, when God will command something else.

Then consider those men of the world who did not know God, and who committed so many sins that they could not all be written down. Because of their guilt, God punished [the world] with the waters of the flood, and covered [it], and all the people in the world died. And consider how great his wrath was then, the lashings that God gave the sinners, to make it rain forty days and forty nights, on everyone the same. View the greatness of God, who willed that Noah should escape with his six married sons and all the married animals: in that ark, they were saved.

Consider the fury and bellowing and fright and noise, such that it seemed the sky and the world were mixing together when that water and wind joined; that the land was being cut off and turning into sea; and God was giving the commandment not to come out.

And consider that land, that world: robbed, laid waste, and so very hurt.

Consider, after this, how the people multiplied, became gentiles, and worshipped idols; how holy prophets and patriarchs came from the people of Israel, the descendents of Noah; and how, because of the hue and cry raised by those holy prophets, there came Jesus Christ, God and true man.

And you must consider how he labored thirty-three years, and was martyred and died crucified, and was resurrected and rose to heaven, and sent the Holy Spirit to the holy apostles, who later spread throughout the world to preach the faith and gospel of Jesus Christ: whosoever shall be baptized and believe shall be saved.

And you must consider this: on Judgment Day, God will come in majesty for the welfare of the good, humble, poor little tame lambs. For them, heaven; and as for the proud and wicked rich men who are fond of gold, silver, and riches, he will sentence them to unending punishment, according to their works and their pride. They will be banished to hell and punished until world without end.

You must also consider the poor Indians, whom the Spaniards have persecuted so—not all the Spaniards, but some of them, including priests and *corregidores* and *encomenderos*. Consider that they not only persecute the Indians, but indeed that they steal their wives and daughters and estates and inheritances, their houses and *chacras* [fields]. In this way you will be able to say why they do not multiply. Consider: the Indians do not multiply in this kingdom.

Consider this: the *corregidor* comes in saying, "I will do justice for you," and he robs. Then the padre enters: "I will make you a Christian; I will baptize and marry and teach you," and he robs and extorts and steals wife and daughter. The *encomendero* and the other Spaniards say: "Justice! Serve the king, because I am his vassal," and he robs and steals everything one has. The noble *caciques* and petty authorities are even worse; they utterly skin the poor unfortunate Indians. But you poor Spaniards are more unfortunate! For you are at such great risk when you die. You came across the sea from Castile to our land to steal from us and to take away our poor possessions.

You must also consider that, when the ambassador of the emperor-king came, the legitimate ruler Wascar Inca immediately offered his peace and friendship. For my grandfather's part, this same Wascar Inca sent his second-in-command, *capac apo* Guaman Mallqui de Ayala, the viceroy of this kingdom, to make peace in the port of Tumbes, where Don Francisco Pizarro and Don Diego de Almagro disembarked. Since that time, my family has never rebelled against the service of His Majesty.

Consider, too, how the Indians of the province of Chile defend their land and their kingdom, and the Christians have not been able to win it, nor will they be able to win it, seeing how much the Indians trouble them.

When all this is considered by His Majesty, he should stand up for the noble *caciques* and the poor Indians of this kingdom. There is no one who can better stand up for them, because he has the best rights by law, and there is no one else but the king who might do this.

You should consider that the ambassadors who were sent by the king tried, out of sheer greed, to rise up in rebellion, and indeed they did rise up to usurp the land, trying to be new Inca kings.

You should consider how they tried to rise up. They came with the express permission of the most holy father, the pope in Rome, and that of the glorious, most Christian emperor Don Carlos. They brought no warrant for killing the Inca king and the most excellent lords and captains of this kingdom. To rise up and usurp the land, first they killed; after they had done that, they rose up to usurp the land and the crown of His Majesty: Don Francisco Pizarro, Don Diego Almagro, Gonzalo Pizarro, Carvajal, and Francisco Hernández Girón. The emperor-king defended himself, spending and toiling to defend himself.

Thus you must consider and put an end to this. For there are no *encomenderos* nor lords of this land other than us, the legitimate owners of the land by the rights of God and by justice and its laws. With the exception of the king, there is no other Spaniard who has the right: all are foreigners *(mitmacs)* in our land, and they are under our command and lordship, which was given to us by God. Consider, Christian.

## PROLOGUE TO THE READER OF "THE CONSIDERATIONS"

YOU MUST CONSIDER, Christian reader, all the chapters of "Considerations."

Look closely within your soul and heart. One captain general of a conquest force composed of more than a thousand soldiers, put together at the expense of the king, has conquered and wreaked great destruction in the service of the king, and the king has heard of this conquest. With great solemnity and festivity, he greets this brave captain general; but not yet, for he wants to see him and grant him favors. His whole pueblo and his wife and children and relatives relate his story to everyone who does not know it. Everyone claims him as a relative and close kin; when he arrives, they receive him with great solemnity and festivity, and invite him and honor him and freely grant him everything he asks; and he deserves it all.

Likewise, the bad captain who has lost this victory and conquest force, and has lost a great number of soldiers because of his laziness or negligence, or out of carelessness, or because he was fainthearted, or because he was careless or slept too much: this captain weeps; he does not want to appear in front of the king; he does not even open his door to him. Thus his wife, father, brothers, and relatives deny him and say that he is not their relative and that they do not know him. He no longer enters his city; he always goes about in hiding. He is denied by the land, by the world.

You should see and consider Christians in the same way. Imagine how such a Christian will appear before the eyes of God, the Virgin Mary, and the saints in heaven; and on earth, in the eyes of the king and his prelates and relatives. The world will deny him, curse him. It will not rejoice; the devil will rejoice. Yet God and king, prelates and Christians will rejoice in the good Christian, who will speak freely with the great and will run without fear through the world.

You must consider this, and restrain yourselves with all these chapters, you Christians in this kingdom: governors, justices, *corregidores,* padres, *encomenderos,* Spaniards, and inspectors.

## HIS MAJESTY QUESTIONS, THE AUTHOR REPLIES

*selected from 974–99*

*[This chapter might be considered an exercise in wishful thinking. Unable to reach the ears of high colonial officials in person, Guaman Poma uses his imagination and his pen to go over their heads, fancifully restoring himself to his grandfather's alleged post as the "second-in-command of the Inca" and engaging in a lengthy direct dialogue with the king of Spain. The primary subject of their imagined dialogue is how to save the Indians of Peru from destruction.]*

HIS ROYAL CATHOLIC MAJESTY questions the author Ayala to learn everything there is to know about the kingdom of the Indies of Peru, for good government and justice, for remedying troubles and misfortunes, for the poor Indians of the kingdom to multiply, and for the reform and good example of the Spaniards, *corregidores,* justices, *doctrina* padres, *encomenderos,* noble *caciques,* and petty authorities.

Hearing His Majesty's questions, the author replies and speaks with His Majesty, saying:

"Your Royal Catholic Majesty, you should listen closely to me. When I have finished, please ask me questions. I am delighted to give you my report on everything in the kingdom, for the memory of the world and Your Majesty's greatness."

Your Royal Catholic Majesty, I will communicate with Your Majesty regarding the service of God our Lord and regarding the service to your royal crown and the increase and welfare of the Indians of this kingdom, because

# KING DON PHILIP III, MONARCH OF THE WORLD.

Ayala, the
author

*The author personally presents the* Chronicle *to His Majesty.*

some people report lies to you, others report the truth, and others give their reports in order to get Your Majesty to grant them a position as bishop, dean, canon, president, *Audiencia* judge, or some other rank and post.

I, as the grandson of the king of Peru, would like to serve Your Majesty; to meet with you face to face; to speak and communicate about these things in your presence. But I cannot travel so far, being eighty years old and infirm.[342] I hope you will be pleased with my thirty years of working in poverty, leaving my house, children, and estates to serve Your Majesty. Therefore, we will meet through writing and sending letters. So, Your Majesty, please ask me questions, and I will reply to them in this way.

His Majesty asks: "Don Felipe, author Ayala, tell me how the Indians of this kingdom had multiplied even before there was an Inca."

I say to Your Majesty that, in those times, there were a king and nobles. [The people] peacefully served the king, mining gold and silver, serving in fields and pastures, and upholding fortresses. Even a little pueblo had many women; the smallest one would have a thousand soldiers. Others had fifty thousand to a hundred thousand. Therefore, they had warfare and fortresses among them.

"**Tell me, Don Felipe Ayala,** about those times: how could there have been so many Indians in the time of the Incas?"

I say to Your Majesty that, in those times, the Inca alone was king, though there were also dukes, counts, marquises, and great noble lords. But they lived under the laws and commandments of the Incas, and, because they had a king, they peacefully served in this kingdom; they multiplied, and had estates, plenty to eat, and their own children and wives.

"**Tell me, author, why** do the Indians not multiply now? Why are they becoming poor?"

I will say to Your Majesty, first, that they do not multiply because all the best women and maidens are taken by the *doctrina* padres, *encomenderos, corregidores,* Spaniards, stewards, deputies, and officers, and their servants. That is why there are so many little mestizos and mestizas in this kingdom. They claim that the women have lovers as a pretext for taking them and their estates from the poor. Because of all these things, all these offenses and harms, the Indians hang themselves, as the *Changas* did in Andahuayllas—that was a small mountain range, once filled with Indian men and women; they prefered to die once and for all rather than face all the harm that was being done to them.

"**Tell me, author, how will** the people multiply?"

---

[342] Guaman Poma seems to use the number eighty as a metaphor for old age. Internal references hint that he was born in the early 1550s, making him around sixty-five years old when he wrote these lines in 1615.

I say to Your Majesty, just as I have written: the padres, priests, *encomenderos, corregidores,* other Spaniards, and noble *caciques* should live as Christians, as Your Majesty has ordained, and not go beyond that. They should let [the people] enjoy their wives and estates, and should leave their maidens alone. There should not be so many kings and justices over the people, and they should let the people multiply, or else be severely punished and removed from their offices and benefices.

**"Tell me, author, how will** the Indians become rich?"

Your Majesty should know that they should keep community estates (which they call *sapsi*), with fields planted with corn, wheat, potatoes, peppers, *macno,* cotton, and grapes, [as well as] textile workshops, dyeworks, coca fields, and fruit orchards. The maidens and widows should spin and weave—ten women working on one piece of cloth. On one portion of the community land (*sapsi*), they should keep Castilian cattle. Each Indian man and woman should have a piece of an estate from their community land (*sapsi*).

Overseeing this, in every province there should be an administrator with a salary set at one seventh [of the income from the community lands]—one main overseer for each province. Whenever there is need, Your Majesty would be able to borrow money and take your royal fifth from the commoners.

With this, the Indians of this kingdom will become rich people; God and Your Majesty's royal crown will be served in this kingdom; and the Indians will increase in this kingdom.

**"Tell me, author: how can** the absent Indians in that kingdom be gathered in?"

I say to Your Majesty that, in every province, these Indian men, women, and children should be gathered into some old pueblo, for they are lost. Give them cropland and bounded pastures, so that they may serve God and Your Majesty. Let them be called your royal crown Indians, and let them pay taxes and tribute, and hold no other office. Their administrator, the noble *cacique,* should be subject to you. No one but the administrator should take a salary from what they pay, in keeping with the Indians' wishes; the rest [of their taxes] should be applied to the service of your royal crown. In this way, [the absent Indians] will be gathered in throughout the kingdom. It should be the administrator's office to gather them.[343]

YOUR ROYAL CATHOLIC MAJESTY. AS YOU MUST KNOW, the dozen learned men and the four notaries of the world[344] set forth, in their council,

---

[343] The following paragraphs on priests are late additions to the manuscript.

[344] That is, the twelve apostles and four evangelists of the Christian Gospels.

an order and a law for the world: that there should be no slaves or tribute for priests, and that no tribute should be paid to priests or to any other such person in the world. Therefore, the *doctrina* padres and priests may not take a salary from the tribute; instead, they must make their living by working at the altar. A priest can make two thousand pesos a year, or one thousand pesos at the very least, from celebrating Mass, offerings, and prayers for the dead, and from gifts, Christmas bonuses, and alms. That would easily provide a man with plenty to be able to dress and eat. But collecting tribute, and calling himself "proprietor," IS NULL AND VOID by the laws of God and the holy Church. He should live from the tithes and the first-fruits paid by the Spanish.

"TELL ME, AUTHOR, how do you expect the priests not to receive a salary?"

I SAY TO YOUR ROYAL CATHOLIC MAJESTY: the first priest in the world was God and living man, Jesus Christ, the priest who came from heaven as a poor man, and who loved the poor more than being rich. Jesus Christ was the living God, who came to bring souls, not silver, back with him from the world. He demanded no tribute, nor did he permit any. Jesus Christ himself left in his place in the world the first priest and general deputy of the Holy Mother Church, St. Peter, and the other apostles and saints. They preferred abject poverty to treasure. They left everything to the poor, searched for Jesus Christ, and saved the souls in heaven. They were all poor, and they demanded no salaries or wages, nor did they seek for treasure or food to eat. They lived from the alms they received, whether many or few, and whatever they had left over they gave to the poor. This was how they spent their lives, by the grace of God and the enlightenment of the Holy Spirit.

From these holy apostles of Jesus Christ there emerged the saints, martyrs, virgins, and confessors; they emerged into the world, and they demanded no tribute or salary at all. They conquered the world with alms. Here, Your Royal Catholic Majesty, you may see the law that God left in the world.

THEREFORE, YOUR MAJESTY should ordain that everything the Indians give should be dedicated to the defense of the Holy Mother Church. Any *doctrina* priest can do well without collecting tribute, being a proprietor, or meddling in matters of justice instead of spending all his time in prayers, humility, and alms. Without hoarding wealth, the hosts of St. Peter may win the world and conquer it for heaven, while the orders of friars stay in their friaries with their vows of religion.

And if they do not like it, Your Majesty may communicate with His Holiness the Pope so that the Indians can enter into studies, the priestly order, proprietorship, and the public order of Christianity.[345] They will take no salaries, being Your Majesty's natives and Indians. Your Majesty will enjoy it all for the defense of the holy Catholic faith of our Christianity, throughout the kingdom of the East and West Indies of this New World, for the service of God and your royal crown.[346]

**"Tell me, author,** how will it be possible for the Indians of that kingdom not to die, become ill from quicksilver poisoning, or suffer hard labor?"

Regarding this, I say to Your Majesty: first, they are greatly harmed by the mine owners and the justices who enter with them. They hang them by their feet, and they whip them while they are hanging with their shameful parts exposed. They force them to work day and night and do not pay them. When they do pay them, they give them only half their wages and steal the other half. They send them out to the low plains, where they die. Of every eleven Indians, only one gets out alive.

What they should do is draw lots. One province should be given six months to rest while the next province comes in.

Also, Your Majesty should order that a grant be given to any Indian, black, or Spaniard who discovers how to cure quicksilver poisoning and heal the ill; let him be paid. In this way, the poor Indians will multiply and will not begrudge the labor.

"Tell me, author, how will the hidden mines of that kingdom be discovered?"

I say to Your Majesty that, as soon as mines are discovered—mines of gold, silver, quicksilver, lead, tin, copper, dyes—as soon as they are discovered, the Spaniards immediately meddle, take them over, and mistreat the Indians. That is why the Indians do not want to report to the mines. If Your Majesty would arrange to grant the mining rights to the discoverer, all the good mines would be discovered, the kingdom would become very rich, and Your Majesty would be very rich—richer than all other kings. Your Majesty will be the greatest monarch in the world; if you carry out what is started here, Your Majesty will be very rich, as will your royal crown. Because of all this, you may enjoy the kingship over all the world, in service to God and your royal crown.

**Your Royal Catholic Majesty,** I tell you that in this kingdom the Indians are coming to an end, and they will come utterly to an end. Twenty years from now, there will be no Indians in this kingdom to serve your royal crown and defend our holy Catholic faith. Without the Indians,

---

[345] Indians were generally excluded from ordination as priests under the colonial regime.
[346] This is the end of the added section on priests. An even later addition on the bottom margin of this page, with remarks on salaried royal judges and lawyers, is only partly legible.

Your Majesty is worth nothing, because, remember, Castile is Castile because of the Indians. His Serenity the emperor-king (may God keep him in heaven) was powerful because of the Indians of this kingdom. Your Majesty's father was also a monarch of great power and renowned strength because of the Indians of this kingdom. The same is true of Your Majesty.

Your Majesty should consider the idea of losing so valuable a kingdom, one which has been so valuable—losing it and seeing the end of all the Indians, for they are already being depopulated. Where there were once a thousand souls, now there are not even one hundred, and all of them are old men and women who can no longer multiply. Even if there are a few unmarried men, they marry old women who cannot give birth. Besides this, they are oppressed with great troubles, disturbed, and robbed. Even their daughters, sons, and married women are being stolen. And there is no remedy, because everyone has joined together—the judges, *corregidores,* deputies, *encomenderos,* stewards, other Spaniards and mestizos, inspectors of the Holy Mother Church, vicars, priests. All work together against the poor; all have joined hands to favor the Spanish Dons and the lady Doñas. They take advantage of all the poor; not only that, but they enter into their possessions, estates, lands, pastures, and houses, by force and against their will.

Writing this is enough to make one cry. None of them report these things to Your Majesty. I will say the truth regarding the value, price, benefits, income, and services that the Indians have had and should have, and which they are losing and will lose throughout the kingdom. Your Majesty should know that you are being served by the Indians when, every six months— twice a year—they pay silver, corn, wheat, clothes, chickens, pullets, local cattle, and other products. In addition, they serve in the mines, the plazas, and the *tambos* (royal inns). They also fix the bridges in your kingdom, and clean the roads and byways. It is from them that the royal fifth, the tithe, the personal tax, and the excise tax are paid, because Your Majesty does not get as much benefit at all from the mestizos, mulattos, or even the Spaniards. Therefore, I place their worth at a very estimable value.

Take care that this kingdom should not lose these Indians, because, if a Spaniard steals and keeps four Indian women to give birth to his little mestizos, he will refuse to recognize them before the bribed judges; nor is there any point, because [Spaniards] have so many [mestizo children] and so many women. This is, first, because the Spaniards look for women in their houses and scattered settlements. They do not leave them alone, day or night. If the women's fathers and mothers defend them, they are mistreated. The Spaniards go to seek them out where they hold their fiestas. They do not allow them to get married or to lead a married life with their husbands. Married Indian women do not have children by their husbands; instead, they give birth to little mestizo children, and then refuse to recognize them. The mestizo children wander around dressed like poor Indians. The whole kingdom is like this.

As soon as an Indian woman appears who has given birth by a poor Indian man, everyone comes down on her right away—the inspector, the vicar, the priest, the *corregidor,* the deputy, the *encomendero.* They punish her, fine her, and banish her to the house of some lady or to the padre's kitchen. There they fornicate with her right away, and she soon gives birth to a mestizo. No one is upset about this. Thus, they prefer to have her living in sin and giving birth to mestizos.

Then they go out to search for more Indian women, since they look on them so favorably, as I have said. When one gives birth to an Indian man's son, they are all thrown into an uproar—it seems like the sky is falling. They punish the mothers and fathers in the public stocks, and they shear the mother's hair. Telling these stories and writing them is an endless task.

"Tell me, author Ayala. You have told me many rueful stories and described how the Indians are coming to an end: they are suffering troubles and cannot multiply because people come in and steal their wives, daughters, and their property in houses and land, utterly skinning them. I do not send my judges to do harm and damage and to rob, but rather to honor the nobles, *caciques,* petty authorities, and the poor Indians, that they might increase and multiply in the service of God and the defense of the holy Catholic faith and in service of my royal crown. Tell me now, author Ayala, how can these things be remedied?"

I say to Your Majesty that all the Spaniards should live like Christians. They should endeavor to marry ladies of equal station, and should leave the poor Indian women to multiply. They should leave their property—their lands and houses—alone; they should return those that they have entered by force, and should pay for the use that they have enjoyed of them. The penalties for these things should be enforced.

Next, whoever deflowers a virgin Indian, makes a married Indian woman give birth, or forces her to fornicate, should be banished for six years to the galleys or to Chile, and all his possessions should be taken as a fine for your royal treasuries and to pay the Indian woman and court expenses. If the judge does not execute this sentence, he deserves the same punishment. All these things should be carried out, and no justice should be against the poor Indians. Those who are not justices—the *doctrina* padres, *encomenderos,* and other Spaniards—should not pretend to be justices. Whoever does so should be well punished, fined, and banished from among the Indians of this kingdom. In this way, the Indians will multiply.

**Your Royal Catholic Majesty,** about the community lands (*sapsi*) of the Indians and the churches, religious brotherhoods, and hospitals: so that these may multiply and increase in this kingdom, it would be beneficial that [the Indians] be asked to give an accounting to [me, as] the second-in-command of the Inca and Your Majesty in this kingdom. They should come give [me] an accounting every sixth month of the year, paying me a salary of one-seventh throughout the kingdom, so that I will be able to lend myself to the service of God and your royal crown, should the need arise, and collect the royal fifth. In this, I will serve God, Your Majesty, the well-being of the Indians of this kingdom, and the increase of wealth.

**Your Royal Catholic Majesty** should request that each noble *cacique,* second-in-command, and petty authority in this kingdom come here to receive their testimonies, so that I may give testimony of what they each deserve; for, as the second-in-command of the Inca and of Your Majesty, I know all about them, their ways and manners. I and my descendents must give these testimonies to you, according to the law, signed in my name in perpetuity. In this way, no one will make himself a *curaca* by force, or take the title of Don or Doña in this kingdom, or wear Spaniards' clothes. They will have to be well-proven, loyal, and Christian, eager to serve God and Your Majesty; and they will favor the poor. Only then will Your Majesty give them titles, throughout the kingdom.

**Your Royal Catholic Majesty,** if one Indian pueblo multiplies while another pueblo wanes or all its Indians die, or only a few are left—for I have seen many pueblos become solitary and empty, such as the pueblos of Uchucmarca and Uruysa;[347] in Uchucmarca there were once twelve thousand soldiers of war, and in Uruysa there were eight thousand soldiers, but neither of them now contains more than fifteen soldiers of tributary age—then it is appropriate for Your Majesty, as the Inca king, to order that title and possession [to the dying pueblo] be given to the other pueblo, so that they might concentrate and settle. [The people of the thriving pueblo] should be given the croplands, pastures, jurisdiction, and property that [the dying pueblo] once held, so that they might possess it. The Indians who multiply in this kingdom should have this grant of titles and lands, in order to serve God and Your Majesty.

**Your Royal Catholic Majesty:** the absent Indians who did not go to the mines or the plazas of this kingdom, whichever each of them was assigned to, should have their names entered on a list. In the name of Your Majesty, they should be sought and brought back. An order should be given to the noble *cacique* [of each province] to bring them back from wherever they have gone in this kingdom. A Spaniard, mestizo, or mulatto should search for them, with costs paid at a salary of one peso per Indian, and they should be brought back in fetters on a packsaddled horse. The Indian

---

[347] In the southeastern corner of Lucanas province, near Tambo Quemado.

should then be handed over, together with his wife and children, to the justice of the mines or plazas.

The Indian should labor as a prisoner, with iron shackles, imprisoned. The constable should be paid the coins for his day labor, and the runaway Indian should be fed at his own expense, and should work until he pays off the cost of his food, his imprisonment, and the king's constable. From this money he should also pay the tribute he owes. This constable should also be fed in the *tambos* and pueblos of this kingdom at no cost or charge, and he should help the *caciques, alcaldes, corregidores,* and priests, for that is in service of God and His Majesty. The constable should also be given a horse at no charge in this kingdom. After [his punishment] is complete, the runaway Indian should be handed over to the noble *cacique,* who will bring him to his own pueblo in this kingdom.

**Your Royal Catholic Majesty:** I will say, with regard to gathering in the absent Indians, that they are of three types. The first are the vagabond runaways; then there are the outsiders; and then there are the orphans.

The first—the vagabond runaways—are the ones who call themselves *quita suwa, puma ranra, chuqui aquilla* [runaway thieves, highwaymen, gang leaders]. They are called vagabonds because they leave their pueblos to be thieves, highwaymen, gamblers, drunks, idlers, coca-eaters, and *quilla wanana* [lazy rebels].

The second are the absent ones—those who have been persecuted with harsh labor and occupations, and who have been offended in their persons and in their wives and children by the *corregidores,* padres, *encomenderos,* and noble *caciques* of these kingdoms. They are called *chicnisca runa, llactamanta carcosca runa, waycasca runa, ima hayca* hacienda-*nta quichusca runa, tunpasca runa, waccha mana yanapacniyoc runa, llactapi cac ancha waccha* [despised people, people expelled from their village, robbed people, people whose estates and possessions have all been stolen, accused people, poor people who have no one to help them, the most orphan-poor in their villages].

The third—Indian orphan boys and girls—are taken from their pueblos to be servant boys and *chinaconas* (maids) for the *corregidores,* padres, *encomenderos,* notaries, deputies, and stewards, who give them as presents to their relatives. They take them by force to the cities, where they abuse and punish them like their black slaves. They cruelly punish and give a bad life to these orphans. Therefore, it is their power that makes these Indian orphans go absent; it is to keep from being so badly harmed that they never return to their pueblos and concentrated settlements. Instead, the orphans go to other cities, where they remain as *yanaconas* and *chinaconas* in this kingdom. These people are called *waccha, lurucha, mana yayayoc mana mamayoc, misqui wicsa, hillo suwa, quilla* muchacho, *mana llamcacoc* muchacho, *quita* muchacho, *quita wausa, chinacona* [orphan-poor, little fruit, fatherless and motherless, sweet bellies, candy thieves, lazy boys, boys who don't work, runaway boys, runaway buggers, *chinaconas*]. These are the things they call each other.

So that they might be gathered into their pueblos and the pueblos be filled with Indians and multiply, Your Majesty should order, first, that the *corregidores* be removed from office and the *doctrina* padres and priests be punished if they commit a single wrong. Remove them from their parishes and do not give them another *doctrina*. They should have to post a bond, and they should be interim priests, not proprietors: this will provide a remedy. Also, *encomenderos* should never be allowed to enter the Indian pueblos. This should be carried out and followed as strictly as any royal decree issued by your royal authorities, the viceroys, the *Audiencia,* or the Holy Council.

The noble *caciques* should be descendants of the great lords of this kingdom, as they have been since the times of *Wari Wiracocha Runa, Wari Runa, Purun Runa, Auca Runa,* and *Incap Runa.* As has been said, they should not be drunks, coca-chewers, or gamblers, and they should be good Christians. Then the absent Indians of this kingdom will be gathered in; they will live tranquilly, be Christians, and multiply, in accordance with Christianity and the service of God and His Majesty.[348]

**Your Royal Catholic Majesty** should know that the Indians should be allowed to rest from the quicksilver mines for a year, while the mines should not rest, to serve Your Majesty.

"But tell me, author, how can the Indians rest while the mines keep working?"

I say to Your Majesty that the Indians who serve in the plazas of [Spanish] cities should trade places; they should go to the mines for one year, while the others go to the plazas and take a rest from the mines. This is because the ones who go to the plaza are not in any risk; therefore, they should go to the mines and work hard. I will say more to Your Majesty: whoever loses all his Indian vassals, loses everything.

"Well, author, tell me what you mean by this declaration."

I say to Your Majesty that the Indians bring Your Majesty his income. I am a prince. I know that, if they come to an end, the land will be left desolate

---

[348] In a late addition on the bottom margins of ms. pp. 987–88, Guaman Poma adds: "Your Royal Catholic Majesty: it is proper and beneficial that the *corregidores* of Indian provinces should be removed, that their salaries be applied to the defense of Your Majesty's royal crown, that a noble *cacique* be selected as provincial *corregidor* each year, and that they be audited, throughout the kingdom. This will bring help and service to your royal crown, and will let the Indians of your kingdom find relief and multiply, because the *corregidores* and interim priests bring no benefit each year; for the well-being of the natives throughout your kingdom."

and solitary. Therefore, Your Majesty should order, under strict penalties, that the nobles and Indians should not be abused, and that no Indian boy under the age of twenty should be sent into the gallery of any quicksilver, silver, or gold mine, nor to smelt ore or work in the quicksilver ovens, because they are tender of age, mere boys. They quickly come down with quicksilver poisoning, and there is no way to heal them; they die, and the Indians come to an end.

"Tell me, author, how to remedy this."

Your Majesty must know that those who enter the galleries should be strong, full-grown Indians who are able to look out for themselves. Also, each Indian should go into the mine for one day, no more. Then another Indian will enter. In this way, they will not contract the illness, and will not die. To carry this out, it would be best that all the Indians who go to serve in the mines be freed for one month from personal service, and that they commend their souls to God, St. Mary, and all the saints and angels. They should rejoice and sing their songs (*taquíes*) with their wives, children, and relatives, because any one of these Indians may die, as so many have died— he may drown or be made cripple or lame, and never see his wife or children again. Therefore, they should confess, take communion, and draw up their wills.

The other Indians should all rejoice in their houses throughout this kingdom. The *corregidor,* padre, and *alcaldes* should leave them alone, because they use [these celebrations] as an excuse to take away everything the poor people own and to skin them. If an Indian man or woman should become a loud drunk, in the morning the justices should give him [or her] fifty lashes for drunkenness—that is, if he has quarreled with his wife or with another Indian. Thus, the padre, *corregidor,* and *alcaldes* are forbidden to go to their houses to search for them, as is stated in the ordinances of Don Francisco de Toledo.

Likewise, Your Majesty should decree that stores of food and water be kept in the mine galleries throughout this kingdom. Then, if [the miners] become caught inside, they may have the help of God, food, and water, so that they can work day and night to clear the mountain and make an opening. In this way those who are trapped in mines may be saved in this kingdom.

**Your Royal Catholic Majesty:** in order that all the Indians of this kingdom might multiply and not go absent, and that they might have many children in the service of God and your royal crown, it is beneficial and essential, first, that the *doctrina* padres all be made interim priests. Second, they should all post bonds, even if they are only to stay in a *doctrina* for one day, because the priests are utterly destroying this kingdom, taking away [the Indians'] estates, wives, and daughters, and fornicating with them all, deflowering girls as young as ten. In order to do this, they raise them in their kitchens, under the pretext of teaching them doctrine. In addition, both the padres and the *corregidores* force them to work and harass them, and for these reasons they go absent.

"Well, tell me, author: don't I send bishops to every city so that they can defend them, do justice, and send out their inspectors to punish [priests who do wrong] and throw them out of their *doctrinas?* Why don't you go there, or send someone, or write a note to the vicar general and the *corregidor* of your province?"

I say to Your Majesty, so that the truth will be known: Your Majesty sends out judges, justices, prelates, bishops, canons, and deans to favor the noble lords and poor Indians. They tell Your Majesty, "I will favor them—yes, of course, I will do justice." But no sooner do they leave the port than they turn into different men. Suddenly, they prefer to favor the rich Spaniards. In proof of this, Your Majesty may take the case of an Indian named Don Cristóbal de León, a great servant of God and Your Majesty.

"Tell me, author, how does he serve God and my crown?"

I say to Your Majesty: whoever defends the poor of Jesus Christ serves God, for that is the word of God in his gospel; and by defending Your Majesty's Indians, he serves your royal crown, for he has been useful to Your Majesty's grandparents and parents, who are all now in heaven. Now he serves Your Majesty, but because he defends the Indians, a padre named Peralta is compiling testimony against him.

In just a short amount of time, [Peralta] has earned twelve thousand pesos, not counting household items and other things, and he plans to move to Spain with that money. Well, imagine, Your Majesty: how could he have earned so much money, since he has no mines or inherited estates? All he has is the labor and the sweat of the poor Indians. [León] complained about this, and he was punished and given shameful penitences by the inspector in the pueblo of Hatun Sora. To make this happen, Peralta's prelate wrote that he should be punished and shown no mercy. The letter that he wrote—I tell you, as proof—was delivered by a padre, Licentiate Francisco de Padilla, and by his brother Rodrigo de Padilla, to the inspector who was investigating poor Don Cristóbal de León. His whole estate was sold, his whole house was burned down; he lent two thousand pesos to the *corregidor* so that he would help him, but the inspector was bribed with two thousand pesos, and poor Don Cristóbal de León was banished.

See, Your Majesty: how can the kingdom help being ruined? Your Majesty will lose this whole kingdom, as valuable and useful as it is in the service of God and our holy Catholic faith and in service of your royal crown.

"Well, tell me, author: since you are the grandson of Topa Inca Yupanqui, the tenth former king, and you are the son of his second-in-command

and viceroy, how is it that you do not favor them in my name and stand up for them?"

That is indeed why I stand up for them, Your Royal Catholic Majesty, as a prince of the Indians of this kingdom. I have suffered such poverty, and I have labored for thirty years in the service of God and Your Majesty. I defend the kingdom, and that is why I am writing this history—to be a memorial, to be placed in the archive, so that justice may be seen.

It would be very beneficial for Your Majesty to send a general inspector to punish the prelates, and, if necessary, to banish them to the court in Spain, for these reasons. The inspector should stay in the city of Los Reyes de Lima and be sent out from there to inspect every city in its jurisdiction.

If Your Majesty does not agree with this idea, then please communicate with His Holiness, so that he might send us his second-in-command, a cardinal who would rank higher than all the priests and prelates, and who could punish or banish anyone who needs punishment—prelates, cathedral chapters, clerics, friars, monasteries, everything relating to the Holy Mother Church. He should also come with a special charge to help the nobles and other poor Indians of this kingdom. Then the Indians will multiply and be tranquil, and will rally to the service of God and Your Majesty in this kingdom.

*[Guaman Poma continues this chapter with a series of detailed recommendations for "remedies" to the problems of Peru: judges and the executors of Indian estates should be audited regularly; no Indian should be able to claim* cacique *status without Guaman Poma's personal approval of their title of nobility; Spaniards who keep Indian servants should be given hefty fines; wandering "absent Indians" should be forced to settle in depopulated provinces, solving both problems at once, and become the king's own Indians (on the model of the Incas'* mitmac *settlers); non-Indians, particularly mestizos, should be strictly prohibited from entering Indian pueblos; all civil officers and priests should be appointed by the king himself; and priests in Indian parishes should post bonds as a guarantee against living with Indian women and giving rise to "so many little mestizos."]*

999    **PROLOGUE: TO THE READER, YOUR ROYAL HOLY CATHOLIC MAJESTY, DON PHILIP III, KING, MONARCH OF THE WORLD**

I say to Your Royal Holy Catholic Majesty—weeping and crying, shouting out to heaven, begging God, the Virgin Mary, and all the saints and angels—I say that we, the poor, are sent so many punishments, misfortunes, and destructions: may God and Your Majesty not permit us to come to an end, or your kingdom to be depopulated.

To avoid this state of affairs, and so that Your Majesty might know what is happening, an inspector of the Holy Mother Church should be sent to each province. After inspecting them, he should gather the noble *cacique,* the administrator-protector and Indian deputy *corregidor,* and the council notary, and he should inspect [these officials], in every pueblo in his district. The inspector and his officers should re-inspect everyone he has inspected: whether they are good or bad; all their expenses in food, money, and clothes; bribes, fines, and bad sentences; *mitayos* and *camaricos;* outrages against virginity and forcing maidens; violations of the Council [of Trent] and of Your Majesty's royal ordinances and decrees; friendships made with the *doctrina* padres; how many days they have lived at the expense of the poor Indians and the *doctrina* padres, and how much cash they have taken from the padres; whether they are angry, wrathful, or proud; whether the padre has punished people and thrown them out of the *doctrina* because they were guilty, or whether he has forced them out without finding them guilty, even though they are good Christians and are following their doctrine in a Christian way; whether it is beneficial to let him remain in the *doctrina* or not. The inspector shall inform Your Majesty and His Lordship the bishop about all these things.

In this way, Your Majesty will find a remedy and will relieve your conscience, for the well-being of the poor people of this kingdom.

Also, no friar or Jesuit should be a *doctrina* priest, because friars belong in friaries all over the world.

Likewise, there should be audits. When a *corregidor* completes his term, he should be audited. Likewise, the judge in each pueblo should be given an audit, as should the judges who come and go in this kingdom. It is a very saintly matter for them to keep Your Majesty informed, in service of God and Your Majesty and for the multiplication, growth, relief, well-being, and conservation of the poor Indians of this kingdom.

*[The next chapter, "Mapamundi of the Indies of Peru" (ms. pp. 1000–87, omitted here) is a catalogue of descriptions of thirty-eight cities, towns, and provinces in colonial South America, from Bogotá and Panamá in the north to Chile and Paraguay in the south.[349] In the conclusion to "Mapamundi," Guaman Poma rails against the greed of the Spanish colonial cities, and in particular against Huamanga, the* corregimiento *capital of his home region, which he predicts will be destroyed by God's wrath in the same way that Arequipa was destroyed in the 1608 earthquake. "Mapamundi" is followed by a brief passage*

---

[349] The title drawing of this chapter—a unique two-page spread depicting Guaman Poma's graphic vision of Peru in map form—has been brilliantly analyzed by Adorno, *Guaman Poma,* pp. 89–119.

*in which Guaman Poma lists (and for the most part criticizes) the "Previous Chroniclers" of the Indies, and contrasts his own sources and methods with theirs (ms. pp. 1088–91). A listing of the "Royal Tambos" of the viceroyalty (ms. pp. 1092–103) rounds out this geographic appendix. Finally, at the end of the book, there comes a very personal chapter, which follows.]*[350]

1104–
1139

## FROM THE WORLD, THE AUTHOR RETURNS TO HIS HOUSE IN THE CENTER OF THIS KINGDOM, THE PROVINCE OF THE ANDAMARCAS, SORAS, AND LUCANAS, AND THE CENTRAL PUEBLO AND HEAD TOWN OF SAN CRISTÓBAL DE SUNTUNTO NUEVA CASTILLA AND SANTIAGO CHIPAO, THE EAGLE AND ROYAL LION OF THIS KINGDOM.[351]

He entered and, first of all, inspected the poor sick people, the old people, and the orphans. He inspected the church, where good things had been constructed. He then saw that the pueblo and province had been brought low, taken over, and destroyed.

FOR THIRTY YEARS he had been serving His Majesty. He now found everything fallen to the ground, and his houses, croplands, and pastures invaded. He found his sons and daughters naked and serving taxpaying Indian commoners. His children, nephews, nieces, and relatives did not recognize him, because he was so old when he returned. He must have been eighty years old, all grey-haired, thin, naked, and barefoot. Before, he would always dress in silks and *cumpis,* and he would relax as a lord and prince, the grandson of the tenth king. He became poor and naked only so that he could manage to see the world, by His Majesty's grace and permission, to serve as an eyewitness. What Christian would do this—leave his children and his estate, valued at twenty thousand [pesos], to wander naked among the poor for thirty years?

---

[350] Guaman Poma added this chapter after he had completed the rest of the book, sewing the pages on which it is written into the bound manuscript. See Rolena Adorno, "A Witness unto Itself: The Integrity of the Autograph Manuscript of Felipe Guaman Poma de Ayala's *El primer nueva corónica y buen gobierno* (1615/1616)," in Adorno and Ivan Boserup, *New Studies of the Autograph Manuscript of Felipe Guaman Poma de Ayala's* Nueva corónica y buen gobierno (Copenhagen: Museum Tusculanum Press, 2003), 76–80.

[351] Eagle and lion: that is, Guaman (*waman,* eagle or falcon) Poma (*puma* or mountain lion). Chipao was the pueblo where he lived for most of the early 1600s. Suntunto (Sondondo) is a pueblo about two miles away where he is thought to have been born.

THE AUTHOR WALKS OVER THE SNOW-BOUND
SIERRA, AND PASSES THROUGH CASTROVIRREYNA,
CHOCLOCOCHA, HUANCAVELICA, THE JAUJA VALLEY,
AND THE PROVINCE OF HUAROCHIRI:
THE AUTHOR AYALA, SERVING HIS MAJESTY FOR THIRTY
YEARS, LEAVING HIS CHILDREN AND LOSING MOST OF HIS
ESTATE, ONLY IN THE SERVICE OF GOD AND HIS MAJESTY,
AND TO FAVOR THE POOR OF JESUS CHRIST:
HE WANDERED IN THE WORLD, CRYING ALL THE WAY,
UNTIL HE WAS ABLE TO PRESENT HIMSELF IN LOS REYES DE
LIMA BEFORE HIS MAJESTY AND HIS ROYAL AUDIENCIA:
PRESENT HIMSELF AND COMPLETE THIS *CHRONICLE* OF
THIS KINGDOM, COMPOSED BY DON FELIPE GUAMAN
POMA DE AYALA[352]

THE AUTHOR, Don Felipe Guaman Poma de Ayala, finished walking through the world when he was eighty years of age.[353] He resolved to return to his own pueblo, where he had houses, croplands, and pastures, and was the noble lord, primary head, administrator-protector, and the general deputy of the *corregidor* of the province of the *Andamarca, Sora,* and *Lucana* Indians by the grace of His Majesty, and a prince of this kingdom.

AND SO IT WAS that he arrived in the pueblos of San Cristóbal de Suntunto and Santiago de Chipao, where an Indian petty authority over ten Indians had been made the noble *curaca* and was calling himself *apo* Don Diego Suyca—this was a tributary Indian who had been punished as a sorcerer, along with his sister. The *corregidor,* Martín de Mendoza, had burned two snakes belonging to him (a *solimán* and a *matacallo*) and other filth. This Indian had come in to serve the new *corregidor,* Juan de León Flores, and Padre Peralta. They loved him because he had five hundred *awasca* [coarsely woven] blankets made for them, and he gave them Indian porters and harassed the Indians with *rescates* and other demands.

In San Cristóbal de Suntunto, the new noble *cacique* was Don Grabiel Caquiamarca, who had Don Francisco Usco (legitimate) as his second-in-command.

And so, the author found the pueblo DESTROYED because of the labor imposed by the *corregidores* and *doctrina* padres of that province, and he

---

[352] This unusually long chapter title runs across the headings of all the pages in the chapter.

[353] The number "seventy-eight" is crossed out and corrected to "eighty" in the manuscript.

**THE AUTHOR WALKS WITH HIS SON, DON FRANCISCO DE AYALA. HE LEAVES THE PROVINCE FOR THE CITY OF LOS REYES DE LIMA, TO GIVE ACCOUNTS TO HIS MAJESTY. POOR, NAKED, AND WALKING IN WINTER.**

Quisiputo
[horse]

Author

Amigo [dog]

Don Francisco de Ayala [child]

Lautaro [dog]

[Lautaro was the name of the *Araucan* leader who resisted the conquest of Chile and nearly retook it from the Spanish. Naming a dog after the resistance leader should not be considered an homage. For the Spanish, giving someone's name to a dog was considered a degrading insult, and it is likely that many Spanish dogs were named Lautaro in Guaman Poma's Peru.]

found that all its Indian men and women had gone absent because of all the labor they were given.

In addition to this, he found Pedro Colla Quispe and Esteban Atapillo OCCUPYING HIS HOUSE AND HOME and his croplands in Chinchay Cocha, along with other Indians who had been sent there by Don Diego Suyca, the tributary Indian, to keep the author from returning, because of everything the author had seen.

The other poor Indian men and women **began to weep** from all their labor and misfortunes in their own pueblo and province; and **his arrival greatly grieved** Don Diego Suyca, Don Cristóbal de León, the other tributary Indians who were pretending to be nobles, and the *corregidor,* notary, deputies, and the Spaniards who rob the Indians, as well as all the priests of those *doctrinas,* all of whom skin the poor people.

HE WAS VERY tired and very poor. The author did not own a single grain of corn or anything else, after walking all over the world for so many years, serving God, His Majesty, His Holiness, and the viceroys, great lords, dukes, counts, marquises, and the royal councils of His Majesty in Castile and in this kingdom, in service of the royal crown and for the well-being, profit, increase, and multiplication of His Majesty's poor Indians.

THIS BEING THE STATE OF THINGS, the author decided to go and present himself before His Majesty, so that all his service and labor of so many years could be put into effect. Then the tributary Indians who had forcibly made themselves *curacas* told the priests and *doctrina* padres to throw the author out of the province.

The [priests] then told the *corregidor,* Juan de León Flores. This *corregidor* ordered the author and the former *corregidor,* Pedro López de Toledo, to be called before him. Then the author informed him that he had held official posts and offices; that he was a noble *cacique,* the highest one in the province; that his grandfathers had been the *apo* Waman Chawa and Don Martín Guaman Mallqui de Ayala, prince and high noble of this kingdom and the second-in-command and viceroy of Topa Inca Yupanqui, the tenth king, Wayna Capac Inca, the eleventh king, and Topa Cusiwalpa Wascar Inca, the twelfth Inca king, whom he had served; and that later, in the same office, he had served God and the emperor-king Don Carlos of glorious memory, and king Don Philip II; and that the author had later served the king and monarch of the whole world that God had created, DON PHILIP III, the monarch of the world.

INFORMED of all these things, the former *corregidor* Pedro López de Toledo replied that it was all a lie, deserving of punishment, and that if [the author] had arrived when he was in office, he would have punished him.

The [new] *corregidor,* Juan de León Flores, then replied to him that he should honor the author, seat him on a chair, and help him in his affairs.

**The author replied** to the *corregidor* that he preferred not to be honored by selling the poor of Jesus Christ, and asked how he could demand, on top of the obligatory tribute and cloth, that the people of his pueblo of Santiago de Chipao weave eighty pieces of cloth, and much more in the other pueblos—five hundred pieces; and he also kept shops in the pueblos, and other *rescates,* and he demanded a hundred Indian porters and other *rescates* and burdens from the poor Indians.

**The author then told him to quit** giving the poor so much labor; if he did that, they could become great friends.

The *corregidor* replied that he was going to make [the Indians] work, that he had asked His Excellency [the viceroy] for permission to do this, and that [the viceroy] was marrying a young woman from his house and his secretary favored him, so he feared no one. Therefore, he did not feel like returning [the author] to his rightful position, nor did he feel like returning his houses and croplands to him. So he threw [the author] out of the province, refusing to obey His Majesty's royal commands. That was when the author began to summon and protest this *corregidor* and his notary.

Therefore, he came to the **city of Los Reyes** de Lima to present himself before His Majesty in favor of the poor. These are the things that happened to the author along the way: his two mules died in the snow from cold, and he continued with one horse and all his poverty. On the road, he met two Christian men, friends of the poor, named Pedro Mosquera and Francisco Juárez. They took the author and comforted him, and he arrived at the sugar mill of Choclococha, where he saw the silver mines of Asto Huaraca and the chapel of Our Lady of Peña de Francia, his patron saint. A Christian man named Miguel Machado and his wife were at the mines, and they comforted him and showed him mercy.

**From there, he departed for the city** of Castrovirreyna de Coyca Pallca, where the conquest had occurred. The author walked there, very poor, and presented himself before a most Christian noble gentleman named **Don Fernando de Castro,** the governor, who gave him some money to buy clothing, and the mine owners Juan de la Cruz Orellana and Antonio de Bendieta honored and comforted him. The padre and vicar of the mining town, a *criollo* from Ica and a most Christian man, gave him money and comforted and honored him.

**THIS BEING THE STATE OF THINGS,** his horse, which cost fifty pesos, was stolen on the orders of the Protector of the Indians, a man named Juan de Mora y Carvajal. He complained about this, but he never attained justice. Therefore, the author left it, and he said this prayer in thanks to God: "See,

Lord God in heaven, how this man, a Protector of the Indians, has harmed the author. What will he do, then, to the poor Indians of Jesus Christ?"

**THIS BEING THE STATE OF THINGS,** a tumult and damage occurred among the poor when the *doctrina* priest from San Cristóbal collected testimony from the *Yauyo* and *Wacho* Indians. They say that the padre had demanded that they give him Indian men to bear his *rescates,* and many unmarried women to weave cloth and do other dealings and labors. [The local leader] Don Pedro talked back, and because of that, to cause harm and damage to the Indians, [the priest] collected testimony, calling [Don Pedro] a sorcerer who worshipped stones. To do this, he began to hang the old men and women and the young children, one by one, and to torture them until they were forced to speak falsely. Because of the pain, they said that they kept *wacas* (idols); they showed various kinds of stones.

In this way, they brought one hundred Indians and whipped them cruelly in front of the judge of Castrovirreyna. Kept in the jail, without food or clothes, eighty tributary Indians, old men, and women died, as did the noble, Don Pedro. The padre stole all their finery—the silver table settings, and the *topos* [silver ornaments] and clothing they used for singing and dancing in their fiestas, such as *aquilla, topos,* and outfits made all of silver, and their clothing made of *cumpi, awasca, wacra,* feathers, *chacpac,* and red wool. He collected these things from everyone's houses, and he made [the silver] into table settings and the wool into bed covers.

**OH, MY GREAT GOD,** St. Mary, our Lord, our Catholic King on high! Have pity on Your poor children, Your creatures, who cost You so much trouble, punishment, torments, and death, and were redeemed by Your precious blood! Have pity, Jesus Christ, on Your poor! Oh, lord, our king, see how eighty lives were lost from your estates! The padre does not care about it, nor does the *corregidor,* because they aim to skin and rob the poor of all they are worth. The *corregidor* skins them, and carries off twelve thousand [pesos] and other things. Afterwards, that same *corregidor* delivers justice: he hangs a poor Indian for stealing something, or he banishes his Indian women to other cities for having lovers, but he does not notice the theft of twenty thousand pesos from the community chest. The *corregidor* and the padre get one share, the *encomendero* gets another. In this kingdom, this is how they skin and make use of the poor of Jesus Christ.

**Oh, the Sodomy of Spanish Christians!**[354] How is it that God does not make [the earth] swallow you or kill you? One Theatine friar said in a sermon

---

[354] Here and in other passages (ms. pp. 109, 681, 716, and 1085–86), Guaman Poma uses the biblical Sodom as a symbol of pride and greed that leads to heavenly retribution (cf. Ezekiel 16:49). He does not interpret "sodomy" as a sexual offense.

that all the Indians would die and be finished off in the mines and at the hands of the *corregidores,* Spaniards, and priests and padres in this kingdom.

**And so, since I had seen so much** torture of the poor, and had heard in the Theatine padre's sermon how they all wished us ill, and had seen the deaths of eighty Indians, I determined to go to the pueblo of San Cristóbal, where I found an Indian petty authority over ten, named Don Juan Quilli, whom I served for a salary of fifty pesos. He gave me a light chestnut horse to pay me for ten pesos of this amount. This petty authority's wife seemed to be of Spanish stock. Their legitimate daughter, for her part, seemed to be of the stock of *cholos* or mestizos, and the licentiate [priest] kept this Indian woman in his kitchen, along with other unmarried women—some to prepare meals, others to bake bread, others to sew.

Then one day a deputy *corregidor* arrived. This same padre complained to the deputy that many Indian women in that town had lovers. Then the deputy, joining up with the padre, banished three beautiful Indian women to go serve their mother in the town of Huancavelica, where Spaniards could fornicate with them and create a stock of mestizos, and where they could be more wicked, half Spanish and half whore. Even when His Majesty orders the Indians to gather in and multiply, [the Spaniards] remove them [from their pueblos] in this way, and there is no remedy. This goes against what His Majesty has decreed. And [the priest] took away other Indian women, besides.

**You see, dear God:** how will the poor multiply? Here, the author and Don Juan Quilli said that, since they had no power, they were banishing the Indian women from the pueblo. In this way, the Indians are coming to an end, and His Majesty is being grievously harmed. Beyond this, His Majesty and His Lordship the bishop did great harm in giving the *doctrinas* to *doctrina* padres who are mere children and young men, when they ought to be past seventy, the age when they make good priests. [The author] mentioned this bit of advice in front of the daughter of Don Juan Quilli, and later, that same María told it to the padre at midnight. So the next morning, the padre immediately spoke to the author, and the padre ordered him to leave, and to say nothing to anyone, and not to encourage the Indians, because if he did, he would seat him on top of a llama and whip him.[355] The priest said he did not want to see him again; he called the *alcalde* and the *fiscal,* and threw him out.

**And so, dear God, where are you?** Do you not hear me, to remedy your poor? For me, I have had more than enough of trying to remedy this. As things are, how should the Indians live married lives and multiply?

---

[355] A standard shaming punishment, used especially for blasphemy and other religious crimes.

Now you will say, "Oh, what bad doctrine! What bad, troublemaking Indians!"

**In another pueblo,** Don Pedro got mixed up in another lawsuit, a brew of lies and wickedness, in the pueblo of Chinchay Yunga. It was brought by another friar who was a *doctrina* padre, out to destroy his pueblo. That is why in Castile they keep all the friars closed up in their friaries, and the clerics in their houses, where they will not cause lawsuits. Here, everything is lies. Thus, this padre frightened all the Indians; even the author was frightened by this padre. What more, then, will he do to my poor, faint-hearted, incapable Indians?

Not to mention too many things, or to wear you out with weeping about the poor, this incident happened in the year 1614. On Ash Wednesday, the author was listening to a frightening sermon by this padre, in which he was saying that he was going to kill, skin, and cure the Indians like so many scabby sheep. When the author heard the bad words in this sermon, he left immediately, right away, to keep from witnessing such tortures of the poor. He was tired of witnessing such things in the world, but he needed to know about it, because eighty souls had died—the treasure of His Majesty, **who mourns them as his own things** that had cost him his own labor, as proprietor and king.

Now you will say that God—and therefore, His Royal Catholic Majesty—are not here at present, because wherever God is, there is the Catholic king with his eyes.

Christians: everyone who informs His Majesty serves God and His Majesty. Their eyes, and the author's eyes, are the eyes of the king himself. He has seen all this as an eyewitness and has wandered all over the world to see and to bring his justice and remedy to the poor.

**Therefore, the author returned** to the road once more to give advice and propose remedies to His Majesty. And so he once more returned to walking, leaving the town a very poor man.

**God was pleased,** as was his mother St. Mary Peña de Francia. He comforted and clothed [the author], through the mercy of the mother of God. Thus, he performed a miracle upon the poor gentleman author. He therefore walked on to the city of Castrovirreyna, where his travels once more turned.

**There he once more** found nothing but misery. An *Aymara* Indian from the pueblo of Huaquirca had stolen a chair and other small items [from him]; this Indian's name was Don Pedro de León Cautillo. Beyond this, [the author's] eldest son ran away and left him, Don Francisco de Ayala, because he saw that he was poor and had no way to feed him. He was now so poor and afflicted that there was no one who would help him or loan him even one real. Here you can see all the poverty he suffered through, in order to serve God our Lord, favor the poor of Jesus Christ, and give an accounting of this kingdom to His Majesty for the remedy and salvation of spirits.

When the author found himself in the pueblo of San Cristóbal, he met a man from the town of Piscoy who, while eating dinner with Don Juan Quilli, the Indian petty authority of ten Indians from that pueblo, had asked Don Juan Quilli why he did not marry his daughter to some Indian so that she would not continue giving birth to more mestizos. He had also said that it seemed bad for her to be in the padre's kitchen, and that it was dishonorable to be so burdened with mestizos.

**Later, the same Spaniard** asked the author why he was wearing himself out and wasting his time, old as he was, instead of making cloth and *rescates* and everything the *corregidor*, deputies, *doctrina* padres, *encomenderos*, and other Spaniards demanded.

**The author replied, saying:** "Señor, the ordinances of Don Francisco de Toledo and the other viceroys do not order me to make cloth, *rescates*, or anything for them or anyone else. They set a salary for such things, to be paid every year and every six months."

**The Spaniard replied:** "Son, let me tell you, as a man who knows about these things: Don Pedro de Mena, a very rich man from Collao, was also once a deputy *corregidor*. Being so rich, this *corregidor* made four thousand pieces of *awasca* cloth to sell in Potosí. He did the same for me and for the padre and the *encomendero*. You should know that the ordinances of Don Francisco de Toledo and all the other viceroys are fine for the Indians, but they're not for the Spaniards—the Spaniards' laws and ordinances stayed back in Castile. We're free. That's why I'm telling you: don't wear yourself out. Weave, start spinning yarn. That way, you'll finish, and they'll be happy."

**The author replied, saying:** "Señor, my hope is that Jesus Christ will return to judge the wicked and punish them, and to bring the good people into Glory. It is good and it is a saintly thing to favor the poor of Jesus Christ."

**This man replied and said that** the *encomendero* of Chinchay had demanded an Indian, Don Andrés, be made the governor [of his pueblo]. "So they had to remove the legitimate one and put him in. If the noble doesn't make good with the *corregidor* and the padre and the *encomendero*, and if he doesn't live well with the Spaniards, they'll either remove him or whip him to death. So you see, son, what kind of end awaits troublemakers and those who don't do what Indians are supposed to do in this kingdom."

**The author replied:** "Señor, I have not come to make trouble, but rather to inform His Majesty and to relieve his royal conscience, and I am going to fulfill that duty. What can all of them do to me? God is my witness, and Santa María Peña de Francia and all God's saints and angels will favor me. I am also a proprietor, the lord of my land, the legitimate heir of *capac apo* Waman Chawa, the most excellent lord of this kingdom. I am also the grandson of

Topa Inca Yupanqui, the tenth king of this kingdom and a great wise man, because my mother, the *Coya* Doña Juana Curi Ocllo, was a legitimate *Coya* or lady and queen of this kingdom. Therefore, prince Don Melchor Carlos Paullo Topa Wiracocha Inca, who went away to Castile, was my uncle, and other Inca lords or princes who are still living are uncles of mine.

"My father served God and His Majesty all his life, as have I. Like **waman, the king of birds, he flies farther,** or flew farther, in the service of God and His Majesty, serving for thirty years.[356] Like *puma,* the king of beasts, he was feared; from his birth, he was the second-in-command and viceroy of Topa Inca Yupanqui, married to his legitimate daughter, Doña Juana Curi Ocllo. As such, he served God and His Majesty. Like Ayala, the loyal Ayala, like the loyal gentleman from the House of Ayala in Spain and Biscay, so he served God and His Majesty all his life, until the day he died. He served the padre like a son or a grandson. He was like the *condor* or vulture that can catch a scent forty leagues off; so he served and caught scents in the service of God and His Majesty for forty years, never stopping. Like *chawa* or cruel, he was very cruel against all tyrants, in service of God and His Majesty. Thus, he was a great Christian prince, who defended the faith and the church of God and who defended the royal crown of His Majesty: Ayala."

**The man replied** and said: "Son, just go to Castile. The king will give you a grant for all your services, and for being a native proprietor, if that's what you are."

**The author replied** and said, "Señor, I am an old man of eighty years. I cannot remedy that. May God remedy it, and His Majesty: he can; it is in his hands."

*[Guaman Poma continues the tale of his journey to Lima as he passes through Castrovirreyna, Huancavelica, the Jauja valley, and Huancayo, then up river and across country to Huarochiri and the* tambo *of Chorrillo, on the main road to the capital. Along the way, he finds one consistent theme: "how the Spaniards have justice and the Indians have none in this kingdom, nor is there anyone who will stand up for them."]*[357]

---

[356] In this paragraph, Guaman Poma explains the symbolic significance of his family names: *waman* (Guaman), eagle or falcon; *puma* (Poma), puma or mountain lion; Ayala, a noble Spanish surname; *condor,* the condor; and *chawa,* raw or cruel. Chawa was his grandfather's name.

[357] Guaman Poma draws special attention to the activities of Padre Francisco de Ávila (c. 1573–1647), the priest of Huarochiri best known to posterity as a prime mover in the "extirpation of idolatries" campaign in central Peru and the probable collector of the Huarochiri manuscript, the longest colonial-era account of Andean mythology written in Quechua. In Guaman Poma's account, Ávila used imprisonment and torture to get Indians to confess to "idolatry" so that he could confiscate their possessions.

**From there, the author** passed on to the pueblo and *tambo* of Sisicaya. The noble *cacique,* a Christian named Don Martín, son of Don Diego, was not there at the time; he was at the chapel of **ST. MARTIN** in Chontay, because his Indians were cleaning the irrigation canals for that community. There he received the author with love and charity; he comforted him, showed him mercy and alms, and gave him new clothes for the love of God and St. Martin, and because [the author] was poor, old, and ill.

The author passed on through the swamps and climbed up the hill of Aysahuillca, where he ran into a poor man named Diego de Aguayo from the city of Chuquisaca. He was an extremely poor man. The author and this man met on the sandy plain that leads up to the city of Lima. As they traveled on, they met another man, a mule driver, very stiff and haughty—God save us! **HE PRETENDED TO BE A JUSTICE,** and he threatened the poor man as an excuse to try to take a mule that the poor man had with him. He asked him where he was coming from, and where he had gotten the mule, and how it could it be that it wasn't dying from the trip, and that it looked like his own mule, as much as one egg looks like another egg. He said all these things only in an attempt to take away the poor man's mule on that road.

**So the author and the poor man went on.** They entered the city of Los Reyes de Lima very late in the day, and could not find a place to stay nor anyone who would come to their aid. Because they were so poor, they slept in an entryway without tasting a bite for supper, and their beasts of burden went without hay because of their great poverty.

From there, [the next day] they went on beyond the Callejón del Cercado, and they entered a house just past the convent of discalced nuns.[358] They were thrown out in the street, because they looked so poor and ragged, even though they begged by the love of God and his mother St. Mary. They had no pity for the poor author.

**The author sold off** the miserable possessions he had, in order to get a little money to sustain him in his poverty. Then he went to the church of Our Lady of Peña de Francia [in the convent] of Santa Clara, because of the devotion that the author held for the Mother of God. Afterwards, he went to the chapel of Las Ánimas del Purgatorio [The Souls in Purgatory], because of his devotion to charity and love for his fellow man. Out of his love towards the poor of Jesus Christ our Lord, he bore everything with patience. He rented a house in the city, and paid twenty reales a month for it, as a poor man, and for the sake of other poor people whom he brought in for the love of God.

---

[358] This Carmelite convent, on Avenida Tacna, was founded in 1535 by Fernando Pizarro. The women who were allowed to join elite convents such as this one were the daughters of the wealthiest and most established families in Peru.

**HERE YOU SEE,** Christians, how you meddle beyond your station. If you are a Jew, a taxpaying commoner, or a day laborer, why do you pretend to be a justice? Why do you try to find out about other people's lives, when you do not know your own? You ask the poor man questions out of greed for his mule; you do not ask so that you can give him alms, not even eight reales, or four. I see everyone pretending to be justices; they do everything with the sole aim of taking away that mule. The world is upside down: this is a sign that there is no God and there is no king—they are in Rome and Castile. There is justice for the poor people—for punishing them; for the rich, there is no punishment. May God, who can, remedy this, amen. Here you see the author's reason for laboring and making himself poor: to find a remedy for all this.

♦ **IT SEEMS THAT** the author suffered harsh labor for love of the poor of Jesus Christ, leaving behind everything he had—estates and children—solely in the service of God and His Majesty. Even in the natural state of the Indians of this kingdom, he was a very great lord and gentleman, so he necessarily had to defend his kingdom, and to speak and communicate with the great, high LORD, KING, and monarch of the world, who towers above all the kings and emperors of Christendom and of the infidel Moors, Turks, Englishmen, and every other nation in the world that God created, everything the sun orbits day and night all over the world.

**WHO COULD DARE** write to, speak with, or approach any personage who is such a great Christian Catholic lord as His Royal Catholic Majesty? He did dare, as the vassal of his royal crown and as his gentleman in this kingdom of the Indies of the New World; that is, as a prince (meaning an *auqui*) of this kingdom—A GRANDSON OF the tenth king, Topa Inca Yupanqui, and a legitimate son of Doña Juana Curi Ocllo, Coya (*Coya* means queen) of Peru.

**Therefore, he had to write** and labor over this *New Chronicle and Good Government of This Kingdom,* in service to God and His Majesty and for the well-being, increase, conservation, and multiplication of the Indians of this kingdom, in service to God and to His Majesty's royal crown.

The author, after entering the city of Los Reyes de Lima, saw it swarming with absent and runaway Indians who had turned themselves into *yanaconas* and tradesmen, though they are low *mitayo* Indians and tributaries. They wear collars, dress like Spaniards, and carry swords; others cut their hair short so that they will not have to pay tribute or serve in the mines. Here you see the world turned upside down. When they see these absent Indians, other Indians leave their pueblos, and there is no one left to pay the tribute or to serve in the mines.

Likewise, the author saw many Indian whores, bearing many little mestizos and mulattos, all wearing petticoats, ankle boots, and coifs. Even if they are married, they still go around with Spaniards and blacks. Therefore, other women do not want to marry Indian men. Nor do they want to leave the city, because they do not want to abandon their whorish lives, so the outlying settlements of the city are full of Indian women, and there is no remedy. They do offense to the service of God our Lord and His Majesty, and thus the Indians of this kingdom do not multiply.

The emancipated blacks, mulattos, and mestizos should pay tribute or personal tax to His Majesty and to their *doctrinas,* and they should be resettled in the cities and towns. The women should pay to the community treasury, or else perform labor, following the laws of Peru in this kingdom.

*[A final chapter, "Months and Years" (ms. pp. 1140–77, omitted here), gives a month-by-month description of labors and festivities in the rural Andean world under the colonial regime. The book ends with the following brief epilogue.]*

1178    ## IN EYES AND SPIRIT I REJOICE ABOUT THE CHRISTIANS OF THE WORLD

SEE HERE THE CHRISTIANS of the world: some will weep; others will laugh; others will curse. Others will commend me to God. Others, out of sheer wrath, will throw away this book; others will want to hold this book and *Chronicle* in their hands, to restrain their spirits, consciences, and hearts, and to live by the law of God—the Ten Commandments, the holy gospel, and everything decreed by the Holy Mother Church of Rome, the most Holy Father Pope, and everything that His Majesty decrees. You should know that there is only one God and one king and his justice. The proud, like Lucifer, will be punished in this world—or, if not, in the next world, by the punishments of God.

Therefore, Christians, fear God and be humble before God and his justice, and before the king and your lords; and, for clerics, before your prelates. Even if a prelate comes in as gentle as a lamb, you would turn him fierce; you are looking to have him punish you. If he does not, your prelate will be punished by God for your faults.

Therefore I beg for you to restrain yourselves, and for each of you to see what it is that you are. If you are a gentleman or an hidalgo, you will seem very goodly. But if you are a commoner, a Jew, or a Moor, mestizo, or mulatto, as God created you, do not pretend to be a gentleman by force. Noble *caciques* are of long lineage: commoner Indians, do not pretend to be lords. Rather, let each one appear according to his nature, as God created him and ordained in the world.

Thus, this *Chronicle* is for the whole world and all of Christendom. Even the infidels should read it, for the good justice, public order, and law of the world.

*[At the end of the book, Guaman Poma draws up his own Table of Contents (ms. pp. 1179–87), in imitation of the printed books of his era. The last two pages of the manuscript display a drawing of the Spanish royal coat of arms (ms. p. 1189) and the following colophon.]*

# CHRONICLE

*1188*

## END OF THE *NEW CHRONICLE AND GOOD GOVERNMENT OF THIS KINGDOM*

Completed by Don Felipe Guaman Poma de Ayala, prince and author from the Indies of the Kingdom of Peru, from the city and surroundings of San Cristóbal de Suntunto de Nueva Castilla, in the province of the Andamarcas, Soras, and Lucanas of the Royal Crown.

From the City of Los Reyes de Lima, Royal Court
and Capital of Peru
Presented to <the gentlemen>. . . .[359]

---

[359] The final two words, "*los señores,*" are crossed out, and the sentence is left unfinished.

# GLOSSARY[1]

**absent Indians:** See OUTSIDER INDIANS.

**apo (Q, *apu*):** Great lord. See also *CAPAC APO.*

**alcalde:** A local or regional official in the colonial system.

**alcalde mayor:** a Spanish provincial magistrate who held both executive and judicial powers, roughly equivalent to a *corregidor.*

**alcalde ordinario:** a local official, generally translated here as "justice of the peace"; in Indian pueblos, *caciques* were typically chosen as *alcaldes.* Other types of *alcaldes* mentioned are the Spanish officials in charge of regulating mines, *plazas,* fields, and *tambos.*

**Audiencia:** The high court and ruling body of colonial Spanish Peru, presided over by the viceroy when he was resident in Lima. *Audiencias* were also established in Bogotá, Charcas, Quito, and Chile.

**audit (S, *residencia*):** More than a financial audit, this was a legal review of the entire term of an official, mandated by Spanish law at the end of his tenure in office. In a system where the top officials at each level of government (*alcalde, corregidor,* viceroy) was both the executive and the head judge, the *residencia* was the only check on corruption.

**ayllu (Q):** The most basic Andean social group; translated by Guaman Poma as *parcialidad,* "band" or lineage-based ethnic group.

**bachiller:** A man with a baccalaureate or bachelor degree, most commonly a priest; in general, a professional such as a priest or lawyer. Also, a fast talker, windbag, charlatan.

**caciques:** Usually found in the phrase "noble *caciques*" (*caciques principales*). Indians descended from the pre-Hispanic Andean nobility, who continued to govern locally under Spanish rule. This was the colonial title (from a Caribbean language) that the Spanish bestowed on the indigenous leaders they recognized and used as intermediaries to rule their empire. The parallel Quechua term was *curaca.*

**camaricos (colonial S, from Q *kamariku*):** Gifts; specifically, forced gifts of food and traveling gear from Indians to their colonial lords.

**cantor:** A member of the church choir. In Indian *pueblos,* the cantors (especially the *maestro cantor,* master cantor or choirmaster) were lay religious

---

[1] The Spanish (S) and Quechua (Q) are given for terms as needed. When there are variations between the Cusco Quechua of the Incas and the Ayacucho Quechua spoken by Guaman Poma, I indicate the Cusco version first, followed by the Ayacucho. For example, Cusco Quechua pronounces *khipu* with an aspirated ("breathy") *kh,* while Ayacucho Quechua does not distinguish the aspiration: Q, *khipu, kipu.*

specialists who, together with the FISCAL, effectively controlled the daily functioning of the church.

*capac apo* (**Q,** *qhapaq apu, qapaq apu*): "Powerful lord," the title of the ruling Inca.

*chicha:* Corn beer, a mildly alcoholic drink brewed from fermented corn.

*china or chinacona* (**Q,** *china,* "**female,**" *chinakuna,* "**females**"): A female servant; specifically, a young Indian woman removed from her community and attached to a Spanish patron. See also YANACONA.

**citizen** (**S,** *vecino*): Only members of the very highest levels of conquest society were given the honorable title of *vecino,* "citizen of a Spanish city." In Guaman Poma's time, *vecino* and *encomendero* were almost synonymous. Most inhabitants of colonial cities (including most Spaniards) were considered mere "residents."

**commoners:** Anyone (Indian or Spanish) who does not have noble status. Spanish commoners are generally called *pecheros* (see TAXPAYERS). **Indian commoners** (*indios; indios comunes; indios particulares; indios bajos; tributarios; mitayos*) formed the vast majority of the population in Guaman Poma's Peru; they paid tribute, usually in the form of unpaid labor, to their Inca and Spanish rulers (see MITAYOS; TRIBUTARIES).

**corregidor:** The district governor or top Spanish official in a colonial province.

**curaca** (**Q,** *kuraka*): See CACIQUES.

**doctor:** A man with a doctorate, most commonly a priest with a doctorate in theology (few medical practitioners, *médicos,* held doctorates). Also, a doctor of the church: an eminent theologian recognized with this title by the Catholic church.

**doctrina:** Catholic doctrine; used as a synonym for the catechism as well. Also a rural Indian parish (the smallest Catholic jurisdiction), and the church at its center. This term was used instead of the standard Spanish term *parroquia* (parish) to distinguish Indian from non-Indian parishes, under the theory that Indians were "new to the faith" and needed to be taught the proper church doctrine, even generations after the conquest.

**doctrina padres** (*S, padres y curas de las doctrinas, padres doctrinantes):* The Catholic clergymen who were sent to serve as parish priests for Indians in their pueblos and villages. Some *doctrina padres* were ordained priests, but many were friars—members of religious orders, such as Franciscans—who were given special dispensation to serve as priests in colonial Indian villages.

**Don, Doña:** These Spanish titles (placed before a person's first name) were strictly reserved for use by only the nobility in the sixteenth century. Over the years, their use extended to ever lower social ranks; Guaman Poma harshly criticizes the beginning of this trend.

**emperor-king (S, *rey emperador*):** The grandson of Ferdinand and Isabel, who inherited the united crown of Spain as Charles I (1516–1556) and the Holy Roman Empire as Charles V or Carlos V (1518–1556). His son Philip II (1556–1598) did not inherit the Empire, making Charles the only "emperor-king."

**encomendero:** Someone given a royal concession to exploit the tribute and labor from one or more Indian communities in exchange for promising (usually only in theory) to care for the spiritual needs of "his Indians." *Encomenderos* made up the wealthiest class of Spanish colonists in the first century after conquest.

**fiscal:** An Indian official who ran the lay religious hierarchy in an Indian pueblo, together with the master cantor. The *fiscales* were generally responsible for instructing children in the Catholic Catechism (see *DOCTRINA*): as well as for managing pueblo funds for religious celebrations, often with little or no interaction with the Spanish priest. (In other contexts, the term *fiscal* is translated here as "legal counsel.")

**hanega:** A dry measure, also called a *fanega;* roughly 1.5 bushels (55 liters).

**inspector (S, *visitador*):** A man appointed, with the powers of a judge, to do a "tour of inspection" (*visita*) of the colonial officials within a jurisdiction. A pastoral inspector tours (*visita*) the priests in a diocese, while a civil inspector tours the civil officials (corregidores, deputies, alcaldes) in a set of civil jurisdictions.

**khipu, kipu:** See *QUIPU*.

**ladino:** Someone (here, usually an Indian) who has become fluent in Spanish as a second language.

**licentiate (S, *licenciado*):** A man with a university degree roughly equivalent, in terms of the length of study, to a bachelor's degree; usually employed as a lawyer.

**man of letters (S, *letrado*):** A man with a post-elementary education, a rare status at the time. See also *BACHILLER, LICENTIATE*.

**mestizo:** A person of mixed descent, usually Indian and Spanish. In the early colonial era, the legitimate children of the rare marriages between Spanish men and Indian women were often raised as and considered to be Spaniards; mestizos were thus presumed to be the illegitimate children of Spanish men and Indian concubines or rape victims.

**mita (colonial S, from Q *mit'a*, *mita*):** A forced labor obligation imposed on tributary Indians under the colonial regime, typically two months per year for able-bodied men. The Andean precursor of the *mita* was a reciprocal labor obligation: if a noble performed a service for a community, for example, he could call on that community's labor in return. The colonial *mita* eliminated the concept of reciprocal obligations. See *MITAYO, MITAYA,* and *PLAZA.*

**mitmac (Q *mitmaq*):** Under Inca rule, an ally of Cusco who was granted land and given favored treatment to resettle in a recently conquered or restive territory of the empire, as a means of imperial control. Guaman Poma sometimes uses *mitmac* as an alternative term for *outsider Indian* (*indio forastero*) under colonial rule, and at times he refers to Spanish colonists as *mitmacs* from Castile.

**mitayo, mitaya (colonial S, from Q *mit'ayoq, mitayoq*):** An Indian commoner called upon to perform *mita* labor. *Mitaya* is the Spanish feminine form of the word, for women doing forced labor. Also, a synonym for Indian *COMMONERS.*

**mulatto:** A person of black and Spanish (or at times black and Indian) descent.

**nobles (S, *principales*):** The indigenous Andean nobility. See *CACIQUE.*

**Old Christian (S, *cristiano viejo*):** A Spaniard who could trace his Christian ancestry back at least three generations on all sides and who was therefore considered not to be "stained" by Jewish or Moorish "blood." This was the keystone concept of Castilian racial-religious prejudice, but Guaman Poma insists that, by the legal criteria defining the term, Indians had better claim to call themselves Old Christians than the Spaniards in Peru.

**outsider Indians (S, *indios forasteros;* also "absent Indians," *indios ausentes*):** Indians (particularly young men) who uprooted themselves and wandered to other communities to avoid the tribute and labor obligations that fell most heavily on Indians living in their own communities. Most outsider Indians lived a marginal existence, but they escaped some of the onerous burdens of the colonial system. See also *MITMAC.*

**pacarico (Q, *paqariku;* from *paqariy,* dawn):** The legendary or mythic place of origin of an Andean people. Also, a night-long celebration with dancing and drinking, much criticized by Guaman Poma.

**personal service (S, *servicio personal*):** Labor obligations imposed on tributary Indians, including the *mita* as well as random requisitions by individual Spaniards such as priests or travelers in the *tambos.*

**petty authorities (S, *mandoncillos*):** Guaman Poma's translation of *kamachikuqkuna:* local Indian officials (usually commoners) under both Inca and colonial Spanish rule. Following the hierarchical Incaic system, he distinguishes among *mandoncillos* of five, ten, fifty, one hundred, and five hundred households.

**plaza:** The central public square of any Spanish city or town, usually located between the church building and the highest local government office. "Indians who serve in the plazas" (*indios de la plaza*) were tributary Indians who fulfilled their *mita* obligation by waiting in the plaza of the nearest Spanish city and offering their services as day laborers to Spanish estate owners.

**protector of the Indians (S,** *protector de indios***):** A colonial official (almost always Spanish) in charge of representing the legal rights of the Indians in a province.

**pueblo.** An indigenous Andean community, as reorganized under colonial rule. Colonial Spanish drew a distinction between pueblos (generally seen as rural and "Indian") and small Spanish communities (*villas* and *aldeas,* translated here as "towns" and "hamlets").

**quadroon (S,** *cuarterón***):** A person with one African and three non-African grandparents; more generally, a light-skinned person of partial black ancestry.

*quipu* **(Q,** *khipu, kipu***):** An Andean system of recording accounts using a series of colored strings and a complex variety of knots. An expert in keeping such accounts was called *quipucamayoc* (*khipukamayoq, kipukamayoq*), which Guaman Poma glosses as "overseer" and "warehouse supervisor."

**rescates:** A system of forced trading that was one of the most lucrative enterprises for many provincial Spanish colonial officials. Guaman Poma uses the term to refer to the whole system, fueled entirely by unpaid Indian labor, in which colonial officials organized the forced manufacture of goods (the textbook case is having Indian women spin yarn and weave it into cloth ); then had the goods transported on the backs of Indian men; and finally sold the goods in Spanish markets or, more often, disposed of them in forced sales to Indians elsewhere in the province.

**royal fifth (S,** *quinto real***):** The king's tribute, a levy of 20 percent (in theory) on all mining production and certain other goods.

*runa* **(Q):** Man; people; a people or ethnic group.

**second-in-command (S,** *segunda persona***):** Guaman Poma's Spanish translation of a Quechua concept of dual rulership. Andean communities and kingdoms typically had two subcommunities and two rulers (most often conceptualized as "upper" and "lower"). In line with this model of rulership, Guaman Poma viewed the viceroy of Peru as a *segunda persona* of the Spanish king.

**Spaniard, Spanish (S,** *español***):** Guaman Poma uses this term to refer to all Europeans, and sometimes to all non-Andeans, in much the same way that Europeans considered all the peoples of the Americas to be "Indians."

**steward (S, *mayordomo*):** Administrators hired by the owners of colonial Spanish business undertakings, farms, and wealthy households to handle day-to-day operations; the *mayordomo* was the highest-ranking Spaniard that most indigenous workers came into contact with on a regular basis. Guaman Poma also uses *mayordomo* as a translation for *surqukuq* (Q), the Incaic official in charge of granaries.

**stock (S, *casta*, "stock, lineage"):** A precursor of the idea of "race" in European and Euro-American thought.

***tambo* (Q, *tampu*):** An inn originally set up under Inca rule to provide travelers with stopping places along the remarkable Inca road system. Guaman Poma saw the colonial-era *tambos* as dens of immorality.

**taxpayers (S, *pecheros*):** In Spain, only commoners (including the peasants who made up most of the population) were subject to paying the personal tax (*pecho*), so the terms *pechero* and commoner were synonymous. Guaman Poma complains that Spanish commoners in Peru were not subject to personal taxes, and that the term *pecheros* was reserved for Spaniards while Indians in the same social position were called tributaries. He insists that Spanish and Indian commoners be treated the same.

**Tawantinsuyu:** The Quechua name ("Four Sectors Together") for the Inca empire, which was ruled from the central Andean city of Cusco by a ruling elite of the Inca lineage. Guaman Poma describes this expansive empire as follows: "Tawantinsuyu is the name for everything from the mountains of Chile to the other end of the mountains in Nuevo Reino [Bogotá], from the Southern Sea [the Pacific Ocean] to the Northern Sea [the Caribbean]: the whole range, all the mountains, the whole chain, the plains, the seaside sands" (ms. p. 343).

**tributaries (S, *tributarios*):** A synonym for Indian COMMONERS, who were required to pay fixed amounts annually to their overlord. After the conquest, tribute was diverted to the local Spanish ENCOMENDERO, or to the king in areas without *encomenderos*. Tribute was usually paid in agricultural products or cloth in the early years.

**viceroy (S, *virrey*):** The representative of the king of Spain and the president of the AUDIENCIA of Lima; held the highest executive, judicial, and legislative powers in the viceroyalty of Peru.

***waca* (Q, *waqa*):** Guaman Poma glosses this as "idol," but natural features in the landscape (especially mountains, cliffs, crags, and large rocks) were often considered *waqa*, which might be translated as "embodying spiritual force." It is usually spelled *huaca* or *guaca* in colonial texts.

**Wiracocha (Q, *wira qucha*, literally "lake of fat," metaphorically "place of power"):** The name of a pre-conquest deity or culture hero from the Huarochiri region, treated by Guaman Poma as an imperfect image of the Christian God. Used after the conquest as the Quechua term for Spaniards. Usually spelled *Viracocha* in colonial texts.

**yanacona (colonial S, from Q *yanakuna*, pl. of *yana*, personal retainers in the households of Andean nobility and royalty):** Servant; in particular, a male Indian servant removed from his community and attached to a Spanish patron. Indian slavery was prohibited in Spanish law by the time of the conquest of Peru, but the conquerors took advantage of this Andean social class and began recruiting Andeans as their personal *yanaconas*. Since *yanaconas* were exempt from paying tribute, some Indian commoners found it to their advantage to become *yanaconas*. The *Cañari, Chachapoya,* and *Wanca* ethnic groups, early military allies of the Spanish against the Incas, had all become *yanaconas* from Guaman Poma's point of view. See also CHINA OR CHINACONA.

# INDEX

*acllacuna (aclla)* ("temple virgin"), 67,
    77, 83, 94, 117
Adorno, Rolena, x, xii, xxiii, xxvii,
    xxx, xxxi, 5, 95, 135, 169, 348
Albornoz, Cristóbal de, x, 84, 88, 92,
    219–21
Allen, Catherine, 271n
Almagro, Diego de, xvii–xix, 6, 9, 19,
    20, 46, 100, 103–109, 112–15,
    117–19, 125, 133, 137, 141, 150,
    290, 295, 331, 332; the younger,
    137, 141, 150, 260, 282, 283,
    290
ancestral peoples of the Andes (*Wari
    Wiracocha Runa, Wari Runa,
    Purun Runa, Auca Runa*), 5, 23–
    25, 25, 27, 28, 29, 31, 32, 36, 38,
    72, 97, 142, 151, 148, 271, 290,
    291, 300, 343; *pacarimoc runa*
    (founding people), 25, 27, 32
Andean civilization, xiii–xiv; Andean
    astrology and medicine, 277–80;
    agriculture, 275–76, 300, 302,
    320–21. *See also* Tawantinsuyu;
    Inca
Andesuyu, xiv, 6, 7, 51, 53, 58, 76,
    95, 97, 145, 158, 162
Apcara (town in central Peru), x, 4,
    95, 308
Arequipa, 37, 41, 56, 58, 94, 125,
    207, 347
Atawalpa (son of Wayna Capac, Inca),
    xv–xviii, xxx, 5, 21, 34, 39, 44,
    46, 72, 101–105, 107–20, 125,
    133, 135, 217, 290; war against
    brother Wascar, xvii–xviii, 108,
    114, 115, 141
Audiencia (high court of colonial
    Spanish America), 145, 1156,
    163–69, 177, 180–81, 215, 230,
    241, 247, 249, 254, 269, 283,
    309, 335, 343, 349, 362, 367

audit (*residencia*), 1, 166, 168, 169,
    176, 178, 179, 181, 182, 185,
    189, 242, 244, 247, 249, 251–52,
    274, 308, 347, 362
Ávalos de Ayala, Luis de (father of
    Martín de Ayala), 10, 120, 121,
    282, 290
Ayala, Martín de (GP's half–brother),
    viii–ix, 8–13, 107, 120, 161–62,
    257. *See also* Guaman Mallqui
    Ayala, Don Martín
Beatriz Coya (married brother, Sayri
    Topa Inca), 147
Benalcázar, Sebastián de, 109–11
biblical references: Genesis, 15–17,
    159n; Adam and Eve, xxiii–xxv, 8,
    15–16, 23, 26–27, 31–32, 38, 50,
    97, 187, 258, 313, 330; Noah, 5,
    17, 23, 25, 31–32, 97, 289, 330–
    31; Sodom, 230, 353; Ten Com-
    mandments, 28, 46, 152, 173,
    202, 217, 255, 270, 275, 287,
    324, 360; King David, 1, 16, 23,
    239; Psalms, 1; Isaiah, 26;
    Habakkuk, 25, gospels, 39, 331,
    336; divine punishments, 41, 230,
    317, 330. *See also* God
blacks, 15, 231–39, 245, 260, 304
Boserup, Ivan, x, xxx, 348
*caciques*, x, 1, 3, 9, 73, 79, 135, 156,
    158–61, 162, 168–70, 171, 175,
    176, 178, 182, 213, 217, 223–24,
    226–28, 231, 234, 238–41, 244,
    246, 248–49, 258, 263, 264,
    266–67, 270, 272, 274, 284–86,
    299–300, 305, 308–9, 319, 328–
    29, 331–33, 336, 340–43, 346–
    47, 349, 351, 358, 360, 362
Cajamarca, xvii, xviii, 9, 19, 109–10
*camarico* ("gifts" taken from Indians),
    109, 187, 191, 221, 248, 253,
    254, 257, 294, 299, 328, 347, 362